C++ PRIMER

Stanley B. Lippman

AT&T Bell Laboratories

ADDISON-WESLEY PUBLISHING COMPANY

Reading, Massachusetts, • Menlo Park, California • New York
Don Mills, Ontario • Wokingham, England • Amsterdam • Bonn
Sydney • Singapore • Tokyo • Madrid • San Juan

Library of Congress Cataloging-in-Publication Data

Lippman, Stanley B.
  A C++ Primer / by Stanley B. Lippman
    p.   cm.
  Includes index.
  ISBN 0-201-16487-6
  1. C++ (Computer program language)   I. Title. II. Title: C plus
plus primer
QA76.73.C15L57 1989
005.13'3--dc19   88-35096
                                                                    CIP

Reprinted with corrections March, 1990.

This book was typeset in Palatino and Courier by the author, using a Linotron 100 photo-typesetter and a DEC VAX 8550 computer running UNIX® System V, Release 2.

UNIX is a registered trademark of AT&T. MS-DOS is a registered trademark of Microsoft Corporation. DEC and VAX are trademarks of Digital Equipment Corporation. Ada is a trademark of the Ada Joint Program Office, Department of Defense, United States Government.

FGHIJ-DO-943210

To Beth,
who makes this,
and all things,
possible.

Preface

The C++ programming language was developed at AT&T Bell Laboratories in the early 1980's by Bjarne Stroustrup. It is an evolution of the C programming language, which extends C in three important ways:

1. provides support for creating and using data abstractions,

2. provides support for object-oriented design and programming, and

3. provides various nice improvements over existing C constructs,

all while retaining C's simplicity of expression and speed of execution.

C++ is already widely available and is in wide use for real application and systems development. Within six months of its initial release from AT&T in late 1985, there were commercial ports of C++ available on over 24 systems, ranging from PCs to large mainframes. Since then, more ports have been made, and C++ is now available directly from several computer vendors. Additionally, in 1988 the first native compilers were produced for the PC and workstation markets. Papers documenting user experience with C++ have appeared in various conferences and technical publications.

Perhaps because of its rapid spread, C++ use has outpaced the availability of tutorial and other educational materials. This book takes a large step toward filling this gap. The primary reference is Stroustrup's *The C++ Programming Language*, which defines and describes the language as of its initial release. Since that release, the C++ language has continued to evolve as new features were added in response to early user experience. This book provides a comprehensive introduction to C++ as reflected in its latest release, Release 2.0. Additionally, it provides a consciously tutorial approach to describing the language. Knowledge of C is not assumed, although familiarity with some modern, block structured language is. This book is intended as a *first* book on C++; it is not intended as a *first* book on programming!

Much of the power of C++ comes from its support for new ways of programming and new ways of thinking about programming problems. Learning to use C++ effectively, therefore, requires more than simply learning a new set of syntax and semantics. To facilitate this larger learning, the book is organized around a series of extended examples. These examples are used both to introduce the details of various language features, and to motivate them as well. By learning language features in the context of a full example, it becomes clear why such features are useful, providing a sense of when and how one would make use of them for real world problem solving. Additionally, this focus on examples, which can and should be executed, allows early use of concepts that will be explained more fully as the reader's knowledge base is built up. Early examples can and do contain simple uses of fundamental C++ concepts, giving a flavor for the kinds of programming one can do in C++ without requiring complete understanding of the details of design and implementation.

Structure of this Book

Fundamental to C++ are various facilities that allow the user to extend the language itself by defining new data types which then can be used with the flexibility and simplicity of built-in data types. The first step to mastery is to understand the base language itself. Chapters 0 through 4 focus on the language at this level, while Chapters 5 through 8 extend the discussion of the facilities which support creation of user-defined types.

Chapter 0 introduces the essential elements of a C++ program and the details of how to get a C++ program entered and executed. Data types, expressions and statements are the subject of Chapters 1 and 2. Chapter 1 includes a discussion and example of the C++ class introducing this fundamental notion which will be expanded on throughout the book. Chapter 3 introduces functions, while Chapter 4 extends the discussion to encompass name overloading and functions for free store management. Proficient programmers, and especially C programmers, may be tempted to skip these chapters. Don't. New concepts are included throughout these sections and even the most experienced C programmer will benefit from skimming the material and working through the examples in the text and the exercises. Chapters 5 and 6 focus on the class mechanism and how it supports design and implementation of abstract data types. By creating new types to describe the problem domain, C++ allows the programmer to write applications with much less concern for the various bookkeeping aspects that make programming tedious. The implementation of types fundamental to the application can be implemented once and reused, allowing the programmer to concentrate on the problem rather than the details of the implementation. Additionally, facilities for encapsulating the data can dramatically simplify subsequent maintenance and change.

Object-oriented programming and the facilities in C++ which support it are the topics of Chapters 7 and 8. Chapter 7 introduces inheritance. Through inheritance, the programmer can capture type relationships that are interdependent. The classic example is that of shapes. All shapes share certain attributes: location on the plane, logic to rotate the shape, draw the shape, etc. Inheritance allows these common attributes to be shared from the application's viewpoint while the implementation of each specific shape need worry only about providing definitions for those attributes which actually differ from one shape to the next. Fundamental to object-oriented approaches is the ability to choose at runtime which exact function will be invoked. For example, at runtime we must be able to tell a shape to rotate and know that the appropriate logic for a circle or square will be invoked depending on the actual type of the shape that is being rotated. In C++ this is handled through the virtual function mechanism which is the topic of Chapter 8. Chapter 8 also introduces the more complicated inheritance hierarchies that are made possible through virtual base classes.

Like its predecessor C, all input and output is actually handled through a standard library. For Release 2.0 this library has been greatly expanded. A tutorial introduction is provided in Appendix A.

As noted above, C++ has evolved since its initial commercial release. Features new to Release 2.0 include

- Multiple inheritance and virtual base classes.

- Recursive memberwise initialization and assignment.

- Type safe linkage to other languages.

- Overloading of operators new, delete, ->, and , (comma).

- Static and const member functions.

Appendix D considers how these language extensions impact users of earlier releases of C++. While as with any programming language the rate of change in C++ will slow with its greater use, Appendix B examines two features likely to be added to the language.

While C++ is based on C there are obviously quite a number of features in C++ that are not present in C. Similarly, there are a few features common to both C and C++ but in which there are slight differences in actual implementation. These are the topic of Appendix C.

Implementation Notes

The programs in this book were directly taken from source files that were compiled on a DEC VAX 8550 running UNIX System V Release 2. All programs and program fragments were compiled using internal versions of Release 2.0 of C++ currently under development at Bell Laboratories.

Portions of this book have been used in tutorials presented by the author at professional conferences. Drafts of the manuscript have served as both start-up and reference material for internal AT&T Bell Laboratories projects beginning to program in C++. Many of the programs and program fragments in this book have been used as part of the verification suite during the development of Release 2.0 .

The C++ language described in this book is based on the May 1989 draft of the C++ Reference Manual currently under development by Stroustrup. The Reference Manual is included in the AT&T C++ Language System, Release 2.0 documentation.

C++ is available from AT&T, Software Sales and Marketing, P.O. Box 25000, Greensboro, NC 27420, USA (telephone 800-828-UNIX) or from your local sales organization for the UNIX System.

Acknowledgements

This book is the result of many invisible hands helping to keep its author on course. My most heartfelt thanks go to Barbara Moo. Her encouragement, advice, and close reading of innumerable drafts of the manuscript have been invaluable. The opening two sections of this Preface are her work. Special thanks also go to Bjarne Stroustrup for his help and encouragement, and for the wonderful language he has given us. Thanks, also, to Stephen Dewhurst, who provided much early support as I was *first* learning C++.

Martin Carroll, William Hopkins, Brian Kernighan, Andrew Koenig, and Alexis Layton provided especially detailed and perceptive comments. Their reviews have improved this book considerably. Phil Brown, James Coplein, Elizabeth Flanagan, David Jordan, Don Kretsch, Craig Rubin, and Judy Ward reviewed various drafts of the manuscript and provided many helpful comments. David Prosser clarified many ANSI C questions. Jerry Schwarz, who implemented the iostream package, provided the original documentation on which Appendix A is based. His detailed and thoughtful review of that appendix is much appreciated.

The following individuals provided reviews of the manuscript for Addison-Wesley: Steven Bellovin, Victor Milenkovic, Norman Kerth, Justin Smith, Jon Forrest, Darrell Long, and Maurice Herlihy.

I am deeply apreciative to Brian Kernighan and Andrew Koenig for making available a number of typesetting tools.

References

[1] Carlo Ghezzi and Mehdi Jazayeri: *Programming Language Concepts*, John Wiley & Sons, NY, 1982.

[2] Adele Goldberg and David Robson: *SMALLTALK-80: The Language and Its Implementation*, Addison-Wesley, Reading, MA, 1983.

[3] Samuel P. Harbison and Guy L. Steele, Jr.: *C: A Reference Manual*, 2nd edition, Prentice-Hall, Englewood Cliffs, NJ, 1987.

[4] Ralph Johnson and Brian Foote: *Designing Reusable Classes*, Journal of Object-Oriented Programming, June/July 1988, pp.22–35.

[5] Brian W. Kernighan and Dennis M. Ritchie: *The C Programming Language*, 2nd edition, Prentice-Hall, Englewood Cliffs, NJ, 1988.

[6] Andrew Koenig: *C Traps and PitFalls*, Addison-Wesley, Reading, MA, 1989.

[7] Andrew Koenig: *What is C++, Anyway?*, Journal of Object-Oriented Programming, April/May 1988, pp.48–52.

[8] Andrew Koenig: *An Example of Dynamic Binding in C++*, Journal of Object-Oriented Programming, August/September 1988, pp.60–62.

[9] Stanley Lippman and Barbara Moo: *C++: From Research to Practice*, Proc. of the USENIX C++ Conference, Denver, CO, October 17–21, 1988, pp.123–136.

[10] Stanley Lippman and Bjarne Stroustrup: *Pointers to Class Members in C++*, Proc. of the USENIX C++ Conference, Denver, CO, October 17–21, 1988, pp.305–326.

[11] Stanley Lippman: *What is* this?, The C++ Report, March 1989, pp. 6–7.

[12] Barbara Liskov and John Guttag: *Abstraction and Specification in Program Development*, McGraw-Hill, NY, 1986.

[13] Ravi Sethi: *Programming Languages Concepts and Constructs*, Addison-Wesley, Reading, MA, 1989. (Two chapters on C++).

[14] Bjarne Stroustrup: *The C++ Programming Language*, Addison-Wesley, Reading, MA, 1986.

[15] Bjarne Stroustrup: *Multiple Inheritance for C++*, Proc. EUUG Spring'87 Conference, Helsinki, May, 1987.

[16] Bjarne Stroustrup: *What is Object-Oriented Programming?*, Proc. of the USENIX C++ Workshop, Santa Fe, NM, November 9–10, 1987, pp.159–180.

[17] Bjarne Stroustrup: *The Evolution of C++ 1985 to 1987*, Proc. of the USENIX C++ Workshop, Santa Fe, NM, November 9–10, 1987, pp.1–21.

[18] Bjarne Stroustrup: *Possible Directions for C++*, Proc. of the USENIX C++ Workshop, Santa Fe, NM, November 9–10, 1987, pp.399–416.

[19] Bjarne Stroustrup: *Type-safe Linkage for C++*, Proc. of the USENIX C++ Conference, Denver, CO, October 17–21, 1988, pp.193–211.

[20] Bjarne Stroustrup: *Parameterized Types for C++*, Proc. of the USENIX C++ Conference, Denver, CO, October 17–21, 1988, pp.1–18.

A Note on This Printing

The following individuals have pointed out errors in the previous printings of this book: David Beckedorff, Dag Bruck, John Eldridge, Jim Humelsine, Dave Jordan, Ami Kleinman, Andy Koenig, Danny Lippman, Tim O'Konski, Clovis Tondo, and Steve Vinoski. My grateful thanks to all!

CONTENTS

Chapter 0: **Getting Started**

For the individual first learning C++, two questions naturally arise:

1. What is a C++ program, anyway? How is one written?

2. Once it is written, how does one get the program to run?

This chapter presents the basic knowledge and procedures for turning C++ source code into executable programs.

0.1   Problem Solving

Programs often are written in response to some problem or task to be solved. Let's look at an example. A book store enters into a file the title and publisher of each book it sells. The information is entered in the order the books are sold. Every two weeks the owner by hand computes the number of copies of each title sold and the number sold from each publisher. The list is alphabetized by publisher and used for purposes of reordering. You have been asked to supply a program to do this work.

One method of solving a big problem is to break it down into a number of smaller problems. Hopefully, these smaller problems are easier to solve. Our book store problem divides nicely into four subproblems, or tasks:

1. Read in the sales file.

2. Count the sales by title and by publisher.

3. Sort the titles by publisher.

4. Write out the results.

Items 1, 3, and 4 represent problems we know how to solve; they do not need to be broken down further. Item 2, however, is still a little more than we know how to do. So we reapply our method to this item:

2a. Sort the sales by publisher.

2b. Within each publisher, sort the sales by title.

2c. Compare adjacent titles within each publisher group. For each matching pair, increment an occurrence count of the first and delete the second.

1

Items 2a, 2b, and 2c also now represent problems that we know how to solve. Since we can solve all the subproblems that we have generated, we have in effect solved the original, bigger problem. Moreover, we see that the original order of tasks was incorrect. The sequence of actions required is the following:

1. Read in the sales file.

2. Sort the sales file — first, by publisher, then, by title within publisher.

3. Compact duplicate titles.

4. Write out the results into a new file.

The resulting sequence of actions is referred to as an *algorithm*. The next step is to translate our algorithm into a particular programming language — in this case, C++.

0.2   The C++ Program

In C++, an action is referred to as an *expression*. An expression terminated by a semicolon is referred to as a *statement*. The smallest independent unit in a C++ program is a statement. In natural language, an analogous construct is the sentence. The following, for example, are statements in C++:

```
int value;
value = 7 + 1;
cout << value;
```

The first statement is referred to as a *declaration* statement. It defines an area of computer memory associated with the name value that can hold integer values. The second statement is referred to as an *assignment* statement. It places in the area of computer memory associated with the name value the result of adding together 7 and 1. The third statement is an *output* statement. cout is the output destination associated with the user's terminal. << is the output operator. The statement writes to cout, that is, the user's terminal, the value stored in the area of computer memory associated with the name value.

Statements are logically grouped into named units referred to as *functions*. For example, all the statements necessary to read in the sales file are organized into a function called readIn(). Similarly, we organize a sort(), compact(), and print() function.

In C++, every program must contain a function called main(), supplied by the programmer, before the program can be run. Here is how main() might be defined for the preceding algorithm:

```
int main()
{
    readIn();
    sort();
    compact();
    print();
    return 0;
}
```

A C++ program begins execution with the first statement of `main()`. In this case, the program begins by executing the function `readIn()`. Program execution continues by sequentially executing the statements within `main()`. A program terminates normally following execution of the last statement of `main()`.

A function consists of four parts: a return type, the function name, an argument list, and the function body. The first three parts are collectively referred to as the *function prototype*. The argument list, enclosed within parentheses, contains a comma-separated list of zero or more arguments. The function body is enclosed within a pair of braces ("{ }"). It consists of a sequence of program statements.

In this instance, the body of `main()` *calls* for execution the functions `readIn()`, `sort()`, `compact()`, and `print()`. When these have completed, the statement `return 0;` is executed. `return`, a predefined C++ statement, provides a method of terminating the execution of a function. When supplied with a value, such as 0, that value becomes the *return value* of the function. In this case, a return value of 0 indicates the successful completion of `main()`.

Let's turn now to how the program is made ready for execution. First we must provide definitions of `readIn()`, `sort()`, `compact()`, and `print()`. At this point, the following dummy instances are good enough:

```
void readIn()  { cout << "readIn()\n"; }
void sort()    { cout << "sort()\n"; }
void compact() { cout << "compact()\n"; }
void print()   { cout << "print()\n"; }
```

`void` is used to specify a function that does not provide a return value. As defined, each function will simply announce its presence on the user's terminal when invoked by `main()`. Later, we can replace these dummy instances with the actual functions as they are implemented. This sort of incremental method of building programs provides a useful measure of control over the programming errors we inevitably make. Trying to get a program to work all at once is simply too complicated and confusing.

A program source file consists of two parts — a file name and a file suffix. The file suffix serves to identify the contents of the file. This suffix will vary among the different implementations of C++. Under the UNIX operating system, the C++ file may end either with ".c" or ".C". The lower case ".c" reflects the very close ties between the C++ and C programming languages. (All C program source files must end with ".c".) To distinguish a C++ source file, use the ".C" file suffix.†

Enter the following complete program into a C++ source file.

```
#include <stream.h>

void read() { cout << "read()\n"; }
void sort() { cout << "sort()\n"; }
void compact() { cout << "compact()\n"; }
void write() { cout << "write()\n"; }

int main() {
    read();
    sort();
    compact();
    write();
    return 0;
}
```

stream.h is referred to as a *header file*. It contains information about cout that is necessary to our program. #include is referred to as a preprocessor directive. It causes the contents of stream.h to be read into our text file. Section 0.5 (page 13) discusses preprocessor directives.

Once the program has been entered into a file, the next step is to compile it. This is done as follows ($ is the system prompt):

```
$ CC prog1.C
```

The command name used to invoke the C++ compiler will vary among different implementations. CC is the command name for the *AT&T C++ Language System, Release 2.0*. Check the reference manual or ask your system administrator for the C++ command name on your system.

Part of the compiler's job is to analyze the program text for "correctness." A compiler cannot detect if the meaning of a program is correct, but it can detect errors in the *form* of the program. Two common forms of program error are the following:

---

†Under MS-DOS, however, the ".C" suffix is not available — MS-DOS does not distinguish between lower- and uppercase letters. Implementations of C++ under MS-DOS support the following file suffixes:

- cxx (x is a "+" rotated 45 degrees).

- cpp (p stands for "plus").

1. *Syntax errors.* The programmer has made a "grammatical error" in the
   C++ language. For example,

```
int main ( {    // error: missing ')'
    readIn():   // error: illegal character ':'
    sort();
    compact();
    print();
    return 0    // error: missing ';'
}
```

2. *Type errors.* Data in C++ has an associated type. The value 10, for
   example, is an integer. The word "hello" surrounded by double quotation marks is a string. If a function expecting an integer argument is
   given a string, a type error is signaled by the compiler.

An error message will contain a line number and a brief description of
what the compiler believes that you have done wrong. It is a good practice to correct errors in the sequence they are reported. Often a single error
can have a cascading effect and cause a compiler to report more errors
than actually are present. Once you have corrected your program text, the
program should be recompiled.

A second part of the compiler's job is to translate formally correct program text. This translation, referred to as *code generation*, typically generates object or assembly instruction text understood by the computer on
which the program is to be run.

The result of a successful compilation is an executable file. By default,
on the author's system, this file is called a.out. It can be executed as follows:

```
$ a.out
```

Output of the program looks like this:

```
readIn()
sort()
compact()
print()
```

The command option -o name allows the programmer to specify a name
for the program file other than a.out. For example, the command line

```
$ CC -o prog1 prog1.C
```

will create the executable file prog1. To run the program, the user will
write

```
$ prog1
```

In addition to the language compiler and C++ command, a C++ implementation provides a set of standard libraries. Program libraries are a collection of precompiled functions. In C++, for example, input and output
are supported within the C++ standard library. Programmers can use
library functions within their programs in the same way they use functions
they themselves have written.

At its best, a program library allows an expert to package his or her
knowledge for use by the general programmer. Few of us, for example,
know how electricity works; most of us, however, know how to turn on a
switch. A good library can be as easy to use as a light switch. In the next
section, we look at the C++ input/output library.

0.3   A First Look at Input/Output

Input and output are not part of the C++ language, but are supported by a
library written in C++ known as the iostream library. Appendix A looks at
this library in detail.† In this section, enough information is introduced to
get the reader started.

Input coming from the user's terminal, referred to as *standard input*, is
"tied" to the predefined iostream cin (pronounced "see-in"). Output
directed to the user's terminal, referred to as *standard output*, is tied to the
predefined iostream cout (pronounced "see-out").

The output operator ("<<") is used to direct a value to standard output.
For example,

```
cout << "The sum of 7 + 3 = ";
cout << 7 + 3;
cout << "\n";
```

The two character sequence \n represents the *newline* character. When
written, the newline character causes the output to be directed to the next
line. Successive occurrences of the output operator can be concatenated.
For example,

```
cout << "The sum of 7 + 3 = " << 7 + 3 << "\n";
```

Each successive output operator is applied in turn to cout. For readability, the concatenated output statement may span several lines. The following three lines make up a single output statement:

---

†Those readers with a C++ implementation not based on Release 2.0 will have an earlier
version of the library called the *stream* library. The examples in the book use a subset common
to both versions.

```
cout << "The sum of "
     << v1 << " + "
     << v2 << " = " << v1 + v2 << "\n";
```

Similarly, the input operator (">>") is used to read a value from standard input. For example, the following program implements a simple algorithm to read in two values, determine the larger of the two values, and write out the value that is largest.

```
#include <stream.h>

void read2( int&, int& );
int max( int, int );
void writeMax( int );

main() {
    int val1, val2;

    read2( val1, val2 );
    int maxVal = max( val1, val2 );
    writeMax( maxVal );
    return 0;
}

void read2( int& v1, int& v2)
{
    cout << "\nPlease enter two numeric values: ";
    cin >> v1 >> v2;
}

int max( int v1, int v2)
{
    if ( v1 > v2 )
        return v1;
    else
        return v2;
}

void writeMax( int val )
{
    cout << val << " is the largest value.\n";
}
```

but note call ← *(handwritten annotation)*

pass by reference *(handwritten annotation)*

A few remarks should be made about this program. The three function names are listed before the definition of main(). The initial listing, referred to as a *forward declaration,* informs the program that these functions exist and that their definition occurs somewhere else in the program, either later in this file or in a separate file. A function must always be declared to the program before it can be called. A forward declaration is one way to do this.

val1 and val2 are referred to as *symbolic variables*. The statement

```
int val1, val2;
```

defines these variables to the program. Variables must also be made known to the program before they can be used. Variables are discussed in detail in Chapter 1.

v1 and v2, referred to as *formal arguments*, make up the argument list of both read2() and max(). val is the single formal argument of writeMax(). The significance of their declaration is looked at in Section 3.6 (page 117) in the discussion of how arguments are passed to functions.

The reader may have noticed that main() is declared slightly differently this time. It does not explicitly specify a return type. This is permissible in C++: a function that does not indicate a return type is presumed to return an integer value.

When compiled and executed, the program outputs the following (the user entered the values 17 and 124):

```
Please enter two numeric values: 17 124
124 is the largest value.
```

The two values entered by the user, 17 and 124, are separated by a blank. Blanks, tabs and newlines are referred to as *white space* in C++. The statement

```
cin >> v1 >> v2;
```

correctly reads in the two values because the input operator (">>") discards all white space that it encounters.

Forward declarations of cin and cout are contained within stream.h. If the programmer should forget to include this file, each reference to either cin or cout will be flagged as a type error by the compiler. The storage of forward declarations is the primary use of header files. (Section 4.5 (page 173) considers header files in detail.)

A third predefined iostream, cerr (pronounced "see-err"), referred to as *standard error*, is also "tied" to the user's terminal. cerr is used to alert the user to some exceptional condition in the program during execution. For example, the following code segment prevents the programmer from dividing by zero:

```
if ( v2 == 0 ) {
    cerr << "\nerror: attempt to divide by zero";
    return;
}
v3 = v1/v2;
```

The following program reads a character at a time from standard input until *end-of-file* is encountered. It keeps a count of both the number of characters and the number of lines it reads. Its output is of the following form:

```
lineCount characterCount
```

Here is the implementation:

```
#include <stream.h>

main () {
    char ch;
    int lineCnt=0,  charCnt=0;

    while ( cin.get(ch) )
    {
        switch ( ch )
        {
          case '\t':
          case ' ':
                break;
          case '\n':
                ++lineCnt;
                break;
          default:
                ++charCnt;
                break;
        }
    }
    cout << lineCnt << " " << charCnt << "\n";
    return 0;
}
```

get() is an iostream function which reads one character at a time, placing that character in its argument — in this case, ch. The two character sequence \t represents the *tab* character.

The switch statement provides a form of conditional testing on a value. If the value matches an explicit case, the statements following that case are executed. If there is no match, the statements following default are executed. Each newline character that is read increments by 1 the value of lineCnt. charCnt is incremented by 1 each time a character is read that is not a tab, blank or newline. The while statement, referred to as a *loop*, provides for the repeated execution of a set of statements as long as some condition holds true. In this case, the `switch` statement is executed for as long as `get()` reads in another character from standard input. (The `while` and `switch` statements are discussed in Chapter 2.)

Exercise 0-1. Enter the program in the file `prog2.<some-suffix>` and compile it into an executable file named `prog2`.

□

Exercise 0-2. Run the program against the text of the previous exercise. Run it against the text of its own program source file. Run it against text consisting only of white space. Run it against text consisting only of end-of-file.

□

Exercise 0-3. Modify the the program to keep a separate count of tabs (`tabCnt`) and blank lines (`blankCnt`). Have the output look as follows:

```
        Total Characters: xx

    Lines:   x
    Chars:   x
    Tabs:    x
    Blanks:  x
```

□

0.4   A Word about Comments

Comments serve as an aid to the human readers of our programs; they are a form of engineering etiquette. They may summarize a function's algorithm, identify the purpose of a variable, or clarify an otherwise obscure segment of code. Comments do not increase the size of the executable program. They are stripped from the program by the compiler before code generation.

There are two comment delimiters in C++. The comment pair ("/* */") is the same comment delimiter used in the C language. The beginning of a comment is indicated by a "/*". The compiler will treat everything that falls between the "/*" and a matching "*/" as part of the comment. A comment pair can be placed anywhere a tab, space, or newline is permitted and can span multiple lines of a program. For example,

```
/*
 * This is a first look at a C++ class definition.
 * Classes are used both in data abstraction and
 * object-oriented programming.  An implementation
 * of the Screen class is presented in Chapter 5.
 */

class Screen {
/* This is referred to as the class body */
public:
    void home();          /* move cursor to 0,0 */
    void refresh();       /* redraw Screen        */
private:
/* Classes support ''information hiding''.   */
/* Information hiding restricts a program's  */
/* access to the internal representation of  */
/* a class (its data).  This is done through */
/* use of the ''private:'' label             */
    char *cursor; /* current Screen position */
};
```

Too many comments intermixed with the program code can obscure the code. Surrounded as it is by comments, for example, the declaration of cursor is very nearly hidden. In general, it is preferable to place a comment block above the text that it is explaining.

Comment pairs do not nest. That is, one comment pair cannot occur within a second pair. Try the following program, which will generate many compiler errors, on your system. How would you fix it?

```
#include <stream.h>

/*
 * comment pairs /* */ do not nest.
 * "do not nest" is considered source code,
 * as are both these lines and the next.
 */

main() {
    cout << "hello, world\n";
}
```

The second comment delimiter, indicated by a double slash ("//"), serves to delimit a single line comment. Everything on the program line to the right of the delimiter is treated as a comment and ignored by the compiler. For example,

```
#include <stream.h>
#include "myIO.h"
int isOdd( int );

main() {
    int v1, v2;         // hold values from user

    read2( v1, v2 ); // declared in myIO.h

    if ( isOdd( v1 ) == 1 )
        cout << v1
            << " is odd\n";

    if ( isOdd( v2 ) == 1 )
        cout << v2
            << " is odd\n";

    return 0;
}

isOdd( int val ) {
/* return 1 if val is odd; otherwise, return 0
 * % is the modulus operator: 3 % 2 yields 1. */

    return(val % 2 != 0);
}
```

This program determines whether values are even or odd. It reuses the read2() function defined in the previous section; the read2() function prototype has been stored in a header file named myIO.h. When the program is compiled and executed, its output looks as follows (the values 497 and −25 are entered by the user):

```
Please enter two numeric values: 497 -25
497 is odd
-25 is odd
```

The two characters of either comment delimiter must not be separated by white space. The following two lines, for example, are *not* treated as comments, but, rather, as program text:

```
/ * not a comment: white space not allowed */
/ / also not a comment: must be //
```

Programs typically contain a mixture of both comment forms. Multiline explanations are generally set off between comment pairs. Half-line and single-line remarks are more often delineated by the double slash.

0.5   Preprocessor Directives

Provided with the standard libraries are a set of standard header files, such as `stream.h`. These header files contain all the information a user requires in order to make use of these libraries. In order to access a variable or function defined within the standard libraries, we must include the associated header file into our program.

Header files are made a part of our program by the `include` *directive*. Directives are specified by placing a pound sign ("#") in the very first column of a line in our program. Directives are processed prior to the invocation of the language compiler. The program that handles directives is referred to as the *preprocessor*.

The `#include` directive reads in the contents of the named file. It takes one of two forms:

```
#include <stream.h>
#include "myIO.h"
```

If the file name is enclosed by angle brackets ("<>") the file is presumed to be a predefined, or *standard*, header file. The search to find it will examine a predefined set of locations, which can be modified by specifying the `-I` option to the `CC` command.† For example,

```
$ CC -I incl -I/usr/local/include prog1.c
```

tells the preprocessor to look first in the directory `incl` and then in the directory `/usr/local/include` before looking in the predefined set of locations. The first located instance of the file terminates the search.

If the file name is enclosed by a pair of quotation marks, the file is presumed to be a user-supplied header file. The search to find it begins in the current directory. If it is not found, then the predefined set of locations is examined. The `-I` option also works with user-supplied header files.

The included file may itself contain a `#include` directive. Because of nested include files, a header file may sometimes be pulled in multiple times for a single source file. Conditional directives can be used to guard against the multiple processing of a header file. For example,

```
#ifndef STRING_H
#define STRING_H
/* String.h contents go here */
#endif
```

The conditional directive `#ifndef` evaluates as true if the name that

---

†Those using other implementations should refer to the reference guide for their C++ command to find the name of the analogous command option.

follows it is not yet defined. When a conditional directive evaluates as true, the subsequent lines until a #endif is encountered are included. If the conditional directive evaluates as false, the lines between it and the #endif directive are ignored.

The #define directive defines the name that follows it. In this case, it defines STRING_H. If the String.h header file is included again, the #ifndef directive will evaluate to false; the contents of String.h will not be included a second time.

The #ifdef directive evaluates as true if the name which follows it is defined. For example,

```
#ifdef u3b2
/* system specific code
 * for AT&T 3B computers goes here */
#endif

#ifdef sun
/* system specific code
 * for Sun computers goes here */
#endif
```

C++ predefines the name __cplusplus (two underscores). A user who wishes to mix C and C++ program code might write the following:

```
#ifdef __cplusplus
extern min( int, int );
int *pi = new int;
#else
extern min();
int *pi;
#endif
```

The statements between the #else directive and the #endif directive will be included if the #ifdef or #ifndef directive evaluates to false.

The preprocessor is closely tied to the C language (and is often called *cpp*, the C preprocessor). Many implementations simply use the underlying C preprocessor and therefore do not recognize the C++ single-line comment delimiter. If you wish to include a comment on a #define directive line, it is safest to use the C comment pair notation:

```
#ifdef u3b2
#define SYSV      /* UNIX System V */
#endif
```

Chapter 1: **The C++ Data Types**

C++ provides a predefined set of data types, operators to manipulate those types, and a small set of statements for program flow control. These elements form an alphabet with which many large, complex real-world systems can be written. At this basic level C++ is a simple language. Its expressive power arises from its support for mechanisms that allow the programmer to define new data abstractions.

The first step in mastering C++ — understanding the basic language — is the topic of this chapter and the next one. This chapter discusses the predefined data types and looks at the mechanisms for constructing new types, while Chapter 2 examines the predefined operators and statements.

The program text we write and program data we manipulate are stored as a sequence of bits in the memory of the computer. A *bit* is a single cell, holding a value of 0 or 1. In physical terms this value is an electrical charge which is either "off" or "on." A typical segment of computer memory might look as follows:

...0001101101110001011001000001111011...

This collection of bits at this level is without structure. It is difficult to speak of this bit stream in any meaningful way.

Structure is imposed on the bit stream by considering the bits in aggregates referred to as *bytes* and *words*. Generally, a byte is composed of 8 bits. A word is typically composed of either 16 or 32 bits. Byte and word sizes vary from one computer to the next. We speak of these values as being *machine dependent*. Fig. 1.1 illustrates our bit stream organized into four addressable byte rows.

The organization of memory allows us to refer to a particular collection of bits. Thus, it is possible to speak of the word at address 1024 or the byte at address 1040, allowing us to say, for example, that the byte at address 1032 is not equal to the byte at address 1048.

It is still not possible, however, to speak meaningfully of the content of the byte at address 1032. Why? Because we do not know how to interpret its bit sequence. To speak of the meaning of the byte at address 1032, we must know the type of the value being represented.

Type abstraction allows for a meaningful interpretation of fixed-length bit sequences at a particular address. Characters, integers, and floating

15

1024	0	0	0	1	1	0	1	1
1032	0	1	1	1	0	0	0	1
1040	0	1	1	0	0	1	0	0
1048	0	0	1	1	1	0	1	1

Figure 1.1 Addressable Machine Memory

point numbers are examples of data types. Other types include memory addresses and the machine instructions that drive the workings of the computer.

C++ provides a predefined set of data types, which allow the representation of integers and floating point numbers and of individual characters.

- The type char can be used to represent individual characters or small integers. A char is represented in a machine byte.

- The type int can be used to represent integer values. Typically, an int is represented in a machine word.

C++ also provides short and long integer types. The actual size of these types is machine dependent. char, short, int, and long are referred to collectively as the *integral types*. Integral types may be either signed or unsigned. The difference is in the interpretation of the type's left-most bit. In a signed type, the left-most bit serves as the *sign bit*, while the remaining bits represent the value. In an unsigned type, all the bits represent the value. If the sign bit is set to 1, the value is interpreted as negative; if 0, positive. An 8 bit signed char may represent the values −128 through 127; an unsigned char, 0 through 255.

The types float and double represent floating point single and double precision values.† Typically, floats are represented in one word; doubles, in two words. The actual sizes are machine dependent. The choice of a data type is determined by the range of values that it is expected to hold. For example, if the values are guaranteed never to exceed 255 or to be less than 0, then an unsigned char is a sufficient data type. If the values are expected to exceed 255, however, then one of the larger data types is necessary.

---

†A third floating point data type, long double, is likely to be added to C++ in the near future. long double is proposed for inclusion in the ANSI C language standard.

1.1 Constant Values

When a value such as 1 occurs in a program, it is referred to as a *literal constant*: literal because we can speak of it only in terms of its value; constant because its value cannot be changed.

Every literal has an associated type. 1, for example, is of type int. 3.14159 is a literal constant of type double. We refer to a literal constant as *nonaddressable*; although its value is stored somewhere in the computer's memory, we have no means of accessing that address.

Literal integer constants can be written in decimal, octal, or hexadecimal notation. (This does not change the bit representation of the value.) The value 20, for example, can be written in any of the following three ways:

```
20     // decimal
024    // octal
0x14   // hexadecimal
```

Prepending a 0 (zero) to a literal integer constant will cause it to be interpreted as being octal notation. Prepending either 0x or 0X will cause a literal integer constant to be interpreted as being hexadecimal notation. (Appendix A discusses printing values in octal or hexadecimal notation.)

A literal integer constant can be specified as being of type long by following its value with either L or l (the letter "ell" in either uppercase or lowercase). Using the lowercase letter in general should be avoided since it is easily mistaken for the number 1. In a similar manner, a literal integer constant can be specified as being unsigned by following its value with either a U or u. An unsigned long literal constant can also be specified. For example,

```
128u    1024UL    1L    8Lu
```

A floating point literal constant can be written in either scientific or common decimal notation. Using scientific notation, the exponent can be written as either E or e. A literal floating point constant can be specified as being of type float by following its value with either F or f. Examples of floating point literal constants follow:

```
3.14159F       0.1f        0.0
3e1            1.0E-3      2.
```

A printable literal character constant can be written by enclosing the character within single quotation marks. For example,

```
'a'        '2'         ','         ' '  (blank)
```

Selected nonprintable characters, the single and double quotation marks, and the backslash can be represented by the following escape sequences:

```
newline              \n
horizontal tab       \t
vertical tab         \v
backspace            \b
carriage return      \r
formfeed             \f
alert (bell)         \a
backslash            \\
question mark        \?
single quote         \'
double quote         \"
```

A generalized escape sequence can also be used. It takes the form

```
\ooo
```

where ooo represents a sequence of up to three octal digits. The value of the octal digits represents the numerical value of the character in the machine's character set. The following examples are representations of literal constants using the ASCII character set:

```
\7 (bell)            \12 (newline)
\0 (null)            \062 ('2')
```

A string literal constant is composed of zero or more characters enclosed in double quotation marks. Nonprintable characters can be represented by their escape sequence. A string literal can extend across multiple source program lines. A backslash as the last character on a line indicates that the string literal is continued on the next line. The following are examples of string literal constants:

```
"" (null string)
"a"
"\nCC\toptions\tfile:[cC]\n"
"a multi-line \
string literal signals its \
continuation with a backslash"
```

A string literal is of type *array of characters*. It consists of both the string literal and a terminating null character added by the compiler. For example, while 'a' represents the single character a, "a" represents the single character a followed by the null character. The null character is used to signal the end of the string.

1.2   Symbolic Variables

Imagine that we are given the problem of computing 2 to the power of 10. Our first attempt might look as follows:

```
#include <stream.h>

main() {
    // a first solution
    cout << "2 raised to the power of 10: ";
    cout << 2 * 2 * 2 * 2 * 2 * 2 * 2 * 2 * 2 * 2;
    cout << "\n";
    return 0;
}
```

This works, although we might double or triple check to make sure that exactly 10 literal instances of 2 are being multiplied. Otherwise we're satisfied. Our program correctly generates the answer 1024.

We're next asked to compute 2 raised to the power of 17 and then to the power of 23. Changing our program each time is a pain. Worse, it seems remarkably easy to produce an answer with one too few or too many instances of 2. Being careful, however, we have avoided mistakes.

Finally we are asked to produce a table listing the powers of 2 from 0 through 31. Using literal constants in a straight code sequence requires 64 lines of the following form:

```
cout << "2 raised to the power of X\t";
cout << 2 * ... * 2;
```

where X will increase by one with each code pair.

At this point, if not earlier, we realize that there must be a better way. As indeed there is. The solution involves two program capabilities that we have not yet formally introduced:

1. Symbolic variables, which allow for the storage and retrieval of values.

2. Flow of control statements, which allow for the repeated execution of a segment of code.

For example, here is a second method of computing 2 raised to the power of 10:

```
#include <stream.h>

main() {
    // a second more general solution
    int value = 2;
    int pow = 10;

    cout << value
        << " raised to the power of "
        << pow << ": \t";

    for ( int i = 1, res = 1; i <= pow; ++i ) {
        res = res * value;
    }

    cout << res << "\n";
    return 0;
}
```

The statement beginning with `for` is referred to as a *loop*: as long as i is less than or equal to pow, the body of the `for` loop (enclosed by braces) is executed. The `for` loop is referred to as a *flow of control* statement. (Program statements are discussed in detail in Chapter 2.)

value, pow, res, and i are symbolic variables that allow for the storage, modification, and retrieval of values. They are the topic of the following subsections. First, however, let's apply another level of generalization to the program by extracting the portion of the program that computes the exponential value and defining it as a separate function:

```
unsigned int
pow( int val, int exp )
{
    // compute val raised to exp power
    for ( unsigned int res = 1; exp > 0; --exp )
        res = res * val;
    return res;
}
```

Each program task that requires computing an exponential value now need only call pow() with its particular set of arguments. Generating a table of the powers of 2 can be done as follows:

```
#include <stream.h>

extern unsigned int pow( int, int );
main() {
    int val = 2;
    int exp = 16;

    cout << "\nThe Powers of 2\n";
    for ( int i = 0; i <= exp; ++i )
        cout << i << ": " << pow( val, i ) << "\n";
    return 0;
}
```

The output of this program is presented in Table 1.1.

The Powers of 2

0: 1
1: 2
2: 4
3: 8
4: 16
5: 32
6: 64
7: 128
8: 256
9: 512
10: 1024
11: 2048
12: 4096
13: 8192
14: 16384
15: 32768
16: 65536

Table 1.1 Powers of 2

This implementation of pow() does not handle a number of special conditions, including negative exponents and resulting values that are very large.

Exercise 1-1. What would happen if pow() were passed a negative second argument? How would you modify pow() to handle this?

☐

Exercise 1-2. Every data type has upper and lower bounds to the range of values it can hold, determined by the size in bits of its type representation. How does this affect the implementation of `pow()`? How would you modify `pow()` to handle a call such as `pow(2,48)`? □

What Is a Variable?

A symbolic variable is identified by a user-supplied name. Each variable is of a particular data type. For example, the following statement declares a variable `ch` of the data type `char`:

```
char ch;
```

`char` is a *type specifier*. `short`, `int`, `long`, `float`, and `double` also serve as type specifiers. In general, any declaration must begin with a type specifier. The data type determines the amount of storage allocated to the variable and the set of operations that can be performed on the variable. (For our purposes, a `char` will be a byte of size 8 bits.)

Both a symbolic variable and a literal constant maintain storage and have an associated type. The difference is that a symbolic variable is *addressable*. That is, there are two values associated with a symbolic variable:

1. Its data value, stored at some location in memory. This is sometimes referred to as a variable's *rvalue* (pronounced "are-value").

2. Its location value; that is, the address in memory at which its data value is stored. This is sometimes referred to as a variable's *lvalue* (pronounced "ell-value").

In the expression

```
ch = ch - '0';
```

the symbolic variable `ch` appears on both the right- and left-hand sides of the assignment operator. The right-hand instance is *read*. Its data value is fetched from its memory location. The character literal `'0'` is then subtracted from that value. The term rvalue is derived from the variable's position to the right of the assignment operator. An rvalue may be read but not altered. You might think of rvalue as meaning *read value*.

The left-hand instance is *written*. The result of the subtraction operation is stored at the location value of `ch`; its previous value is overwritten. The term lvalue is derived from the variable's position to the left of the assignment operator. You might think of lvalue as meaning *location value*.

ch is referred to as an *object*. An object represents a region of memory. ch represents a region of memory of size 1 byte.

The *definition* of a variable causes storage to be allocated. A definition introduces the variable's name and its type. Optionally, an initial value for the variable may also be introduced. There must be one and only one definition of a variable in a program.

The *declaration* of a variable announces that the variable exists and is defined somewhere else. It consists of the variable's name and its type preceded by the keyword extern. (For a full discussion, see Section 3.9 (page 124) on program scope.) A declaration is *not* a definition. A declaration does not result in an allocation of storage. Rather, it is an assertion that a definition of the variable exists elsewhere in the program. A variable can be declared multiple times in a program.

In C++, a variable must be defined or declared to the program before it is used.

The Name of a Variable

The name of a variable, its *identifier*, can be composed of letters, digits, and the underscore character. It must begin with either a letter or an underscore. Upper- and lowercase letters are distinct. There is no language-imposed limit on the permissible length of a name, which varies among implementations.

C++ reserves a set of words for use within the language as keywords. The predefined type specifiers, for example, are all reserved keywords. The keyword identifiers may not be reused as program identifiers. Table 1.2 lists the reserved keywords in C++.†

There are a number of generally accepted conventions in naming identifiers, most concerning the human readability of programs:

- An identifier is normally written in lowercase letters.

- An identifier is provided with a mnemonic name; that is, a name which gives some indication of its use in a program.

- A multiword identifier either places an underscore between each word or capitalizes the first letter of each embedded word. For example, one writes is_empty or isEmpty, not isempty.

---

†Note that template is a proposed keyword for a possible future extension to C++ to support *parameterized types*. Appendix B examines possible future directions for C++.

asm	delete	if	register	template
auto	do	inline	return	try
break	double	int	short	typedef
case	else	long	signed	union
catch	enum	new	sizeof	unsigned
char	extern	operator	static	virtual
class	float	overload	struct	void
const	for	private	switch	volatile
continue	friend	protected	this	while
default	goto	public		

Table 1.2 C++ Keywords

Variable Definitions

A simple definition consists of a type specifier followed by a name. The definition is terminated by a semicolon. Examples of simple definitions follow:

```
double salary;
double wage;
int month;
int day;
int year;
unsigned long distance;
```

When more than one identifier of a type is being defined, a comma-separated list of identifiers may follow the type specifier. The list may span multiple lines. It is terminated by a semicolon. For example, the preceding definitions can be rewritten as follows:

```
double salary, wage;
int month,
    day, year;
unsigned long distance;
```

A simple definition specifies the type and identifier of a variable. It does not provide a first value. A variable without a first value is spoken of as *uninitialized*. An uninitialized variable is not without a value; rather, its value is said to be *undefined*. This is because the memory storage allocated for the variable is not swept clean. Whatever was stored there by the previous use of the memory remains. When an uninitialized variable is read, its arbitrary bit pattern is interpreted as its value. This value may vary from one execution of a program to another. The following program example illustrates the arbitrary nature of uninitialized data:

```
#include <stream.h>

const iterations = 2;
void func() {
// illustrate danger of uninitialized variables

    int value1, value2; // uninitialized
    static int depth = 0;

    if ( depth < iterations ) {
        ++depth;
        func();
    }
    else depth = 0;

    cout << "\nvalue1:\t" << value1;
    cout << "\tvalue2:\t" << value2;
    cout << "\tsum:\t" << value1 + value2;
}

main() {
    for ( int i = 0; i < iterations; ++i )
        func();
}
```

When this program is compiled and executed, it produces the following rather surprising output (moreover, these results will vary each time the program is compiled and executed):

```
value1: 0           value2: 74924    sum:       74924
value1: 0           value2: 68748    sum:       68748
value1: 0           value2: 68756    sum:       68756
value1: 148620   value2: 2350     sum:       150970
value1: 2147479844          value2: 671088640
            sum:       -1476398812
value1: 0           value2: 68756    sum:       68756
```

In the program, iterations is referred to as a *symbolic constant*. This is indicated by the keyword const. Symbolic constants are discussed in Section 1.5 (page 36) in this chapter. depth is referred to as a *local static variable*. The meaning of the keyword static is explained in Section 3.10 (page 132) in the discussion of scope. func() is referred to as a *recursive function*. Section 3.1 (page 105) discusses recursive functions.

A first value may be specified in the definition of a variable. A variable with a declared first value is spoken of as an *initialized* variable. Examples of initialized variables include the following:

```
#include <math.h>

double price = 109.99, discount = 0.16,
       salePrice = price * discount;

int val = getValue();
unsigned absVal = abs( val );
```

abs(), a predefined function stored in the math library, returns the absolute value of its argument. getValue() is a user-defined function that returns a random integer value. A variable may be initialized with an arbitrarily complex expression.

1.3   Pointer Types

A pointer variable holds values that are the addresses of objects in memory. Through a pointer, an object can be referenced indirectly. Typical uses of pointers are the creation of linked lists and the management of objects allocated during program execution.

Every pointer has an associated type. The data type specifies the type of data object the pointer will address. A pointer of type int, for example, will point to an object of type int. In order to point to an object of type double, a pointer of type double is defined.

The storage allocated a pointer is the size necessary to hold a memory address. This means that a pointer of type int and a pointer of type double are usually the same size. The pointer's associated type specifies how the contents and size of the memory it addresses should be interpreted. The following are examples of pointer variable definitions:

```
int *ip1, *ip2;
unsigned char *ucp;
double *dp;
```

A pointer definition is specified by prefixing the identifier with the dereference operator ("*"). In a comma-separated definition list, the dereference operator must precede each identifier intended to serve as a pointer. In the following example, lp is interpreted as a pointer to a long and lp2 is interpreted as a data object of type long and not as a pointer type:

```
long *lp, lp2;
```

In this next example, fp is interpreted as a data object of type float and fp2 is interpreted as a pointer to a float:

```
float fp, *fp2;
```

For clarity, it is preferable to write

```
char *cp;
```

rather than

```
char* cp;
```

Too often, a programmer, later wishing to define a second character pointer, will incorrectly modify this definition as follows:

```
char* cp, cp2;
```

A pointer may be initialized with the lvalue of a data object of the same type. Recall that an object appearing on the right-hand side of the assignment operator yields its rvalue. To obtain an object's lvalue, a special operator must be applied. This operator is referred to as the *address-of* operator; its symbol is the ampersand ("&"). For example,

```
int i = 1024;
int *ip = &i; // assign ip the address of i
```

A pointer may also be initialized with another pointer of the same type. In this case, the address-of operator is prohibited:

```
int *ip2 = ip;
```

It is always an error to initialize a pointer to a data object's rvalue. The following declaration will be flagged as illegal during compilation:

```
int i = 1024;
int *ip = i; // error
```

It is also an error to initialize a pointer to an lvalue of an object of a different type. The following definitions of uip and uip2 will be flagged as illegal during compilation:

```
int i = 1024, *ip = &i; // ok
unsigned int *uip = &i, // illegal
             *uip2 = ip; // illegal
```

C++ is a *strongly typed* language. All initializations and assignments of values are checked at compile time to be sure the types of these values are correctly matched. If they are not and if a rule exists for matching them, the compiler will apply that rule. This rule is referred to as a *type conversion*. (See Section 2.10 (page 80) for a discussion.) If there is no rule, the statement is flagged as an error. This is the desirable action since initialization or assignment without a conversion rule is unsafe and will likely result in a program error during execution.

It should be obvious why assigning an object's rvalue to a pointer is unsafe. The pointer will assume the value is a memory address. An attempt to either read or write to that "address" will be disastrous.

The danger in assigning to a pointer the lvalue of an object of a different type is more subtle. It goes back to the idea that a pointer's type specifies how the addressed memory should be interpreted.

For example, although an `int` pointer and a `double` pointer can each hold the same memory address, the size of the memory read and written through the two pointers will differ by the different sizes of an `int` and a `double`. Additionally, the organization and meaning of the bit sequences may differ between data types.

This is not to say that the programmer cannot convert a pointer of one type to a pointer to another type. Since this is potentially unsafe, however, the programmer must do it explicitly. (Section 2.10 (page 84) discusses explicit type conversions, referred to as *casts*.)

A pointer of any type may be assigned a value of 0, indicating that a pointer is not currently addressing a data object. A value of 0, when used as a pointer value, is sometimes referred to as *NULL*. There is also a special pointer type, `void*`, which may be assigned the address of an object of any data type. (Section 2.10 (page 84) discusses the `void*` pointer type.)

In order to access the object a pointer addresses, the dereference operator must be applied. For example,

```
int i = 1024;
int *ip = &i; // ip now points to i
int k = *ip;  // k now contains 1024
```

Were the dereference operator not applied, k would be initialized to the address of i and not to i's value, resulting in a compile time error:

```
int *ip = &i; // ip now points to i
int k = ip;   // error
```

In order to assign a value to the object a pointer addresses, the dereference operator must be applied to the pointer. For example,

```
int *ip = &i; // ip now points to i

*ip = k;            // i = k
*ip = abs( *ip ); // i = abs(i);
*ip = *ip + 1;     // i = i + 1;
```

The following two assignment statements have very different results, although both are legal. The first statement increases the address that the pointer ip contains; the second increases the value of the data object that ip addresses.

```
int i, j, k;
int *ip = &i;

*ip = *ip + 2; // add two to i (i = i + 2)
ip = ip + 2;   // add to the address ip contains
```

A pointer may have its address value added to or subtracted by an integral value. This sort of pointer manipulation, referred to as *pointer arithmetic,* may at first appear slightly nonintuitive until we realize that the addition is of data objects and not of discrete decimal values. That is, the addition of 2 to a pointer increases the value of the address it contains by the size of two objects of its type. For example, allowing that a char is 1 byte, an int is 4 bytes, and a double is 8, the addition of 2 to a pointer increases its address value by 2, 8, or 16 depending on whether the pointer is of type char, int, or double.

Exercise 1-3. Given the following definitions:

```
int ival = 1024;
int *iptr;
double *dptr;
```

which of the following assignments, if any, are illegal? Explain why.

```
(a) ival = *iptr;          (b) ival = iptr;
(c) *iptr = ival;          (d) iptr = ival;
(e) *iptr = &ival;         (f) iptr = &ival;
(g) dptr = iptr;           (h) dptr = *iptr;
```

☐

Exercise 1-4. A variable is assigned one of only three possible values: 0, 128, and 255. Discuss the advantages and disadvantages of declaring the variable to be of the following data types:

```
(a) double          (c) unsigned char
(b) int             (d) char
```

☐

String Pointers

The most frequently defined pointer to a predefined data type is char*. This is because all string manipulation in C++ is done through character pointers. This subsection considers the use of char* in detail. In Chapter 6, we will define a String class type.

The type of a literal string constant is a pointer to the first character of the string. This means that every string constant is of type `char*`. We may declare a variable of type `char*` and initialize it to a string, as follows:

```
char *st = "The expense of spirit\n";
```

The following program, which is intended to compute the length of `st`, uses pointer arithmetic to advance through the string. The idea is to terminate the loop statement when the null character the compiler places at the end of every literal string constant is encountered. Unfortunately, we have coded the program incorrectly. Can you see the error?

```
#include <stream.h>
char *st = "The expense of spirit\n";

main() {
    int len = 0;

    while ( st++ != '\0' )
        ++len;

    cout << len << ": " << st;
    return 0;
}
```

This program fails because `st` is not dereferenced. That is,

```
st++ != '\0'
```

tests whether or not the address `st` points to is the null character, not whether the character that it addresses is null. The condition will always evaluate as true since each iteration of the loop adds one to the address of `st`. The program will execute forever, or until the system stops it. A loop such as this is referred to as an *infinite loop*.

Our second version of the program corrects this mistake. It runs to completion. Unfortunately, its output is in error. The string that `st` addresses is not printed out. Can you see the mistake we've made this time?

```
#include <stream.h>
char *st = "The expense of spirit\n";

main() {
    int len = 0;

    while ( *st++ != '\0' )
        ++len;

    cout << len << ": " << st;
    return 0;
}
```

The mistake in this case is that st no longer addresses the string literal constant. It has been advanced to point to the terminating null character. This is the character the program directs to standard output. Somehow we must return to the address of the string. Here is one solution:

```
st -= len;
cout << len << ": " << st;
```

The program is compiled and executed. Its output, however, is still incorrect. It now generates the following:

```
22: he expense of spirit
```

This reflects something of the nature of programming. Can you see the mistake we've made this time?

The terminating null character of the string is not being taken into account. st must be repositioned the length of the string *plus one*. The following line is correct:

```
st -= len + 1;
```

When compiled and executed, the program correctly outputs the following:

```
22: The expense of spirit
```

The program is now correct. In terms of program style, however, it is still less than perfect. The statement

```
st -= len + 1;
```

has been added to correct the error introduced by directly incrementing st. The reassignment of st does not fit into the original logic of the program, however, and the program is now a little less easy to understand.

In a program this small, of course, one obscure statement may not seem very serious. Consider, however, that this statement represents 20% of the executable statements in our program. Extrapolate that to a program of 10,000 lines and the problem is no longer trivial. A program correction like this is often referred to as a *patch* — something stretched over a hole in an existing program.

We patched our program by compensating for a logic error in the original design. A better solution is to correct the original design flaw. One solution is to define a second character pointer and initialize it with st. For example,

```
char *p = st;
```

p can now be used in our computation of the length of st, while st is left unchanged:

```
while ( *p++ != '\0' )
```

Let's look at another improvement to our program — one that permits our work to be used by others. As it is coded now, there is no way for another program to calculate the length of a string except by rewriting or copying our work. Either alternative is wasteful.

A more productive alternative is to separate out the code that calculates the length of a string. By placing that code in a separate function, it becomes available to any programmer on our system. Here is how we might define stringLength():

```
#include <stream.h>

void stringLength( char *st )
{ // calculate length of st
    int len = 0;
    char *p = st;

    while ( *p++ )
        ++len;

    cout << len << ": " << st ;
}
```

The definition

```
char *p = st;
```

corrects the design flaw of the original program. The statement

```
while ( *p++ )
```

is a shorthand notation for

```
while ( *p++ != '\0' )
```

Now we can modify main() to take advantage of the stringLength() function:

```
extern void stringLength( char* );
char *st = "The expense of spirit\n";

main() {
    stringLength( st );
    return 0;
}
```

stringLength() is stored in the file string.C. Compiling and executing this program is done as follows:

```
$ CC main.C string.C
$ a.out
22: The expense of spirit
$
```

The design of stringLength() reflects the needs of our original program too closely. It is not general enough to serve most other programs. For example, imagine that we are asked to write a function that determines whether two strings are equal. We might design our algorithm as follows:

- Test whether the two pointers address the same string. If they do, the strings are equal.

- Otherwise, test whether the lengths of the two strings are the same. If they are not, the two strings are unequal.

- Otherwise, test whether the characters of the two strings are equal. If they are, the two strings are equal. Otherwise, the two strings are unequal.

stringLength(), as we have designed it, cannot be used with this new function. A more general design would have it simply return the length of the string. Any display of that string should be left to the program that calls stringLength(). Here is our new implementation:

```
int stringLength( char *st )
{ // return length of st
    int len = 0;

    while ( *st++ )
        ++len;

    return len;
}
```

It may surprise the reader to see that this version of stringLength() again directly increments st. This does not present a problem in this new implementation for the following two reasons:

1. Unlike those earlier versions, this `stringLength()` implementation does not access st after st has been modified, and so the change to st does not matter.

2. Any changes made to the value of st within `stringLength()` disappear when `stringLength()` completes execution. st is said to be *passed-by-value* to the `stringLength()` function. This means, in effect, that `stringLength()` manipulates only a copy of st. (Section 3.6 (page 117) discusses pass-by-value in detail.)

`stringLength()` can now be called by any program wishing to calculate the length of a string. For the purposes of our program, the `main()` function must be reimplemented:

```
...
main() {
    int len = stringLength( st );
    cout << len << ": " << st;
    return 0;
}
```

`stringLength()` performs the same service that the `strlen()` library function performs. By including the standard header file `string.h`, the programmer can utilize a large number of useful string functions, including the following:

```
// copy src into dst
char *strcpy( char *dst, char *src );

// compare two strings.  return 0 if equal.
int strcmp( char *s1, char *s2 );

// return the length of st
int strlen( char *st );
```

For more details and a full list of the string library functions, refer to your library reference manual.

Exercise 1-5. Explain the difference between 0, '0', '\0', and "0".

□

Exercise 1-6. Given the following set of variable definitions,

```
int *ip1, ip2;
char ch, *cp;
```

which of the following assignments are type violations? Explain why.

```
(a)  ip1 = "All happy families are alike";
(b)  cp = 0;                  (c)  cp = '\0';
(d)  ip1 = 0;                 (e)  ip1 = '\0';
(f)  cp = &'a';               (g)  cp = &ch;
(h)  ip1 = ip2;               (i)  *ip1 = ip2;
```

☐

1.4 Reference Types

A reference type is defined by following the type specifier with the address-of operator. The definition of a reference object must specify an initialization. For example,

```
int val = 10;

int &refVal = val;  // ok
int &refVal2;       // error: uninitialized
```

A reference type, sometimes referred to as an *alias*, serves as an alternative name for the object with which it has been initialized. All operations applied to the reference act on the object to which it refers. For example,

```
refVal += 2;
```

adds 2 to val, setting it to 12.

```
int ii = refVal;
```

assigns ii the value currently associated with val, while

```
int *pi = &refVal;
```

initializes pi with the address of val.

A reference can be thought of as a special kind of pointer — one to which object syntax may be applied. For example,

```
( *pi == refVal && pi == &refVal )
```

is always true if both pi and refVal address the same object. Unlike a pointer, however, a reference must be initialized and, once initialized, a reference cannot be made to alias another object.

A declaration list of two or more reference objects must precede each identifier with an address-of operator. For example,

```
int i;

// one reference, r1; one object, r2
int &r1 = i, r2 = i;

// one object, r1; one reference, r2
int r1, &r2 = i;

// two references, r1 and r2
int &r1 = i, &r2 = i;
```

A reference may be initialized with an rvalue. In this case, an internal temporary is generated and initialized with the rvalue. The reference is then initialized with the temporary. For example,

```
int &ir = 1024;
```

becomes

```
int T1 = 1024;
int &ir = T1;
```

Initialization of a reference with an object that does not exactly match in type will also result in the generation of an internal temporary. For example,

```
unsigned int ui = 20;
int &ir = ui;
```

becomes

```
int T2 = int(ui);
int &ir = T2;
```

The primary use of a reference type is as an argument or return type of a function, especially when applied to user-defined class types. Section 3.7 (page 119) discusses how reference types are used in this manner.

1.5   Constant Types

There are two problems with the following `for` loop statement, both concerning the use of 512 as an upper bound.

```
for (int i = 0; i < 512; ++i );
```

The first problem is readability. What does it mean to test i against 512? What is the loop doing, that is, that makes 512 matter? (In this example, 512 is referred to as a *magic number*, one whose significance is not evident within the context of its use. It's as if the number had been plucked from thin air.)

The second problem is maintainability. Imagine that the program is 10,000 lines. This `for` loop header appears in 4% of the code. The value 512 must now be doubled to 1024. The 400 occurrences of 512 must be found and converted. Overlooking even one instance breaks the program.

The solution to both problems is the use of an identifier initialized to 512. By choosing a mnemonic name, perhaps `bufSize`, we make the program more readable. The test is now against the identifier rather than the literal constant:

```
i < bufSize
```

The 400 occurrences no longer need to be touched in the case where `bufSize` is changed. Rather, only the one line that initializes `bufSize` requires change. Not only is this significantly less work, but the likelihood of making an error is reduced significantly. The cost of the solution is one additional variable. The value 512 is now said to be *localized*.

```
int bufSize = 512; // input buffer size
// ...

for ( int i = 0; i < bufSize; ++i )
// ...
```

The problem with this solution is that `bufSize` is an lvalue. It is possible for `bufSize` to be accidentally changed from within the program. For example, here is a common error made by a programmer coming to C++ from a Pascal-derived language:

```
// accidentally changes the value of bufSize
if ( bufSize = 1 )
    // ...
```

In C++, "=" is the assignment operator and "==" is the equality operator. Pascal and languages derived from it use "=" as the equality operator. The programmer has accidentally changed `bufSize`'s value to 1, which will result in a difficult-to-trace program error. (Often such an error is difficult to find because the programmer does not *see* the code as being wrong — the reason many compilers issue a warning for this type of assignment.)

The `const` type modifier provides a solution. It transforms a symbolic variable into a *symbolic constant*. For example,

```
const int bufSize = 512; // input buffer size
```

defines `bufSize` to be a symbolic constant initialized with the value 512. Any attempt to change that value from within the program will result in a compile-time error. A symbolic constant is referred to as a *read-only* variable.

Since a `const` variable may not be modified once it has been defined, it *must* be initialized. The definition of an uninitialized symbolic constant will result in a compile-time error. For example,

```
const double PI; // error: uninitialized const
```

It is also a compile-time error to assign the address of a symbolic constant to a pointer. Otherwise, the constant value could be changed indirectly through the pointer. For example,

```
const double minWage = 3.60;
double *p = &minWage; // error

*p += 1.40;
```

The programmer, however, may declare a pointer that addresses a constant. For example,

```
const double *pc;
```

`pc` is a pointer to a `const` object of type `double`. `pc`, itself, however, is not a constant. This means the following:

1. `pc` can be changed to address a different variable of type double at any time within the program.

2. The value of the object addressed by `pc` cannot be modified through `pc`.

For example,

```
pc = &minWage; // ok
double d;
pc = &d; // ok
d = 3.14159; // ok
*pc = 3.14159; // error
```

The address of a `const` variable can only be assigned to a pointer to a constant, such as `pc`. A pointer to a constant, however, can also be assigned the address of an ordinary variable, such as

```
pc = &d;
```

Although d is not a constant, the programmer is assured that its value cannot be modified through `pc`. Pointers to `const` objects are most often defined as the formal arguments of a function. Section 3.6 (page 119) examines this use of pointers to constants.

The programmer may also define a `const` pointer. For example,

```
int errNumb; // possible error status of program
int *const curErr = &errNumb; // constant pointer
```

curErr is a constant pointer to an object of type int. The programmer can modify the value of the object curErr addresses:

```
if ( *curErr ) {
    errorHandler();
    *curErr = 0;
}
```

but cannot modify the address that curErr contains:

```
curErr = &myErrNumb; // error
```

A constant pointer to a const object may also be defined:

```
const int pass = 1;
const int *const true = &pass;
```

In this case, neither the value of the object addressed by true nor the address itself can be changed.

Exercise 1-7. Explain the meaning of the following five definitions. Identify any illegal definitions.

(a) `int i;`   (d) `int *const cpi;`
(b) `const int ic;`   (e) `const int *const cpic;`
(c) `const int *pic;`

☐

Exercise 1-8. Which of the following initializations are legal? Explain why.

(a) `int i = 'a';`
(b) `const int ic = i;`
(c) `const int *pic = &ic;`
(d) `int *const cpi = &ic;`
(e) `const int *const cpic = &ic;`

☐

Exercise 1-9. Based on the definitions in the previous exercise, which of the following assignments are legal? Explain why.

(a) `i = ic;`   (d) `pic = cpic;`
(b) `pic = &ic;`   (e) `cpic = &ic;`
(c) `cpi = pic;`   (f) `ic = *cpic;`

☐

1.6   Enumeration Types

An enumeration is a set of symbolic integral constants. The elements of an enumeration differ from their equivalent const declarations in that there is no addressable storage associated with the elements of an enumeration. It is an error to apply the address-of operator to an enumeration element.

An enumeration is declared with the enum keyword and a comma-separated list of identifiers enclosed in braces. By default, the first identifier is assigned the value 0. Each subsequent identifier is assigned a value one greater than the value of the identifier that immediately precedes it. For example, the following declaration associates FALSE with 0 and TRUE with 1.

```
enum { FALSE, TRUE }; // FALSE == 0, TRUE == 1
```

A value may also be explicitly assigned to an element of the enumeration. This value need not be unique. As before, in the absence of an explicit assignment, the value assigned an element is one greater than its immediately preceding element. In the following example, FALSE and FAIL are assigned the value 0, while PASS and TRUE are assigned the value 1:

```
enum { FALSE, FAIL = 0, PASS, TRUE = 1 };
```

An enumeration may optionally be provided with a *tag name*. Each named enumeration defines a unique type and can be used as a type specifier for declaring identifiers. For example,

```
enum TestStatus { NOT_RUN=-1, FAIL, PASS };
enum Boolean { FALSE, TRUE };

main() {
    const testSize = 100;
    TestStatus testSuite[ testSize ];
    Boolean found = FALSE;

    for ( int i = 0; i < testSize; ++i )
        testSuite[ i ] = NOT_RUN;
}
```

Named enumerations were not distinct types in the definition of the C++ language prior to Release 2.0. For backward compatibility, therefore, type violations in the initialization and assignment of an identifier of an enumeration are not flagged as errors in the current AT&T implementation. Warnings, however, are issued, and should not be ignored. For example,

```
main() {
    TestStatus test = NOT_RUN;
    Boolean found = FALSE;

    test = -1; // error: TestStatus = int
    test = 10; // error: TestStatus = int
    test = found; // error: TestStatus = Boolean
    test = FALSE; // error: TestStatus = const Boolean
    int st = test; // ok: implicit conversion
}
```

By declaring `test` to be of the TestStatus enumeration type, the programmer enlists the compiler's help in making sure that `test` is only assigned one of its three valid values. In addition, the use of an enumeration tag name provides a helpful form of program documentation.

1.7 Array Types

An array is a collection of objects of a single data type. The individual objects are not named; rather, each one is accessed by its position in the array. This form of access is referred to as *indexing* or *subscripting*. For example,

```
int i;
```

declares a single integer object, while

```
int ia[ 10 ];
```

declares an array of 10 integer objects. Each object is referred to as an *element* of `ia`. Thus

```
i = ia[ 2 ];
```

assigns `i` the value stored in the element of `ia` indexed by 2. Similarly,

```
ia[ 7 ] = i;
```

assigns the element of `ia` indexed by 7 the value of `i`.

An array definition consists of a type specifier, an identifier and a *dimension*. The dimension, which specifies the number of elements contained in the array, is enclosed in a bracket pair ("[ ]"). An array must be given a dimension size greater than or equal to one. The dimension value must be a constant expression; that is, it must be possible to compute the value of the dimension at compile time. This means that a variable may not be used to specify the dimension of an array. The following are examples of legal array definitions:

```
const bufSize = 512,
      stackSize = 25,
      maxFiles = 20,
      staffSize = 27;

char inputBuffer[ bufSize ];
int tokenStack[ stackSize ];
char *fileTable[ maxFiles - 3 ];
double salaries[ staffSize ];
```

Note that the elements of an array are numbered beginning with 0. For an array of 10 elements, the correct index values are 0 through 9, not 1 through 10. This is a common source of program error. For example, the following for loop *steps through* the 10 elements of an array, initializing each to the value of its index:

```
const SIZE = 10;
int ia[ SIZE ];

main() {
    for ( int i = 0; i < SIZE; ++i )
        ia[ i ] = i;
}
```

An array may be initialized explicitly by specifying a comma-separated list of values enclosed in braces. (This ability is restricted to arrays defined outside a function. The distinction between definitions inside and outside a function is discussed in Chapter 3.) For example,

```
const SZ = 3;
int ia[ SZ ] = { 0, 1, 2 };
```

An explicitly initialized array need not specify a dimension value. The compiler will determine the array size by the number of elements listed:

```
// an array of dimension 3
int ia[] = { 0, 1, 2 };
```

If the dimension size is specified, the number of elements provided must not exceed that size. Otherwise, a compile-time error results. If the dimension size is greater than the number of listed elements, the array elements not initialized explicitly will be set to 0.

```
// ia ==> { 0, 1, 2, 0, 0 }
const SZ = 5;
int ia[ SZ ] = { 0, 1, 2 };
```

A character array may be initialized with either a list of comma-separated character literals enclosed in braces or a string constant. Note, however, that the two forms are *not* equivalent. The string constant contains the additional terminating null character. For example,

```
char ca1[] = { 'C', '+', '+' };
char ca2[] = "C++";
```

ca1 is of dimension 3; ca2 is of dimension 4. The following declaration will be flagged as an error:

```
// error: "Pascal" is 7 elements
char ch3[6] = "Pascal";
```

An array may not be initialized with another array, nor may one array be assigned to another:

```
const int SZ = 3;
int ia[SZ] = { 0, 1, 2 };

int ia2[] = ia; // error
int ia3[ SZ ];

ia3 = ia; // error
```

To copy one array into another, each element must be copied in turn. This operation is common enough to make it a candidate for a general function; let's call it copyArray().

copyArray() requires two arrays, one to receive the copied values and one to hold the values to be copied. We'll call them target and source. These will be two arguments to the function.

In general, a distinct function is required for each distinct array type we wish to copy, such as an array of integers or an array of floating-point values, even though the actual C++ code to perform the array copy may be the same.† For the purposes of our example, we will define copyArray() to take two integer arrays. Our initial function prototype looks as follows:

```
void copyArray( int target[], int source[] );
```

An array, when passed to a function, is converted to a pointer to its *zeroth* element; the size information, in effect, is lost. A function being passed an array must somehow be told of its size. One way of doing this is to pass a second argument containing the size of the array. copyArray() is implemented as follows:

---

†With the introduction of *parameterized types*, this constraint will be lifted. See Appendix B, for a discussion.

```
void copyArray( int target[], int source[],
                int targetSize, int sourceSize )
{ /* copy source to target
  * set additional target elements to 0 */

    int upperBound = targetSize;

    if ( targetSize > sourceSize )
        upperBound = sourceSize;

    for ( int i = 0; i < upperBound; ++i )
        target[ i ] = source[ i ];

    while ( i < targetSize )
        target[ i++ ] = 0;
}
```

Any expression that results in an integral value can be used to index into an array. The language, however, provides no compile- or run-time range checking of the index. Nothing stops a programmer from stepping across an array boundary except his or her attention to detail and program testing. It is not inconceivable for a program to compile and execute and still be entirely wrong.

Exercise 1-10. Which of the following array definitions are illegal? Explain why.

```
int getSize();
int bufSize = 1024;

(a)  int ia[ bufSize ];       (c)  int ia[ 4 * 7 - 14 ];
(b)  int ia[ getSize() ];     (d)  int ia[ 2 * 7 - 14 ];
```

□

Exercise 1-11. Why is the following initialization an error?

```
char st[ 11 ] = "fundamental";
```

□

Exercise 1-12. There are two indexing errors with regard to the array ia in the following code fragment. Identify them.

```
main() {
    const max = 10;
    int ia[ max ];
    for ( int index = 1; index <= max; ++index )
        ia[ index ] = index;
    // ...
}
```

□

Multidimensional Arrays

Multidimensional arrays can also be defined. Each dimension is specified with its own bracket pair. For example,

```
int ia[ 4 ][ 3 ];
```

defines a two-dimensional array. The first dimension is referred to as the *row* dimension; the second, the *column* dimension. That is, ia is a two-dimensional array of four rows of three elements each. A two-dimensional array is also referred to as a matrix.

Multidimensional arrays may also be initialized.

```
int ia[ 4 ][ 3 ] = {
    { 0, 1, 2 },
    { 3, 4, 5 },
    { 6, 7, 8 },
    { 9, 10, 11 }
};
```

The nested braces, which indicate the intended row, are optional. The following initialization is equivalent, although less clear.

```
int ia[4][3] = { 0,1,2,3,4,5,6,7,8,9,10,11 };
```

The following definition initializes the first element of each row. The remaining elements are initialized to 0.

```
int ia[ 4 ][ 3 ] = { {0}, {3}, {6}, {9} };
```

Were the nested braces left off, the results would be very different. The following definition

```
int ia[ 4 ][ 3 ] = { 0, 1, 2, 3 };
```

initializes the first three elements of the first row and the first element of the second. The remaining elements are initialized to 0.

Indexing into a multidimensional array requires a bracket pair for each dimension. For example, the following pair of nested `for` loops initializes a two dimensional array.

```
main()
{
    const rowSize = 4;
    const colSize = 3;
    int ia[ rowSize ][ colSize ];

    for ( int i = 0; i < rowSize; ++i )
        for ( int j = 0; j < colSize; ++j )
            ia[ i ][ j ] = i + j;
}
```

In the Pascal or Ada programming language, a multidimensional array is indexed by a comma-separated list of values enclosed in a bracket pair. Although the expression

```
ia[ 1, 2 ]
```

is a legal construct in both C++ and Ada, its meaning is very different in the two languages.

- In Ada, the expression indexes the second element of the first row. It evaluates to the integer value of that element.

- In C++, the expression indexes the *third* row of `ia` (the rows and columns, recall, are indexed beginning with 0). It evaluates to a pointer of type `int*` addressing the zeroth element of that row.

In C++, the expression

```
ia[ 1, 2 ]
```

is treated as a comma expression yielding a single integer value — in this case,

```
ia[ 2 ]
```

A comma expression is a series of expressions separated by a comma. These expressions are evaluated from left to right. The result of a comma expression is the value of the right-most expression. The value of the following comma expression, for example, is 3.

```
7, 6+4, ia[0][0] = 0, 4-1; // comma expression
```

Relationship of Array and Pointer Types

The definition of an array consists of four distinct elements: the type specifier, the identifier, the index operator ("[ ]"), and, within the operator, the dimension. For example,

```
char buf[ 8 ];
```

defines `buf` to be an array of 8 elements of type `char`.

Subscripting occurs by applying the index operator to the array identifier:

```
buf[ 0 ];
```

returns the value of the initial element contained in `buf`.

What, however, if the index operator is omitted? What is the value of the array identifier itself?

```
buf;
```

The array identifier returns the address in memory of the first element contained in `buf`. This is equivalent to

```
&buf[ 0 ];
```

Recall that the application of the address-of operator to a data object returns a pointer of that object's type. In this case, the object is of type `char`, which means that `buf` must return a value of type `char*`. If this is so, then a pointer can be set to an array identifier. For example,

```
char *pBuf = buf; // ok
```

`pBuf` and `buf` are now equivalent. Each evaluates to the address of the first element of the array. To address the next element, then, the following two methods must also be equivalent:

```
// equivalent addressing methods
pBuf + 1 ;
&buf[ 1 ];
```

More generally,

```
for ( int i = 0; i < arraySize; ++i )
{
        pBuf + i;
        &buf[ i ];
}
```

From this, it follows that

```
// two equivalent accessing methods
*pBuf;
buf[ 0 ];
```

are equivalent forms. Each returns the value of the zeroth element of the array. To access the next element, the programmer could write either of the following:

```
*(pBuf + 1 );
buf[ 1 ];
```

or, more generally,

```
*(pBuf + index);
buf[ index ];
```

These two methods for addressing an array element can be used interchangeably. In particular, programmers new to C++ often feel uncomfortable with pointer syntax. Initially, they may wish to apply the indexing operator to pointers that address arrays. The following implementation of a string concatenation function is an example.

```
#include <stream.h>
char *catString( char *st1, char *st2 )
{ // append st2 to st1 if two distinct strings

    // if st1 does not address a string
    // but st2 does, return st2
    if ( st1 == 0 && st2 )
        return st2;

    // unless st1 and st2 address distinct
    // strings, return st1
    if ( st2 == 0 || st1 == st2 )
        return st1;

    for ( int i = 0; st1[ i ] != '\0'; ++i )
        ; // step through to end of st1

    for ( int j = 0; st2[ j ] != '\0'; ++i, ++j )
        st1[ i ] = st2[ j ];
    st1[ i ] = '\0';
    return st1;

}
```

The equivalence between a pointer and an array has to do with the access, or addressing, of a contiguous block of memory. The methods by which an array identifier and pointer come to address that memory, however, are very different.

An array definition causes a block of storage to be allocated. The array identifier is initialized with the address of this storage, which cannot be changed within the program. The effect is to handle the array identifier as a constant. The attempt to increment buf in the following program is, therefore, illegal. An array identifier is not an lvalue.

```
char buf[] = "rampion";
main() {
    int cnt = 0;
    while ( *buf ) {
        ++cnt;
        ++buf; // error: may not increment buf
    }
}
```

The definition of a pointer provides it with only the storage sufficient to hold the value of a memory address. The programmer must first set a pointer to address some previously allocated object or chunk of storage before it may be safely used. This is often done by allocating memory during program execution through use of the new operator. (See Section 4.1 (page 135) for a discussion.)

Exercise 1-13. Although the following program compiles without either a warning or an error message, there is something wrong. What is the problem? How would you fix it?

```
char buf[] = "fiddleferns";

main() {
    char *ptr = 0;
    for ( int i = 0; buf[ i ] != '\0'; ++i );
        ptr[ i ] = buf[ i ];
}
```

☐ *Class = data types + operations*

1.8 Class Types

A user-defined data type in C++, referred to as a *class*, is an aggregate of named data elements, possibly of different types, and a set of operations designed to manipulate that data. Typically, a class is used to introduce a new data type into the program; a well-designed class can be used as easily as a predefined data type. Classes are discussed in detail in Chapters 5 - 8. Because they are the central concept in C++, this section introduces them through an extended example — the design of an integer array class.

more irritating aspects of a predefined array type are the

... .n array must be a constant expression. The programmer,
however, does not always know at compile time how large an array is
necessary. A more flexible array type would permit the programmer to
specify (or modify) the array dimension during the execution of the
program.

2. There is no range-checking of an array index. The following program
fragment, for example, uses the wrong upper bounds constant for the
array it is initializing. Although the program runs to completion, its
results will likely prove incorrect because of its modification of memory
outside the boundary of the array.

```
const int SIZE = 25;
const int SZ = 10;
int ia[ SZ ];
// ...

main() {
    // not caught during program execution
    for ( int i = 0; i < SIZE; ++i )
        ia[ i ] = i;
    // ...
}
```

3. It is necessary to pass the size of an array to a function along with the
array. Array arguments would be easier to use if an array knew its size.

4. It would be nice to be able to copy one array to another in a single
statement. For example,

```
int ia[ SZ ];
int ia2[ SZ ] = ia; // not supported
```

In this section, a class is defined which supports these four additional
characteristics of an array. Moreover, the syntax for using objects of the
array class will be as simple as that for "ordinary" arrays. The design of a
class type is discussed in detail in Chapter 6. At this point, we will simply
present the definition of the array class and discuss its implementation.
Here is what it looks like:

(handwritten: class head)

(handwritten: class tag)

```
const int ArraySize = 24; // default size

class IntArray {
public:
    // operations performed on arrays
    IntArray( int sz = ArraySize );
    IntArray( const IntArray& );
    ~IntArray() { delete ia; }
    IntArray& operator=( const IntArray& );
    int& operator[]( int );
    int getSize() { return size; }
protected:
    // internal data representation
    int size;
    int *ia;
};
```

(handwritten annotations: ordinary alloc. of array with possible default size; init. one array w/another; copy array; over loaded operators; (read) access function; 2 constructors; destructor; info. hiding)

A class definition consists of two parts: the *class head*, composed of the keyword `class` and a tag name, and the *class body*, enclosed by braces and terminated with a semicolon.

A class tag name represents a new data type. It serves as a type specifier in the same way as do the built-in type specifiers. The following are examples of how variables of the IntArray class may be defined:

```
const int SZ = 10;
int mySize;
int ia[SZ]; // predefined array
IntArray myArray( mySize ), iA( SZ );
IntArray *pA = &myArray;
IntArray iA2; // 24 elements by default
```

The class body contains the member definitions. The class members consist of both the operations that can be performed by the class, and the data necessary to represent the class abstraction. In our case, an integer array is represented by two data members:

1. `size`, which holds the number of elements represented by the array.

2. `ia`, which addresses the memory in which the elements are contained.

The `protected` and `public` keywords control access to the class members. Members that occur in a `public` section of the class body can be accessed from anywhere within the general program. Members that, in this case, occur in the `protected` section can be accessed only by the member functions of the IntArray class. This access restriction is referred to as *information hiding*.

In general, only the member functions of a class are permitted to access the class data members. This provides two primary benefits:

1. Should the data representation of the class change, only the class member functions, not user programs, need to be modified.

2. Should there be an error in the manipulation of a class data member, only the small set of class member functions, not an entire program, need to be examined.

Three *member functions* of IntArray — special initialization and deallocation functions — use the class tag name as their name. Although defined by the class designer, they are invoked automatically by the compiler. The function preceded by the tilde ("~"), the deallocation function, is referred to as a *destructor*. The other two are initialization functions; they are referred to as *constructors*. The constructor

```
IntArray( int sz = ArraySize );
```

handles "ordinary" declarations. sz represents the array size requested by the user. If the user does not care to request a size, by default the array will contain ArraySize elements. This is the size of iA2 in the definition

```
IntArray iA2;
```

Here is an implementation of this instance of IntArray(). It introduces the operator new. The new operator handles *dynamic memory allocation*. Section 4.1 (page 135) discusses operator new.

```
IntArray::IntArray( int sz )
{
    size = sz;

    // allocate an integer array of size
    // and set ia to point to it
    ia = new int[ size ];

    // initialize array
    for ( int i = 0; i < sz; ++i )
        ia[ i ] = 0;
}
```

The double colon ("::") operator is referred to as the scope operator. It tells the compiler that the IntArray function being defined is a member of the IntArray class. A class member function can access its own class members directly. When we write

```
size = sz;
```

size refers to the data member of the class variable for which the member function has been invoked. In our example, size is the data member of iA2.

The second instance of `IntArray()` handles initialization of one IntArray object with another. It is invoked automatically whenever there is a definition of the following form:

```
IntArray iA3 = myArray;
```

This implementation looks much like the other, except that the array elements and size are copied:

```
IntArray::IntArray( const IntArray &iA )
{
    size = iA.size;
    ia = new int[ size ];
    for ( int i = 0; i < size; ++i )
        ia[ i ] = iA.ia[ i ];
}
```

In order to access the class members of a particular class variable, a member selector operator must be used:

1. The dot operator (".") is used whenever the programmer wishes to access either a data member or member function of a particular class object.

2. The arrow operator ("->") is used whenever the programmer wishes to access a member of a particular class object through a class pointer.

For example,

```
iA.size;
```

is read as meaning the following: *Select the* `size` *data member of the class object* `iA`.

The assignment of one array object with another is handled by

```
IntArray& operator=( IntArray& );
```

The odd-looking function name is part of the mechanism that allows a class to overload the C++ operators to have meaning when applied to class objects. (Section 6.3 (page 254) discusses class operator overloading in detail.) Here is an implementation of this function. Notice that it resizes the target array to be the same size as the array to be copied.

```
IntArray& IntArray::operator=( const IntArray &iA )
{
    delete ia; // free up existing memory
    size = iA.size; // resize target
    ia = new int[ size ]; // get new memory
    for ( int i = 0; i < size; ++i )
        ia[ i ] = iA.ia[ i ]; // copy
    return *this;
}
```

See Section 5.4 (page 196) for a discussion of the statement

```
return *this;
```

The overloaded assignment operator will be invoked automatically whenever one IntArray object is assigned to another. For example,

```
ia2 = myArray;
```

The array class will not be of much practical interest unless users can easily index into a class object. The following loop construct must be supported:

```
for ( int i = 0; i < upperBound; ++i )
    myArray[ i ] = myArray[ i ] + i;
```

where upperBound has been set with the size value of the IntArray object myArray. This can all be accomplished with the member functions getSize() and operator[]. getSize(), referred to as an *access function*, provides read access of an otherwise private value. Because it is so small, its definition is included within the definition of the class. upperBound may either be assigned the value of getSize(),

```
upperBound = myArray.getSize();
```

or getSize() can replace upperBound in the for loop:

```
for ( int i = 0; i < myArray.getSize(); ++i )
```

The subscript operator function is not much larger than getSize() but somewhat trickier to implement because it must support *both* read and write capabilities. The read portion is simple: accept an index value and return the appropriate element. This provides for a statement of the following form:

```
int i = myArray[ someValue ];
```

The subscript operator must also provide for a statement of the form:

```
myArray[ i ] = someValue;
```

In order for myArray[i] to appear on the left-hand side of the assignment operator, it must evaluate to an lvalue. This is done by specifying its
return value as a reference type (a reference, recall, serves as an alias for
another variable — Section 3.7 (page 121) discusses a reference return
value.) The implementation of this member function can now be coded as
follows:

```
int& IntArray::operator[](int index)
{
      return ia[index];
}
```

   Typically, the class definition and any associated constant values or
typedef names are stored in a header file. The header file is named with
the class tag name. In this case, the header file is called IntArray.h. All
programs wishing to use the IntArray class will include this header file.
Similarly, the member functions of a class are typically stored in a program
text file named with the class tag name. In this case, the member functions
will be placed in the file IntArray.C. To use these functions, a program
must link them into its executable. Rather than require that these functions
be recompiled with each program wishing to utilize the IntArray class, we
can precompile the functions and store them in a library. This is done as
follows:

```
$ CC -c IntArray.C
$ ar cr IntArray.a IntArray.o
```

ar is a command to create an *ar*chive library provided on the UNIX system.
The characters cr that follow it represent two command line options.
IntArray.o, an object file, contains the machine language representation
of the C++ program code. It is generated when the compiler is given the
command-line option -c. IntArray.a is the name we wish given to the
the IntArray class library we are about to create. To use this library, the
programmer can place its name explicitly on the command line when compiling a program:

```
$ CC main.c IntArray.a
```

This will cause the IntArray member functions to be included in the executable version of the program.

Exercise 1-14. The IntArray class illustrated here provides a minimum
number of operations. List some additional functionality that you believe
an array class should provide for its users.

□

Exercise 1-15. One useful capability would be the ability to initialize an IntArray object with an integer array. Describe a general algorithm to implement the following constructor:

```
IntArray::IntArray( int *ia, int size );
```

It should support the following definition:

```
int ia[ 4 ] = { 0, 1, 2, 3 };
IntArray myIA( ia, 4 );
```

☐

IntArray represents one important use of the C++ class mechanism. IntArray is referred to as an *abstract data type*. Programmers can use the IntArray class in much the same way that they can use the predefined C++ data types. This aspect of classes is considered in detail in Chapters 5 and 6.

A second important use of the class mechanism is to define subtype relationships. For example, IntArrayRC is a type of integer array class that also provides range checking of its subscript values. It is implemented through a mechanism referred to as *inheritance*. Here is the definition of IntArrayRC:

```
#include "IntArray.h"

class IntArrayRC : public IntArray {
public:
    // constructors are not inherited
    IntArrayRC( int = ArraySize );
    int& operator[]( int );
protected:
    void rangeCheck( int );
};
```

inheritance n/ public base type to create subtype

IntArrayRC needs to define only those aspects of its implementation that are different or in addition to the implementation of IntArray:

1   It must provide its own instance of the subscript operator, one that provides range checking.

2   It must provide a function to do the actual range checking.

3   It must provide its own set of automatic initialization functions — that is, its own set of constructors.

The data members and member functions of IntArray are all available to IntArrayRC as if IntArrayRC had explicitly defined them itself. This is the meaning of

this subclass
is derived from
base class   INHERITANCE

```
class IntArrayRC : public IntArray
```
could be "private"
see p. 71

The colon (":") defines IntArrayRC to be *derived* from IntArray. A derived class inherits (that is, shares) the members of the class it is derived from. IntArrayRC can be thought of as extending the IntArray class by providing the additional feature of subscript range checking. The subscript operator is implemented as follows:

```
int& IntArrayRC::operator[]( int index )
{
    rangeCheck( index );
    return ia[ index ];
}
```

rangeCheck() tests each index value. If the index is invalid, it issues an error message and causes the program to stop. exit(), which causes termination of the program, is an operating system call. The argument passed to exit() becomes the return value of the program. The function prototype of exit() is contained in the system header file stdlib.h. Here is the implementation of rangeCheck():

```
#include <stdlib.h>
#include <stream.h>

enum { ERR_RANGE = 17 };

void IntArrayRC::rangeCheck( int index )
{
    if ( index < 0 || index >= size ) {
        cerr << "Index out of bounds for IntArrayRC: "
            << "\n\tsize: " << size
            << "\tindex: " << index << "\n";
        exit( ERR_RANGE );
    }
}
```

Because constructors are not inherited by the derived class, IntArrayRC must define a constructor instance of its own to accept a possible dimension size. Here is its implementations:

```
// IntArrayRC need only pass its argument
// to its base class IntArray constructor
IntArrayRC::IntArrayRC( int sz )
        : IntArray( sz )
        {} // null body
```

The portion of the constructor marked off by the colon is referred to as a *member initialization list*. It provides the mechanism by which the

IntArray constructor is passed its argument. The body of the IntArrayRC constructor is null since its job is only to pass its dimension argument to the IntArray constructor. Here is an example of how an IntArrayRC object can be used:

```
#include "IntArrayRC.h"

const size = 12;
main()
{
    IntArrayRC ia( size );

    // subscript error: 1 .. size
    for ( int i = 1; i <= size; ++i )
        ia[ i ] = i;
}
```

This program incorrectly indexes ia from 1 to size rather than from 0 to size−1. When compiled and executed, the program results in the following output:

```
Index out of bounds for IntArrayRC:
        size: 12            index: 12
```

As this program example illustrates, range checking can provide an important safeguard in the use of an array type. Range checking, however, is also an expensive run-time overhead. An application might wish to combine IntArray and IntArrayRC class types in different portions of its code. Class inheritance supports this in two ways:

1. The class derived from, referred to as a *base class*, can be assigned objects of a derived class. For example,

```
#include "IntArray.h"

void swap( IntArray &ia, int i, int j )
{
    // swap elements i and j within ia
    int tmp = ia[ i ];
    ia[ i ] = ia[ j ];
    ia[ j ] = tmp;
}
```

swap() can be passed arguments of an IntArray class or arguments of any class derived from IntArray, such as IntArrayRC. For example, given the following two class objects:

```
IntArray ia1;
IntArrayRC ia2;
```

the following two calls of `swap()` are legal:

```
swap( ia1, 4, 7 );
swap( ia2, 4, 7 );
```

This ability of assigning derived class objects to objects of a base class allows inherited classes to be used interchangeably.

There is one problem, however. The subscript operator is implemented differently in the two integer array classes. When we call

```
swap( ia1, 4, 7 );
```

the IntArray subscript operator must be used. When, however, we call

```
swap( ia2, 4, 7 );
```

the IntArrayRC subscript operator must be used. The subscript operator to be used by `swap()` must change with each call, depending on the actual class type of its argument. This is resolved automatically by the language compiler in C++ through a mechanism referred to as *class virtual functions*.

2. Virtual class member functions are inherited members, such as the subscript operator, whose implementation is dependent on its class type.

To make the subscript operator virtual, we must modify its declaration in the IntArray class body:

```
class IntArray {
public:
    virtual int& operator[]( int );
    ...
};
```

That's it. Each invocation of `swap()` will now call the appropriate subscript operator as determined by the actual class type with which `swap()` is called. Here is an example:

```
#include <stream.h>
#include "IntArray.h"
#include "IntArrayRC.h"

void swap( IntArray&, int, int );

main() {
    const size = 10;
    IntArray ia1( size );
    IntArrayRC ia2( size );

    // error: should be size-1
    cout << "swap() with IntArray ia1\n";
    swap( ia1, 1, size );
    cout << "swap() with IntArrayRC ia2\n";
    swap( ia2, 1, size );
}
```

When compiled and executed, the program generates the following results:

```
swap() with IntArray ia1
swap() with IntArrayRC ia2
Index out of bounds for IntArrayRC:
        size: 10          index: 10
```

Inheritance and virtual functions are the two primary components of *object-oriented programming*. They are considered at length in Chapters 7 and 8.

Exercise 1-16. List another specialized instance of an IntArray class. What additional operations or data does it require? Is it necessary to replace any of the IntArray operations? Which ones? □

1.9   Typedef Names

Arrays and pointers can be thought of as *derived types*. They are constructed from other types by applying the subscript and dereference operators to the definition of a particular variable; these operators can be thought of as type constructors. The derived type may then be further derived, such as in the definition of an array of pointers:

```
char *winter[ 3 ];
char *spring[] = { "March", "April", "May" };
```

winter and spring are arrays. Each contains three elements of type `char*`. `spring` is initialized. The statement

```
char *cruellestMonth = spring[ 1 ];
```

initializes `cruellestMonth` to "April", the character string addressed by the second element of `spring`.

The following two output statements are equivalent:

```
main() {
   cout << "Lilacs breed in " << spring[ 1 ];
   cout << "Lilacs breed in "
        << cruellestMonth;
}
```

The `typedef` mechanism provides a general facility for introducing mnemonic synonyms for existing predefined, derived, and user-defined data types. For example,

```
class IntArray;

typedef double wages;
typedef IntArray testScores;
typedef unsigned int bitVector;
typedef char *string;
typedef string monthTable[3];
```

These typedef names can serve as type specifiers within the program:

```
const classSize = 93;

string myName = "stan";
wages hourly, weekly;
testScores finalExam( classSize );
monthTable summer, fall = {
            "September", "October", "November" };
```

A typedef definition begins with the keyword `typedef`, followed by the data type and identifier. The identifier, or typedef name, does not introduce a new type, but rather a synonym for the existing data type. A typedef name may appear anywhere in a program that a type name may appear.

A typedef name can serve as a program documentation aid. It can also reduce the notational complexity of a declaration. Typedef names, for example, are typically used to improve the readability of definitions of pointers to functions and pointers to class member functions. (These pointer types are discussed in Chapters 4 and 5.)

A typedef name can also be used to encapsulate machine-dependent aspects of a program. On some machines, for example, an `int` may be large enough to contain a set of values; on others, a `long` may be required. By replacing the explicit type with a typedef, only one statement will require change when the program is *ported* from one machine to another.

lvalue - location (write)
rvalue - read

Chapter 2: **Expressions and Statements**

Data types were the focus of Chapter 1. We looked at the predefined data types, methods of defining new data types, and how to define data objects. In this chapter we look at the predefined operations that can be used to manipulate that data. These operations consist of a predefined set of operators and a set of statements with which to organize these operators and to direct the flow of program execution. In Chapter 3 the focus will be the function, a mechanism through which the user can define his or her own set of operations.

2.1 What Is an Expression?

An expression is composed of one or more *operations*. The objects of the operation(s) are referred to as *operands*. The operations are represented by *operators*. For example, in C++ the test for equality is represented by the operator "==".

Operators that act on one operand are referred to as *unary* operators, while operators that act on two operands are referred to as *binary* operators. The operands of a binary operator are distinguished as the *left* or *right* operand. Some operators represent both a unary and binary operation. For example,

```
*ptr
```

represents the unary dereference operator. It returns the value stored in the object `ptr` addresses. However,

```
var1 * var2
```

represents the binary multiplication operator. It computes the product of its two operands, `var1` and `var2`.

The evaluation of an expression performs one or more operations, yielding a result. Except when noted otherwise, the result of an expression is an rvalue. The data type of the result of an expression is in general determined by the data type of the operand(s). When more than one data type is present, type conversions take place following a predefined set of rules. Section 2.10 (page 80) considers type conversions in some detail.

When two or more operators are combined, the expression is referred

63

to as a *compound expression*. The order of operator evaluation is determined by the *precedence* and *associativity* of the operators. (This will be explained after we look at the predefined set of operators.)

The simplest form of an expression consists of a single literal constant or variable. This "operand" is without an operator. The result is the operand's rvalue. For example, here are three simple expressions:

```
3.14159
"melancholia"
upperBound
```

The result of `3.14159` is `3.14159`. Its type is `double`. The result of `melancholia` is the address in memory of the first element of the string. Its type is `char*`. The result of `upperBound` is its rvalue. Its type is determined by its definition.

The following sections discuss the predefined C++ operators, presented in their presumed order of familiarity.

2.2   Arithmetic Operators

Operator	Function	Use
`*`	multiplication	expr * expr
`/`	division	expr / expr
`%`	modulus (remainder)	expr % expr
`+`	addition	expr + expr
`−`	subtraction	expr − expr

Table 2.1 Arithmetic Operators

Division between integers results in an integer. If the quotient contains a fractional part, it is truncated. For example,

```
21 / 6;
21 / 7;
```

both result in a value of 3.

The modulus operator ("`%`") computes the remainder of division between two values. It can be applied only to operands of the integral types. The left operand of the modulus operator is the dividend. The divisor is the operator's right operand. Both operands must be of an integral data type. The following are examples of both legal and illegal expressions using the modulus operator:

```
3.14 % 3 // error: floating point operand
21 % 6   // ok: result is 3
21 % 7   // ok: result is 0

int i;
double f;

i % 2    // ok: non-zero result indicates i is odd
i % f    // error: floating point operand
```

In certain instances, the evaluation of an arithmetic expression will result in an incorrect or undefined value. These occurrences are referred to as *arithmetic exceptions*. An exception may be due to the nature of mathematics — such as division by zero — or due to the nature of computers — such as *overflow*. For example, an unsigned char of 8 bits can hold the range of values 0 through 255. The following multiplication assigns an unsigned char the value 256.

```
unsigned char uc = 32;
int i = 8;
uc = i * uc; // overflow
```

To represent 256, 9 bits are required. The assignment of 256 to uc, therefore, results in an overflow of the memory allocated for its data type. The actual value uc contains is undefined and will vary across different machines.

2.3   Equality, Relational and Logical Operators

The equality, relational and logical operators evaluate to either true or false. A truth condition yields 1; a false condition yields 0.

The logical AND ("&&") operator evaluates to true only if both its operands evaluate to true. The logical OR ("||") operator evaluates to true if either of its operands evaluate to true. The operands are guaranteed to be evaluated from left to right. Evaluation stops as soon as the truth or falsity of the expression is determined. Given the forms

```
expr1 && expr2
expr1 || expr2
```

expr2 is guaranteed not to be evaluated if either of the following is true:

- In a logical AND expression, expr1 evaluates to false, or

- In a logical OR expression, expr1 evaluates to true.

A valuable use of the logical AND operator is to have expr1 evaluate

oper	function	use
!	logical NOT	!expr
<	less than	expr < expr
<=	less than or equal	expr <= expr
>	greater than	expr > expr
>=	greater than or equal	expr >= expr
==	equality	expr == expr
!=	inequality	expr != expr
&&	logical AND	expr && expr
||	logical OR	expr || expr

Table 2.2 Equality, Relational and Logical Operators

to false in the presence of some boundary condition that would make the evaluation of `expr2` dangerous. For example,

```
while ( ptr != 0 &&
        ptr->value < upperBound &&
        notFound( ia[ ptr->value ] ))
```

A pointer with a value of 0 is not addressing an object. Applying the member selection operator to a 0-valued pointer is always trouble. The first logical AND operand prevents that possibility. Equally troublesome is an out-of-bounds array index. The second operand guards against that possibility. The third operand is safe to evaluate only when the first two operands return true.

The logical NOT operator ("!") evaluates to true if its operand has a value of zero; otherwise, it evaluates to false. For example,

```
int found = 0;
while ( !found ) {
    found = lookup( *ptr++ );
    if ( ptr == endPtr ) // at end
        return 0;
}
return ptr;
```

The expression

```
( !found )
```

returns true as long as `found` is equal to 0.

Use of the logical NOT is in part a question of style. For example,

```
( !found )
```

is clear in its meaning: *not found*. Is it as clear, however, what the following condition tests?

```
!strcmp( string1, string2 )
```

strcmp() is a C library routine that compares its two string arguments
for equality. A return value of 0 indicates that the two strings are equal.

```
!strcmp( string1, string2 )
```

means, *if* string1 *is not equal to* string2. Use of the logical NOT notation in this case may actually obscure the condition under test.

2.4   Assignment Operators

The left operand of the assignment operator ("=") must be an lvalue. The
effect of an assignment is to store a new value in the left operand's associated storage. For example, given the following three definitions:

```
int i;
int *ip;
int ia[ 4 ];
```

the following are all legal assignments:

```
ip = &i;
i = ia[ 0 ] + 1;
ia[ *ip ] = 1024;
*ip = i * 2 + ia[ i ];
```

The result of an assignment operator is the value of the expression on
the right hand side of the operator. The data type of the result is that of
the left operand.

Assignment operators can be concatenated provided that each of the
operands being assigned is of the same general data type. For example,

```
main()
{
    int i, j;
    i = j = 0; // ok: each assigned 0
    // ...
}
```

i and j are each assigned 0. The order of evaluation is right to left.

Assignment operator concatenation also allows for notational compaction, as in the following rewrite of the IntArray constructor (see Section 1.8
(page 52) for its original implementation):

```
IntArray::IntArray( int sz ) {
    ia = new int[ size = sz ];
    // ...
}
```

Use of this notation is a matter of personal style. Be careful, however, that compactness does not slip over the edge into obscurity.

The compound assignment operator also provides a measure of notational compactness. For example,

```
int arraySum( int ia[], int sz ) {
    int sum = 0;
    for ( int i = 0; i < sz; ++i )
        sum += ia[ i ];
    return sum;
}
```

The general syntactic form of the compound assignment operator is

```
a op= b;
```

where op may be one of the following ten operators: `+=`, `-=`, `*=`, `/=`, `%=`, `<<=`, `>>=`, `&=`, `^=`, `|=`. Each compound operator is equivalent to the following "longhand" assignment:

```
a = a op b;
```

The longhand notation for summing a vector, for example, is

```
sum = sum + ia[ i ];
```

Exercise 2-1. The following is illegal. Why? How would you correct it?

```
main() {
    int i = j = k = 0;
}
```

☐

Exercise 2-2. The following is also illegal. Why? How would you correct it?

```
main() {
    int i, j;
    int *ip;

    i = j = ip = 0;
}
```

☐

2.5   Increment and Decrement Operators

The increment ("++") and decrement ("−−") operators provide a convenient notational compaction for adding or subtracting 1 from a variable. Both operators should be thought of as assignment operators; the operand must be an lvalue. Each operator has a *prefix* and *postfix* form. For example,

```
main() {
    int c;
        ++c; // prefix increment
        c++; // postfix increment
}
```

Let's illustrate the use of the post- and prefix forms of the operators by defining a stack class, IntStack, to hold integer values. IntStack will perform two operations:

1. push(int v), which places the value of v at the top of the stack.

2. pop(), which returns the value stored at the top of the stack.

In addition, there are two possible exception conditions:

1. *overflow*: attempting to push() onto a stack which is full.

2. *underflow*: attempting to pop() a stack which is empty.

IntStack will be represented as an array of integers. Therefore, the following members are required:

```
int size;
int *ia;
int top;
```

top will always index the top element of the stack. This means that an empty stack will set top equal to −1. A full stack is indicated by top having the value size−1.

The boolean functions isEmpty() and isFull() are trivial to write:

```
typedef int Boolean;
extern const int BOS; // Bottom Of Stack

Boolean IntStack::isEmpty() { return (top == BOS ); }
Boolean IntStack::isFull()  { return (top == size-1); }
```

The implementation of push() illustrates the prefix form of the increment operator. Recall that top points to the current stack top. The new item must be placed in the element one greater than the current value of top:

```
void IntStack::push( int v )
{ // add v to the top of stack
      if ( isFull() )
            grow(); // enlarge stack

      ia[ ++top ] = v;
}
```

The prefix form of ++ increments the value of top *before* that value is used as an index into ia. It is a compact notation for the following two statements:

```
top = top + 1;
ia[ top ] = v;
```

grow() resizes the stack by some predetermined amount. Section 4.1 (page 137) contains the implementation of grow().

The implementation of pop() illustrates the postfix form of the decrement operator. Recall again that top points to the current stack top. After the stack is popped, top must be decremented.

```
int IntStack::pop()
{ // return the topmost element of stack
      if ( isEmpty() )
            // report error and exit()
            ;

      return ia[ top-- ];
}
```

The postfix form of −− decrements the value of top *after* that value is used as an index into ia. It is a compact notation for the following statement pair:

```
ia[ top ];
top = top - 1;
```

The execution of the return statement follows the decrement of top.

All that remains for the definition of IntStack is the management of its stack. Since the internal representation of our stack class is the same as that of the IntArray class defined earlier, we will reuse the IntArray implementation by deriving IntStack from IntArray (see Section 1.8 (page 51) for the definition of the IntArray class):

```
#include "IntArray.h"
typedef int Boolean;
const int BOS = -1; // Bottom Of Stack

class IntStack : private IntArray {
public:
    IntStack( int sz = ARRAY_SIZE )
        : IntArray( sz ), top( BOS ) {}
    Boolean isEmpty();
    Boolean isFull();
    void push( int );
    int pop();
    void grow() {}
protected:
    int top;
};
```

inheritance w/ private base class (re-use rather than subtype)

In the earlier derivation of IntArrayRC, IntArray was declared to be a `public` base class. In the derivation of IntStack, IntArray is declared to be a `private` base class. One difference between a private and public base class is that a private base class cannot be assigned objects of its derived class. For example,

```
extern swap( IntArray&, int, int );
IntArray ia;
IntArrayRC ia1;
IntStack is;

ia = ia1; // ok: public base class
ia = is;  // error: private base class

swap( ia1, 4, 7 ); // ok: public base class
swap( is, 4, 7 );  // error: private base class
```

A second difference between a private and public base class is that the inherited members of a private base class are treated as private members of the derived class. This means that the public interface of the IntArray class cannot be accessed through an IntStack class object. For example,

```
int bottom = is[0]; // error: operator[] private
```

Class inheritance can be used in two primary ways:

1. As a method of creating a subtype of an existing class, as in the derivation of IntArrayRC from the IntArray class in Chapter 1.

2. As a method of *reusing* an implementation to create a new class type, as in the derivation of IntStack from the IntArray class.

IntStack is not a subtype of IntArray. It does not share the operations that are applied to objects of the IntArray class. By making IntArray a private base class of IntStack, users of IntStack are prohibited from accidentally applying the IntArray operations on an IntStack class object. Additionally, were an IntStack class object assigned accidentally to an IntArray class object, the integrity of the stack could seriously be compromised. Preventing just such an accident is a second reason for making IntArray a private base class of IntStack. A private base class cannot be assigned a class object of its derived class.

Here is an example of using an IntStack object:

```
#include <stream.h>
#include "IntStack.h"

IntStack myStack;

const DEPTH = 7;
main() {
    for ( int i = 0; i < DEPTH; ++i )
        myStack.push(i);

    for ( i = 0; i < DEPTH; ++i )
        cout << myStack.pop() << "\t";

    cout << "\n";
}
```

When this program is compiled and executed, it generates the following results:

```
6       5       4       3       2       1       0
```

Exercise 2-3. Why do you think C++ wasn't named ++C? □

2.6 sizeof Operator

The sizeof operator returns the size, in bytes, of an expression or type specifier. It may occur in either of two forms:

```
sizeof (type-specifier);
sizeof expr;
```

Here is an example of how both forms of the sizeof operator are used:

```
int ia[] = { 0, 1, 2 };
const sz = sizeof ia / sizeof( int );
```

This next program illustrates the use of the `sizeof` operator on a wide variety of type specifiers.

```
#include <stream.h>
#include "IntStack.h"

main() {
    cout << "int :\t\t" << sizeof( int );
    cout << "\nint* :\t\t" << sizeof( int* );
    cout << "\nint& :\t\t" << sizeof( int& );
    cout << "\nint[3] :\t" << sizeof( int[3] );

    cout << "\n\n";   // to separate output

    cout << "IntStack :\t" << sizeof( IntStack );
    cout << "\nIntStack* :\t" << sizeof( IntStack* );
    cout << "\nIntStack& :\t" << sizeof( IntStack& );
    cout << "\nIntStack[3] :\t" << sizeof( IntStack[3] );
    cout << "\n";
}
```

When compiled and executed, the program generates the following output on a particular machine:

```
int :            4
int* :           4
int& :           4
int[3] :         12

IntStack :       12
IntStack* :      4
IntStack& :      4
IntStack[3] :    36
```

2.7 Arithmetic if Operator

The arithmetic `if` operator, the only ternary operator in C++, has the following syntactic form:

```
expr1 ? expr2 : expr3;
```

`expr1` is always evaluated. If it evaluates to a true condition — that is, any nonzero value — `expr2` is evaluated; otherwise, `expr3` is evaluated. The following program illustrates how the arithmetic if operator might be used.

```
#include <stream.h>

main() {
     int i = 10, j = 20, k = 30;

     cout << "\nThe larger value of "
          << i << " and " << j << " is "
          << ( i > j ? i : j );

     cout << "\nThe value of " << i << " is"
          << ( i % 2 ? " " : " not " )
          << "odd";

     // the arithmetic if can be nested, but
     // too deep a nesting will be difficult to read
     // max is set to the largest of 3 variables
     int max = ( (i > j)
          ? (( i > k) ? i : k)
          : ( j > k ) ? j : k);

     cout << "\nThe larger value of "
          << i << ", " << j << " and " << k
          << " is " << max << "\n";
}
```

When compiled and executed, the program generates the following output:

```
The larger value of 10 and 20 is 20
The value of 10 is not odd
The larger value of 10, 20 and 30 is 30
```

2.8 Bitwise Operators

A bitwise operator interprets its operand(s) as an ordered collection of bits. Each bit may contain either a 0 (off) or a 1 (on) value. A bitwise operator allows the programmer to test and set individual bits or bit subsets.

The operands of the bitwise operators must be of an integral type. Although they may be either signed or unsigned, unsigned operands are recommended. How the "sign bit" is handled in a number of the bitwise operations may differ across implementations; programs that work under one implementation may fail under another. Thus the use of unsigned operands makes for more portable programs.

First we will examine how each operator works. Then we will consider an example of how bitwise operators might be used. In Section 6.4 (page

Operator	Function	Use
˜	bitwise NOT	˜expr
<<	left shift	expr1 << expr2
>>	right shift	expr1 >> expr2
&	bitwise AND	expr1 & expr2
^	bitwise XOR	expr1 ^ expr2
|	bitwise OR	expr1 | expr2

Table 2.3 Bitwise Operators

272) we will implement a BitVector class.

The bitwise NOT operator ("˜") flips the bits of its operand. Each 1 bit is set to 0; each 0 bit is set to 1.

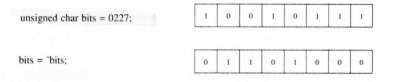

The bitwise shift operators ("<<, >>") shift the bits of the left operand some number of positions either to the left or right.

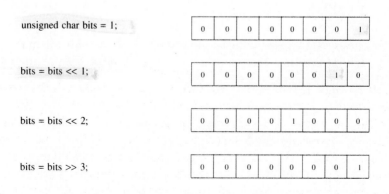

The operand's excess bits are discarded. The left shift operator ("<<") inserts 0-valued bits in from the right. The right shift operator (">>")

inserts 0-valued bits in from the left if the operand is unsigned. If the operand is signed, it may either insert copies of the sign bit or insert 0-valued bits; this behavior is machine dependent.

The bitwise AND operator ("&") takes two integral operands. For each bit position, the result is a 1-bit if both operands contain 1-bits; otherwise, the result is a 0-bit. (This operator should not be confused with the logical AND operator ("&&").)

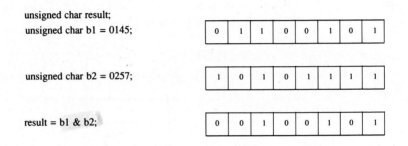

```
unsigned char result;
unsigned char b1 = 0145;        | 0 | 1 | 1 | 0 | 0 | 1 | 0 | 1 |


unsigned char b2 = 0257;        | 1 | 0 | 1 | 0 | 1 | 1 | 1 | 1 |


result = b1 & b2;               | 0 | 0 | 1 | 0 | 0 | 1 | 0 | 1 |
```

The bitwise XOR (exclusive or) operator ("^") takes two integral operands. For each bit position, the result is a 1-bit if either but not both operands contain a 1-bit; otherwise, the result is a 0-bit.

```
result = b1 ^ b2;               | 1 | 1 | 0 | 0 | 1 | 0 | 1 | 0 |
```

The bitwise OR (inclusive or) operator ("|") takes two integral operands. For each bit position, the result is a 1-bit if either or both operands contain a 1-bit; otherwise, the result is a 0-bit.

```
result = b1 | b2;               | 1 | 1 | 1 | 0 | 1 | 1 | 1 | 1 |
```

A variable utilized as a discrete collection of bits is referred to as a *bit vector*. Bit vectors are an efficient method of keeping *yes/no* information on a set of items or conditions.

Here is an example. A teacher has 30 students in a class. Each week the class is given a pass/fail quiz. A bit vector will be used to track the results of each quiz.

```
unsigned int quiz1 = 0;
```

The teacher must be able to turn on and off and to test individual bits. For example, student 27 has taken a make-up quiz and passed. The teacher must turn bit 27 on. The first step is to set the 27th bit of an integer to 1, while all the other bits remain 0. This can be done with the left shift operator ("<<") and the integer constant 1:

1

0	0	0	0	0	0	0	0
0	0	0	0	0	0	0	0
0	0	0	0	0	0	0	0
0	0	0	0	0	0	0	1

1 << 27

0	0	0	0	1	0	0	0
0	0	0	0	0	0	0	0
0	0	0	0	0	0	0	0
0	0	0	0	0	0	0	0

If this value is bitwise ORed with `quiz1`, all but the 27th bit will remain unchanged. The 27th bit is turned on:

```
quiz1 |= 1<<27;
```

Imagine that the teacher reexamined the quiz and discovered that student 27 actually had failed the make-up. The teacher must now turn off bit 27. This time the integer must have all the bits except the 27th turned on. Notice that this is the inverse of the previous integer. Applying the bitwise NOT to the previous integer will turn on every bit but the 27th:

1	1	1	1	0	1	1	1
1	1	1	1	1	1	1	1
1	1	1	1	1	1	1	1
1	1	1	1	1	1	1	1

˜(1 << 27)

If this value is bitwise ANDed with `quiz1`, all but the 27th bit will remain unchanged. The 27th bit is turned off:

```
quiz1 &= ˜(1<<27);
```

Here is how the teacher can determine the on or off status of a bit. Consider student 27 again. The first step is to set the 27th bit of an integer to 1. The bitwise AND of this value with `quiz1` will evaluate to true if bit 27 of `quiz1` is also on; otherwise, it will return 0 (false):

```
int hasPassed = quiz1 & (1<<27);
```

Exercise 2-4. Given the following two definitions:

```
unsigned int ui1 = 3, ui2 = 7;
```

What is the result of each of the following expressions?

```
(a)   ui1 & ui2           (c)   ui1 | ui2
(b)   ui1 && ui2          (d)   ui1 || ui2
```

□

Exercise 2-5. What is the effect of assigning 0377 to a variable of type `unsigned char` in terms of its bit pattern? Draw a picture.

□

Exercise 2-6. How might a programmer isolate the second byte of a variable of type `int` using the bitwise operators?

□

Exercise 2-7. There is a method of generating the powers of two using the left shift operator and the literal constant 1. Generate a table of the first 16 values. □

2.9 Precedence

Operator precedence, that is, the order in which operators are evaluated in a compound expression, is important to learn in order to avoid many common sources of program error. What, for example, is the result of the following arithmetic expression?

```
6 + 3 * 4 / 2 + 2
```

A purely left-to-right evaluation yields a value of 20. Other possible results include 9, 14, and 36. Which is correct? 14.

In C++, multiplication and division have a higher precedence than addition. This means that they are evaluated first. Multiplication and division have the same precedence, however. Operators which have the same precedence are evaluated from left to right. The order of expression evaluation is therefore the following:

```
1.  3 * 4 => 12
2.  12 / 2 => 6
3.  6 + 6 => 12
4.  12 + 2 => 14
```

Here is a compound expression insidiously in error. The problem is that the inequality operator ("!=") has a higher precedence than the assignment operator:

```
while ( ch = nextChar() != '\0' )
```

The programmer's intention is to assign ch the next character then test that character to see whether it is null. The behavior of the code, however, is to test the next character to see whether it is null. ch is then assigned the truth or false value of the test. The next character is never assigned.

Precedence can be overridden by the use of parentheses, which mark off subexpressions. In the evaluation of a compound expression, the first action is to evaluate all parenthetical subexpressions. Each subexpression is replaced by its result; evaluation continues. Innermost parentheses are evaluated before outer pairs. For example,

```
4 * 5 + 7 * 2 ==> 34
4 * ( 5 + 7 * 2 ) ==> 76
4 * ( (5 + 7) * 2 ) ==> 96
```

Here is the earlier compound expression properly parenthesized to reflect the programmer's intentions:

```
while ( (ch = nextChar()) != '\0' )
```

Table 2.4 presents the full set of C++ operators in order of precedence. 17R should be read as "precedence level 17, right to left associativity."

Similarly, 7L should be read as "precedence level 7, left to right associativity." The higher the precedence level, the greater the precedence of the operator.

Exercise 2-8. Using Table 2.4, identify the order of evaluation of the following compound expressions:

```
(a)    ! ptr == ptr->next
(b)    ~ uc ^ 0377 & ui << 4
(c)    ch = buf[ bp++ ] != '\0'
```

☐

Exercise 2-9. The three expressions in the previous exercise all evaluate in an order contrary to the intentions of the programmer. Parenthesize them to evaluate in an order you imagine to be the intention of the programmer.

☐

Exercise 2-10. Why does the following fail to compile? How would you fix it?

```
void doSomething();

main()
{
    int i = doSomething(), 0;
}
```

☐

2.10   Type Conversion

At the machine level, all data types melt away into a contiguous stream of bits. Type information is a kind of prescription: "take x number of bits and interpret them using the following pattern...."

Converting one predefined type into another typically will change one or both properties of the type but not the underlying bit pattern. The size may widen or narrow, and of course the intepretation will change.

Some conversions are not safe; typically, a compiler will warn about these. Conversions from a wider data type to a narrower data type are one category of unsafe type conversion. Here are three examples of potentially unsafe conversions:

HIGH

Level	Operator	Function
17R	: :	global scope (unary)
17L	: :	class scope (binary)
16L	->,.	member selectors
16L	[ ]	array index
16L	( )	function call
16L	( )	type construction
16L	sizeof	size in bytes
15R	++,--	increment,decrement
15R	~	bitwise NOT
15R	!	logical NOT
15R	+,-	unary minus, plus
15R	*,&	dereference, address-of
15R	( )	type conversion (cast)
15R	new,delete	free store management
14L	->*,.*	member pointer selectors
13L	*,/,%	multiplicative operators
12L	+,-	arithmetic operators
11L	<<,>>	bitwise shift
10L	<,<=,>,>=	relational operators
9L	==,!=	equality, inequality
8L	&	bitwise AND
7L	^	bitwise XOR
6L	|	bitwise OR
5L	&&	logical AND
4L	||	logical OR
3L	?:	arithmetic if
2R	=,*=,/=	assignment operators
2R	%=,+=,-=,<<=	
2R	>>=,&=,|=,^=	
1L	,	comma operator

LOW

Table 2.4 Operator Precedence and Associativity

R = right-to-left associativity
L = left-to-right

```
long lval;
unsigned char uc;

int (3.14159);
(signed char) uc;
short (lval);
```

The following two notations,

```
type (expr)
(type) expr
```

are referred to as *casts*. They represent an explicit request by the programmer to convert expr into type.

The three cases illustrate the potential dangers of narrowing type conversions.

In the first case, the fractional part is lost. For example,

```
// 3.14159 != 3.0
3.14159 != double (int (3.14159) );
```

In the second case, for half the possible values of uc (128 - 255), the interpretation of the bit pattern has changed. The left-most bit is now the sign bit.

In the third case, for any value of lval which requires bits beyond the size of a short, the result of the conversion is undefined.

Some conversions are safe on some machines but involve narrowing on others. On most machines, for example, an int is the same size as either a short or long but not both. One of the following conversions will be unsafe on any machine that does not implement short, int, and long as three distinct sizes:

```
unsigned short us;
unsigned int ui;

int( us );
long( ui );
```

The whole issue of type conversion can be quite bewildering, but it is something of which programmers must be aware. The next two subsections look at implicit and explicit type conversions. Section 6.5 (page 282) discusses user-defined conversions for class types.

Implicit Type Conversions

An implicit type conversion is a conversion performed by the compiler without programmer intervention. An implicit conversion is applied generally whenever differing data types are intermixed. Such a conversion is performed following a set of predefined rules referred to as the *standard conversions*.

Assigning a value to an object converts the value to the type of the object. Passing a value to a call of a function converts the value to the type of the function argument. For example,

```
void ff( int );

int val = 3.14159; // conversion to int 3
ff( 3.14159 );     // conversion to int 3
```

In both cases, the double literal 3.14159 is implicitly converted to type int by the compiler. A warning is issued since the conversion involves a narrowing.

In an arithmetic expression, the widest data type present becomes the target conversion type. For example,

```
val + 3.14159;
```

The widest data type of this arithmetic expression is of type double. val is implicitly converted to double by widening (also referred to as *type promotion*). Its value 3 becomes 3.0 and is added to 3.14159. The result of the expression is 6.14159.

Note that the value of val remains 3. The type conversion is applied to a copy of val's value. A variable is not written in the process of type conversion.

```
val = val + 3.14159;
```

Two conversions occur. The value of val is promoted to double. The result, 6.14159, is then narrowed to type int. This narrowed value is then assigned to val. val now contains the value 6.

The behavior is exactly the same when this expression is written as

```
val += 3.14159;
```

For example, the resulting value of the following two statements is 23, not 20:

```
int i = 10;
i *= 2.3; // 23, not 20
```

The truncation of the double literal constant occurs after the multiplication.

Explicit Conversions

It is somewhat wasteful to perform two conversions for the compound expression

```
i = i + 3.14159;
```

Since the target data type is int, it seems more sensible to narrow the double operand rather than promote i to double, then narrow the sum to int.

One reason for an explicit cast is to override the usual standard conversions. For example,

```
i = i + int(3.14159);
```

3.14159 is now converted to int, yielding the value 3. This is added to and then assigned to i.

A predefined standard conversion allows a pointer to any data type to be assigned to a pointer to type void*. A void* pointer is used whenever the exact type of an object is either unknown or will vary under particular circumstances. A void* pointer is sometimes referred to as a *generic* pointer because of its ability to address objects of any data types.

However, a void* pointer may not be dereferenced directly. (There is no type information to guide the compiler in interpreting the underlying bit pattern.) Rather, a void* pointer must first be converted to a pointer to a particular type.

In C++, however, there is *no* predefined conversion of a void* pointer to a pointer to a particular type since it is potentially unsafe. For example, attempting to assign a void* pointer to a pointer to anything other than void* will result in a compile-time error:

```
int i;
void *vp;
int *ip = &i;
double *dp;

vp = ip; // ok
dp = vp; // error: no standard conversion: unsafe
```

A second reason for an explicit cast is to override type checking. C++, in general, permits a value to be explicitly cast to any data type. By providing an explicit cast, the programmer assumes responsibility for the safety of the type conversion. For example,

```
dp = (int*)vp; // ok: explicit cast
*dp = 3.14;    // trouble if dp addresses i
```

A third reason for an explicit cast is to disambiguate a situation in which more than one conversion is possible. We will look at this case more closely in Section 4.3 (page 161) in our discussion of overloading function names.

Given the following set of identifiers:

```
char ch;                    unsigned char unChar;
short sh;                   unsigned short unShort;
int intVal;                 unsigned int unInt;
long longVal;               float fl;
```

Exercise 2-11. Identify which of the following assignments are unsafe because of possible narrowing:

```
(a)  sh = intVal              (d)  longVal = unInt
(b)  intVal = longVal         (e)  unInt = fl
(c)  sh = unChar              (f)  intVal = unShort
```

□

Exercise 2-12. Identify the data type of the following expressions:

```
(a)   'a' - 3
(b)   intVal * longVal - ch
(c)   fl + longVal / sh
(d)   unInt + (unsigned int) longVal
(e)   ch + unChar + longVal + unInt
```

□

2.11   Statements

Statements form the smallest executable unit within a C++ program. Statements are terminated with a semicolon; their simplest form is the empty, or null, statement. It takes the following form:

```
; // null statement
```

A null statement is useful in those instances where the syntax of the language requires the presence of a statement but where the logic of the program does not. This is occasionally the case with the while and for loop statements. For example,

```
while ( *string++ = *inBuf++ )
          ; // null statement
```

The presence of an unnecessary null statement will not generate a compile-time error. (The author once used an ALGOL68 compiler at Columbia University that flagged every null statement as a fatal error. Imagine being up at 3 A.M. waiting 40 minutes to compile a program, only to have an extraneous semicolon terminate the compilation.)

```
int val;; // additional null statement
```

is composed of two statements: the declaration statement `int val` and the null statement.

A declaration followed by a semicolon is a *declaration statement*, the only statement that can be specified outside a function. An expression followed by a semicolon is an *expression statement*.

Compound Statements and Blocks

A number of syntactic constructs in the language permit only a single statement to be specified. The logic of the program, however, may require that a sequence of two or more statements be executed. In these cases a compound statement can be used. For example,

```
if ( account.balance - withdrawal < 0 )
{ // compound statement
    issueNotice( account.number );
    chargePenalty( account.number );
}
```

A compound statement is a sequence of statements enclosed by a pair of braces. The compound statement is treated as a single unit and may appear anywhere in the program where a single statement may appear. A compound statement need not be terminated with a semicolon.

A compound statement containing one or more declaration statements is referred to as a *block*. Blocks are considered in detail in Section 3.10 (page 130) in the discussion of scope.

2.12   Statement Flow Control

The default flow of statement execution is sequential. Every C++ program begins with the first statement of `main()`. Each statement in turn is executed. When the final statement is executed, the program is done.

Except in the simplest programs, sequential program execution is inadequate to the problems we must solve. Through our program examples we have already seen the conditional `if` statement and the `while` and `for` loop statements. The following subsections review the entire C++ statement set.

2.13   if Statement

An `if` statement tests a particular condition. Whenever that condition evaluates as true, an action or set of actions is executed. Otherwise, the action(s) are ignored.

The syntactic form of the `if` statement is the following:

```
if ( expression )
    statement;
```

The *expression* must be enclosed in parentheses. If it evaluates to a non-zero value, the condition is considered as true and the *statement* is executed.

For example, let's provide a member function to return the minimum value contained in an IntArray class object. In addition, we must keep track of the number of occurrences of that value. The function's logic will require two conditional statements:

1. If a current value is equal to the minimum value, increment a counter by one.

2. If a current value is less than the minimum value, assign the minimum value this current value and reset the counter to 1.

The actual array of values will be stepped through using a `for` loop. To find the minimum value, each element must be examined.

This function requires two variables: one to hold the minimum value, and a second to hold the count of its occurrences. The maximum number of occurrences is equal to the size of the array. The data type to hold the count of the occurrences, therefore, must be the same size as the data type of `size`, the data member of IntArray that holds the array dimension.

```
int minVal = ?; // what value?
int occurs = ?; // what value?
```

`minVal` must be initialized with a first value against which the elements of the array can be tested. One approach is to initialize `minVal` with the largest possible integer value. Provided that `occurs` is initialized to `0`, this will work in every case. It is not, however, the best strategy.

Let's look at the possible outcomes of testing for the minimum value.

- If the array is sorted in ascending order, the first array element is the minimum value of the array. This best case requires only one assignment to `minVal`.

- If the array is sorted in descending order, the last array element is the minimum value of the array. This worst case requires n assignments.

- The array is unsorted and the elements are entered in a random order. On average, the minimum value will occur somewhere in the middle. This average case requires that possibly half the elements be assigned to `minVal`.

In *all* cases, by making `minVal`'s initial value the first element of the array, we are guaranteed to save one assignment. In addition, only `n-1` elements need be examined. This will be the strategy of the function.

Two `if` statements are required:

```
if minVal > ia[ i ] ... // new minVal
if minVal == ia[ i ] ... // another occurrence of minVal
```

A somewhat common programmer error in the use of the `if` statement is to not provide a compound statement when multiple statements must be executed upon a condition evaluating as true. This can be a very difficult error to uncover since the text of the program looks correct For example,

```
if ( minVal > ia[ i ] )
    minVal = ia[ i ];
    occurs = 1; // not part of if statement
```

Contrary to the indentation and intention of the programmer,

```
occurs = 1;
```

is not treated as part of the `if` statement but rather is executed unconditionally following evaluation of the `if` statement. Here is the `if` statement written correctly:

```
if ( minVal > ia[ i ] ) {
    minVal = ia[ i ];
    occurs = 1;
}
```

Our second `if` statement looks as follows:

```
if ( minVal == ia[ i ] )
    ++occurs;
```

Notice that the order of the `if` statements is significant. Our function will always be off by 1 if we place them in the following order:

```
if ( minVal > ia[ i ] ) {
    minVal = ia[ i ];
    occurs = 1;
}
```

```
// potential error if minVal
// has just been set to ia[i]
if ( minVal == ia[ i ] )
    ++occurs;
```

Not only is the execution of both if statements on the same value potentially dangerous, it is also unnecessary. The same element cannot be both less than minVal and equal to it. If one condition is true, the other condition can be ignored safely. The if statement allows for this kind of *either-or* condition by providing an else clause.

The syntactic form of the if-else statement is the following:

```
if ( expression )
    statement-1;
else
    statement-2;
```

If the *expression* evaluates to a nonzero value, the condition is considered to be true and *statement-1* is executed; otherwise, *statement-2* is executed. Note that if *statement-1* is not a compound statement, it must be terminated by a semicolon. Programmers familiar with either Pascal or Ada, in which the semicolon following *statement-1* is illegal, often fail to provide the necessary semicolon. For example,

```
if ( minVal == ia[ i ] )
    ++occurs; // terminating ';' required
else
if ( minVal > ia[ i ] ) {
    minVal = ia[ i ];
    occurs = 1;
}
```

In this example, *statement-2* is itself an if statement. If minVal is less than the element, no action is taken.

In the following example, one of the three statements is always executed:

```
if ( minVal < ia[ i ] )
    ; // null statement
else
if ( minVal > ia[ i ] ) {
    minVal = ia[ i ];
    occurs = 1;
}
else // minVal == ia[ i ]
    ++occurs;
```

The if-else statement introduces a source of potential ambiguity referred to as *the dangling-else* problem. This problem occurs when a statement contains more `if` than `else` clauses. The question then arises, with which `if` does the additional `else` clause properly match up? For example,

```
if ( minVal <= ia[ i ] )
    if ( minVal == ia[ i ]
        ++occurs;
else {
    minVal = ia[ i ];
    occurs = 1;
}
```

The indentation indicates the programmer's belief that the `else` should match up with the outer `if` clause. In C++, however, the dangling-else ambiguity is resolved by matching the `else` with the last occurring unmatched `if`. In this case, the actual evaluation of the `if-else` statement is as follows:

```
if ( minVal <= ia[ i ] )
{ // effect of dangling-else resolution
    if ( minVal == ia[ i ]
        ++occurs;
    else {
        minVal = ia[ i ];
        occurs = 1;
    }
}
```

One method of overriding the default dangling-else matching is to place the last occurring `if` in a compound statement:

```
if ( minVal <= ia[ i ] )
{ // override the default resolution
    if ( minVal == ia[ i ]
        ++occurs;
}
else {
    minVal = ia[ i ];
    occurs = 1;
}
```

Some coding styles recommend *always* using compound statement braces to avoid possible confusion and error in later modifications of the code.

Section 1.8 (page 51) introduces the IntArray class. Here is an implementation of the IntArray member function `min()`:

```
#include "IntArray.h"

IntArray::min( int &occurs ) {
    int minVal = ia[ 0 ];
    occurs = 1;

    for ( int i = 1; i < size; ++i ) {
        if ( minVal == ia[ i ] )
            ++occurs;
        else
        if ( minVal > ia[ i ] ) {
            minVal = ia[ i ];
            occurs = 1;
        }
    }

    return minVal;
}
```

location (write)

read

In order to pass both the minimum value and the number of its occurrences, min() utilizes an argument of an integer reference type. A reference argument type passes the lvalue of the actual argument into the function; a nonreference argument passes the rvalue. *Pass-by-reference* *(write)* allows the actual argument to be assigned to from within the function. Here is an example of how it might be used:

```
#include <stream.h>
#include "IntArray.h"

IntArray myArray;

main() {
    // initialize the array in descending order
    for ( int i = myArray.getSize()-2; i >= 0; --i )
        myArray[ i ] = i;

    // insert a second copy of 0, the lowest value
    myArray[ myArray.getSize()-1 ] = 0;

    int number = 0;
    int low = myArray.min( number );

    cout << "\nlow: " << low
         << " number: " << number << "\n";
}
```

When compiled and executed, this program generates the following output:

```
low: 0 number: 2
```

Section 3.7 (page 119) considers the reference type and pass-by-reference mechanism in detail.

Exercise 2-13. Change the declaration of `occurs` in the argument list of `min()` to be a nonreference argument type and rerun the program. □

2.14   switch Statement

Deeply nested `if-else` statements can often be correct syntactically and yet not express the intended logic of the programmer. Unintended `else-if` matchings are more likely to pass unnoticed, for example. Modifications to the statements are also much harder to get right. As an alternative method of choosing among a set of mutually exclusive choices, C++ provides the `switch` statement.

For example, suppose that we have been asked to count the number of occurrences of each of the five vowels in random segments of text. (The conventional wisdom is that e is the most frequently occurring vowel.) Our program logic is as follows:

- read each character in turn until there are no more characters to read;

- compare each character to the set of vowels;

- if the character matches one of the vowels, add 1 to that vowel's count;

- display results.

The program was used to analyze the previous section of this book. Here is the output, which verifies the conventional wisdom regarding the frequency of the vowel e:

```
aCnt:    394
eCnt:    721
iCnt:    461
oCnt:    349
uCnt:    186
```

The program is implemented as a five-way `switch` statement with a truth condition for each vowel. In a `switch` statement, the truth condition is implemented as a `case` label. The Vowels enumeration is used to enhance the readability of the program text. The program is implemented as follows:

```
#include <stream.h>

enum Vowels { a='a', e='e', i='i', o='o', u='u' };
main()
{
    char ch;
    int aCnt=0, eCnt=0, iCnt=0, oCnt=0, uCnt=0;

    while ( cin >> ch )
      switch ( ch ) {
            case a:
                  ++aCnt;
                  break;
            case e:
                  ++eCnt;
                  break;
            case i:
                  ++iCnt;
                  break;
            case o:
                  ++oCnt;
                  break;
            case u:
                  ++uCnt;
                  break;
      }; // end switch(ch)

      cout << "aCnt: \t" << aCnt << "\n";
      cout << "eCnt: \t" << eCnt << "\n";
      cout << "iCnt: \t" << iCnt << "\n";
      cout << "oCnt: \t" << oCnt << "\n";
      cout << "uCnt: \t" << uCnt << "\n";
}
```

There is a problem in the logic of the program, however. For example, how does the program handle the following input?

```
UNIX
```

The capital U and the capital I are not recognized as vowels. Our program fails to count vowels occurring as uppercase characters. Before we fix our program, however, let's look more closely at the switch statement.

The value following the case keyword, referred to as the *case label*, must be followed by a colon. Each case label must be a constant expression of an integral type. No two case labels may have the same value; if they do a compile-time error occurs.

When the switch statement is executed, its expression is evaluated and compared to each case label in turn. If the expression is equal to a case label, execution begins with the first statement following the case label. If there is no match between the expression and the set of case labels, no action is taken.

A common misconception is that only the statements defined for the matched case label are executed. Rather, execution begins there and continues across case boundaries until the end of the switch statement is encountered. Let's look more closely at this other common cause of program error. Here is our earlier switch statement, modified slightly:

```
switch ( ch ) {
    case a: ++aCnt;
    case e: ++eCnt;
    case i: ++iCnt;
    case o: ++oCnt;
    case u: ++uCnt;
}; // end switch(ch)

cout << ch << "\n"; // for illustration
```

If ch is set to i, execution begins following case i:. iCnt is incremented. Execution, however, does not stop there, but continues across case boundaries until the closing brace of the switch statement. oCnt and uCnt are also both incremented. If ch is next set to e, eCnt, iCnt, oCnt, and uCnt are all incremented.

The programmer must explicitly tell the compiler to stop statement execution within the switch statement. This is done by specifying a break statement after each execution unit within the switch statement. Under most conditions, the last statement of a case label is break.

When a break statement is encountered, the switch statement is terminated. Control shifts to the statement immediately following the closing brace of the switch. In the example, this statement is

```
cout << ch << "\n"; // for illustration
```

A case label that deliberately omits a break statement should in most cases provide a comment stating that the omission is deliberate. If obvious from the context, however, the comment may be left out safely.

When might the programmer wish to omit a break statement from a case label? One circumstance is when a set of values are all to be handled by the same sequence of actions. Each element of the range must be provided with its own case label. For example, recall our earlier program that failed to read uppercase vowels — here is a corrected implementation:

```
switch (ch ) {
    case A:
    case a:
        ++aCnt;
        break;
    // ...
    case U:
    case u:
        ++uCnt;
        break;
};
```

The switch statement provides the equivalent of an unconditional
else clause. This is the default label. If no case label matches the value
of the switch expression and the default label is present, the statements
following the default label will be executed. For example, let's add a
default case to our switch statement. The default case will count the
number of consonants:

```
#include <ctype.h>

// ...
switch (ch) {
    case A:
    case a:
        ++aCnt;
        break;
    // ...
    case U:
    case u:
        ++uCnt;
        break;
    default:
        if isalpha( ch )
            ++conCnt;
        break;
};
```

isalpha() is a C library routine; it evaluates to true if its argument is a
letter of the alphabet. To use it, the programmer must include the system
header file ctype.h.

Although it is not strictly necessary to specify a break statement in the
last label of a switch statement, the safest course is to always provide
one. If an additional case label is added later to the bottom of the switch
statement, the absence of the break statement may suddenly become significant.

Exercise 2-14. Modify the program so that it also counts the number of spaces read.

☐

Exercise 2-15. Modify the program so that it counts the number of occurrences of the following two-character sequences: ff, fl, and fi. ☐

Iterative Statements

Many program activities involve performing a fixed set of statements against a collection of similar objects. A bank program, for example, may be written to process checks. For each check, the program must, among other actions,

- read in the check,

- verify that it has a correct account number,

- verify that the account has funds sufficient to cover the amount of the check,

- debit the account for the amount of the check, and

- record the transaction.

To repeat this sequence of code for each check is hardly reasonable. Rather, the language provides iterative control statements, called *loops*, that allow the program to repeat execution of the single instance of the fixed set of statements.

A loop cycles over a body of code for as long as a specified condition remains true. The bank program would probably specify the following truth condition:

```
while there exists a check to be processed
```

This loop will terminate when the last check has been processed; that is, when the specified condition becomes false. This specified condition is sometimes referred to as a *loop control*.

C++ supports three loop constructs: the while, do, and for statements. The main distinction among them is the method of loop control. For all three statements, a true condition is any nonzero value. A zero value indicates a false condition.

2.15   while Statement

The syntactic form of the `while` loop is as follows:

```
while ( expression )
    statement;
```

For as many iterations as the *expression* evaluates to a true condition, the *statement* (or compound statement) is executed. The sequence is as follows:

1. Evaluate the expression.

2. Execute the statement if the condition is true.

If the first evaluation of the expression tests false, the statement is never executed. For example, the algorithm to count vowels introduced in the earlier subsection on the `switch` statement requires that characters from the input stream be read in one character at a time until the end of the file is reached. The `while` loop is a perfect candidate for implementing this:

```
char ch;
while ( cin >> ch )
    switch( ch ) {
        ...
```

Because the entire `switch` is considered a single statement, it does not need to be placed in a compound statement.

The `while` loop is particularly appropriate for manipulating strings and other pointer types. For example,

```
ff( const char *st )
{
    int len = 0;
    const char *tp = st;

    // compute length of st
    while ( *tp++ ) ++len;

    // now copy st
    char *s = new char[ len + 1];
    while ( *s++ = *st++ )
        ; // null statement

    // ... rest of function
}
```

Exercise 2-16. Implement a function to determine if two strings are equal.

□

Exercise 2-17. Implement a function which returns the number of occurrences of a character within a string.

□

Exercise 2-18. Implement a function which determines if a substring occurs within a string. □

2.16   for Statement

A `for` loop is used most commonly to step through a fixed-length data structure such as an array. We have utilized it a number of times already. The syntactic form of the `for` loop is as follows:

```
for ( init-statement; expression-1; expression-2 )
    statement;
```

init-statement can be either a declaration or an expression. It is generally used to initialize or assign to one or a set of variables. It may be null. The following are all legal instances of the *init-statement*:

```
for ( int i = 0; ...
for ( ; /* null init-statement */ ...
for ( i = 0; ...
for ( int lo = 0, hi = max, mid = max/2; ...
for ( char *ptr = getStr(); ...
for ( i = 0, ptr = buf, dbl = 0.0; ...
```

expression-1 serves as the loop control. For as many iterations as *expression-1* evaluates as a true condition, *statement* is executed. *statement* may either be a single or a compound statement. If the first evaluation of *expression-1* evaluates to false, *statement* is never executed. The following are all legal instances of *expression-1*:

```
(...; index < arraySize; ... )
(...; ptr; ... )
(...; *st1++ = *st2++; ... )
(...; ch = getNextChar(); ... )
```

expression-2 is evaluated after each iteration of the loop. It is generally used to modify the variables initialized in *init-statement*. If the first evaluation of *expression-1* evaluates to false, *expression-2* is never executed. The following are all legal instances of *expression-2*:

```
( ...; ...; ++i )
( ...; ...; ptr = ptr->next )
( ...; ...; ++i, --j, ++cnt )
( ...; ...; ) // null instance
```

Given the following for loop:

```
const int sz = 24;
int ia[ sz ];

for ( int i = 0; i < sz; ++i )
    ia[ i ] = i;
```

the order of evaluation is as follows:

1. *init-statement* is executed once at the start of the loop. In this example, i is defined and initialized to 0.

2. *expression-1* is executed. A true condition, any value other than 0, causes execution of *statement*. A false condition terminates the loop. An initial false condition results in *statement* never being executed.

   In this example, i is compared to sz. For as long as i is less than sz,

   ```
   ia[ i ] = i;
   ```

   is executed.

3. *expression-2* is executed. Typically, this modifies the variable(s) initialized in *init-statement*. In the example, i is incremented by 1.

This constitutes one complete iteration of the for loop. Step 2 is now repeated. This process can be modeled as the following equivalent while loop:

```
init-statement;
while ( expression-1 )
{
    statement;
    expression-2;
}
```

Exercise 2-19. Implement a function to compare two arrays for equality. Be sure to define what it means for two arrays to be equal.

☐

Exercise 2-20. Implement a function to search an array for a particular value. If the value is found, return its array index. What should the function do if the value is not found? ☐

2.17   do Statement

Imagine that we have been asked to write an interactive program that converts miles into kilometers. The outline of the program looks like this:

```
int more = 1;  // dummy value to start loop

while ( more ) {
    val = getValue();
    val = convertValue(val);
    printValue(val);
    more = doMore();
}
```

The problem here is that the loop control is set up within the loop body. With the for and while loop, however, unless the loop control evaluates to true, the loop body will never be executed. This means that the programmer must provide a first value to start the loop going. The do loop guarantees that its loop body is always executed at least once. It does not require a forced startup.

The syntactic form of the do loop is as follows:

```
do
    statement;
while ( expression );
```

statement is executed before *expression* is evaluated. If the condition evaluates as false, the do loop terminates. Our program outline now looks as follows:

```
int more;

do {
    val = getValue();
    val = convertValue(val);
    printValue(val);
    more = doMore(); }
while ( more );
```

Jump Statements

Jump statements unconditionally transfer program control within a function. Jump statements include the break, continue, and goto statements. The following sections look at each jump statement in turn.

2.18 break Statement

A break statement terminates the smallest enclosing while, do, for, or switch statement. Execution resumes at the statement immediately following the terminated statement. For example, IntArray requires a member function that searches the array for the first occurrence of a particular value. If it is found, the function returns its index; otherwise, the function returns −1. This is implemented as follows:

```
#include "IntArray.h"

IntArray::search( int val )
{ // val in ia? return index; otherwise, -1
    int loc = -1;
    for ( int i = 0; i < size; ++i )
        if ( val == ia[ i ] ) {
            loc = i;
            break;
        }
    return loc;
}
```

If a match is found, there is no reason to continue looking. break terminates the for loop. The return statement immediately following the for loop is executed.

2.19 continue Statement

A continue statement causes the current iteration of the nearest enclosing while, do, or for loop to terminate. In the case of the while and do loops, execution resumes with the loop control evaluation. In the case of the for loop, execution resumes with the evaluation of *expression-2*. Unlike the break statement, which terminates the loop, the continue statement terminates only the current iteration. For example, the following program fragment reads in a program text file one word at a time. Every word that begins with an underscore will be processed; otherwise, the current loop iteration is terminated:

```
while ( cin >> inBuf ) {
    if ( inBuf[0] != '_' )
        continue; // terminate iteration
    // ... process string ...
}
```

2.20   goto Statement

If the `break` and `continue` statements did not exist, the programmer would need some way to jump out of a loop or `switch` statement. The `goto` statement provides just such a facility, one rarely used in programming today. The `goto` statement transfers program control unconditionally. The target destination of a `goto` is a label. The target label and `goto` must appear in the same function.

The syntactic form of the `goto` statement is

```
goto label;
```

where *label* is a user-supplied identifier. A label may be used only as the target of a `goto` and must be terminated by a colon.

A label may not immediately precede a closing right brace. A `null` statement following the label is the typical method of handling this constraint. For example,

```
        end: ; //null statement
    }
```

A `goto` statement may not jump over the definition of a variable with an explicit or implicit initializer unless the definition occurs in a block and the entire block is jumped over. The following program, for example, is illegal:

```
        #include "IntArray.h"
        extern int getValue();
        extern void processArray( IntArray& );

        main() {
            int sz = getValue();
            if ( sz <= 0 )
                goto end; // illegal jump

            IntArray myArray( sz );
            processArray( myArray );

        end: ;
        }
```

`myArray` has an implicit initializer — the IntArray class constructor.

Exercise 2-21. Rewrite the instance of `main()` so that it is no longer illegal. □

Chapter 3: **Functions and Scope**

A function can be thought of as a user-defined operation. In general, a function is represented by a name, not an operator. The operands of a function, referred to as its *arguments*, are specified in a comma-separated *argument list* enclosed in parentheses. The result of a function is referred to as its *return type*. A function that does not yield a value has a return type of void. The actual actions a function performs are specified in the *body* of the function. The function body is enclosed in braces ("{}") and is sometimes referred to as a block. Here are some examples of functions:

```
inline int abs( int i )
{ // return the absolute value of i
    return( i < 0 ? -i : i );
}

inline int min( int v1, int v2 )
{ // return the smaller of two values
    return( v1 <= v2 ? v1 : v2 );
}

gcd( int v1, int v2 )
{ // return the greatest common denominator
    int temp;
    while ( v2 ) {
        temp = v2;
        v2 = v1 % v2;
        v1 = temp;
    }
    return v1;
}
```

A function is evaluated whenever the call operator ("()") is applied to the function's name. If the function expects to receive arguments, these arguments, referred to as the *actual arguments* of the call, are placed inside the call operator. Each argument is separated by a comma. This is referred to as *passing arguments* to a function. In the following example, main() calls abs() twice and min() and gcd() once each. It is defined in the file main.C.

```
#include <stream.h>
#include "localMath.h"

main() {
  int i, j;

  // get values from standard input
  cout << "Value: "; cin >> i;
  cout << "Value: "; cin >> j;

  cout << "\nmin: " << min( i, j ) << "\n";
  i = abs( i ); j = abs( j );
  cout << "gcd: " << gcd( i, j ) << "\n";
}
```

A function call can cause one of two things to occur. If the function has been declared *inline,* the body of the function is expanded at the point of its call during compilation; otherwise, the function is invoked at run time. A function invocation causes program control to transfer to the function being invoked; execution of the currently active function is suspended. When evaluation of the called function completes, the suspended function resumes execution at the point immediately following the call. Function invocation is managed on the program's *run-time stack.*

If a function is not declared to the program before it is used, a compile-time error will result.

The function definition, of course, serves as its declaration. However, a function may only be defined once in a program. Typically the definition resides in its own text file or in a text file containing it and other related functions. A function is usually used in files other than the one containing its definition. Therefore an additional method of declaring a function is required.

The declaration of a function consists of its return type, name, and argument list. These three elements are referred to as the *function prototype.* A function prototype may appear multiple times in a file without penalty.

To compile `main.C`, `abs()`, `min()`, and `gcd()` must first be declared; otherwise, each of their calls within `main()` will generate a compile-time error. The three prototypes look as follows (the prototype need not specify an argument's name, only its type):

```
int abs( int );
int min( int, int );
int gcd( int, int );
```

Function prototypes (and the definition of inline functions) are best placed within header files. These header files can then be included whenever the declarations are required. This way, all files share a common declaration; should that declaration have to be modified, only that one instance need be changed.

The header file might be called `localMath.h`. It might look as follows (inline functions are defined in header files, not in program text files):

```
int gcd( int, int );

// inlines are placed within header file
inline abs(int i) { return( i<0 ? -i : i ); }
inline min(int v1,int v2) { return( v1<=v2 ? v1 : v2 ); }
```

Compilation of the program is done as follows:

```
$ CC main.C gcd.C
```

Execution of the program produces the following results:

```
Value: 15
Value: 123

min: 15
gcd: 3
```

3.1 Recursion

A function that calls itself, either directly or indirectly, is referred to as a *recursive function*. `gcd()`, for example, can be rewritten as a recursive function:

```
rgcd( int v1, int v2 )
{
    if (v2 == 0 )
        return v1;
    return rgcd( v2, v1%v2 );
}
```

A recursive function must always define a *stopping condition*; otherwise, the function will recur "forever." In the case of `rgcd()`, the stopping condition is a remainder of 0.

The call

```
rgcd( 15, 123 );
```

evaluates to 3. Table 3.1 traces the execution.

The last call, `rgcd(3,0)`, satisfies the stopping condition. It returns the greatest common denominator, 3. This value successively becomes the return value of each prior call. The value is said to *percolate* upward.

v1	v2	return
15	123	rgcd(123, 15)
123	15	rgcd(15, 3)
15	3	rgcd(3, 0)
3	0	3

Table 3.1 Trace of rgcd(15,123)

A recursive function is likely to run slower than its nonrecursive (or *iterative*) counterpart due to the overhead associated with the invocation of a function. The function code, however, is likely to be smaller and less complex.

A factorial of a number is the product of its counting sequence beginning with 1. The factorial of 5, for example, is 120; that is,

```
1 x 2 x 3 x 4 x 5 = 120
```

Computing the factorial of a number lends itself to a recursive solution:

```
unsigned long
factorial( int val ) {
    if ( val > 1 )
        return val * factorial( val-1 );
    return val;
}
```

The stopping condition in this case is when val contains a value of 1.

Exercise 3-1. Rewrite factorial() as an iterative function.

□

Exercise 3-2. What would happen if the stopping condition were as follows?

```
if ( val != 0 )
```

□

Exercise 3-3. Why do you think the return value is specified as an unsigned long while the argument is of type int? □

3.2   Inline Functions

A question not as yet addressed directly is why `min()` was defined as a function. To reduce the amount of code duplication is not the reason. It actually requires one more character to write

```
min( i, j );
```

then to write the function directly:

```
i < j ? i : j;
```

The benefits of making it a function include the following:

- It is generally easier to read a call of `min()` than an instance of the *arithmetic if*, especially when `i` and `j` are complex expressions.

- It is easier to change one localized instance than 300 occurrences within an application. For example, if it is decided the test should read

  ```
  i <= j
  ```

  finding every coded occurrence would be tedious and prone to error.

- There is a uniform semantics. Each test is guaranteed to be implemented the same.

- The function instance provides full type checking of its arguments. Type errors are caught at compile-time.

- The function can be reused rather than rewritten by other applications.

There is, however, one serious drawback to making `min()` a function: It is significantly slower. The two arguments must be copied, machine registers must be saved, the program must branch to a new location. The handwritten code is simply faster.

```
int minVal =  i <= j  ? i : j;
int minVal2 = min( i, j );
```

Inline functions provide a solution. A function specified as inline is expanded "in line" at the point of call.

```
int minVal2 = min( i, j );
```

is expanded during compilation into

```
int minVal2 = ( i <= j ) ? i : j;
```

The run-time overhead of making `min()` a function is removed.

   `min()` is declared inline by specifying the `inline` keyword in its definition. Note, however, that the inline specification is only a recommendation to the compiler. A recursive function, such as `gcd()`, for example, cannot be completely expanded inline (although its first invocation may). A 1,200 line function is also likely not to be expanded inline. In general the inline mechanism is meant to optimize small, straight-line, frequently called functions.

3.3   Strong Type Checking

`gcd()` expects two arguments of type `int`. What happens if its arguments are of type `float` or type `char*`? What happens if `gcd()` is passed only one argument or more than two?

`gcd()`'s primary operation is performing modulo arithmetic on its two values. Modulo arithmetic may not be applied to nonintegral operands. Therefore the call

```
gcd( 3.14, 6.29 );
```

is likely to fail during execution. A worse result would be for it to return some invalid value (worse because the invalid result may go unnoticed, or, if found, may be quite difficult to trace). What could possibly be the result of the following call?

```
gcd( "hello", "world" );
```

Or the accidental concatenation of two values in this call?

```
gcd( 24312 );
```

The only desirable result of attempting to compile either of the latter two calls of `gcd()` is a compile-time error; any attempt to execute these calls invites disaster. In C++, these two calls do result in compile-time error messages of the following general form:

```
// gcd( "hello", "world" )
error: invalid argument types (char*, char*) --
       expecting (int, int )

// gcd( 24312 )
error: missing value for argument two
```

What of the earlier call in which `gcd()` is passed two arguments of type `double`? Flagging the call as a type error is correct but perhaps too severe. Rather, the arguments are implicitly converted to `int`, fulfilling the type requirements of the argument list. Because it is a narrowing conversion, a warning is issued. The call becomes

```
gcd( 3, 6 );
```

which returns a value of 3.

C++ is a *strongly typed* language. Both the argument list and the return type of every function call are *type checked* during compilation. If there is a type mismatch between an actual type and a type declared in the function prototype, an implicit conversion will be applied if possible. If an implicit conversion is not possible or if the number of arguments is incorrect, a compile-time error is issued.

The function prototype provides the compiler with the type information necessary for it to perform compile-time type checking. This is why a function may not be called until it has first been declared.†

3.4 Returning a Value

The return type of a function may be a predefined, user-defined, or derived type (such as a pointer or reference type). The following are examples of possible function return types:

```
double sqrt( double );
char *strcpy( char*, const char* );
IntArray &IntArray::qsort();
TreeNode *TreeNode::inOrder();
void error( const char* ... );
```

Arrays and functions are an exception in that neither of them may be declared as a return type. Either a pointer to an array or a pointer to a function, however, may be declared as the return type of a function. A function that does not return a value should declare a return type of `void`. A function without an explicit return value by default is assumed to return a value of type `int`.

The following two declarations of `isEqual()` are equivalent; both describe `isEqual()` as having a return type of `int`:

```
int isEqual( long*, long* );
isEqual( long*, long* );
```

The `return` statement terminates the function currently executing. Program control literally returns to the function from which the now-terminated function was called. There are two forms of the `return` statement:

---

†This type checking ability is considered so valuable, in fact, that the ANSI committee for the C language has adopted the C++ function prototype for the ANSI C language.

```
return;
return expression;
```

A `return` statement is not strictly necessary in a function that declares a return type of `void`. It is used primarily to effect a premature termination of the function. (This use of the `return` statement parallels the use of the `break` statement inside a loop.) An implicit return is effected upon completion of a function's final statement. For example,

```
void dCopy( double *src, double *dst, int sz )
{ // copy src array into dst
   // simplifying assumption: arrays are same size

   // if either array is empty, quit
   if ( src == 0 || dst == 0 )
       return;

   if ( src == dst ) // no need to copy
       return;

   if ( sz <= 0 ) // nothing to copy
       return;

   // still here?  copy.
   for ( int i = 0; i < sz; ++i )
       dst[ i ] = src[ i ];

   // no explicit return necessary
}
```

The second form of the return statement specifies the function result. It may be an arbitrarily complex expression; it may itself contain a function call. Implementation of `factorial()`, for example, contains the following return:

```
return val * factorial( val-1 );
```

If the actual return value does not exactly match the declared return type, an implicit conversion will be applied if possible. For historical reasons, it is not an error for a function that does not explicitly declare a `void` type not to return a value. However, in general a warning will be issued. `main()` is a good example of a function that programmers typically fail to provide with a return statement. The programmer should be careful to provide a return value at each termination point in the function. For example,

```
enum Boolean { FALSE, TRUE };

Boolean isEqual( char *s1, char *s2 )
{ // if s1 == s2, return TRUE; else FALSE

    // if either are null, not equal
    if ( s1 == 0 || s2 == 0 )
        return FALSE;

    if ( s1 == s2 ) // the same string
        return TRUE;

    while ( *s1 == *s2++ )
        if ( *s1++ == '\0' )
            return TRUE;

    // still here: not equal
    return FALSE;
}
```

A function may return only one value. If the program's logic requires that multiple values be returned, the programmer might do any of the following:

- A variable defined outside a function is referred to as a *global variable*. A global variable is able to be accessed from within any function, provided it has been properly declared. The programmer can assign a second "return" value to a global variable. The advantage of this strategy is its simplicity. The disadvantage is that it is nonintuitive, by which is meant that it is unclear from a call of the function that this variable is being set. This makes it difficult for others programmers to understand or make changes to the code. This act of setting a global variable from within a function is referred to as a *side effect*.

- Return an aggregate data type that contains the multiple values. For this sort of use, a class in general is more flexible than an array. In addition, a programmer can return only a pointer to an array; the programmer may return a class object, pointer, or reference to a class.

- The formal arguments may be defined as either pointer or reference types. This will provide access to the lvalues of these arguments. They may then be directly set to contain some value. (This method is discussed in the Section 3.6 (page 118) later in this chapter.)

3.5   The Function Argument List

The different functions of a program can communicate by two methods. (By *communicate* is meant a shared access to values.) One method makes use of global program variables; the second, of a function's formal argument list.

The general accessibility of a global variable from anywhere within the program is both its main benefit and its most significant liability. The visibility of a global variable makes it a convenient method of communication between the different parts of a program. The drawbacks to relying on global variables to communicate between functions are as follows:

- The functions that utilize the global variable depend on the existence and type of that global variable, making the reuse of that function in a different context much more difficult.

- If the program must be modified, global dependencies increase the likelihood of introducing bugs. Moreover, introducing local changes requires an understanding of the entire program.

- If a global variable gets an incorrect value, the entire program must be searched to determine where the error occurs; there is no localization.

- Recursion is more difficult to get right when the function makes use of a global variable.

The argument list provides an alternative method of communication between a function and the general program. The argument list, together with the function's return type, defines the *public interface* of the function. A program that limits its knowledge of a function to the function's public interface should not have to change if the function changes. Similarly, a function that is self-contained can be used across programs; it need not be limited to a specific application.

Omitting an argument or passing an argument of the wrong type are common sources of serious run-time program error in the pre-ANSI C language. With the introduction of strong type checking in C++, these interface errors are almost always caught at compile time.

The likelihood of error in passing arguments increases with the size of the argument list — some functions in FORTRAN take 32 arguments. As a general rule, eight arguments should be the maximum. If a function is written with larger argument lists, perhaps it is trying to do too much; a better design might be to divide it into two (or more) more specialized functions.

As an alternative to a large argument list, the programmer might define a class type to contain the argument values. This has two benefits:

1. The complexity of the argument list is significantly reduced.

2. Validity checks of the argument values can be performed by class member functions rather than inside the function. This reduces the size of the function and makes it easier to understand.

Argument List Syntax

The argument list of a function may not be omitted. A function that does not take any arguments can be represented either with an empty argument list or an argument list containing the single keyword void. For example, both of the following declarations of fork() are equivalent:

```
// equivalent declarations
int fork();
int fork( void );
```

The argument list is referred to as the *signature* of a function because the argument list is often used to distinguish one instance of a function from another. The name and signature of a function uniquely identify it. (Section 4.3 (page 152) on overloading functions discusses this idea more fully.)

The signature consists of a comma-separated list of argument types. A name may optionally follow each type specifier. The shorthand comma-separated type declaration syntax is an error within the signature. For example,

```
min( int v1, v2 ); // error
min( int v1, int v2 ); // ok
```

No two argument names appearing in a signature may be the same. The argument name allows the argument to be accessed from within the body of the function. Therefore the argument name is unnecessary in a function declaration. If present, its name should serve as a documentation aid. For example,

```
print( int *array, int size );
```

There is no language-imposed penalty for specifying a different name for an argument in the declaration(s) and definition of a function. The human reader of the program, however, may become confused.

A Special Signature: Ellipses ...

It is sometimes impossible to list the type and number of all the arguments that might be passed to a function. In these cases, ellipses ("...") can be specified within the function signature.

Ellipses suspend type checking. Their presence tells the compiler that zero or more arguments may follow and that the types of the arguments are unknown. Ellipses may take either of two forms:

```
foo( arg_list, ... );
foo( ... );
```

In the first form, the comma following the argument list is optional.

The standard C library output function `printf()` is an example in which ellipses are necessary. `printf()` always takes a character string as its first argument. Whether it takes additional arguments is determined by its first argument, referred to as a format string. Metacharacters, set off by `%`, indicate the presence of additional arguments. For example,

```
printf( "hello, world\n" );
```

takes a single string argument. However,

```
printf( "hello, %s\n", userName );
```

takes two arguments. The `%` indicates the presence of a second argument; the `s` indicates that the type of the argument is *string*.

`printf()` is declared in C++ as follows:

```
printf( const char* ... );
```

This requires that every call of `printf()` be passed a first argument of type `char*`. After that, anything goes.

The following two declarations are *not* equivalent:

```
void f();
void f( ... );
```

In the first instance, `f()` is declared as a function that takes no arguments; in the second, `f()` is declared as a function that may take zero arguments or more. The calls

```
f( someValue );
f( cnt, a, b, c );
```

are legal invocations of the second declaration only. The call

```
f();
```

is a legal invocation of both functions.

A Special Signature: Default Initializers

A default value is a value that, although not universally applicable, is judged to be appropriate in a majority of cases. A default value frees the individual from having to attend to every small detail. Under the UNIX system, for example, by default each text file created by the author has read and write permission for him but only read permission for all others. If he wishes to either loosen or tighten the permissions on his files, the UNIX system supports a simple mechanism by which he can modify or replace the default values.

A function may specify a default value for one or more of its arguments using initialization syntax within the signature. A function to create and initialize a two-dimensional character array intended to simulate a terminal screen, for example, can provide default values for the height, width, and background character of the screen:

```
char * screenInit( int height = 24, int width = 80,
                   char background = ' ' );
```

A function that provides default argument initializers can be invoked with or without a corresponding actual argument. If an argument is provided, it overrides the default value; otherwise, the default value is used. Each of the following calls of screenInit() is correct:

```
char *cursor;

// equivalent to screenInit(24,80,' ')
cursor = screenInit();

// equivalent to screenInit(66,80,' ')
cursor = screenInit( 66 );

// equivalent to screenInit(66,256,' ')
cursor = screenInit(66, 256);

cursor = screenInit(66, 256, '#');
```

Note that it is impossible to supply a character value for background without also supplying height and width values. Arguments to the call are resolved *positionally*. Part of the work of designing a function with default initializers is the arrangement of arguments within the signature such that those most likely to take a user-specified value occur first. The design assumption within screenInit() (possibly arrived at through experimentation) is that height is the value most likely to be supplied by the user.

A function may specify default initializers for all or only a subset of its arguments. The rightmost uninitialized argument must be supplied with a default initializer before any argument to its left may be supplied. Again, this is because arguments to a call of the function are resolved positionally. A default argument initializer is not limited to a constant expression.

An argument can have its default initializer specified only once in a file. The following, for example, is illegal:

```
ff( int = 0 ); // in ff.h

#include "ff.h"
ff( int i = 0 ) { ... } // error
```

By convention, the default initializer is specified in the function declaration contained in the public header file, and not in the function definition.

Succeeding declarations of a function may specify additional default initializers — a useful method of customizing a general function for a specific application. The UNIX system library function chmod() changes the protection level of a file. Its function prototype is found in the system header file stdlib.h. It is declared as follows:

```
chmod( char *filePath, int protMode );
```

where protMode represents a file-protection mode and filePath represents the name and path location of the file. A particular application is always changing a file's protection mode to *read-only*. Rather than indicate that each time, chmod() is redeclared to supply the value by default:

```
#include <stdlib.h>
chmod( char *filePath, int protMode=0444 );
```

Given the following function prototype declared in a header file:

```
ff( int a, int b, int c = 0 ); // ff.h
```

how can we redeclare ff() in our file to provide b with a default initializer? The following is illegal — it respecifies c's default initializer:

```
#include "ff.h"
ff( int a, int b = 0, int c = 0 ); // error
```

The following also seems illegal, but in fact is the correct redeclaration:

```
#include "ff.h"
ff( int a, int b = 0, int c ); // ok
```

At the point of this redeclaration of ff(), b is the rightmost argument without a default initializer. Therefore, the rule that the default initializer be assigned positionally beginning with the rightmost argument has not been violated. In fact, we can now redeclare ff() a third time:

```
#include "ff.h"
ff( int a, int b = 0, int c ); // ok
ff( int a = 0, int b, int c ); // ok
```

3.6   Argument Passing

Functions are allocated storage on a structure referred to as the program's *run-time stack*. That storage remains on the stack until the function is terminated. At that point, the storage is automatically popped. The entire storage area of the function is referred to as the *activation record*.

The argument list of a function describes its *formal arguments*. Each formal argument is provided storage within the activation record. The storage size of an argument is determined by its type specifier. The expressions found between the parentheses of a function call are referred to as the *actual arguments* of the call. Argument passing is the process of initializing the storage of the formal arguments by the actual arguments.

The default initialization method of argument passing in C++ is to copy the rvalues of the actual arguments into the storage of the formal arguments. This is referred to as *pass-by-value*.

Under pass-by-value, the function never accesses the actual arguments of the call. The values the function manipulates are its own local copies; these are stored on the stack. In general, changes made to these values are not reflected in the values of the actual arguments. Once the function terminates and the stack of the function's activation record is popped, these local values are lost.

Under pass-by-value, the contents of the actual arguments are not changed. This means that a programmer need not save and restore argument values when making a function call. Without a pass-by-value mechanism, each formal argument not declared `const` would have to be considered potentially altered with each function call. Pass-by-value has the least potential for harm and requires the least work by the general user. Pass-by-value is a reasonable default mechanism for argument passing.

Pass-by-value, however, is not suitable for every function. Situations under which pass-by-value is unsuitable include the following:

- When a large class object must be passed as an argument. The time and space costs to allocate and copy the class object onto the stack are often too high for real-world program applications.

- When the values of the argument must be modified. The function `swap()` is an example of where the user wants to change the values of the actual arguments but cannot do so under pass-by-value.

```
void swap( int v1, int v2 ) {
    int tmp = v2;
    v2 = v1;
    v1 = tmp;
}
```

swap() exchanges the local copies of its arguments. The actual variables passed to swap() are unchanged. This is illustrated in the following program, which calls swap:

```
#include <stream.h>
void swap( int, int );

main() {
    int i = 10;
    int j = 20;

    cout << "Before swap():\ti: "
         << i << "\tj: " << j << "\n";

    swap( i, j );

    cout << "After swap():\ti: "
         << i << "\tj: " << j << "\n";
}
```

Compiling and executing this program results in the following output:

```
Before swap():   i: 10    j: 20
After swap():    i: 10    j: 20
```

pass by reference (1)

Two alternatives to pass-by-value are available to the programmer. In one instance, the formal arguments are declared as pointers. swap(), for example, could be rewritten as follows:

```
void pswap( int *v1, int *v2 ) {
    int tmp = *v2;
    *v2 = *v1;
    *v1 = tmp;
}
```

main() must be modified to declare and call pswap(). The programmer must now pass the address of the two objects, not the objects themselves:

```
pswap( &i, &j );
```

Compiling and executing this revised program shows the output to be correct:

```
Before swap():   i: 10    j: 20
After swap():    i: 20    j: 10
```

When the argument is declared only to save the expense of copying, declare it as a const argument:

```
void print( const BigClassObject* );
```

This way, readers of the program (and the compiler) know that the function does not change the object addressed by the argument.

The second alternative to pass-by-value is to declare the formal arguments to be type reference. swap(), for example, could be rewritten as follows:

```
void rswap( int &v1, int &v2 ) {
    int tmp = v2;
    v2 = v1;
    v1 = tmp;
}
```

The call of rswap() in main() looks the same as the original call of swap():

```
rswap( i, j );
```

Compiling and executing the program will show that the values of i and j are properly exchanged.

3.7   A Reference Argument

A reference argument passes the lvalue of its actual argument to the function. This has the two following effects:

1. Modifications to the argument made within the function change the actual argument and not a local copy. This is why rswap() works.

2. There is no performance penalty in passing large class objects to a function. Under pass-by-value, the entire class object is copied with each function call.

If the reference argument type is not modified within the function, it is a good practice to declare it as const. Note, however, that it is illegal to declare x to be const in the following example:

```
class X;
int foo( X& );
int bar( const X& x ) {
    // const passed to nonconst reference
    return foo( x );    // error
}
```

x cannot be passed as an argument to foo() unless the signature of foo() is modified either to const X& or X.

A reference argument of a predefined integral or floating-point type can behave unexpectedly when passed an actual argument that does not exactly match its data type. This is because a temporary object of the exact type is generated, assigned the rvalue of the actual argument, *then* passed to the function. For example, here is what will occur when rswap() is invoked with an unsigned int:

```
int i = 10;
unsigned int ui = 20;

rswap( i, ui );
```

becomes

```
int T2 = int(ui);
rswap( i, T2 );
```

Execution of this call of rswap() results in the following *incorrect* output:

```
Before swap():  i: 10    j: 20
After swap():   i: 20    j: 20
```

ui remains unchanged because it is never passed to rswap(). Rather, T2, the temporary generated because of type mismatch, is passed. The result is a simulation of pass-by-value. (The compiler should issue a warning.)

Reference arguments are most appropriate for use with user-defined class types when an exact match can be predicted and object size is a concern. The predefined data types do not work as well with reference semantics. Counting unsigned, there are eight flavors of integers, seven of which will always mismatch any integral reference argument. In cases where the type of the actual argument cannot be predicted, it is not safe to depend on pass-by-reference semantics.

A pointer argument permits the object it addresses to be modified from within the function. What if we wish, however, to modify the pointer itself? Then we declare a pointer reference:

```
void prswap( int *&v1, int *&v2 ) {
      int *tmp = v2;
      v2 = v1;
      v1 = tmp;
}
```

The declaration

```
int *&p1;
```

should be read from right to left: p1 is a reference to a pointer to an object of type int. The modified implementation of main() will look as follows:

```
#include <stream.h>
void prswap( int *&v1, int *&v2 );

main() {
      int i = 10;
      int j = 20;

      int *pi = &i;
      int *pj = &j;

      cout << "Before swap():\tpi: "
            << *pi << "\tpj: " << *pj << "\n";

      prswap( pi, pj );

      cout << "After swap():\tpi: "
            << *pi << "\tpj: " << *pj << "\n";
}
```

When compiled and executed, the program generates the following output:

```
Before swap():   pi: 10   pj: 20
After swap():    pi: 20   pj: 10
```

By default, the return type is also passed by value. For large class objects, a pointer or reference return type is more efficient; the object itself is not copied.

A second use of a reference return type allows a function to be made the target of an assignment. The reference in effect returns the lvalue of the object to which it refers. This is particularly important in a function such as the subscript operator for the IntArray class, which must support both read and write capabilities:

```
int& IntArray::operator[]( int index ) {
    return ia[ index ];
}

IntArray myArray( 8 );
myArray[ 2 ] = myArray[ 1 ] + myArray[ 0 ];
```

Section 1.8 (page 51) contains the definition of the IntArray class.

3.8   An Array Argument

Arrays in C++ are never passed by value. Rather, an array is passed as a pointer to its initial element. For example,

```
void putValues( int[ 10 ] );
```

is treated by the compiler as having been declared as

```
void putValues( int* );
```

The array's size is not relevant to the declaration of the formal argument. The following three declarations are equivalent:

```
// three equivalent declarations of putValues
void putValues( int* );
void putValues( int[] );
void putValues( int[ 10 ] );
```

This has two implications for the programmer:

- The changes to an array argument within the called function are made to the actual array of the call, not to a local copy. In cases where the array of the call must remain unchanged, programmers will themselves need to simulate pass-by-value.

- The size of an array is not part of its argument type. The function being passed an array does not know its actual size and neither does the compiler. There is no checking of array sizes. For example,

```
void putValues( int[ 10 ] ); // treated as int*
main() {
    int i, j[ 2 ];
    putValues( &i ); // ok: int*; run-time error
    putValues( j );  // ok: int*; run-time error
    return 0;
}
```

The extent of the argument type checking confirms that both calls of putValues() are provided with an argument of type int*.

By convention, string character arrays encode their termination point with a null character. All other array types, however, including character arrays, which wish to handle embedded nulls, must in some way make their size known when passed as formal arguments to a function. One common method is to provide an additional argument that contains the array's size.

```
void putValues( int[], int size );
main() {
    int i, j[ 2 ];
    putValues( &i, 1 );
    putValues( j , 2 );
    return 0;
}
```

putValues() prints out the values of an array in the following format:

```
( 10 )< 0, 1, 2, 3, 4, 5, 6, 7, 8, 9 >
```

where 10 represents the size of the array. Here is an implementation:

```
#include <stream.h>

const lineLength = 12; // elements to a line
void putValues( int *ia, int sz ) {
    cout << "( " << sz << " )< ";
    for ( int i = 0; i < sz; ++i ) {
        if ( i % lineLength == 0 && i )
            cout << "\n\t"; // line filled
        cout << ia[ i ];

        // separate all but last element
        if ( i % lineLength != lineLength-1 &&
            i != sz-1 )
                cout << ", ";
    }
    cout << " >\n";
}
```

A multidimensional array declared as a formal argument must specify the size of all its dimensions beyond that of its first. For example,

```
void putValues( int matrix[][10], int rowSize );
```

declares matrix to be a two-dimensional array. Each matrix row consists of 10 column elements. matrix may equivalently be declared as

```
int (*matrix)[10];
```

This declares matrix to be a pointer to an array of 10 elements.

```
matrix += 1;
```

will advance `matrix` the size of its second dimension and point it to its next row — a reason why the size of the second dimension must be supplied. The parentheses around `matrix` are necessary because of the higher precedence of the index operator.

```
int *matrix[ 10 ];
```

declares `matrix` to be an array of 10 integer pointers.

3.9   Program Scope

Earlier it was stated that every identifier in a program must be unique. This does not mean, however, that a name can be used only once in a program: a name can be reused provided that there is some *context* by which to distinguish between the different instances. One context is the signature of a function. In the last section, for example, `putValues()` is used as the name of two functions. Each has a unique, distinguishing signature.

A second, more general context is *scope*. C++ supports three kinds of scope: *file* scope, *local* scope, and *class* scope. File scope is that portion of the program text that is not contained within either a function or a class definition. File scope is the outermost scope of a program. It is said to *enclose* both local and class scope.

In general, local scope is that portion of the program text contained within the definition of a function. Each function is considered to represent a distinct local scope. Within a function, each compound statement (or block) containing one or more declaration statements maintains an associated local scope. Local block scopes can be nested. The argument list is treated as being within the local scope of the function. The argument list is *not* considered to be within the enclosing file scope.

Section 5.8 (page 217) presents a full discussion of class scope. There are two salient points to make now:

1. Each class is considered to represent a distinct class scope.

2. Member functions are treated as being within the scope of their class.

A global variable without an explicit initializer is guaranteed by the language to have its storage initialized to 0. Thus, in the following two definitions, both `i` and `j` have an initial value of 0:

```
int i = 0;
int j;
```

The value of an uninitialized local variable is undefined.

A name may be reused in distinct scopes without penalty. In the following program fragment, for example, there are four unique instances of ia:

```
void swap( int *ia, int, int );
void sort( int *ia, int sz );
void putValues( int *ia, int sz );

int ia[] = { 4, 7, 0, 9, 2, 5, 8, 3, 6, 1 };

const SZ = 10;
main() {
    int i, j;

    // ...
    swap( ia, i, j );
    sort( ia, SZ );
    putValues( ia, SZ );
}
```

Every variable has an associated scope which, together with its name, uniquely identifies it. A variable is visible to the program only from within its scope. A local variable, for example, may be accessed only within the function within which it is defined — the reason why its name may be reused within other scopes without conflict.

A variable defined at file scope is visible to the entire program. There are three cases under which its visibility is constrained:

1. A local variable may reuse a global variable's name. The global variable is now said to be hidden by the local instance. What if the programmer must access the now-hidden global instance? The scope operator provides a solution.

2. A global variable is defined in one file but also used in a second file or multiple files. How does the programmer declare the variable in these other files? Use of the `extern` keyword provides a solution.

3. Two global variables defined in separate program files reuse the same name but are intended to refer to different program entities. Each by itself compiles cleanly. When compiled together, the variable is flagged as being multiply defined, and compilation stops. How does the programmer compile the program without having to change all the instances of one of the variables? Use of the `static` keyword provides a solution.

These three cases are the subject of the following three subsections.

The Scope Operator

The scope operator ("::") provides a solution to the problem of accessing a hidden global variable. An identifier prefixed with the scope operator will access the global instance. In the following example, contrived to illustrate how the scope operator may be used, the function computes a Fibonacci series. There are two definitions of the variable max. The global instance indicates the maximum value for the series. The local instance indicates the desired length of the series. (Recall, the formal arguments of a function occur within the function's local scope.) Both instances of max must be accessed within the function. Every unqualified reference to max, however, refers to the local instance. In order to access the global instance, the scope operator must be used — ::max. Here is an implementation:

```
#include <stream.h>

const max = 65000;
const lineLength = 12;

void fibonacci( int max ) {
    if ( max < 2 ) return;
    cout << "0 1 ";

    for ( int i = 3, v1 = 0, v2 = 1, cur;
            i <= max; ++i ) {
                cur = v1 + v2;
                if ( cur > ::max ) break;
                cout << cur << " ";
                v1 = v2;
                v2 = cur;
                if ( i % lineLength == 0 )
                        cout << "\n";
            }
}
```

Here is an implementation of main() to exercise the function:

```
#include <stream.h>
void fibonacci( int );

main() {
    cout << "Fibonacci Series: 16\n";
    fibonacci( 16 );
    return 0;
}
```

Compiling and executing the program produces the following output:

```
Fibonacci Series: 16
0 1 1 2 3 5 8 13 21 34 55 89
144 233 377 610
```

extern Variables

The `extern` keyword provides a method of declaring a variable without defining it. Similar in effect to the function prototype, it says that elsewhere in the program an identifier of this type is defined.

```
extern int i;
```

is a "pledge" to the program that elsewhere there exists the definition

```
int i;
```

The `extern` declaration does not cause storage to be allocated. It may appear multiple times within a program. Typically, however, it is declared once in a public header file to be included when necessary.

The `extern` keyword may also be specified in a function prototype. Its only effect is to make the implicit "defined elsewhere" nature of the prototype explicit. It takes the following form:

```
extern void putValues( int*, int );
```

The declaration of an extern variable with an explicit initializer is treated as a definition of that variable. Storage is allocated and any subsequent definitions of that variable in the same scope is flagged as an error. For example,

```
extern const bufSize = 512; // definition
```

static Global Variable

A global identifier preceded by the keyword `static` will be invisible outside the file in which it is defined. Variables and functions only of interest within the file in which they are defined are declared static. In this way, they cannot clash with global identifiers in other files that accidentally reuse the same names.

Static identifiers at file scope are spoken of as having *internal linkage*. (Nonstatic global identifiers are said to have *external linkage*.) By default, inline functions and `const` definitions are static.

Here is an example of when a function might be declared static. The file is `sort.C`. It contains three functions: `bsort()`, `qsort()`, and `swap()`.

bsort() and qsort() provide for sorting an array in ascending order.
swap() is invoked by both functions but is not intended for general use.
For our example, it is declared static. (It may alternatively be declared
inline.)

file scope

```
static void swap ( int *ia, int i, int j )
{ // swap two elements of an array
    int tmp = ia[ i ];
    ia[ i ] = ia[ j ];
    ia[ j ] = tmp;
}

void bsort( int* ia, int sz )
{ // bubble sort
    for ( int i = 0; i < sz; i++ )
        for ( int j = i; j < sz; j++ )
            if ( ia[i] > ia[j] )
                swap( ia, i, j );
}
```

```
1   void qsort( int *ia, int low, int high ) {
2   // stopping condition for recursion
3       if ( low < high ) {
4           int lo = low;
5           int hi = high + 1;
6           int elem = ia[ low ];
7
8           for (;;) {
9               while ( ia[ ++lo ] <= elem ) ;
10              while ( ia[ --hi ] > elem ) ;
11
12              if ( lo < hi )
13                  swap( ia, lo, hi );
14              else break;
15          } // end, for(;;)
16
17          swap( ia, low, hi );
18          qsort( ia, low, hi - 1 );
19          qsort( ia, hi + 1, high );
20      } // end, if ( low < high )
21  }
```

qsort() is an implementation of C.A.R Hoare's *quicksort* algorithm.
Let's look at the function in detail. low and high represent the lower and
upper bounds of the array. qsort(), a recursive function, applies itself to
progressively smaller subarrays. The stopping condition is when the lower
bound is equal to (or greater) than the upper bound (line 3).

elem (line 6), is referred to as the *partition element*. All array elements
less than elem are moved to the left of elem; all elements greater are
moved to the right. The array is now partitioned into two subarrays.
qsort() is recursively applied to each (lines 18 – 19).

The purpose of the for(;;) loop is to perform the partition (lines 8 –
15). At each iteration of the loop, lo is advanced to index the first element of ia greater than elem (line 9). Similarly, hi is decremented to
index the "endmost" element of ia equal to or less than elem (line 10). If
lo is no longer less than hi, the elements have been partitioned and we
break the loop; otherwise, the elements are swapped and the next loop
iteration begins (lines 12 – 14).

Although the array has been partitioned, elem is still located at
ia[low]. The swap() on line 17 places elem in its final position in the
array. qsort() is then applied to the two subarrays.

The following implementation of main() to execute the two sorting
functions utilizes putValues() to print the arrays.

```
#include <stream.h>
#include "sort.h"  /* bsort(), qsort() */
#include "print.h" /* putValues() */

// for illustration, predefine arrays
int ia1 [10]={ 26, 5, 37, 1, 61, 11, 59, 15, 48, 19};
int ia2 [16]={ 503, 87, 512, 61, 908, 170, 897, 275,
          653, 426, 154, 509, 612, 677, 765, 703 };

main() {
  cout << "\nBubblesort of first array";
  bsort( ia1, 10 );
  putValues( ia1, 10 );

  cout << "\nQuicksort of second array";
  qsort( ia2, 0, 15 );
  putValues( ia2, 16 );
}
```

When compiled and executed, the program produces the following output:

```
Bubblesort of first array
( 10 )< 1, 5, 11, 15, 19, 26, 37, 48
        59, 61 >

Quicksort of second array
( 16 )< 61, 87, 154, 170, 275, 426, 503, 509
         512, 612, 653, 677, 703, 765, 897, 908 >
```

3.10 Local Scope

In general, local variables are allocated storage at the time a function is invoked; they are said to *come into* or *enter scope*. This storage is allocated from the program's run-time stack and is part of the activation record of the function. An uninitialized local variable will contain a random bit pattern left over from a previous use of that storage. Its value is spoken of as *undefined*.

Upon termination of the function, its activation record is popped from the run-time stack. In effect, the storage associated with the local variables is deallocated. The variables are said to *go out of* or *exit scope* upon termination of the function. Any values they contain are lost.

Because the storage associated with local variables is deallocated upon termination of the function, the address of a local variable should never be passed outside its scope. Here is an example,

```
#include <stream.h>

const strLen = 8;
char *globalString;

char *trouble() {
    char localString[ strLen ];

    cout << "Enter string: ";
    cin >> localString;
    return localString; // dangerous
}

main() { globalString = trouble(); ... }
```

globalString is set to the address of the local character array, localString. Unfortunately, localString's storage is deallocated on completion of trouble(). On the reentry into main(), globalString is addressing technically unallocated memory.

When the address of a local variable is passed outside its scope, it is referred to as a *dangling reference*. This is a serious programmer error because the contents of the addressed memory are unpredictable. If the bits at that address are somehow relevant, the program may run to completion but provide invalid results.

Local scopes may be nested. Any block that contains a declaration statement maintains its own local scope. For example, the following defines two levels of local scope, performing a binary search of a sorted array.

```
const notFound = -1;

int binSearch( int *ia, int sz, int val )
{ // local scope: level #1
  // contains ia, sz, val, low, high
     int low = 0;
     int high = sz - 1;

     while ( low <= high )
     { // local scope: level #2
          int mid = ( low + high )/2;
          if ( val == ia[ mid ] )
               return mid;
          if ( val < ia[ mid ] )
               high = mid - 1;
          else low = mid + 1;
     }    // end, local scope: level #2

     return notFound;
}   // end, local scope: level #1
```

The while loop of binSearch() defines a nested local scope. It contains
one identifier, the integer mid, enclosed by binSearch()'s local scope. It
contains the argument members ia, sz, and val, plus the local variables
high and low. The global scope encloses both local scopes. It contains
one identifier, the integer constant notFound.

When a reference is made to an identifier, the immediate scope in
which the reference occurs is searched. If a definition is found, the reference is resolved; if not, the enclosing scope is searched. This process continues until either the reference is resolved or global scope has been
exhausted. If the latter occurs, the reference is flagged as an error. Use of
the scope operator ("::") limits the search to global scope.

A for loop permits the definition of variables within its control structure. For example,

```
for ( int i = 0; i < arrayBound; ++i )
```

Variables defined inside the for loop control are entered into the same
scope as the for statement itself, as if the for statement were written like
this:

```
int i;
for ( i = 0; i < arrayBound; ++i )
```

This permits the programmer to access the control variables after completion of the loop. For example,

```
const notFound = -1;

findElement( int *ia, int sz, int val )
{
    for ( int i = 0; i < sz; ++i )
        if ( ia[ i ] == val ) break;

    if ( i == sz ) return notFound;
    return i;
}
```

This does not permit the programmer, however, to reuse the name of control variables within the same scope. For example,

```
fooBar( int *ia, int sz ) {
    for (int i=0; i<sz; ++i) ... // defines i
    for (int i=0; i<sz; ++i) ... // error: i redefined
    for (i=0; i<sz; ++i) ...       // ok
}
```

static Local Variables

It is desirable to declare an identifier as a local variable whenever its use is confined to a function or a nested block. When the value of that variable must persist across invocations, however, an ordinary local variable cannot be used. Its value will be discarded each time it exits scope.

The solution in this case is to declare the identifier as static. A *static local variable* has permanent storage. Its value persists across invocations; its access remains limited to its local scope. For example, here is a version of gcd() that traces the depth of its recursion using a static local variable:

```
#include <stream.h>

traceGcd( int v1, int v2 )
{
    static int depth = 1;        // one-time init
    cout << "depth #" << depth++ << "\n";

    if (v2 == 0 )
        return v1;
    return traceGcd( v2, v1%v2 );
}
```

The value associated with the static local variable depth persists across invocations of traceGcd(). The initialization is performed only once. The following small program exercises traceGcd():

```
#include <stream.h>
extern traceGcd(int, int);

main() {
    int rslt = traceGcd( 15, 123 );
    cout << "gcd of (15,123): " << rslt << "\n";
}
```

When compiled and executed, the program generates the following results:

```
depth #1
depth #2
depth #3
depth #4
gcd of (15,123): 3
```

register Local Variables

Local variables heavily used within a function can be specified with the keyword `register`. If possible, the compiler will load the variable into a machine register. If it cannot, the variable remains in memory. Array indices are obvious candidates for register variables:

```
for ( register int i = 0; i < sz; ++i )
    ia[ i ] = i;
```

A formal argument can also be declared as a register variable:

```
class iList {
public:
    int value;
    iList *next;
};

int find( register iList *ptr, int val )
{  // find val in linked list

    while ( ptr ) {
        if ( ptr->value == val )
            return 1;
        ptr = ptr->next;
    }  •
    return 0;
}
```

Register variables may increase the speed of a function if the variables selected are used heavily.

4: **The Free Store and Name Overloading**

This chapter considers two fundamental concepts: the program free store and function name overloading. The program free store allows for run-time memory allocation. The implementation of the IntArray class in Chapter 1 provided us with a brief first look at run time memory allocation. In this chapter, we look at it in detail.

Function name overloading allows multiple function instances that provide a common operation on different argument types to share a common name. If you have written an arithmetic expression in a programming language, you have used a predefined overloaded function. In this chapter, we see how to define our own.

4.1 Free Store Allocation

Every program is provided with a pool of unallocated memory that it may utilize during execution. This pool of available memory is referred to as the program's *free store*, and by using it, the IntArray class can defer allocation of its array member until run time. Let's reexamine how this is done:

```
IntArray::IntArray( int sz )
{
    size = sz;
    ia = new int[ size ];
    for ( int i = 0; i < sz; ++i )
        ia[ i ] = 0;
}
```

IntArray has two data members, `size` and `ia`. `ia`, an integer pointer, will address the array allocated on the free store. One aspect of free store memory is that it is unnamed. Objects allocated on the free store are manipulated indirectly through pointers. A second aspect of free store memory is that it is uninitialized and must therefore always be set before it is used. This is the purpose of the `for` loop setting each element of `ia` to 0. `size`, of course, contains the size of the array.

Free store memory is allocated by applying operator `new` to a type specifier, including that of a class name. Either a single object or an array of objects can be allocated. For example,

```
int *pi = new int;
```

allocates one object of type int. Operator new returns a pointer to that object to which pi is initialized.

```
IntArray *pia = new IntArray( 1024 );
```

allocates an IntArray class object. The parentheses following the class name, if present, supply arguments to the class constructor. In this case, pia is initialized to point to an IntArray object of 1024 elements. If the parentheses are not present, as in

```
IntArray *pia2 = new IntArray;
```

then the class must either define a constructor that does not require arguments or else define no constructors at all.

An array is allocated from the free store by following the type specifier with a bracket-enclosed dimension. The dimension can be an arbitrarily complex expression. Operator new returns a pointer to the first element of the array. For example,

```
#include <string.h>
char *copyStr( const char *s )
{
    char *ps = new char[ strlen(s) + 1 ];
    strcpy( ps, s );
    return ps;
}
```

Arrays of class objects can also be allocated. For example,

```
IntArray *pia = new IntArray[ someSize ];
```

allocates an array of IntArray objects of some size.

The allocation of memory at run time is referred to as *dynamic memory allocation*. We say that the array addressed by ia is allocated *dynamically*. The storage of ia itself, however, is allocated during compilation — the reason why ia can be a named object. Allocation that occurs during compilation is spoken of as *static memory allocation*. We say that the pointer ia is allocated *statically*.

An object's lifetime, that period of time during program execution during which storage is bound to the object, is referred to as an object's *extent*. Variables defined at file scope are spoken of as having *static extent*. Storage is allocated before program start-up and remains bound to the variable throughout program execution. Variables defined at local scope are spoken of as having *local extent*. Storage is allocated at each entry into the local scope; on exit, the storage is freed up. A static local variable exhibits static extent.

Objects allocated on the free store are spoken of as having *dynamic extent*. Storage allocated through the use of operator `new` remains bound to an object until explicitly deallocated by the programmer. Explicit deallocation is achieved by applying operator `delete` to a pointer addressing the dynamic object. Let's look at an example.

IntArray::grow() expands the array `ia` addressed by half its size. First a new, larger array is allocated. Then the values of the old array are copied and the additional elements are initialized to 0. Finally, the old array is explicitly deallocated by applying operator `delete`.

```
void IntArray::grow()
{
  int *oldia = ia;
  int oldSize = size;

  size += size/2 + 1;
  ia = new int[ size ];

  // copy elements of old array into new
  for ( int i = 0; i < oldSize; ++i )
        ia[ i ] = oldia[ i ];

  // initialize remaining elements to 0
  for ( ; i < size; ++i )
        ia[ i ] = 0;

  delete oldia;
}
```

`oldia` has local extent; it is deallocated automatically upon termination of the function. The array `oldia` addresses, however, is not. Its extent is dynamic and persists across local scope boundaries. If the array `oldia` addresses is not explicitly deallocated using operator `delete`, the memory bound to the array is lost to the program.

```
delete oldia;
```

returns the storage to the free store.

When deleting an array of class objects, the size of the array must also be made known to the delete operator. This is necessary in order that the proper number of class destructors are invoked. For example, given the following array,

```
IntArray *pia = new IntArray[ size ];
```

the delete operator applied to `pia` looks as follows:

```
delete [size] pia;
```

The `delete` operator must be applied only to memory that has been allocated by operator `new`. Applying operator `delete` to memory not allocated on the free store is likely to result in undefined program behavior during execution. There is, however, no penalty for applying operator `delete` to a pointer set to 0 — that is, that does not address an object. The following are examples of safe and unsafe applications of operator `delete`:

```
void f() {
    int i;
    char *str = "dwarves";
    int *pi = &i;
    IntArray *pia = 0;
    double *pd = new double;

    delete str; // dangerous
    delete pi;  // dangerous
    delete pia; // safe
    delete pd;  // safe
}
```

The program's free store is not infinite; during the course of program execution it may become exhausted. (Failure to delete objects no longer needed, of course, will speed up exhaustion of the free store.) By default, `new` returns 0 when insufficient free store is available to satisfy its request.

The programmer cannot safely ignore the possibility that `new` has returned 0. Our `grow()` function, for example, will fail if `new` is unable to allocate the requested memory. Our code, recall, looks as follows:

```
ia = new int[ size ];

// trouble if new returns 0
for ( int i = 0; i < oldSize; ++i )
    ia[ i ] = oldia[ i ];
```

The programmer must prevent the execution of the `for` loop on a zero-valued `ia`. The simplest method of doing this is to insert a test on `ia` following the call of `new`. For example,

```
ia = new int[ size ];
if ( !ia ) {
    error("IntArray::grow(): free store exhausted");
}
```

where `error()` is a general function defined by the programmer to report errors and exit gracefully.

Here is a small program that illustrates the use of `grow()`:

```
#include <stream.h>
#include "IntArray.h"

IntArray ia( 10 );
main() {
    cout << "size: " << ia.getSize() << "\n";
    for ( int i = 0; i < ia.getSize(); ++i )
        ia[i] = i*2; // initialize

    ia.grow();
    cout << "new size: " << ia.getSize() << "\n";

    for ( i = 0; i < ia.getSize(); ++i )
        cout << ia[i] << " ";
}
```

When compiled and executed, the program generates the following output:

```
size: 10
new size: 16
0 2 4 6 8 10 12 14 16 18 0 0 0 0 0 0
```

Here is a function designed to illustrate the exhaustion of free store. Implemented as a recursive function, its stopping condition is a return value of 0 from `new`.

```
#include <stream.h>

void exhaustFreeStore( unsigned long chunk ) {
    static int depth = 1;
    static int report = 0;

    ++depth; // keep track of invocations
    double *ptr = new double[ chunk ];
    if ( ptr )
        exhaustFreeStore( chunk );

    // free store exhausted
    delete ptr;
    if ( !report++ )
        cout << "Free Store Exhausted:"
            << "\tchunk: " << chunk
            << "\tdepth: " << depth << "\n";
}
```

Executing `exhaustFreeStore()` four times with different-sized arguments produced the following results:

```
Free Store Exhausted:    chunk: 1000000    depth: 4
Free Store Exhausted:    chunk: 100000     depth: 22
Free Store Exhausted:    chunk: 10000      depth: 209
Free Store Exhausted:    chunk: 1000       depth: 2072
```

The C++ library provides some help in keeping watch over the free store. The exception handler _new_handler is discussed in Section 4.4 (page 170) later in this chapter.

The programmer may also place an object allocated from the free store at a specific address. The form of this invocation of operator new looks as follows:

```
new (place_address) type-specifier
```

where *place_address* must be a pointer. In order to use this instance of operator new, the header file new.h must be included. This facility allows the programmer to preallocate memory which at a later time will contain objects specified by this form of operator new. For example,

```
#include <stream.h>
#include <new.h>

const Chunk = 16;
class Foo { public: int val; Foo(){ val = 0; }};

// preallocate memory, but no Foo objects
char *buf = new char[ sizeof(Foo) * Chunk ];

main() {
  // construct Chunk Foo objects for buf
  Foo *pb = new (buf) Foo[ Chunk ];

  // check that objects were placed in buf
  if ( (char*)pb == buf )
    cout << "Operator new worked!: pb: "
         << pb << " buf: " << (void*)buf << "\n";
}
```

When compiled and executed, this program generates the following output:

```
Operator new worked!: pb: 0x234cc buf: 0x234cc
```

There is one possibly confusing aspect to this program. This is the cast of buf to void*. This is necessary because the output operator, when passed a char* operand, prints the "null terminated string" that it addresses. By casting buf to void*, the output operator knows to print the address value of buf. This is because the output operator is *overloaded* to take two different pointer argument types: `char*` and `void*`. Over-loaded functions are discussed in a subsequent section of this chapter.

Although this instance of operator `new` is used primarily with class types, it may also be used with the built-in data types. For example,

```
#include <new.h>
int *pi = new int;

main() {
   int *pi2 = new (pi) int;
}
```

4.2   A Link List Example

In this section, a rudimentary integer list class, which we shall call IntList, is implemented in order to illustrate both pointer manipulation and the use of operators `new` and `delete`. At minimum, IntList must support two values — the integer value of the list item and the address value of the next item of the list. These may be represented as follows:

```
int val;
ListItem *next;
```

A list is a sequence of items. An item contains a value and a pointer, possibly null, of the next item on the list. A list may be empty; that is, there may be a list of no items:

```
IntList il; // the empty list
```

A list may grow by adding items. These items may be inserted at the beginning of the list:

```
il.insert( someValue );
```

or appended to the end of the list:

```
il.append( someValue );
```

A list may shrink by removing items (provided that the list is not empty):

```
il.remove( someValue );
```

A user must be able to display the items of a list:

```
il.display();
```

Here is a first program we would like to write using the IntList class:

```
#include "IntList.h"

const SZ = 12;
main() {
    IntList il;
    il.display();

    for ( int i = 0; i < SZ; ++i )
        il.insert( i );
    il.display();

    IntList il2;
    for ( i = 0; i < SZ; ++i )
        il2.append( i );
    il2.display();

    return 0;
}
```

When compiled and executed, this program will generate the following output:

```
( empty )
( 11 10 9 8 7 6 5 4 3 2 1 0 )
( 0 1 2 3 4 5 6 7 8 9 10 11 )
```

The first step in implementing this program is to define the IntList class. This is the first place where we can go wrong. An incorrect design choice would be to declare both val and next as members of IntList. For example,

```
class IntList {
public:
    IntList( int = ??? );
    // ...
private:
    int val;
    IntList *next;
};
```

There are several problems with this design. They all stem from a confusion between a list object and an item of the list. For example, this design does not allow an empty list to be represented. There is no way to distinguish between a list of one item and the empty list. The question marks in the signature of the IntList constructor are intended to underscore the problem. There is no default value which val can be initialized with in order to indicate the empty list. Other problems have to do with what `insert()` and `remove()` mean when the IntList object also serves as the first item of its list.

The IntList design must distinguish between the items on the list and the list object itself. One way to do this is to define both an IntList and IntItem class. Here is our definition of IntItem:

```
class IntList;
class IntItem {
    friend class IntList;
private:
    IntItem(int v=0) { val = v; next = 0; }
    IntItem *next;
    int val;
};
```

IntItem is referred to as a *private class*. Only IntList is permitted to create and manipulate IntItem objects. This is the meaning of the friend declaration. Section 5.5 (page 200) discusses friends in detail. Section 5.1 (page 181) examines the issue of private and public. IntList is implemented as follows:

```
class IntItem;
class IntList {
public:
    IntList(int val) { list = new IntItem( val ); }
    IntList() { list = 0; }
    // ...
private:
    IntItem *list;
};
```

Exercise 4-1. Why does IntList need both constructors? Why not, for example, simply define

```
IntList( int val = 0 );
```

□

Exercise 4-2. An additional IntList member might be

```
int len; // length of list
```

which maintains a count of the list items. Discuss the pros and cons of declaring this member. □

The next step is to implement the member functions which support user manipulation of the IntList object. `insert()` places a new IntItem at the front of the list. It is implemented as follows:

```
IntList::insert( int val )
{ // add to the front of the list
    IntItem *pt = new IntItem( val );
    pt->next = list;
    list = pt;
    return val;
}
```

append() is slightly more complicated. It must add the new IntItem to the end of the list. An auxiliary function, atEnd(), returns a pointer to the last list item:

```
IntItem *IntList::atEnd()
{ // return pointer to last item on list
    IntItem *prv, *pt;
    for ( prv=pt=list; pt; prv=pt, pt=pt->next )
            ;  // null statement
    return prv;
}
```

append() must test for the special case of an empty list. The implementation looks as follows:

```
IntList::append( int val )
{ // add to the back of the list
    IntItem *pt = new IntItem( val );
    if ( list == 0 )
        list = pt;
    else
        (atEnd())->next = pt;
    return val;
}
```

Exercise 4-3. Discuss the pros and cons of keeping an IntList member

```
IntItem *endList;
```

How might this change the implementation of append()? □

Users of the list class must be able to display the elements of the list. This is done by the display() member function. The list values are displayed within parentheses, 16 to a line. It looks like this:

```
#include <stream.h>
const int lineLength = 16;

IntList::display()
{ // display val member of list
    if ( list == 0 ) {
        cout << "( empty )\n";
        return 0;
    }

    cout << "( ";
    int cnt = 0; // number of items displayed
    IntItem *pt = list;

    while ( pt ) {
        if ( ++cnt % lineLength == 1 && cnt != 1 )
            cout << "\n   ";
        cout << pt->val << " ";
        pt = pt->next;
    }

    cout << ")\n";
    return cnt;
}
```

The test

```
if ( ++cnt % linelength == 1
        && cnt != 1 )
```

insures that the closing right parenthesis is not output on a line by itself.
The full specification of the `IntList.h` header file up to this point looks
as follows:

```
class IntList; // forward declaration

class IntItem {
    friend class IntList;
private:
    IntItem(int v=0) { val = v; next = 0; }
    IntItem *next;
    int val;
};
```

```
class IntList {
public:
    IntList(int val) { list = new IntItem( val ); }
    IntList() { list = 0; }
    display();
    insert( int=0 );
    append( int=0 );
private:
    IntItem *atEnd();
    IntItem *list;
};
```

The user must be able to remove items from a list or to remove an entire list. It is the choice of the class designer whether an attempt at removing an item from an empty list is an error. In either case, a predicate function, isEmpty(), is valuable to users of the class:

```
class IntItem { /* ... */ };

class IntList {
public:
    isEmpty() { return list == 0; }
    // ...
private:
    IntItem *list;
};
```

The removal of the entire list might be implemented as follows. Note that it returns a count of the number of items removed.

```
IntList::remove()
{ // delete the entire list
    IntItem *tmp, *pt = list;
    int cnt = 0;

    while ( pt ) {
        tmp = pt;
        pt = pt->next;
        ++cnt;
        delete tmp;
    }

    list = 0;
    return cnt;
}
```

Alternatively, a user may wish to remove all items containing a particular value. A special case to look out for is when the value to be removed is the first item on the list. In this case, the list member must itself be updated.

```
IntList::remove( int val )
{ // delete all entries with value val
    IntItem *prv, *tmp, *pt = list;
    int cnt = 0;

    // while the first item on list == val
    while ( pt && pt->val == val ) {
         tmp = pt->next; // save pointer to next
         delete pt;
         ++cnt;
         pt = tmp;
    }

    if ((list = pt) == 0 )
        return cnt; // list empty
    prv = pt; pt = pt->next;

    while ( pt ) { // iterate through list
       if ( pt->val == val ) {
            tmp = prv->next = pt->next;
            delete pt;
            ++cnt;
            pt = tmp;
       }
       else {
            prv = pt;
            pt = pt->next;
       }
    } // end, while (pt)
    return cnt;
}
```

Another useful member function is length(). length() returns the number of items in a list. An empty list should, of course, return a length of 0.

```
IntList::length() {
    int cnt = 0;
    IntItem *pt = list;
    for ( ; pt; pt = pt->next, ++ cnt )
        ; // null statement
    return cnt;
}
```

Here is a second small program to exercise these four member functions (the expanded specification of the header file IntList.h is left as an exercise for the reader):

```
#include "IntList.h"
#include <stream.h>

const SZ = 12;
const ODD = 1;

main() {
    IntList il; // empty list

    if ( // test that empty list is handled
        il.isEmpty() &&
        il.length() == 0 &&
        il.remove() == 0
        )
        cout << "Empty List: ok.\n";

    // every odd item is set to value of ODD
    for ( int i = 0; i < SZ; ++i )
            il.append( i%2 == 0 ? i : ODD );
    il.display();

    // illustrate remove( someValue );
    cout << il.remove( ODD ) << " items of value "
        << ODD << " removed: ";
    il.display();

    // illustrate remove()
    int len = il.length();
    if ( il.remove() == len )
        cout << "All " << len << " items removed: ";
    il.display();
    return 0;
}
```

When compiled and executed, the program generates the following output:

```
Empty List: ok.
( 0 1 2 1 4 1 6 1 8 1 10 1 )
6 items of value 1 removed: ( 0 2 4 6 8 10 )
All 6 items removed: ( empty )
```

Exercise 4-4. Implement IntList::removeFirst(). The return value
of this member function is the value of its val member. Be sure to handle
the case of an empty list.

□

Exercise 4-5. Implement `IntList::removeLast()`. Again, the return value is the value of its `val` member. Be sure to handle the case of an empty list. □

A common operation on a list is the concatenation of one list with another. The operation itself is simple, but the implementation is easy to get wrong. The following, for example, is likely to get the user into trouble:

```
#include "IntList.h"

void IntList::concat( IntList& il )
{
     (atEnd())->next = il.list;
}
```

The problem is that two IntList objects now point to the same sequence of items. The likelihood is that the two class objects will delete the items at different times in the program. If the second class object attempts to access the items already deleted, a dangling reference will occur that will likely cause a run-time program exception. If that does not happen, the possibility exists that when the second class object deletes the items for the second time, the storage might already have been reallocated for a completely different purpose. Again, in all likelihood, the program will crash at run-time. A general solution is to provide a reference count for each list item. Each time an item is removed, its reference count is decremented by one. When the reference count is zero, the item would actually be deleted. An alternative strategy is to copy each list item taking part in the concatenation. This version of `concat()` looks as follows:

```
void IntList::concat( IntList& il )
{ // append il.list to invoking list object
    IntItem *pt = il.list;
    while ( pt ) {
        append( pt->val );
        pt = pt->next;
    }
}
```

An interesting list operation is that of inversion. In this case, the list is reversed, the back becoming the front and vice versa. Although the implementation is short, the pointer manipulations are somewhat tricky and easy to get wrong when you first begin programming with lists. Here is an implementation:

```
void IntList::reverse() {
    IntItem *pt, *prv, *tmp;
    prv = 0;   pt = list; list = atEnd();

    while ( pt != list ) {
        tmp = pt->next;
        pt->next = prv;
        prv = pt;
        pt = tmp;
    }
    list->next = prv;
}
```

The following small program exercises both concat() and reverse():

```
#include "IntList.h"
const SZ = 8;

main() {
    IntList il, il2;
    for ( int i = 0; i < SZ/2; ++i )
        il.append( i );
    for ( i = SZ/2; i < SZ; ++i )
        il2.append( i );

    il.display(); il2.display();
    il.concat( il2 ); il.display(); // concat
    il.reverse(); il.display(); // reverse
    return 0;
}
```

When compiled and executed, the program generates the following output:

```
( 0 1 2 3 )
( 4 5 6 7 )
( 0 1 2 3 4 5 6 7 )
( 7 6 5 4 3 2 1 0 )
```

Exercise 4-6. Implement a member function to add a list item such that its next IntItem is the first value on the list larger than its own value.

□

Exercise 4-7. Modify IntList to have an

```
IntItem *endList;
```

member. When modifying the public member functions, be sure not to break any existing code (the three program examples in this section). □

4.3   Overloaded Function Names

A word is said to be overloaded when it has two or more distinct meanings. The intended meaning of any particular use is determined by its context. If we write

```
static int depth;
```

the meaning of static is determined by the scope in which it appears. It
is either a local static variable or a static variable declared at file scope. (In
the next chapter, we will introduce a third meaning for static, that of a
static class member.)

   In each case, the meaning of static is made clear by providing the context of its use. When that context is missing, we speak of the word as being
ambiguous. An ambiguous word can have two or more meanings, each of
them equally possible.

   In natural language, ambiguity is often deliberate. In literature, for
example, ambiguity can enrich our understanding of a book's characters or
themes. An individual, perhaps, is described as *bound and determined*. One
character might turn to another and say, "People are never *just*." The
human mind can hold different meanings for a word simultaneously.

   Ambiguity, however, does not sit well with a compiler. If the context
in which an identifier or statement occurs is insufficient to make its meaning clear, the compiler will report an error. Ambiguity is an important
issue in overloading function names, the topic of this section, and in class
inheritance, the topic of Chapters 7 and 8.

Why Overload a Function Name?

In C++, two or more functions can be given the same name provided that
each signature is unique, in either the number or the types of their arguments. For example,

```
int max( int, int );
double max( double, double );
Complex &max( const Complex&, const Complex& );
```

A separate implementation of max() is required for each unique argument
type. Each, however, performs the same general action; each returns the
larger of its two arguments.

   From a user's viewpoint, there is only one operation, that of determining a maximum value. The implementation details of how that is accomplished are of little general interest. With function overloading, the user
can simply write the following:

```
int i = max( j, k );
Complex c = max( a, b );
```

The arithmetic operators provide an analogy. The expression

```
1 + 3
```

invokes the addition operation for integer operands, while the expression

```
1.0 + 3.0
```

invokes a different addition operation that handles floating-point operands.

The implementation is transparent to the user because the addition operator ("+") is overloaded to represent the different instances. It's the responsibility of the compiler, not the programmer, to distinguish between these different instances. Function-name overloading provides a similar transparency to user-defined functions.

Without the ability to overload a function name, each instance must be given its own unique name. For example, our set of max() functions becomes the following:

```
int max( int, int );
double fmax( double, double );
Complex &Cmax( const Complex&, const Complex& );
```

This lexical complexity is not intrinsic to the problem of determining the larger of two objects of different data types, but rather reflects a limitation of the programming environment — each identifier occurring at the same scope must be unique. Such complexity presents a practical problem to the programmer, who must either remember or look up each name.

Function-name overloading relieves the programmer of this lexical complexity.

How to Overload a Function Name

When a function name is declared more than once in a program, the compiler will interpret the second (and subsequent) declarations as follows:

- If both the return type and signature of the two functions match exactly, the second is treated as a redeclaration of the first. For example,

```
// declares the same function
extern void print( int *ia, int sz );
void print( int *array, int size );
```

Argument names are irrelevant in signature comparisons.

- If the signatures of the two functions match exactly but the return types differ, the second declaration is treated as an erroneous redeclaration of the first and is flagged at compile time as an error. For example,

```
unsigned int max( int*, int sz );
extern int max( int *ia, int ); // error
```

A function's return type is not considered when distinguishing between overloaded instances.

- If the signatures of the two functions differ in either the number or type of their arguments, the two function instances are considered to be overloaded. For example,

```
extern void print( int *, int );
void print( double *da, int sz );
```

A typedef name provides an alternative name for an existing data type; it does not create a new data type. The following two instances of search() are treated as having exactly the same signature. The declaration of the second instance results in a compile-time error because, although it declares the same signature, it declares a different return type.

```
// typedef does not introduce a new type
typedef char *string;

extern int search( string );
extern char *search( char* ); // error
```

When Not to Overload a Function Name

Overloading allows a set of functions that perform a similar operation, such as print(), to be collected under a common mnemonic name. The resolution of which function instance is meant is transparent to the user, removing the lexical complexity of providing each function with a unique name, such as iPrint() and iaPrint().

Given the benefit, when is it not beneficial to overload a function name? One instance is when the collection does not perform a similar operation. For example, here is a set of functions that operate on a common data abstraction. They may at first seem as likely candidates for overloading:

```
void setDate( Date&, int, int, int );
Date& convertDate( char* );
void printDate( const Date& );
```

These functions operate on the same data type but do not share the same operation. In this case the lexical complexity is a programmer convention that associates a set of functions with a common data type. The C++ class mechanism makes this sort of convention unnecessary. These functions should be made member functions of the Date class. For example,

```
class Date {
public:
    set( int, int, int );
    Date &convert( char* );
    void print();
    // ...
};
```

The following set of five member functions for a Screen class perform various move operations. Again, it might first be thought to overload this set under the name move().

```
Screen& moveHome();
Screen& moveAbs( int, int );
Screen& moveRel( int, int, char *direction );
Screen& moveX( int );
Screen& moveY( int );
```

The last two instances cannot both be overloaded; their signatures are exactly the same. To provide a unique signature, we could compress the two functions into one:

```
Screen& move( int, char xy );
```

This provides a unique signature. Moreover, if studies show that the x or y axis is moved more frequently, a default value may be specified:

```
Screen& move( int, char xy = 'x' );
```

Studies might also show that the most frequent movement is one position forward on the x axis. If a default value is supplied for the first argument, however, the signature is no longer unique:

```
Screen& move( int sz = 1, char xy = 'x' );
```

Now both move() and moveHome() can be called without arguments. An argument with a default initializer need not be considered when attempting to match the intended instance of an overloaded function call.

At this point the programmer might question the wisdom of overloading these two functions. It almost seems as if overloading in this case is a process of discarding information. Although cursor movement is a general operation shared by all these functions, the specific nature of that movement is unique among certain of these functions.

moveHome(), a special case of cursor movement, is another case in point. The name moveHome() conveys more information than does move(). The program might be best served with a special function name:

```
inline Screen&
Screen::home()
{
    return move( 0, 0 );
}
```

This leaves the second and third movement functions. Again, they can be overloaded. Just as easily, however, they might be compressed into one instance by using a default argument initializer:

```
move( int, int, char* = 0 );
```

Programmers are best served by not thinking of each language feature as the next mountain to climb. Use of a feature should follow from the logic of the application and not simply because it is there.

Resolving an Overloaded Function Call

The signature of a function distinguishes one instance from another in an overloaded function set. For example, here are four distinct instances of print():

```
extern void print( unsigned int );
extern void print( char* );
extern void print( char );
extern void print( int );
```

A call to an overloaded function is resolved to a particular instance through a process referred to as *argument matching*, which can be thought of as a process of disambiguation. Argument matching involves comparing the actual arguments of the call with the formal arguments of each declared instance. There are three possible outcomes of a call of an overloaded function:

1. A match. The call is resolved to a particular instance. For example, each of the following three calls of print() results in a match:

    ```
    unsigned a;

    print( 'a' ); // matches print(char);
    print( "a" ); // matches print(char*);
    print( a );   // matches print(unsigned);
    ```

2. No match. The actual argument cannot be made to match an argument of the defined instances. Each of the following two calls of print() results in no match:

```
int *ip;
SmallInt si;

print( ip ); // error: no match
print( si ); // error: no match
```

3. Ambiguous match. The actual argument can match more than one
defined instance. The following call, an example of an ambiguous
match, can match each instance of print() except the one that takes
an argument of type char*.

```
unsigned long ul;

print( ul );   // error: ambiguous
```

Matching can be achieved in one of three ways, in the following order
of precedence:

1. An exact match. The type of the actual argument exactly matches the
type of one defined instance. For example,

```
extern ff( int );
extern ff( char* );

f( 0 ); // matches ff(int)
```

0 is of type int. The call exactly matches ff(int).

2. A match through application of a standard conversion. If no exact
match is found, an attempt is made to achieve a match through a standard conversion of the actual argument. For example,

```
class X;
extern ff( X& );
extern ff( char* );

ff( 0 );   // matches ff(char*)
```

3. A match through application of a user-defined conversion. If no exact
match or match by a standard conversion is found, a user-defined
conversion is attempted. For example,

```
class SmallInt {
public:
    operator int();
    // ...
};

SmallInt si;
extern ff( char* );
extern ff( int );

ff( si ); // matches ff(int)
```

`operator int()` is referred to as a conversion operator. Conversion operators allow a class to define its own set of "standard" conversions. Section 6.5 (page 282) looks at these user-defined conversions in detail.

Details of an Exact Match

Actual arguments of type `char`, `short`, and `float` are handled as a special case with regard to an exact match. There are two passes made over the set of overloaded functions whenever there is an actual argument of one of these types.

In the first pass, an attempt is made to match the arguments exactly. For example,

```
ff( char );
ff( long );

ff( 'a' ); // ff(char)
```

The character constant exactly matches the overloaded instance that takes a formal argument of type `char`. The search for a match is complete.

If there is no exact match on the first pass, the following promotions take place:

- An argument of type `char`, `unsigned char`, or `short` is promoted to type `int`. An argument of type `unsigned short` is promoted to type `int` if the machine size of an `int` is larger than that of a `short`; otherwise, it is promoted to type `unsigned int`.

- An argument of type `float` is promoted to type `double`.

In the second pass, an attempt is made to match the argument exactly in its promoted type. For example,

```
ff( int );
ff( short );
ff( long );

ff( 'a' ); // ff(int);
```

The character constant exactly matches the overloaded instance that takes a formal argument of type int. The matching of either type short or type long requires application of a standard conversion. The search for a match is complete.

An actual argument of type int cannot match exactly a formal argument of either char or short. Similarly, a double does not match exactly an argument of type float. For example, given the following pair of overloaded functions,

```
ff( long )
ff( float );
```

the following call is ambiguous:

```
ff( 3.14 ); // error: ambiguous
```

The literal constant 3.14 is of type double. It matches neither instance exactly. A match is achieved with either instance by means of a standard conversion. Since there are two conversions possible, the call is flagged as ambiguous. No one standard conversion is given precedence over another. The programmer can resolve the ambiguity either by an explicit cast, such as the following:

```
ff( long( 3.14 )); // ff( long )
```

or use of the float constant suffix:

```
ff( 3.14F ); // ff( float )
```

In the following example, given the following declarations:

```
ff( unsigned );
ff( int );
ff( char );
```

a call with an actual argument of type unsigned char matches the formal argument of type int. The other two instances both require application of a standard conversion.

```
unsigned char uc;
ff( uc ); // ff(int)
```

Argument matching can distinguish between const and "ordinary" pointer and reference arguments. For example,

```
extern void ff( const char* );
extern void ff( char* );

char *cp;
const char *pcc;

ff( pcc );    // ff( const char* )
ff( cp );     // ff( char* )
ff( 0 );      // error: ambiguous
```

The last call is ambiguous because zero is an exact match of type int. It
can only match either pointer instance of ff() through application of a
standard conversion. The conversion of zero to a pointer type matches
both instances of ff().

Each named enumeration defines a unique type that matches exactly
only its enumerated elements and identifiers of the enumeration type. For
example,

```
enum Bool { FALSE, TRUE } found;
enum Stat { FAIL, PASS };

extern void ff( Bool );
extern void ff( Stat );
extern void ff( int );

ff( PASS );   // ff( Stat )
ff( 0 );      // ff( int )
ff( found ); // ff( Bool )
```

An exact match can be overridden by the use of an explicit cast. For
example, given the following set of overloaded functions,

```
extern void ff(int);
extern void ff(void *);
```

the call

```
ff( 0xffbc );
```

matches ff(int) exactly since 0xffbc is a literal integer constant written
in hexadecimal notation. The programmer can force the void* instance of
ff() to be invoked, however, by providing an explicit cast. This is done as
follows:

```
ff( (void *)0xffbc ); // ff( void* )
```

An explicit cast of an actual argument causes the argument to match the
type of the cast exactly.

Details of a Match by Standard Conversion

If there is no resolution of an overloaded function call by means of an exact match, a match is attempted by application of a standard type conversion. For example,

```
extern ff( char* );
extern ff( double );

ff( 'a' ); // ff( double );
```

Through the application of a standard type conversion to an actual argument of the function call,

1. any numeric type will match a formal argument of any other numeric type, including unsigned;

2. enumeration types will match a formal argument of numeric type;

3. zero will match both a formal argument of a pointer type and a formal argument of a numeric type; and,

4 a pointer of any type will match a formal argument of void*.
   Here are some examples:

```
extern ff( char* );
extern ff( void* );
extern ff( double );

main() {        // int i;
    ff( i );    // matches ff( double );
    ff( &i );   // matches ff( void* );
    ff( "a" );  // matches ff( char* );
}
```

All standard conversions are treated as requiring equal work. The conversion of a char to an unsigned char, for example, does not take precedence over the conversion of a char to a double. Closeness of type is not considered. If more than one match is possible by application of the standard conversions, the call is ambiguous and is is flagged at compile time as an error: For example, given the following pair of overloaded functions,

```
extern ff( unsigned );
extern ff( float );
```

each of the following calls matches both instances. Each call is ambiguous and is flagged as an error.

```
// each call is ambiguous
ff( 'a' );
ff( 0 );
ff( 2uL );
ff( 3.14159 );
```

Ambiguity can be resolved by an explicit cast.

Reference Argument Matching

A temporary variable is generated whenever a reference argument is passed either an rvalue or an identifier whose type does not match the type of the reference exactly. (Section 3.7 (page 120) presents a discussion of the generation of temporaries for reference arguments.) In the case where two or more standard conversions are possible for the resolution of an overloaded function call, a conversion that does not require the generation of a temporary takes precedence over one that does.

In the following call, for example, a match requires the application of a standard conversion in both instances. The conversion of an int to short, however, does not require the generation of a temporary whereas the conversion to char& does. The conversion to short, therefore, takes precedence. There is no ambiguity.

```
extern ff( char& );
extern ff( short );
int i;

ff( i );    // ff(short), standard conversion
```

If the argument of type short was also declared to be a reference argument, however, the call would be ambiguous since both instances would then require the generation of a temporary. Note that the generation of a temporary is not taken into account in the case of an exact match:

```
ff( 'a' ); // ff(char&), exact match
```

Multiple Argument Calls

A call with multiple arguments is resolved by applying the matching rules to each argument in turn. The function chosen is the one for which the resolution of each argument *is the same or better* than for the other functions in the overloaded set. For example,

```
extern ff( char*, int );
extern ff( int, int );

// ff( int, int )
ff( 0, 'a' );
```

The instance of `ff()` taking two arguments of type `int` is invoked because

1. Its first argument is better. `0` is an exact match of a formal argument of type `int`.

2. Its second argument is the same. `'a'` equally matches the second argument of both functions.

A call is considered ambiguous if no one function instance contains a better match. In the following example, both instances of `min()` require two standard conversions to achieve a match:

```
int i, j;
extern min( long, long );
extern min( double, double );

// error: ambiguous, no ``best'' match
min( i, j );
```

A call is also considered ambiguous if more than one function instance contains a better match. For example,

```
extern foo( int, int );
extern foo( double, double );

// error: ambiguous: two ``best'' matches
foo( 'a', 3.14F );
```

In this case, both instances of `foo()` contain one exact match.

Default Argument Initializers

An overloaded function instance with default argument initializers will match a call that provides all or some subset of its arguments. For example,

```
extern ff( int );
extern ff( long, int = 0 );

main() {
    ff( 2L );    // matches ff( long, 0 );
    ff( 0, 0 ); // matches ff( long, int );
    ff( 0 );     // matches ff( int );
    ff( 3.14 ); // error: ambiguous
}
```

The last call is ambiguous because both instances can match through application of a standard conversion. There is no precedence given to ff(int) because it has exactly one argument.

Overloading and Scope

The overloaded set of function instances associated with a particular name must all be declared within the same scope. A locally declared function, for example, hides rather than overloads a function instance declared at file scope. For example,

```
extern void print( char* );
extern void print( double ); // overloads print

void fooBar( int ival )
{
    // separate scope: hides both instances of print
    extern void print( int );

    // error: print(char*) is not visible in this scope
    print( "Value: " );
    print( ival );       // ok: print(int);
}
```

Since each user-defined class maintains its own scope, the member functions of two distinct classes can never overload one another.

Exercise 4-8. How should the following error() function be defined in order to handle the following calls:

```
error( "Array out of bounds: ", index, upperBound );
error( "Division by zero" );
error( "Invalid selection", selectVal );
```

□

Overloading Operator new

Operator `new` can be overloaded by the programmer. The predefined instance has the following prototype:

```
void *operator new( long size );
```

where `size` represents the storage requirements of the type in bytes. Every user-defined instance of operator `new` must return a `void*` and specify a first argument of type `long`. For example, a second overloaded instance of operator `new` is provided by the standard C++ library. Its prototype looks as follows:

```
void *operator new( long size, void *memAddress );
```

The `size` argument is provided automatically by the compiler. Additional arguments must be specified in a comma-separated argument list placed between the keyword `new` and the type specifier:

```
#include <new.h>
char buf[ sizeof(IntArray) ];

main() {
    // default instance of new
    IntArray *pa = new IntArray( 10 );

    // operator new( long, void* )
    IntArray *pbuf = new (buf) IntArray( 10 );
}
```

4.4   Pointers to Functions

We have been asked to provide a general sorting function. In most cases the quick sort algorithm is appropriate. Users need only write the following:

```
sort( array, lowBound, highBound );
```

Under some circumstances, however, quicksort is inappropriate. If the array is arranged in descending order, for example, a merge sort will perform better. If storage is at a premium, a heap sort is most appropriate. For a small set of elements, a bubble sort usually is good enough.

The `sort()` function must provide some facility for specifying an alternative sorting algorithm. The problem is how to provide the flexibility required in a few cases without overly complicating the general use of the function. Typically, the solution is a default value. In this case, the default value is the `quickSort()` function.

A second requirement is the ability to change sorting algorithms without requiring a change to user code, allowing the code to be fine-tuned after it is up and running. Typically, this can be accomplished by having the user code manipulate a function argument or pointer. In this case the argument would need to be a sorting function. Since a function, however, cannot be passed as an argument, a pointer to a function would need to be used.

This section considers how both these requirements can be met.

The Type of a Pointer to Function

What will a pointer to function look like? What will its type be? How will it be declared? Here is the declaration of quickSort():

```
void quickSort( int*, int, int );
```

The function name, of course, is not part of its type. A function's type is determined by its return value and argument list signature. A pointer to quickSort() must specify the same signature and return type:

```
void *pf( int*, int, int );
```

This is almost correct. The problem is that the compiler interprets the statement as the definition of a function pf() taking three arguments and returning a pointer of type void*. The dereference operator is associated with the type specifier, not pf. Parentheses are necessary to associate the dereference operator with pf:

```
void (*pf)( int*, int, int );
```

This statement declares pf to be a pointer to a function taking three arguments and with a return type of void — that is, a pointer of the same type as quicksort().

Other functions may or may not have the same function type. The following three sort functions share the same type:

```
void bubbleSort( int*, int, int );
void mergeSort( int*, int, int );
void heapSort( int*, int, int );
```

However, both min() and max() declare functions of a different type:

```
int min( int*, int sz );
int max( int*, int sz );
```

A pointer to these two functions will be defined like this:

```
int (*pfi)( int*, int );
```

There are as many distinct function types as there are distinct combinations of function signatures and return types.

Initialization and Assignment

Recall that an array identifier evaluates as a pointer to its first element when not modified by the subscript operator. A function name, when not modified by the call operator, evaluates as a pointer to a function of its type. For example,

```
quickSort;
```

evaluates as an unnamed pointer of the type

```
void (*)( int*, int, int );
```

Applying the address-of operator to the function name also yields a pointer to its function type. Thus, both quicksort and &quicksort evaluate to the same type. A pointer to a function is initialized as follows:

```
void (*pfv)( int*, int, int ) = quickSort;
void (*pfv2)(int*, int, int ) = pfv;
```

Assignment is similar:

```
pfv = quickSort;
pfv2 = pfv;
```

An initialization or assignment is legal only if the argument list and return type match exactly. Otherwise, a compile-time error message is issued. For example,

```
extern int min( int*, int );
extern void (*pfv)( int*, int, int ) = 0;
extern int (*pfi)( int*, int ) = 0;
main() {
    pfi = min; // ok
    pfv = min; // error
    pfv = pfi; // error
}
```

A function pointer can be initialized with and assigned zero.

Pointers can also address instances of an overloaded function. When a function is overloaded, the compiler resolves the instance by finding an exact match of the return type and the signature. If no instance matches exactly, the initialization or assignment results in a compile-time error. For example,

```
extern void ff( char );
extern void ff( unsigned );

void ( *pf )(char) = ff; // ok: void f(char)
void ( *pf2 )(int) = ff; // error: no exact match
```

Invocation

The dereference operator is not required in order to invoke a function through a pointer. Both the direct and indirect calls of a function are written the same. For example,

```
#include <stream.h>

extern min( int*, int );
int (*pf)( int*, int ) = min;

const int iaSize = 5;
int ia[ iaSize ] = { 7, 4, 9, 2, 5 };

main() {
    cout << "Direct call: min: "
        << min( ia, iaSize ) << "\n";

    cout << "Indirect call: min: "
        << pf( ia, iaSize ) << "\n";
}

min( int* ia, int sz)
{
    int minVal = ia[ 0 ];
    for ( int i = 0; i < sz; ++i )
        if ( minVal > ia[ i ] )
            minVal = ia[ i ];
    return minVal;
}
```

The call

```
pf( ia, iaSize );
```

is a shorthand notation for the explicit pointer notation:

```
(*pf)( ia, iaSize );
```

The two forms are equivalent.

Arrays, Arguments, and Return Type

An array of pointers to functions can be declared. For example,

```
int (*testCases[10])();
```

declares `testCases` to be an array of ten elements. Each element is a pointer to a function taking no arguments and with a return type of `int`. Execution of the elements of `testCases` might look as follows:

```
extern const SIZE = 10;
extern int (*testCases[SIZE])();
extern int testResults[SIZE];

void runtests() {
    for ( int i = 0; i < SIZE; ++i )
        testResults[ i ] = testCases[ i ]();
}
```

An array of pointers to functions may be initialized as follows:

```
extern void quickSort( int*, int, int );
extern void mergeSort( int*, int, int );
extern void heapSort( int*, int, int );
extern void bubbleSort( int*, int, int );

void ( *sortFuncs[] )( int*, int, int ) =
{
    quickSort,
    mergeSort,
    heapSort,
    bubbleSort
};
```

A pointer to `sortFuncs`, which can also be declared, is of the type "pointer to an array of pointers to functions." The definition will look like this:

```
void ( **pfSort )( int*, int, int ) = sortFuncs;
```

The two dereference operators declare `pfSort` to be a pointer to a pointer.

```
*pfSort;
```

evaluates to the address of `sortFuncs`.

```
**pfSort;
```

evaluates to the address of `quickSort()`, the first element of `sortFuncs` — the equivalent of writing

```
*pfSort[ 0 ];
```

To execute `quickSort()` through `pfSort`, the programmer would write either of the following:

```
// equivalent invocations
pfSort[ 0 ]( ia, 0, iaSize-1 ); // shorthand
(*pfSort[ 0 ])( ia, 0, iaSize-1 ); // explicit
```

Pointers to functions can also be declared as arguments to functions and can be provided with default values.

```
extern void quickSort( int*, int, int );
void sort( int*, int, int,
            void (*)(int*,int,int)=quickSort );
```

A simple definition of `sort()` might look as follows:

```
void sort( int *ia, int low, int high,
            void (*pf)(int*, int, int))
{
    if ( !ia ) return;
    if ( !pf ) return;
    if ( high < low + 2 ) return;
    pf( ia, low, high );
}
```

`sort()` might be called in any of the following ways:

```
// normally, these would be in a header file
extern int *ia;
extern const iaSize;
extern void quickSort( int*, int, int );
extern void bubbleSort( int*, int, int );

typedef void (*PFV)( int*, int, int );
extern void sort( int*, int, int, PFV=quickSort );
extern void setSortPointer( PFV& );

PFV mySort;
void ff() {
    sort( ia, 0, iaSize );
    sort( ia, 0, iaSize, bubbleSort );

    setSortPointer( mySort );
    sort( ia, 0, iaSize, mySort );
}
```

A pointer to a function can also be declared as the return type of a function. For example,

```
int ( *ff( int ))( int*, int );
```

declares `ff()` to be a function taking one argument of type `int`. It returns a pointer to a function of type

```
int (*)( int*, int );
```

The use of a typedef name can make the use of a pointer to a function considerably easier to read. For example,

```
typedef int (*PFI)( int*, int );
PFI ff( int );
```

is an equivalent declaration of `ff()`.

Exercise 4-9. Section 3.9 (page 126) defines the function `fibonacci()`. Define a pointer to a function that can point to `fibonacci()`. Invoke the function through this pointer to generate a Fibonacci series of eight elements.

□

Exercise 4-10. Section 3.10 (page 131) defines the function `binSearch()`. Define a function `search()` that can be invoked as follows:

```
extern int size, val, ia[];
int index = search( ia, size, val, binSearch );
```

□

_new_handler

`_new_handler`, a pointer to a function provided in the C++ standard library distributed with the AT&T C++ Language System, is set to `0` by default. The declaration of `_new_handler` looks as follows:

```
void ( *_new_handler )();
```

`_new_handler` is a pointer to a function with a `void` return value and taking no arguments.

When `new` fails, it tests `_new_handler` to see whether it points to a function. If `_new_handler` is not set, `new` will return `0`; if `_new_handler` is set, the function to which it points is invoked.

The function to which `_new_handler` points must be supplied by the user. In addition, `_new_handler` must be explicitly set by the user to point to this function. This can either be done directly, as follows,

```
// to be invoked if new fails
extern void freeStoreException()

// set _new_handler to freeStoreException
_new_handler = freeStoreException;
```

or through the `set_new_handler()` library function. The latter can be accomplished as follows:

```
// new.h contains a declaration of set_new_handler
#include <new.h>

// set _new_handler with library function
set_new_handler( freeStoreException );
```

The purpose of _new_handler, then, is to provide access to a function that is only to be called under the exception condition that the free store is exhausted. Providing _new_handler with a function frees the user from having to test each call of new for failure.

The simplest function with which to provide _new_handler reports the error and causes the program to exit under its own power:

```
#include <stream.h>
#include <stdlib.h>

extern char *progName; // current file
enum Exceptions { FS_EXHAUST = 1, /* ... */ };

void freeStoreException() {
    cerr << progName
        << ": free store exhausted!\n";

    // do any clean-up here ...
    exit( FS_EXHAUST );
}
```

Exercise 4-11. Set `freeStoreException` to _new_handler and rerun the `exhaustFreeStore()` program defined in Section 4.1 (page 139) of this chapter. □

4.5 Type-Safe Linkage

Overloading gives the appearance of permitting multiple occurrences of the same nonstatic function identifier. This is a lexical convenience that holds at the program source level. The downstream components of the compilation system, however, require that each nonstatic function identifier

be uniquely named. For example, most link editors resolve external references lexically. If the link editor sees two or more instances of the identifier
print, it cannot analyze the signature types to distinguish between
instances (by this point in the compilation, that information is usually lost).
Rather, the link editor flags print as multiply defined and quits.

To handle this problem, each function identifier is *encoded* with a
unique internal name. The downstream components of the compilation system see only this encoded name. The exact details of the name transforma-
tion are unimportant; they are likely to vary across implementation. The
general algorithm encodes the type information of the signature and
appends it to the function name. In two special cases, the encoding will
generate linkage errors and the program will fail to compile:

1. Inconsistent declarations of a function within separate files.

2. Calls of functions of other languages, notably C.

This section considers these two special cases.

InterFile Declarations

In the first case, a function is accidentally declared differently in two
separate files; both declarations are meant to represent the same function.
For example, in the file token.C, the function addToken() is defined as
taking one argument of type unsigned char. In the file lex.C, where it
is called, addToken() is declared as taking one argument of type char.

```
// in file token.C
addToken( unsigned char tok ) { /* ... */ }

// in file lex.C
extern addToken( char );
```

A call of addToken() in lex.C will cause the program to fail at the link
edit phase. Arguments of type unsigned char and char are encoded
differently. The addToken() function declared in lex.C will be flagged
as an undefined function. If the program were to compile successfully, the
following scenario might occur.

The compiled program is tested on an AT&T 3B20. The program executes correctly and is sent out to a field location using a VAX 8550. The
program compiles without a hitch. Unfortunately, the first time it is executed, it fails miserably. Not even the simplest test program works.

What happened? Here is part of the set of Token declarations:

```
enum Tokens {
    // ...
    INLINE = 128;
    VIRTUAL = 129;
    // ...
    };
```

The call of `addToken()` looks as follows:

```
curTok = INLINE;
addToken( curTok );
```

`chars` are implemented as a signed type on the 8550. On the 3B20 they are implemented as unsigned. The misdeclaration of `addToken()` does not show up on the 3B20; on the 8850, however, each token with a value greater than 127 causes an overflow.

Because the compiler processes one file at a time, it cannot ordinarily detect type violations across files. As we have seen, these type violations can be a source of serious program error. The internal encoding of function names with their signature provides some measure of interfile type checking of function calls. This error and others like it are caught at link time.

Erroneous declarations of external variables between files, however, cannot be caught during compilation. Errors such as the following reveal themselves only in run-time exceptions or in the incorrect output of the program.

```
// in token.C
unsigned char lastTok = 0;

// in lex.C
extern char lastTok;     // one token history
```

A Word on Header Files

The disciplined use of header files is fundamental to the prevention of this sort of interfile error. A header file provides a centralized location for the declaration of all `extern` variables, function prototypes, class definitions, and inline functions. Files that must declare a variable, function, or class *include* the header file(s).

This provides two safeguards. First, all files are guaranteed to contain the same declaration. Second, should a declaration require updating, only one change to the header file need be made. The possibility of failing to update the declaration in a particular file is removed. Our `addToken()` example would provide a `token.h` header file.

```
// in token.h
enum Tokens { /* ... */ };
extern unsigned char lastTok;
extern addToken( unsigned char );

// in lex.C
#include "token.h"

// in token.C
#include "token.h"
```

Some care should be taken in designing header files. The declarations provided should logically belong together. A header file takes time to compile.
If it is too large or filled with too many disparate elements, programmers
will be reluctant to incur the compile-time cost of including them.

A second consideration is that a header file should never contain a
non-static definition. If two files in the same program include a header file
with an external definition, most link editors will reject the program
because of multiply defined symbols. Because const values are often
required in header files, the default linkage of a const identifier is static.
consts can therefore be defined inside a header file.

Other Language Function Calls

If the programmer wishes to call a function written in another programming language — most notably, C — an escape mechanism is necessary to
inhibit the encoding of the function name. The escape mechanism, referred
to as a *linkage directive*, has a single line and compound syntactic form:

```
extern "C" void exit(int);

extern "C"  {
    printf( const char* ... );
    scanf( const char* ... );
}

extern "C" {
#include <string.h>
}
```

The linkage directive consists of the extern keyword followed by a string
literal, followed by an "ordinary" function prototype. Although the function is written in another language, calls to it are still fully type checked.
Multiple functions may be enclosed within braces. The braces serve as
delimiters and do not introduce a new level of scope.

The linkage directive may be specified only at file scope. The following code fragment is illegal and will be flagged as an error at compile time:

```
char *copy( char *src, char *dst )
{
    // error: linkage directive must be at file scope
    extern "C" strlen( const char* );
    if ( !dst )
        dst = new char[ strlen(src)+1 ];
    // ...
    return dst;
}
```

By moving the linkage directive to file scope, the function will compile:

```
extern "C" strlen( const char* );

char *copy( char *src, char *dst )
{
    if ( !dst )
        dst = new char[ strlen(src)+1 ];
    // ...
    return dst;
}
```

The linkage directive is more appropriately placed, however, within a header file.

If a C++ function is intended to be invoked by routines written in other languages, the function must also be escaped.

The linkage directive may only be specified for one instance of an overloaded function. A program that includes the following two header files is illegal:

```
// in string.h
extern "C" strlen( const char* );

// in String.h
extern "C" strlen( const String& );
```

The overloading of sqrt(), following, illustrates a typical use of the linkage directive:

```
class Complex;
class BigNum;

extern Complex& sqrt( Complex& );
extern "C" double sqrt( double );
extern BigNum& sqrt( BigNum& );
```

The C language `sqrt()` instance is escaped; the additional C++ class instances are not. The order of declarations is not significant.

Exercise 4-12. `exit()`, `printf()`, `malloc()`, `strcpy()`, and `strlen()` are C language library routines. Modify the following C program so that it compiles and links under C++.

```
char *str = "hello";

main()
{   /* C language program */
    char *s, *malloc(), *strcpy();

    s = malloc( strlen(str)+1  );
    strcpy( s, str );
    printf( "%s, world\n", s );
    exit( 0 );
}
```

□

Exercise 4-13. Section 3.10 (page 131) defines the function `binSearch()`. We wish to make it available to programs written in C. How should it be declared? □

Exercise 4-14. The C math library trigonometric functions are declared as follows:

```
double sin( double );
double cos( double );
double tan( double );
```

Show how these declarations would be overloaded to accept arguments of the class types RealNum and Complex. □

Chapter 5: **The C++ Class**

The C++ class mechanism allows users to define their own data types. These types may add functionality to an already existing type — such as the IntArray class introduced in Chapter 1. Classes can also be used to introduce altogether new types, such as a Complex number class or a BitVector class. Classes are typically used to define abstractions that do not map naturally into the predefined or derived data types; for example, a computer Task class, a terminal display Screen class or an Employee or ZooAnimal class. The possible class types are unlimited. In the next four chapters we will implement a number of different classes.

A C++ class has four associated attributes:

1. A collection of *data members*, the representation of the class. There may be zero or more data members of any type in a class.

2. A collection of *member functions*, the set of operations that may be applied to objects of that class. There may be zero or more member functions for a class. They are referred to as the class *interface*.

3. Levels of program access. Members of a class may be specified as `private`, `protected`, or `public`. These levels control access to members from within the program. Typically, the representation of a class is private while the operations that may be performed on the representation are public. This sort of public/private specification is referred to as *information hiding*. A private internal representation is said to be *encapsulated*.

4. An associated class *tag name*, serving as a *type specifier* for the user-defined class. A class name may appear anywhere in a program the predefined type specifiers may appear. Given the class name `Screen`, for example, a user may write

```
Screen myScreen;
Screen *tmpScreen = &myScreen;
Screen& copy( const Screen[] );
```

A class with a private representation and a public set of operations is referred to as an *abstract data type*. In this chapter and Chapter 6 we examine the design, implementation and use of abstract data types in C++.

5.1   The Class Definition

A class definition has two parts: the *class head*, composed of the keyword
`class` followed by the class tag name, and the *class body*, enclosed by a
pair of curly braces, which must be followed by either a semicolon or a
declaration list. For example,

```
class Screen { /* ... */ };
class Screen { /* ... */ } myScreen, yourScreen;
```

Within the class body, the data members, member functions, and levels of
information hiding are specified. The following subsections consider the
various types of specification.

Data Members

The declaration of class data members is the same as for variable declarations with the exception that an explicit initializer is not allowed. For
example, the Screen class may define its representation as follows:

```
class Screen {
    short height; // number of Screen rows
    short width;  // number of Screen columns
    char *cursor; // current Screen position
    char *screen; // screen array (height*width)
};
```

As with variable declarations, it is not necessary to declare the two `short`
members, or the two `char*` members, separately. The following definition
is equivalent:

```
class Screen {
/*
 * height and width refer to row and column
 * cursor points to current Screen position
 * screen addresses array height*width
 */
    short height, width;
    char *cursor, *screen;
};
```

In general, unless there is a reason to do otherwise, declare the
members of a class in order of increasing size. This usually gives optimal
alignment on all machines. The data members can be of any type. For
example,

```
class StackScreen {
    int topStack;
    void (*handler)(); // handles exceptions
    Screen stack[ STACK_SIZE ];
};
```

A class object can be declared as a data member only if its class definition
has already been seen. In cases where a class definition has not been seen,
a forward declaration of the class can be supplied. A forward declaration
permits pointers and references to objects of the class to be declared as
data members. Pointers and references are permitted because both are a
fixed size independent of the type they address. For example, here is a
definition of StackScreen using a forward declaration:

```
class Screen; // forward declaration
class StackScreen {
    // pointer to STACK_SIZE Screen objects
    int topStack;
    Screen *stack;
    void (*handler)();
};
```

A class is not considered defined until the closing brace of the class body is
seen — precluding a class from declaring a member object of its own type.
The class is considered to be declared, however, and may define pointer
and reference data members of its own class type. For example,

```
class LinkScreen {
    Screen window;
    LinkScreen *next;
    LinkScreen *prev;
};
```

Member Functions

Users of the Screen class must perform a wide range of operations on a
Screen class object. A set of cursor movement operations will be required.
The ability to test and set portions of the screen must also be provided.
The user should be able to copy one Screen object to another and indicate
at run time the actual dimensions of the screen. This set of operations to
manipulate a Screen object is declared within the class body. These operations are spoken of as the *member functions* of the class.

The member functions of a class are declared inside the class body. A
declaration consists of the function prototype. For example,

```
class Screen {
public:
    void home();
    void move( int, int );
    char get();
    char get( int, int );
    void checkRange( int, int );
    // ...
};
```

The definition of a member function can also be placed inside the class body. For example,

```
class Screen {
public:
    void home() { cursor = screen; }
    char get() { return *cursor; }
    // ...
};
```

home() positions the cursor at the top left-hand corner of the screen. get() returns the value of the current cursor position. Because they are defined inside the class body, they are *automatically* handled as inline functions.

Member functions larger than one or two lines are best defined outside the class body. This requires a special class syntax to identify the function as a member of its class. For example, here is the definition of checkRange():

```
#include "Screen.h"
#include <stream.h>
#include <stdlib.h>

void Screen::checkRange( int row, int col )
{ // validate coordinates
    if ( row < 1 || row > height ||
         col < 1 || col > width ) {
        cerr << "Screen coordinates ( "
             << row << ", " << col
             << " ) out of bounds.\n";
        exit( -1 );
    }
}
```

A member function defined outside the class body must explicitly declare itself to be inline. For example, the following implementation defines move() to be an inline member function of Screen:

```
inline void
Screen::move( int r, int c )
{ // move cursor to absolute position
     checkRange( r, c ); // valid address?
     int row = (r-1)*width; // row location
     cursor = screen + row + c - 1;
}
```

Member functions are distinguished from ordinary functions by the following attributes:

- Member functions have full access privilege to both the public and private members of the class while, in general, ordinary functions have access only to the public members of the class. Of course, the member functions of one class, in general, have no access privileges to the members of another class.

- Member functions are defined within the scope of their class; ordinary functions are defined at file scope. (Section 5.8 (page 217) considers class scope in detail.)

A member function can overload only other member functions of its class. This is because overloaded functions must occur in the same scope. The following second instance of get(), for example, has no relationship with the nonmember, global get() or a member function get() of another class.

```
inline char
Screen::get( int r, int c )
{
     move( r, c );   // position cursor
     return get();   // other Screen get()
}
```

Information Hiding

It often happens that the internal representation of a class type is modified subsequent to its initial use. For example, imagine that a study is conducted of users of our Screen class, and that it is determined that all the Screen class objects defined are of the dimension 24 x 80. In this case, a less flexible but more efficient representation for the Screen class is the following:

```
const Height = 24;
const Width = 80;
class Screen {
        char screen[ Height ][ Width ];
        short cursor[2];
};
```

Each member function must be reimplemented, but the interface of each function (that is, its signature and return type) will remain unchanged. What is the effect of this change of the internal representation of Screen on users of the class?

- Every program that had direct access to the data members of the old Screen representation is broken. It is necessary to locate and rewrite all those portions of code before the programs can be used again.

- Every program that limited its Screen object access to the Screen member functions requires no change to its working code. Recompilation, however, is necessary.

Information hiding is a formal mechanism for restricting user access to the internal representation of a class type. It is specified by labeled public, private, and protected sections within the class body. Members declared within a public section become public members; those declared within a private or protected section become private or protected members.

- A public member is accessible from anywhere within a program. A class enforcing information hiding limits its public members to the member functions meant to define the functional operations of the class.

- A protected member behaves as a public member to a *derived class*; it behaves as a private member to the rest of the program. (We saw an instance of how protected members are used in the IntArrayRC class derivation in Chapter 1. A full discussion of protected members is deferred until Chapter 7, in which derived classes and the concept of *inheritance* are introduced.)

- A private member can be accessed only by the member functions and *friends* of its class. (See Section 5.5 (page 200) later in this chapter for a discussion of friends.) A class that enforces information hiding declares its data members as private.

The following definition of Screen specifies its public and private sections:

```
class Screen {
public:
    void home(){ move( 1, 1 ); }
    char get() { return *cursor; }
    char get( int, int );
    inline void move( int, int );
    // ...
private:
    short height, width;
    char *cursor, *screen;
};
```

By convention, the public members of a class are presented first. The private members are listed at the bottom of the class body.

A class may contain multiple public, protected, or private labeled sections. Each section remains in effect until either another section label or the closing right brace of the class body is seen. If no label is specified, by default the section immediately following the opening left brace is private.

5.2   Class Objects

The preceding definition of Screen did not cause any memory to be allocated. Memory is allocated for a class with the definition of each class object. The definition

```
    Screen myScreen;
```

for example, allocates a chunk of storage sufficient to contain the four Screen class data members.

Objects of the same class can be initialized and assigned to one another. By default, copying a class object is equivalent to copying all its elements. For example,

```
    // bufScreen.height = myScreen.height
    // bufScreen.width = myScreen.width
    // bufScreen.cursor = myScreen.cursor
    // bufScreen.screen = myScreen.screen
    Screen bufScreen = myScreen;
```

By default, class objects are passed by value as the argument and return type of a function. A pointer to a class object can be initialized or assigned the result either of operator new or of the address-of operator ("&"). For example,

```
Screen *ptr = new Screen;
myScreen = *ptr;
ptr = &bufScreen;
```

Outside the scope of the class, the member selection operators are required to access either the data members or member functions of a class. The class object selector (".") is used with a class object or reference; the class pointer selector ("->") is used with a pointer to a class object. For example,

```
#include "Screen.h"
isEqual( Screen& s1, Screen *s2 )
{ // return 0 if not equal, 1 if equal

    if ( s1.getHeight() != s2->getHeight() ||
         s1.getWidth() != s2->getWidth() )
            return 0;    // not equal

    for ( int i = 0; i < s1.getHeight(); ++i )
        for ( int j = 0; j < s2->getWidth(); ++j )
            if (s1.get( i, j ) != s2->get( i, j ))
                    return 0; // not equal

    // still here?  then screens are equal
    return 1;
}
```

isEqual() is a nonmember function that compares two Screen objects for equality. isEqual() has no access privilege to the private data members of Screen; it must rely on the public member functions of the Screen class.

getHeight() and getWidth(), referred to as access functions, provide read-only access to the private data members of the class. Their implementation is straightforward. For efficiency, they are defined as inline:

```
class Screen {
public:
    int getHeight() { return height; }
    int getWidth() { return width; }
    // ...
private:
    short height, width;
    // ...
};
```

Members of a class may be accessed directly within the scope of the class. Each member function is contained within the scope of its class regardless of whether it is defined within or outside the class body. A member function can access the members of its class without using the member selection operators. For example,

```
#include "String.h"
#include <string.h>

void Screen::copy( Screen& s )
{ // copy one Screen object with another

    delete screen; // free up existing storage
    height = s.height;
    width = s.width;

    screen = cursor = new char[ height * width + 1 ];
    strcpy( screen, s.screen );
}
```

Exercise 5-1. copy() resizes the target Screen object to the size of the Screen object it is to duplicate. Reimplement copy() to allow the source and target Screen objects to be of different sizes.

□

Exercise 5-2. An interesting and possibly dangerous assumption is being made about the characters contained within screen. This assumption allows the screen members to be copied using the strcpy() library function. What is this assumption? Reimplement copy() so that it does not depend on this assumption. □

5.3   Class Member Functions

Member functions provide the set of operations a user may perform on the class type. This set is referred to as the *public interface* of the class. The success or failure of a class depends on the completeness and efficiency of this set of member functions. This section considers the member functions a Screen class requires. It is divided into the following four subsections: manager functions, implementor functions, helping functions, and access functions. These categories of member functions are not part of the C++ language. Rather, they are a method of thinking about the kinds of member functions a class generally requires.

Manager Functions

One set of specialized member functions, manager functions, manage class objects, handling activities such as initialization, assignment, memory management, and type conversion. Manager functions are usually invoked implicitly by the compiler.

An initialization member function, called a *constructor*, is implicitly invoked each time a class object is defined or allocated by operator new. A constructor is specified by giving it the class name. Here is a Screen class constructor:

```
Screen::Screen( int high, int wid, char bkground )
{    // Screen initializer function: constructor

    int sz = high * wid;
    height = high; width = wid;
    cursor = screen = new char[sz+1];

    char *ptr = screen;
    char *endptr = screen + sz;
    while ( ptr != endptr ) *ptr++ = bkground;
    *ptr = '\0'; // end of screen marked by null
}
```

The declaration of the Screen constructor within the class body provides a default high, wid, and bkground argument value.

```
class Screen {
public:
    Screen( int=8, int=40, char='#' );
    // ...
};
```

Each declared Screen object is automatically initialized by the Screen constructor. For example,

```
Screen s1;                      // Screen(8,40,'#')
Screen *ps = new Screen( 20 );  // Screen(20,40,'#')

main() {
    Screen s(24,80,'*');        // Screen(24,80,'*')
    // ...
}
```

Chapter 6 considers constructors and the other manager functions in detail.

Implementor Functions

A second set of member functions, referred to as *implementor* functions, provides the capabilities associated with the class abstraction. A Screen, for example, is expected to support cursor movement such as home() and move(). Additional required cursor movements include forward(), back(), up(), and down(). The member functions forward() and back() move the cursor one character at a time. On reaching the bottom or top of the screen, the cursor wraps around.

```
inline void Screen::forward()
{
    // advance cursor one screen element
    ++cursor;

    // check for bottom of screen; wraparound
    // bottom of screen is null element
    if ( *cursor == '\0' )
        home();
}



inline void Screen::back()
{ // move cursor backward one screen element

    // check for top of screen; wraparound
    if ( cursor == screen )
        bottom();
    else
        --cursor;
}
```

bottom() is an implementor function that sets the cursor to the last column of the screen.

```
inline void Screen::bottom ()
{
  int sz = width*height - 1;
    cursor = screen + sz;
}
```

up() and down() move the cursor up or down one row of the screen. On reaching the top or bottom row of the screen, the cursor does not wrap around, but rather sounds a bell, remaining where it is.

```
const char BELL = '\007';
void inline Screen::up()
{ // move cursor up one row of screen
  // do not wraparound; rather, ring bell

    if ( row() == 1 ) // at top?
        cout.put( BELL );
    else
        cursor -= width;
}

void inline Screen::down()
{
    if ( row() == height ) // at bottom?
        cout.put( BELL );
    else
        cursor += width;
}
```

Exercise 5-3. Additional cursor movements might include moving forward or backward one word, where a word is delimited by white space. Implement wordForward().

□

Exercise 5-4. Another useful capability is to position the cursor at the occurrence of a string. For example,

```
myScreen.find( "this" );
```

Implement find(char*);□

Helping Functions

Another set of member functions carries out auxiliary tasks. Usually these helping functions are not intended to be invoked directly by the user. Rather, they provide support for the other class member functions. Generally, they are declared as private. checkRange(), defined earlier, is a helping function. Here are four additional helping functions. row() returns the current row of the cursor position:

```
inline Screen::row()
{ // return current row
  int pos = cursor - screen + 1;
  return (pos+width-1)/width;
}
```

`col()` returns the current column of the cursor position:

```
inline Screen::col()
{ // return current column
  int pos = cursor - screen + 1;
  return ((pos+width-1) % width)+1;
}
```

`remainingSpace()` returns the amount of space remaining on the screen, not counting the current position:

```
inline Screen::remainingSpace()
{ // current position is no longer remaining
  int sz = width*height;
  return( screen + sz - cursor - 1 );
};
```

`stats()` displays the information returned by the three previous helping functions; it was useful in testing the code incorporated here.

```
void inline Screen::stats()
{
    cout << "row: " << row()<< "\t";
    cout << "col: " << col()<< "\t";
    cout << "rm: " << remainingSpace()<< "\n";
}
```

The following is a small program written to exercise a portion of the member functions implemented thus far.

```
#include "Screen.C"
#include <stream.h>

main()
{ // exercise cursor movements
  Screen x(3,3);
  int sz = x.getHeight() * x.getWidth();

      cout << "Screen Object ( "
          << x.getHeight() << ", " << x.getWidth()
          << " ) ( size: " << sz << " )\n\n";

      x.home();
      for ( int i = 0; i <= sz; ++i )
      { // ``<='' in order to wraparound
            x.stats();
            x.forward(); }
      return 0;
}
```

When compiled and executed, the program generates the following output:

```
Screen Object ( 3, 3 ) ( size: 9 )

row: 1   col: 1   rm: 8
row: 1   col: 2   rm: 7
row: 1   col: 3   rm: 6
row: 2   col: 1   rm: 5
row: 2   col: 2   rm: 4
row: 2   col: 3   rm: 3
row: 3   col: 1   rm: 2
row: 3   col: 2   rm: 1
row: 3   col: 3   rm: 0
row: 1   col: 1   rm: 8
```

Access Functions

Information hiding encapsulates the internal representation of the class object, thereby protecting user code from changes to that representation. Equally important, the internal state of the class object is protected from random program modification. A specific small set of functions provides all write access to the object. If an error occurs, the search space for the mistake is limited to this function set, greatly easing the problems of maintenance and program correctness. Member functions supporting user access to otherwise private data are referred to as *access functions*. So far we have seen only read access functions. Here are two set() functions that allow a user to write to the screen:

```
    void Screen::set( char *s )
    { // write string beginning at screen element

        int space = remainingSpace();
        int len = strlen( s );
        if ( space < len ) {
            cerr << "Screen: warning: truncation: "
                 << "space: " << space
                 << "string length: " << len << "\n";
            len = space;
        }

        for ( int i = 0; i < len; ++i )
            *cursor++ = *s++;

    }
```

```
void Screen::set( char ch )
{
    if ( ch == '\0' )
        cerr << "Screen: warning: "
             << "null character (ignored).\n";
    else *cursor = ch;
}
```

A simplifying assumption of our Screen class implementation is that the screen does not contain embedded null characters. This is the reason that set() does not permit a null character to be written to the screen.

Access functions may also augment the class abstraction by providing a set of predicate operations. The Screen class, for example, might be augmented with a collection of isEqual() functions.

isEqual(char ch) returns true if ch is equal to the character contained at the current cursor location. Its implementation is straightforward:

```
class Screen {
public:
    isEqual( char ch ) { return (ch == *cursor ); }
    // ...
}
```

isEqual(char* s) returns true if the array of characters beginning with the current cursor location is equal to s.

```
#include <string.h>

Screen::isEqual( char *s )
{ // yes? return 1; otherwise, 0

    int len = strlen( s );
    if ( remainingSpace() < len )
        return 0;

    char *p = cursor;
    while ( len-- > 0 )
        if ( *p++ != *s++ )
            return 0;

    return 1;
}
```

isEqual(Screen&) returns true if two screens are equal; that is, the height, width, and contents of the two screens must all be the same.

```
Screen::isEqual( Screen& s )
{
    // first, are they physically unequal?
    if ( width != s.width || height != s.height )
        return 0;

    // do both share the same screen?
    char *p = screen;
    char *q = s.screen;
    if ( p == q ) return 1;

    // be careful not to walk off the Screens
    while ( *p && *p++ == *q++ );

    if ( *p ) // loop broke on not equal
        return 0;

    return 1;
}
```

Exercise 5-5. Compare the nonmember implementation in Section 5.2 (page 184) with this implementation. Why do the two look so different? Are they equivalent? □

const Member Functions

An attempt to modify a nonclass const object from within a program is flagged as a compile-time error. For example,

```
const char blank = ' ';
blank = '\0'; // error
```

A class object, however, ordinarily is not directly modified by the programmer. Rather, the public set of member functions are invoked. In order to enforce the *constness* of a class object, the compiler must distinguish between safe and unsafe member functions. For example,

```
const Screen blankScreen;
blankScreen.display();  // safe
blankScreen.set( '*' ); // unsafe
```

The class designer indicates which member functions are safe by specifying them as const. For example,

```
class Screen {
public:
    char get() const { return *cursor; }
    // ...
};
```

Only member functions specified as const can be invoked by a const class object.

The const keyword is placed between the argument list and body of the member function. A const member function defined outside the class body must specify the const keyword in both its declaration and definition. For example,

```
class Screen {
public:
    isEqual( char ch ) const;
    // ...
private:
    char *cursor;
    // ...
};

Screen::isEqual( char ch ) const
{
    return( ch == *cursor );
}
```

It is illegal to declare as const a member function that modifies a data member. In the following simplified Screen definition, for example,

```
class Screen {
public:
    void ok(char ch) const { *cursor = ch; }
    void error(char *pch) const { cursor = pch; }
    // ...
private:
    char *cursor;
    // ...
};
```

ok() is a legal const member function because it does not change the value of cursor — rather, it changes the value of the object cursor addresses. error(), however, does modify the actual value of cursor and therefore cannot be specified as a const member function. The declaration results in the following error message:

```
error: assignment to member Screen::cursor of
       const class Screen
```

A const member function can be overloaded with a nonconst instance that defines the same signature. For example,

```
class Screen {
public:
    char get(int x, int y);
    char get(int x, int y) const;
    // ...
};
```

In this case, the constness of the class object determines which of the functions is invoked:

```
const Screen cs;
Screen s;

main() {
    char ch = cs.get(0,0); // const member
    ch = s.get(0,0); // nonconst member
}
```

Constructors and destructors are exceptions in that they are not required to be declared const in order to be applied to constant class objects. In general, any class that is expected to be used extensively should declare the permissible member functions for a const class object as const.

Exercise 5-6. Identify those member functions of Screen that may legally be defined as const. □

5.4   The Implicit this Pointer

There is a certain inelegance in the current implementation of the Screen class member functions. Manipulations of a screen tend to occur as a sequence of actions: clear, move, set, display. The programmer is constrained, however, to code each action as a separate statement:

```
Screen myScreen( 3, 3 ), bufScreen;

main() {
    myScreen.clear();
    myScreen.move(2,2);
    myScreen.set('*');
    myScreen.display();

    bufScreen.reSize(5,5)
    bufScreen.display();
}
```

The need to specify a new statement for each action applied to a Screen object is unnecessarily verbose. What we would prefer is to support the concatenation of member calls. For example,

```
main() {
    myScreen.clear().move(2,2).set('*').display();
    bufScreen.reSize(5,5).display();
}
```

This section illustrates how to implement this syntax. First let us examine the class member function itself more closely.

What Is the this Pointer?

Each class object maintains its own copy of the class data members. myScreen has its width, height, cursor, and screen; bufScreen has its own separate set. Both myScreen and bufScreen, however, will call the same copy of any particular member function. There exists only one instance of each class member function. This presents two problems:

1. If only one instance of a member function exists, it cannot be stored inside the class object. That would proliferate function copies with each object defined.

2. If only one instance of a member function exists, how are the particular data members of a class object bound to the data members manipulated within the member function? How, for example, does the cursor manipulated by move() become bound in turn to the cursor belonging to myScreen and bufScreen?

The answer is the this pointer. Each class member function contains a pointer of its class type named this. Within a Screen member function, for example, the this pointer is of type Screen*; within an IntList member function, it is of type IntList*.

The `this` pointer contains the address of the class object through which the member function has been invoked. In this way, the `cursor` manipulated by `home()` becomes bound in turn to the `cursor` belonging to `myScreen` and `bufScreen`.

One way of understanding this is to take a brief look at how one compiler, the AT&T C++ Language System, implements the `this` pointer. It is accomplished in the following two steps:

1. Translate the class member functions. Each class member function is translated into a uniquely named nonmember function with one additional argument — the `this` pointer. For example,

```
home__Screen( Screen *this )
{
    this->cursor = this->screen;
}
```

2. Translate each class member invocation. For example,

```
myScreen.home()
```

is translated into

```
home__Screen( &myScreen );
```

The programmer can reference the `this` pointer explicitly. For example, it is legal, although silly, to write the following:

```
inline void Screen::home()
{
    this->cursor = this->screen;
}
```

There are circumstances, however, when the programmer does need to reference the `this` pointer explicitly.

Using the this Pointer

The `this` pointer is the key to implementing the Screen class concatenation syntax. The member selection operators ("." and "->") are left-associative binary operators. The order of execution is left to right. `myScreen.clear()` is invoked first. For `move()` to be invoked next, `clear()` must return a Screen class object. For `move()` to be invoked correctly, `clear()` must return the `myScreen` object. Each member function must be modified to return the class object that has invoked it. Access to the class object is through the `this` pointer. Here is an implementation of `clear()`:

```
Screen& Screen::clear( char bkground )
{ // reset the cursor and clear the screen
    char *p = cursor = screen;

    while ( *p )
        *p++ = bkground;

    return *this; // return invoking object
}
```

move(), home(), the set() functions, and the four cursor movement functions will all need to add a return *this to their definitions and revise their return types from void to Screen&.

Let's see how these functions can be used — first, from within a member function, then within a nonmember function.

```
Screen&
Screen::lineX( int row, int col, int len, char ch)
{ /* provide straight line in row beginning at col
   *           of length len using character ch   */

    move( row, col );
    for ( int i = 0; i < len; ++i )
        set( ch ).forward();

    return *this;
}
```

The following nonmember function provides the capability of drawing a line of some length down a particular column:

```
Screen& lineY( Screen& s, int row, int col,
               int len, char ch )
{ // provide vertical line at col
    s.move( x, y );
    for ( int i = 0; i < len; ++i )
        s.set(ch).down();

    return s;
}
```

Exercise 5-7. A member function removes the lexical complexity of the member selection operator through the mechanism of the this pointer. To see this more clearly, rewrite lineY() as a Screen member function. □

The Screen member function display() might be implemented as follows:

```
Screen& Screen::display()
{
    char *p;
    for ( int i = 0; i < height; ++i )
    {   // for each row
        cout << "\n";
        int offset = width * i; // row position
        for ( int j = 0; j < width; ++j )
        {   // for each column, write element
            p = screen + offset + j;
            cout.put( *p );
        }
    }
    return *this;
}
```

It is also possible to overwrite the class object addressed by the this pointer, as illustrated by the reSize() member function. reSize() generates a new Screen object. The following assignment replaces the invoking Screen object by this new object:

```
*this = *ps;
```

where ps points to the new Screen object. One implemention of reSize() is as follows:

```
Screen&
Screen::reSize( int h, int w, char bkground )
{ // reSize a screen to height h and width w

    Screen *ps = new Screen( h, w, bkground );
    char *pNew = ps->screen;

    // Is this screen currently allocated?
    // If so, copy old screen contents to new
    if ( screen )
    {
        char *pOld = screen;
        while ( *pOld && *pNew )
            *pNew++ = *pOld++;
        delete screen;
    }

    *this = *ps; // replace Screen object
    return *this;
}
```

Linked list management also often requires having access to the this pointer. For example,

```
class DList { // doubly-linked list
public:
    void append( DList* );
    // ...
private:
    DList *prior, *next;
};

void DList::append( DList *ptr )
{
    ptr->next = next;
    ptr->prior = this;
    next->prior = ptr;
    next = ptr;
}
```

Here is small program to exercise some of the Screen member functions
defined in this and the previous section.

```
#include "Screen.h"
main() {
  Screen x(3,3);
  Screen y(3,3);

  // if equal, return 1
  cout << "isEqual( x, y ): (>1<) "
       << x.isEqual(y) << "\n";

  y.reSize( 6, 6 ); // double it

  cout << "isEqual( x, y ): (>0<) "
       << x.isEqual(y) << "\n";

  // draw a line on the Y axis
  lineY( y,1,1,6,'*' ); lineY( y,1,6,6,'*' );

  // draw a line on the X axix
  y.lineX(1,2,4,'*').lineX(6,2,4,'*').move(3,3);

  // write to screen and display
  y.set("hi").lineX(4,3,2,'^').display();

  // x and y equal in size, but not content
  x.reSize( 6, 6 );
  cout << "\n\nisEqual( x, y ): (>0<) "
       << x.isEqual(y) << "\n";
```

```
    // now, both are equal
    x.copy( y );
    cout << "isEqual( x, y ): (>1<) "
         << x.isEqual(y) << "\n";

    return 0;
}
```

When compiled and executed, the program generates the following output:

```
isEqual( x, y ): (>1<) 1
isEqual( x, y ): (>0<) 0

******
*####*
*#hi#*
*#^^#*
*####*
******

isEqual( x, y ): (>0<) 0
isEqual( x, y ): (>1<) 1
```

where the values surrounded by brackets are the expected values and the values outside the parentheses are the actual values generated by calls of isEqual().

5.5   Friends to a Class

In some instances, the information-hiding access rules are too prohibitive. The friend mechanism gives nonmembers of the class access to the non-public members of a class. Before discussing the rules for declaring a friend, let's first illustrate an instance in which a friend is necessary.

The iostream input and output operators ("$>>$", "$<<$") can be overloaded to handle class types. Once the operators are defined for a class type, objects of the class can be output in the same way as the built-in types. For example,

```
Screen myScreen;
cout << myScreen;
cout << "myScreen: " << myScreen << "\n";
```

The input and output operators both require an iostream object as their left operand, and both return the iostream object upon which they operate. This allows successive input or output operators to be concatenated. For example,

```
((( (cout << "myScreen: ") << myScreen) << "\n")
```

Each parenthetical subexpression returns the iostream object cout, which becomes the left operand of the next outermost expression.

```
cout << myScreen
```

must be implemented as

```
ostream &operator<<( ostream&, Screen& );
```

This implementation, however, precludes defining these operator functions as member functions of Screen.

Here is the declaration of the output operation as a member function of Screen:

```
class Screen {
public:
    ostream &operator<<( ostream& );
    // ...
};
```

The left operand of every member function is an object or pointer to an object of its class. This is why the member function instance of the output operator declares only the one ostream argument. A call of this instance takes the following form:

```
myScreen << cout;
```

It would be very confusing both to the programmer and the human readers of the program to provide this instance. Providing the nonmember instance, however, means that our output operator has no access privilege to the nonpublic members of the Screen class — the very members it is intended to display. This is where the friend mechanism comes in.

A friend is a nonmember of a class that is given access to the nonpublic members of a class. A friend may be a nonmember function, a member function of a previously defined class, or an entire class. In making one class friend to another, the member functions of the friend class are given access to the nonpublic members of the class.

A friend declaration begins with the keyword friend. It may appear only within the class definition. Since friends are nonmembers of the class, they are not affected by the public, private, or protected section in which they are declared within the class body. A stylistic convention is to group all friend declarations immediately following the class header:

```
class Screen {
    friend iostream&
        operator>>( iostream&, Screen& );
    friend iostream&
        operator<<( iostream&, Screen& );
public:
    // ... rest of the Screen class
};
```

How might the output Screen operator be written? The three necessary
data members are the Screen's height and width, and the actual character array that screen addresses. For simplicity, the cursor position
becomes reset to "home" whenever a Screen object is read. The format of
the Screen object output is as follows:

```
<height,width>linearScreenDump
```

The output operator might be implemented as follows:

```
ostream& operator<<( ostream& os, Screen& s )
{
    os << "\n<" << s.height
       << "," << s.width << ">";

    char *p = s.screen;
    while ( *p ) os.put( *p++ );

    return os;
}
```

Here is a simple exercise of the output operator. main() is implemented
as follows:

```
#include <stream.h>
#include "Screen.h"

main() {
  Screen x(4,4,'%');
  cout << x;
  return 0;
}
```

When compiled and executed, it generates the following output:

```
<4,4>%%%%%%%%%%%%%%%%
```

The input operator will read as input the result of the Screen output
operator. Let's store the output in a file named output. An implementation of the input operator is presented next; the verification of the input
format is omitted to save space.

```
istream& operator>>( istream& is, Screen& s )
{ // read Screen object output by operator <<
    int wid, hi;
    char ch;

    // format verification not shown
    // <hi,wid>screenDump
    is >> ch;   // '<'
    is >> hi;   // get height
    is >> ch;   // ','
    is >> wid;  // get width
    is >> ch;   // '>'

    delete s.screen;

    int sz = hi * wid;
    s.height = hi; s.width = wid;
    s.cursor = s.screen = new char[ sz + 1 ];

    char *endptr = s.screen + sz;
    char *ptr = s.screen;
    while ( ptr != endptr ) is.get( *ptr++ );
    *ptr = '\0';

    return is;
}
```

The following small program exercises both the input and output operator instances for the Screen class.

```
#include <stream.h>
#include "Screen.h"

main() {
  Screen x(5,5,'?');
  cout << "Initial Screen: \t" << x;

  cin >> x;
  cout << "\nInput Screen: \t" << x;

  return 0;
}
```

Its input is the output of the previous program. When compiled and executed, it generates the following output:

```
Initial Screen:
<5,5>??????????????????????????
Input Screen:
<4,4>%%%%%%%%%%%%%%%%%%
```

Exercise 5-8. The input operator should verify the correctness of the format that it is reading. Modify it to do that.

□

Exercise 5-9. Implementing the output operator so that it preserves the cursor position is not difficult. The member functions col() and row() can be of help. Reimplement the output operator to preserve the current cursor position.

□

Exercise 5-10. Reimplement the input operator so that it can handle the format of the output operator reimplemented in the preceding exercise. □

A class must specify each instance of an overloaded function it wishes to make a friend to the class. For example,

```
iostream& storeOn( iostream&, Screen& );
BitMap& storeOn( BitMap&, Screen& );

class Screen {
    friend iostream&
        storeOn( iostream&, Screen& );
    friend BitMap&
        storeOn( BitMap&, Screen& );
public:
    // ... rest of the Screen class
};
```

If a function manipulates objects of two distinct classes, the function may either be made a friend to both classes or be made a member function of one class and a friend to the other. Let's look at how this might be done.

In one instance, a function should logically be made a member of both classes. Since this is impossible, the function instead is made a friend to both classes. For example,

```
// forward declarations
class Screen;
class Window;

Screen& isEqual( Screen&, Window& );

class Screen {
    friend Screen& isEqual( Screen&, Window& );
    // ... rest of Screen goes here
};

class Window {
    friend Screen& isEqual( Screen&, Window& );
    // ... rest of Window goes here
};
```

In the second instance, a function logically belongs as a member of one class. It still, however, requires access to the second class. Therefore, it is made a friend to that second class:

```
class Window;
class Screen {
public:
    Screen& copy( Window& );
    // ... remaining Screen members
};

class Window {
    friend Screen& Screen::copy( Window& )
    // ... remaining Window members
};

Screen& Screen::copy( Window& ) { /* ... */ }
```

An entire class may be declared as a friend to a second class. For example,

```
class Window;
class Screen {
        friend class Window;
public:
        // ... rest of the Screen class
};
```

The nonpublic members of the Screen class may now be accessed within any Window member function.

5.6   Static Class Members

It is sometimes necessary that all the objects of a particular class have access to the same variable. This may be some condition flag or counter related to the class that changes dynamically in the course of the program — perhaps a count is needed of how many objects of a class exist at any one point in the program. Sometimes it is simply more efficient to provide one variable for all the objects of one class rather than having each object maintain its own copy. This variable may be a pointer to an error-handling routine for that class or a pointer to the free store of the class. For these cases a static class member can provide a solution.

A static data member acts as a global variable for its class. Two advantages of a static data member over the use of a global variable are the following:

1. Information hiding can be enforced. A static member can be made non-public; a global variable cannot.

2. A static member is not entered into the program's global "name space," thus removing the possibility of an accidental conflict of names.

There is only one instance of a static data member of a class. It is in scope whenever the class is in scope; that is, whenever the class definition is accessible. A static data member is a single shared object accessible to all objects of its class.

A data member is made static by prefixing its declaration with the keyword `static`. Static data members obey the public/private/protected access rules.

For example, in the CoOp class defined next, `costPerShare` is declared a private static member of type double.

```
class CoOp {
friend compareCost( CoOp&, CoOp* );
public:
    CoOp( int, char * );
    inline double monthlyMaint();
    void raiseCost(double incr) { costPerShare += incr; }
    double getCost() { return costPerShare; }
private:
    static double costPerShare;
    int shares;
    char *owner;
};
```

The decision to make `costPerShare` static has two purposes: to conserve storage and to limit the chance of error. Each CoOp object must be able to access `costPerShare`. Although its current value is the same for each object, the value changes over time. Therefore, it cannot be made a constant. But since it is inefficient to have every class object maintain a copy of the same value, we declare it static. By having `costPerShare` static, it need only be updated once and we are assured that each class object is accessing the same value. Were each class object to maintain its own copy, each copy would have to be updated, leading to inefficiency and error.

A static data member is initialized outside the class definition in the same manner as a nonmember variable. The only difference is that the class scope operator syntax must be used. For example, here is how we might initialize `costPerShare`:

```
#include "CoOp.h"
double CoOp::costPerShare = 23.99;
```

As with nonmember variables, only one initialization of a static data member can occur within a program. This means that static member initializations should be placed in a file together with the definitions of the noninline member functions, and not in the class header file. The access level of a static data member pertains only to the read and write access of that member and not to its initialization. This is why `costPerShare` can be initialized at file scope.

Access of a static class member is syntactically identical to access of a nonstatic member. For example,

```
inline double
CoOp::monthlyMaint()
{
    return( costPerShare * shares );
}

// Pointer and Reference arguments in order to
// illustrate object and pointer access
compareCost( CoOp& unit1, CoOp* unit2 )
{
    double maint1, maint2;
    maint1 = unit1.costPerShare * unit1.shares;
    maint2 = unit2->costPerShare * unit2->shares;
    // ...
}
```

Both `unit1.costPerShare` and `unit2->costPerShare` reference the static member `CoOp::costPerShare`.

Because there is only one copy of a class static data member, it can also be accessed directly. This looks as follows:

```
if ( CoOp::costPerShare < 100.00 ))
```

The class scope operator ("CoOp::") must be specified because the static member occurs in the class scope and not the global scope of the program.

The following definition of the friend function `compareCost` is the equivalent of the one just presented:

```
compareCost( CoOp& unit1, CoOp *unit2 )
{
    double maint1, maint2;
    maint1 = CoOp::costPerShare * unit1.shares;
    maint2 = CoOp::costPerShare * unit2->shares;
    // ...
}
```

The two member access functions, `raiseCost()` and `getCost()` access only the static class member `costPerShare`. The problem with this is that each must be called with a particular class object. It is irrelevant which object. The object is required only for the calling syntax since there is only one `costPerShare` instance shared by all class objects. This can result in misleading program code.

Alternatively, a member function which accesses only the static members of a class may also be declared as static. This can be done as follows:

```
class CoOp {
    friend compareCost( CoOp&, CoOp* );
public:
    CoOp( int, char* );
    inline double monthlyMaint();
    static void raiseCost(double incr);
    static double getCost() { return costPerShare; }
private:
    static double costPerShare;
    int shares;
    char *owner;
};

void CoOp::raiseCost(double incr)
{
    costPerShare += incr;
}
```

A static member function does not contain a `this` pointer; therefore, any implicit or explicit reference to the `this` pointer results in a compile-time error. Attempting to access a nonstatic class member is an implicit reference to the `this` pointer. For example, `monthlyMaint()` could not be declared as a static member function since it needs to access the data member `shares`. The definition of a static member function is the same as that of a nonstatic class member function.

A static member function may be invoked through a class object or a pointer to a class object in the same way a nonstatic member function is invoked. It may also be invoked directly using the member class syntax. For example,

```
compareCost( CoOp& unit1, CoOp *unit2 )
{
    // equivalent calls of static member getCost()
    double maint1, maint2;
    if ( CoOp::getCost() == 0 )
        return 0;

    maint1 = unit1.getCost() * unit1.shares;
    maint2 = unit2->getCost() * unit2->shares;
    // ...
}
```

A static class member can be accessed or invoked directly even if no class objects are ever declared.

Exercise 5-11. Given the following class Y, with two static class members and two static member functions:

```
class X {
public:
    X( int i ) { val = i; }
    getVal() { return val; }
private:
    int val;
};

class Y {
public:
    Y( int i );
    static getXval();
    static getCallsXval();
private:
    static X Xval;
    static callsXval;
};
```

Initialize `Xval` to 20 and `callsXval` to 0.

□

Exercise 5-12. Implement the two static member access functions. `callsXval` simply keeps count of how many times `getXval()` is called. □

5.7 Class Member Pointer

Pointers, especially pointers to functions, provide a useful form of program generality. Users of the Screen class, for example, have been asking for a "repeat" function that performs some user-specified operation n times. A nongeneral implementation could be the following:

```
Screen &repeat( char op, int times )
{
    switch( op ) {
        case DOWN: // ... invoke Screen::down()
            break;
        case UP: // ... invoke Screen::up()
            break;
        // ...
    }
}
```

Although this works, it has a number of drawbacks. One problem is that it is too explicitly reliant on the member functions of Screen. Each time a member function is added or removed, `repeat()` must be updated. A second problem is its size. By having to test for each possible member function, the full listing of `repeat()` is large and seems very complex.

An alternative, more general implementation replaces op with a pointer to Screen member function argument type. `repeat()` no longer needs to determine the intended operation. The entire `switch` statement can be removed. The definition and use of pointers to class members is the topic of the following subsections.

The Type of a Class Member

A pointer to a function may not legally be assigned the address of a member function even when the return type and signature of the two match exactly. For example, `pfi`, following, is a pointer to a function taking no arguments and with a return type of int:

```
int (*pfi)();
```

Screen defines two access functions, `getHeight()` and `getWidth()`, which also take no arguments and define a return type of int:

```
inline Screen::getHeight() { return height; }
inline Screen::getWidth()  { return width; }
```

Two nonmember functions, `HeightIs()` and `WidthIs()`, are also defined for purposes of illustration:

```
HeightIs() { return HEIGHT; }
WidthIs()  { return WIDTH; }
```

Assignment of either or both of `HeightIs()` and `WidthIs()` to pfi is legal and correct,

```
pfi = HeightIs;
pfi = WidthIs;
```

The assignment of either Screen member function `getHeight()` or `getWidth()`, however, is a type violation and will generate a compile-time error:

```
// illegal assignment: type violation
pfi = Screen::getHeight;
```

Why is there a type violation? A member function has an additional type attribute absent from a nonmember function — *its class*. A pointer to a member function must match exactly not in two but in three areas:

1. The data type and number of formal arguments; that is, its signature.

2. The return data type.

3. The class type of which it is a member.

The declaration of a pointer to a member function requires an expanded syntax that takes the class type into account. The same also holds true for pointers to class data members. Consider the type of the Screen class member `height`. The complete type of `Screen::height` is "short member of class Screen." Consequently, the complete type of a pointer to `Screen::height` is "pointer to `short` member of class Screen." This is written as follows:

```
short Screen::*
```

A definition of a pointer to a member of class Screen of type `short` looks like this:

```
short Screen::*ps_Screen;
```

ps_Screen can be initialized with the address of `height` as follows:

```
short Screen::*ps_Screen = &Screen::height;
```

Similarly, it can be assigned the address of `width` like this:

```
        ps_Screen = &Screen::width;
```

ps_Screen may be set to either width or height since both are Screen class data members of type short. An attempt to take the address of a nonpublic class member in a portion of the program without access privilege to the class results in a compile-time error.

Exercise 5-13. What is the type of the Screen class members screen and cursor?

□

Exercise 5-14. Define, initialize and assign a pointer to class member for Screen::screen and Screen::cursor. □

A pointer to member function is defined by specifying its return type, signature, and class. For example, a pointer to the Screen members getHeight() and getWidth() is defined as follows:

```
        int (Screen::*)()
```

That is, a pointer to a member function of Screen taking no arguments and returning a value of type int. A pointer to a member function can be initialized and assigned to as follows:

```
        // all pointers to class member may be assigned 0
        int (Screen::*pmf1)() = 0;
        int (Screen::*pmf2)() = Screen::getHeight;

        pmf1 = pmf2;
        pmf2 = Screen::getWidth;
```

Use of a typedef can make the pointer to member syntax easier to read. For example, the following typedef defines Action to be an alternative type name for

```
        Screen& (Screen::*)()
```

that is, a pointer to a member function of Screen taking no arguments and returning a reference to a Screen class object.

```
        typedef Screen& (Screen::*Action)();

        Action deFault = Screen::home;
        Action next = Screen::forward;
```

Exercise 5-15. Define a typedef for each distinct type of Screen member function. □

Pointers to members may be declared as arguments to functions; a default argument initializer may also be specified. For example,

```
action( Screen&, Screen& (Screen::*)() );
```

`action()` is declared as taking two arguments:

1. A reference to a Screen class object.

2. A pointer to a member function of Screen taking no arguments and returning a reference to a Screen class object.

   `action()` can be invoked in any of the following ways:

```
Screen myScreen;
typedef Screen& (Screen::*Action)();
Action deFault = Screen::home;

extern Screen&
action( Screen&, Action = Screen::display );

ff()
{
    action( myScreen );
    action( myScreen, deFault );
    action( myScreen, Screen::bottom );
}
```

Exercise 5-16. Pointers to members may also be declared as class data members. Modify the Screen class definition to contain a pointer to Screen member function of the same type as `home()` and `bottom()`.

□

Exercise 5-17. Modify the existing Screen constructor (or introduce a new constructor) to take a pointer to Screen member argument of the type specified in the previous exercise. Provide a default argument. Provide an access function to allow the user to set this member. □

Using a Pointer to Class Member

Pointers to class members must always be accessed through a specific object of the class. We do this by using the two pointer to member selection operators ("`.*`" for class objects and references and "`->*`" for pointers to class objects.) For example, pointers to member functions are invoked as follows:

```
int (Screen::*pmfi)() = Screen::getHeight;
Screen& (Screen::*pmfS)(Screen&) = Screen::copy;

Screen MyScreen, *BufScreen;

// direct invocation of member function
if (MyScreen.getHeight() == BufScreen->getHeight())
    BufScreen->copy( MyScreen );

// equivalent invocation through pointers to members
if ((MyScreen.*pmfi)() == (BufScreen->*pmfi)())
    (BufScreen->*pmfS)(MyScreen);
```

The calls

```
(myScreen.*pmfi)()
(BufScreen->*pmfi)()
```

require the parentheses because the precedence of the call operator (" () ")
is higher than the precedence of the pointer to member selection operators.
Without the parentheses,

```
myScreen.*pmfi()
```

would be interpreted to mean

```
myScreen.*(pmfi())
```

that is, invoke the function pmfi() and bind its return value to the pointer
to member object selection operator (". *").

Similarly, pointers to data members are accessed in the following
manner:

```
typedef short Screen::*ps_Screen;
Screen myScreen, *tmpScreen = new Screen(10,10);

ff() {
    ps_Screen pH = &Screen::height;
    ps_Screen pW = &Screen::width;

    tmpScreen->*pH = myScreen.*pH;
    tmpScreen->*pW = myScreen.*pW;
}
```

Since height and width are private members of the Screen class, the
initialization of pH and pW within ff() is legal only if ff() is declared a
friend to Screen. Otherwise, ff()'s attempt to take the address of these
private class members will be flagged as an error at compile time.

Here is an implementation of the repeat() member function we discussed at the beginning of this section:

```
typedef Screen& (Screen::*Action)();

Screen&
Screen::repeat( Action op, int times )
{
    for ( int i = 0; i < times; ++i )
            (this->*op)();
    return *this;
}
```

A declaration wishing to provide default arguments for repeat()
might look as follows:

```
class Screen {
public:
    Screen &
        repeat( Action=Screen::forward, int=1 );
    // ...
};
```

Invocation of repeat() might look as follows:

```
Screen myScreen;
myScreen.repeat(); // repeat( Screen::forward, 1 );
myScreen.repeat( Screen::down, 20 );
```

A table of pointers to class members can also be defined. In the following example, Menu is a table of pointers to Screen member functions that
provide for cursor movement. In addition, we define an enumeration,
CursorMovements, to index into Menu.

```
Action Menu[] = {
    Screen::home,
    Screen::forward,
    Screen::back,
    Screen::up,
    Screen::down,
    Screen::bottom
};

enum CursorMovements {
    HOME, FORWARD, BACK, UP, DOWN, BOTTOM
};
```

Next, we provide an overloaded instance of move() that accepts a
CursorMovements argument. Here is its implementation:

```
Screen& Screen::move( CursorMovements cm )
{
    (this->*Menu[ cm ])();
    return *this;
}
```

This instance of move() might be utilized in an interactive program in which the user selects a cursor movement from a menu displayed on the screen.

Exercise 5-18. Define an overloaded instance of repeat() that takes a cursorMovement as an argument. □

Pointers to Static Class Members

Static class members fall outside the pointer to class member syntax Static class members belong to the class and not to any instance of a class object. The declaration of a pointer to a static class member looks the same as that of a pointer to a nonclass member. Dereferencing the pointer does not require a class object. For example, let's look at the CoOp class again:

```
class CoOp {
    friend compareCost( CoOp&, CoOp* );
public:
    CoOp( int, char* );
    inline double monthlyMaint();
    static void raiseCost(double incr);
    static double getCost() { return costPerShare; }
private:
    static double costPerShare;
    int shares;
    char *owner;
};

void CoOp::raiseCost(double incr)
{
    costPerShare += incr;
}
```

The type of &costPerShare is double*; it is not double CoOp::*. The definition of a pointer to costPerShare looks as follows:

```
// not double CoOp::*pd
double *pd = &CoOp::costPerShare;
```

It is dereferenced in the same way as an ordinary pointer is dereferenced. It does not require an associated CoOp class object. For example,

```
Coop unit;
double maint = *pd * unit1.shares;
```

Similarly, the type of `getCost()` is `double (*)()`; it is not `double (CoOP::*)()`. The pointer definition and indirect call to `getCost()` are also handled in the same way as those of nonclass pointers:

```
// not double (CoOp::*pf)()
double (*pf)() = CoOp::getCost;
double maint = pf()*unit.shares;
```

5.8   Class Scope

A class may assume either global or local scope. Although the definition of one class may be nested within the definition of a second, both classes are treated as occurring in the same scope. The nested class is not considered to be a member of the enclosing class or to have any special access privilege to the nonpublic members of that class. For example, Section 4.2 (page 145) defines an IntList and private IntItem class. Here are the *equivalent* definitions, but with the definition of IntItem nested within the definition of IntList:

```
class IntList {
    class IntItem {
        friend class IntList;
    private:
        IntItem(int v=0) { val = v; next = 0; }
        IntItem *next;
        int val;
    };
public:
    IntList(int val) { list = new IntItem( val ); }
    IntList() { list = 0; }
    // ...
private:
    IntItem *atEnd();
    IntItem *list;
};
```

IntItem is neither a member nor a private member of IntList. `list`, an IntItem class object, is a private member of IntList. IntItem and IntList both occur at file scope. IntItem is lexically nested within IntList to indicate to the human reader that it is used only by IntList. `typedef` specifications occurring within a class definition are also treated as occupying the same scope as the enclosing class. For example,

```
class Foo {
    typedef int Bar;
private:
    Bar val; // ok
};

Bar val; // ok: the typedef is visible
```

Every class maintains its own scope. The names of class members are said to be local to the scope of their class. If a variable at file scope has its name reused by a class member, that variable is hidden within the scope of the class. For example,

```
int height;

class FooBar {
public:
    // FooBar::height <== 0
    FooBar() { height = 0; }
private:
    short height;
};
```

Although `height` is not declared until the bottom portion of the Screen definition, `height` is in scope within the entire class body. Were this not the case, the declaration of class data members would always need to be placed first in the class body. The hidden global variable can be accessed through the scope operator. For example:

```
int height;

class FooBar {
public:
    FooBar() { height = ::height; }
private:
    short height;
};
```

In contrast, a variable defined within a function is not visible until its declaration is seen. In the following example, `localFunc()` references two different instances of height.

```
int height = 66;

localFunc() {
    int hi = height; // ::height
    int height = 24; // hides ::height
    hi = height;     // hi <== 24
}
```

The following example is even more confusing. Which instance of
height do you think is referenced?

```
int height = 66;

badPractice() {
    int height = height; // which height?
}
```

A variable is considered defined once its identifier is specified in the
declaration statement. In this case, the reference to height in the initializer accesses the just-defined local instance. This means that height is
being initialized to an undefined value. Here is one solution:

```
int height = 66;

bdPrac() {
    int height = ::height;
}
```

The compiler is not likely to confuse the two instances of the variable;
the human readers of the program, however, might. The preferred solution in this case is to rename the local instance to something other than
height.

A member function occurs within the scope of its class. It also maintains its own local scope, the same as does a nonmember function. If a
class member name is reused within the member function's local scope, the
class member name becomes hidden at the point the local instance is
defined. For example,

```
Screen::badPractice() {
    int hi = height; // Screen::height
    int height = height; // height local instance
}
```

The hidden class member can be accessed through the class scope
operator. For example,

```
Screen::bdPrac() {
    int height = Screen::height;
}
```

It is also possible to access a hidden global variable through the scope operator. For example,

```
Screen::badPractice() {
    int height =
        (Screen::height > ::height)
        ? ::height : Screen::height;
}
```

Scope Resolution

When an identifier appears within a member function of a class, the algorithm to resolve the identifier is as follows:

1. The immediate block containing the identifier is searched for a declaration of the identifier. If a declaration is found, the identifier is resolved; otherwise, the enclosing scope is searched.

2. If the immediate block in which the identifier occurs is a local block nested within a member function, then the enclosing block is that of the member function. The scope of the member function is searched. If a declaration is found, the identifier is resolved; otherwise, the enclosing scope is searched.

3. If the immediate block in which the identifier occurs is the member function itself, then the enclosing scope is that of the class. If a class member has been declared with a member of the same name as the identifier, the identifier is resolved to refer to that member; otherwise, the enclosing scope is searched.

4. For resolving an identifier reference within a class member function, the enclosing scope of a nonderived class is considered to be that of file scope. If a declaration is found, the identifier is resolved; otherwise, the identifier is flagged as an illegal reference to an undeclared variable.

When an identifier is specified with either the file scope or class scope operator, the resolution of that identifier is limited to a search of the explicitly named scope. Let's consider an example. First, we define a set of identifiers.

```
extern f( int ), ff(), f3();
int i = 1024;

class Example {
public:
    f(); // hides ::f( int )
    Example( int ii = 0 ){ i = ii; }
private:
    int i; // hides ::i
    int ff; // hides ::ff()
};
```

An identifier is hidden when its name is reused within an inner scope even if the type of the local instance is different. The global identifiers i, ff(), and f(int) are hidden within the class scope of Example. Within Example::f(), references to these hidden identifiers must be prefixed with the file scope operator.

```
#include "Example.h"

Example::f()
{
    int j;

    // error: file scope f() is hidden
    // Example::f() takes no argument
    j = f( 1 );

    // ok: explicit reference to ::f( int );
    // i is resolved to Example::i;
    j = ::f( i );

    // ok: explicit references
    ::i = ::f( ::ff() );

    // ok: explicit reference is unnecessary
    // file scope f3() is visible within Example
    return( f3() );
}
```

Example::f() can also define local instances of i and f. These local instances will hide the class member instances. To reference the class members, the class scope operator must be used.

```
#include "Example.h"

Example::f()
{
    // hides Example::i
    int i = ff ? Example::i : ( ::ff() ? ::i : 0 );

    // hides Example::f
    float f = (float) Example::f();

    return( i + Example::i + ::i );
}
```

Use of the scope resolution operator limits the lookup of an identifier to the specified scope. The class scope operator cannot be used to reference a file scope identifier. For example, `Example::f3()` will result in an error message declaring `Example::f3()` to be undefined.

```
#include "Example.h"

Example::f()
{
    // ok: ::f3() invoked
    int i = f3();

    // error: Example::f3() undefined
    return( Example::f3() );
}
```

Local Classes

A class can be defined within the local scope of a file. Its class name is visible only within the boundary of its local scope. For example,

```
int doString( char *s )
{
    // local class visible only within doString()
    class String {...};
    String str( s );
}

String str( "gravity" ); // error: String not visible
```

The member functions of a local class must be defined within the class body. The following, for example, is illegal — a function cannot be nested within another function.

```
int doString( char *s )
{
    class String {
    public:
        String& operator=(char*);
    };

    String::operator=(char* s) {} // illegal
}
```

Nor can the member function be defined outside the body of the function its class is defined within — the class name is not visible. For example,

```
int string1(char *s) { class String { ... }; }
int string2(char *s) { class String { ... }; }

// error: no String class visible
String::operator=(char* s) {}
```

In practice, this limits the size and complexity of the member functions of a locally defined class to a few lines of code each. Beyond that, the code becomes difficult for the human reader to understand.

Although a local class is within the scope of its containing function, the variables defined within the scope of that function *are not visible* to the member functions of the local class. For example, the reference to bufSize within String() resolves to the instance defined at file scope, while the reference to bufSize within func() resolves to the local instance.

```
const int bufSize = 1024;
void func() {
    const int bufSize = 512;
    char *ps = new char[bufSize]; // 512

    class String {
    public:
        String() {
            str = new char[ bufSize ]; // 1024 !
        }
        // ...
```

The definition of a local class allows the programmer to limit the visibility of the class name to the function (or block) within which the class is defined. In general, a local class makes sense when its definition is simple and its use is limited to the function within which it is defined.

5.9   Unions: A Space-Saving Class

A union is a special instance of a class. The amount of storage allocated for
a union is the amount necessary to contain its largest data member. Each
member begins at the same memory address. Only one member at a time
may be assigned a value. For example, in a compiler, the lexical analyzer
separates the user's program into a sequence of tokens. The statement

```
int i = 0;
```

is converted into a sequence of five tokens:

1. The type keyword `int`

2. The identifier `i`

3. The operator `=`

4. The integer constant `0`

5. The separator `;`

These tokens are passed from the lexical analyzer to the parser. The first
step of the parser is to identify the token sequence. Information must be
present so that the parser can recognize the token stream as a declaration
— for example, as the sequence

```
Type ID Assign Constant Semicolon
```

Once the parser identifies the general token sequence, it then requires the
particular information of each token. In this case, it must know that

```
Type <==> int
ID <==> i
Constant <==> 0
```

It does not need any further information about Assign and Semicolon.

A representation of a token, therefore, requires two members, `token`
and `value`. `token` will hold a unique number that is assigned to each
possible token. For example, an identifier may be represented by 85, a
semicolon by 72. `value` will hold the particular information about that
token instance. For example, for ID, `value` will contain the string "i"; for
Type, `value` will contain a code representing the type `int`.

The representation of `value` is problematic. Although it will contain
only one value for any given token, `value` can hold multiple data types.
One representation of multiple data types, of course, is a class. The compiler writer can declare `value` to be of class type TokenValue and can then
define TokenValue to contain a member for each possible data type of
`value`.

This representation solves the problem. `value`, however, can be only
one of multiple possible data types for each particular token object. Token-
Value, however, carries around the storage necessary for all the possible
data types. Preferably, TokenValue would maintain storage sufficient only
to hold any one of the multiple possible data types, not storage to hold
them all. A union permits just that. Here is a definition of a TokenValue
union:

```
union TokenValue {
        char cval;
        char *sval;
        int  ival;
        double dval;
};
```

Since the largest data type among the members of TokenValue is `double`,
the size of TokenValue is also of type `double`. The members of a union
by default are public. A union cannot contain either a static data member
or a class object member whose class defines either a constructor or a destructor. Here is an example of how TokenValue might be used:

```
class Token {
public:
        int tok;
        TokenValue val;
};
```

A Token object might be used as follows:

```
lex() {
    Token curToken;
    char *curString;
    int curIval;

    // ...
    case ID: // identifier
        curToken.tok = ID;
        curToken.val.sval = curString;
        break;

    case ICON: // integer constant
        curToken.tok = ICON;
        curToken.val.ival = curIval;
        break;
    // ... etc.
}
```

The danger of using a union is the possibility of accidentally retrieving the current union value through an inappropriate data member. For example, if the last union assignment is an integer value to `ival`, the programmer does not want to retrieve that value through the character pointer `sval`. Doing so will certainly lead to a program error.

To help safeguard against this kind of error, an additional variable is defined whose purpose is to keep track of the type of the value currently stored in the union. This additional variable is referred to as the *discriminant* of the union. This is the role the `tok` member of Token serves. For example,

```
char *idVal;

if ( curToken.tok == ID )
    idVal = curToken.val.sval;
```

A good practice when handling a union object as part of a class is to provide a set of access functions for each union data type. For example,

```
char *Token::getString()
{
    if ( tok == ID )
        return val.sval;
    error( ... );
}
```

The tag name of a union is optional. There is no reason to provide a tag name if the union is going to be used only in one instance. By not providing a tag name, there is one less global identifier to possibly collide with. For example, the following definition of Token is *equivalent* to its previous definition. The only difference is that the union is without a tag name:

```
class Token {
public:
    int tok;
    union {
        char cval;
        char *sval;
        int ival;
        double dval;
    } val;
}
```

There is a special instance of a union referred to as an *anonymous union*. An anonymous union is a union without a tag name that is *not* followed by an object definition. For example, here is a Token class definition containing an anonymous union:

```
class Token {
public:
    int tok;
    // anonymous union
    union {
        char cval;
        char *sval;
        int  ival;
        double dval;
    };
};
```

The data members of an anonymous union can be accessed directly. For example, here is the lex() fragment recoded to use the Token class definition containing an anonymous union:

```
lex() {
    Token curToken;
    char *curString;
    int curIval;

    // ... figure out what the token is
    // ... now set curToken
    case ID:
        curToken.tok = ID;
        curToken.sval = curString;
        break;
    case ICON: // integer constant
        curToken.tok = ICON;
        curToken.ival = curIval;
        break;
    // ... etc.
}
```

An anonymous union removes one level of member selection because the member names of the union enter the enclosing scope. An anonymous union cannot have private or protected members. An anonymous union defined at file scope must be declared static.

5.10   Bit Field: A Space-Saving Member

A special class data member, referred to as a *bit field*, consists of a specified number of bits. A bit field must have an integral data type. It can be either signed or unsigned. For example,

```
class File {
    // ...
    unsigned modified : 1; // bit field
};
```

The bit field identifier is followed by a colon (":") followed by a constant expression specifying the number of bits. modified, for example, is a bit field consisting of a single bit.

Bit fields defined in consecutive order within the class body will, if possible, be packed within adjacent bits of the same integer, thereby providing for storage compaction. For example, in the following declaration, the five bit fields are to be stored in the single unsigned int first associated with the bit field mode.

```
typedef unsigned int Bit;

class File {
public:
    // ...
private:
    Bit mode: 2;
    Bit modified: 1;
    Bit prot_owner: 3;
    Bit prot_group: 3;
    Bit prot_world: 3;
    // ...
};
```

A bit field is accessed in the same manner as the other data members of a class. For example,

```
File::write()
{
    modified = 1;
    // ...
}

File::close()
{
    if ( modified )
        // ... save contents
}
```

Here is a simple example of how a bit field larger than one bit might be used (Section 2.8 (page 74) discusses the bitwise operators utilized in the example):

```
enum { READ = 01, WRITE = 02 }; // File modes

main() {
    File myFile;

    myFile.mode |= READ;
    if (myFile.mode & READ )
        cout << "\nmyFile.mode is set to READ";
}
```

Typically, a set of inline member functions are defined to test the value of a member bit field. For example, File might define isRead() and isWrite().

```
inline File::isRead() { return mode & READ; }
inline File::isWrite() { return mode & WRITE; }

if (myFile.isRead()) /* ... */
```

The address-of operator ("&") cannot be applied to a bit field, and so there can be no pointers to class bit fields. Nor can a bit field be declared to be static.

5.11   Class Argument and Ellipses

An object of a class that defines either a constructor or an instance of the assignment operator cannot be passed as an argument to a function that does not specify an appropriate argument declaration. For example,

```
extern foo( int, ... );

class Screen {
public:
    Screen( const Screen& );
    // ...
};

void bar( int ival, Screen scrObj )
{
    // error:  no Screen argument specified
    foo( ival, scrObj );
}
```

It is possible, however, to pass a pointer to scrObj to foo().

```
#include <stream.h>
#include <string.h>

enum CursorMovements {HOME,FORWARD,BACK,UP,DOWN,BOTTOM};

class Screen {
    friend istream& operator>>(istream&,Screen&);
    friend ostream& operator<<(ostream&,Screen&);
public:
    Screen( int = 8, int = 40, char = '#' );
    ~Screen() { delete screen; }

    Screen& home(){ move(1,1); return *this; }
    Screen& bottom(), forward(), back();
    Screen& up(), down();
    Screen& lineX( int, int, int, char='-' );
    Screen& lineY( int, int, int, char='|' );
    Screen& move( CursorMovements );
    Screen& move( int, int );
    Screen& copy( Screen& );
    Screen& clear( char = '#' );
    Screen& reSize( int, int, char = '#' );
    Screen& display(), stats();
    Screen& set(char*), set(char);

    char get() { return *cursor; }
    char get( int, int );
    int isEqual( Screen& );
    int isEqual( char* );
    int isEqual( char ch ) { return (ch == *cursor ); }
    int getHeight() { return height; }
    int getWidth() { return width; }
private:
    int row(), col();
    int remainingSpace();
    void checkRange(int,int);

    short height, width;
    char *cursor, *screen;
};
```

Figure 5.1 Screen.h

Chapter 6: **Class Member Functions**

This chapter considers the following three categories of member functions that aid in managing classes:

1. Constructors and destructors for the automatic initialization and deinitialization of class objects.

2. Overloaded operator functions that can be applied to class objects using operator notation rather than member function names. For example, rather than the following explicit invocation of the Screen member function isEqual():

```
if ( myScreen.isEqual(yourScreen) )
```

operator overloading allows users of the Screen class to write the following equivalent invocation:

```
if ( myScreen == yourScreen )
```

In addition, a class can take over its own memory management by providing member instances of operators new and delete.

3. Conversion operators that define a set of permissible type conversions for a class. These conversions can be applied implicitly by the compiler in much the same manner as the standard conversions are applied.

The invocation of these special member functions is generally transparent to users of the class. Together, these functions serve to make the syntax and use of a class as "natural" for the programmer as that of a built-in type.

6.1 Class Initialization

A class object is initialized by the initialization of its data members. Provided all the members are public, the object may be initialized using a comma-separated list of values enclosed in braces. For example,

```
class Word {
public:
        int occurs;
        char *string;
};


// explicit member initialization
Word search = { 0, "rosebud" };
```

More generally, C++ supports a mechanism for the automatic initialization of class objects. A special class member function, called a *constructor*, is invoked implicitly by the compiler whenever a class object is defined or allocated through operator new. The constructor is a user-supplied initialization function that is named with the tag name of its class. For example, here is a constructor for Word:

```
class Word {
public:
        Word( char*, int=0 ); // constructor
private:
        int occurs;
        char *string;
};


#include <string.h>
inline Word::Word( char *str, int cnt )
{
        string = new char [ strlen(str) + 1 ];
        strcpy( string, str );
        occurs = cnt;
}
```

The constructor must not specify a return type or explicitly return a value. Otherwise, the definition of a constructor is the same as that of an ordinary member function. In this case, the constructor for Word requires one argument of type char*. An optional second argument of type int may also be supplied. Several examples follow of how a Word object might be defined in the presence of this constructor.

```
#include "Word.h"


// Word::Word( "rosebud", 0 )
Word search = Word( "rosebud" );


// Word::Word( "sleigh", 1 )
Word *ptrAns = new Word( "sleigh", 1 );
```

```
main()
{ // shorthand constructor notations

    // Word::Word( "CitizenKane", 0 )
    Word film( "CitizenKane" );

    // Word::Word( "Orson Welles", 0 )
    Word director = "Orson Welles";
}
```

Constructor Definition

One of the most heavily used data types is that of a string. In C++, however, strings are a derived type (an array of char) without built-in operator support. (There are no assignment or relational operators, for example.) A string type is an inevitable candidate for implementation as an abstract data type. We will use the design of a String class to illustrate the syntax and semantics of constructors, destructors, and overloaded operators. We begin by looking more closely at constructors.

A constructor is identified by assigning it the tag name of a class. It may be overloaded to provide a set of alternative initializations. Our String class, for example, contains two data members:

1. str, of type char*, that addresses the character array of the string.

2. len, of type int, that contains the length of the character array pointed to by str.

Let's declare two String constructors, one to initialize str and a second to initialize len.

```
class String {
public:
        String( int );
        String( char* );
private:
        int len;
        char *str;
};
```

The definition of a class object allocates the storage necessary to contain the nonstatic data members defined for the class. The constructor provides for the initialization of this storage. Here is the definition of our first String constructor:

```
String::String( char *s )
{ // #include <string.h>
    len = strlen( s );
    str = new char[ len + 1 ];
    strcpy( str, s );
}
```

There is nothing complicated about the definition of this constructor. Its power lies in the class mechanism that invokes it implicitly for each class object the user defines that takes an initial character string. `strlen()` and `strcpy()` are string functions of the standard C library. We will provide similar support for our String class. It is worth taking a moment to understand why `str` is not simply assigned the address of `s`:

```
str = s;
```

but rather is allocated its own dynamic storage into which s is copied. The primary reason is that we cannot know for certain the *extent* of the storage in which s is contained:

- If it is of *local extent*, that is, allocated on the run-time stack, then its storage will disappear when the block it is defined in terminates — any subsequent use of `str` will be in error. For example,

```
String *readString().
{ // example of a string with local extent
    char inBuf[ maxLen ];
    cin >> inBuf;
    String *ps = new String( inBuf );
    return ps;
}

String *ps = readString();
```

- If it is of *dynamic extent*, that is, has been allocated from the free store, then it is important that it be deleted before the class object goes out of scope. However, application of the `delete` operator on memory not allocated by operator `new` can cause serious run-time program error.

The moral is that pointer assignment across scopes is potentially dangerous and requires careful management from the programmer. We will come across this problem of pointer assignment again when we consider the initialization and assignment of one class object with another object of its class.

Here is the definition of the second String constructor:

```
String::String( int ln )
{
    len = ln;
    str = new char[ len + 1 ];
    str[0] = '\0';
}
```

The decision to maintain the string length as a separate field might reasonably be questioned. The trade-off is between the required storage and the run-time cost of computing the length. The choice of an explicit length field is based on two factors: First, the length is needed often enough that the savings in time will offset the storage cost (this must be borne out in practice). Second, a String object will be used not only to store an explicit string, but also to provide a fixed-length buffer.

Because the definition of a class object results in an implicit call of a constructor, full type checking of the definition is applied. The following three String object definitions are invalid. In the first case, no argument is supplied. In the second, the argument is of the wrong type. In the third, there is one too many arguments.

```
int len = 1024;

String myString; // error: no argument
String inBuf( &len ); // error: bad type: int*
String search( "rosebud", 7 ); // error: two arguments
```

There are both explicit and shorthand forms for passing arguments to a constructor. The following are all legal forms of defining a String class object:

```
// explicit form: reflects actual invocation
String searchWord = String( "rosebud" );

// abbreviated form: #1
String commonWord( "the" );

// abbreviated form: #2
String inBuf = 1024;

// use of new requires explicit form:
String *ptrBuf = new String( 1024 );
```

An invocation of operator new invokes the constructor for the class after the necessary storage is allocated. If new fails to allocate the required storage, the constructor is *not* executed. The class pointer is set to 0. For example,

```
String *ptrBuf = new String( 1024 );
if ( ptrBuf == 0 )
     cerr << "free store exhausted\n";
```

It is useful to allow the definition of a String object without requiring that an argument be supplied. For example,

```
String tmpStr;
```

This can be done either by providing a default argument to either of the already-defined constructors, or by providing a *default constructor*. A default constructor is one that defines an empty argument list. Arrays of objects of a class with constructors use constructors in the initialization just like individual class objects. If there are fewer initializers in the list than elements in the array, the default constructor is used. If there is no default constructor, the initialization list for the array must be complete. The implementation of a default constructor for the String class might look as follows:

```
#include "String.h"

String::String()
{ // default constructor
     len = 0;
     str = 0;
}
```

A common programmer mistake is the following:

```
String st();
```

This does *not* define a String class object st initialized with the default String constructor. Rather, it declares a function st that takes no arguments and returns a String class object. The following are both correct definitions of st as a class object of String:

```
String st;
String st = String();
```

Exercise 6-1. Define a single String constructor that accepts all the following declarations:

```
String s1( "rosebud", 7 );
String s1( "rosebud", 8 );
String s2( "", 1024 );
String s3( "The Raw and the Cooked" );
String s4;
```

□

Constructors and Information Hiding

A constructor assumes the level of accessibility of the public, private, or protected section in which it is declared. For example, to restrict use of the String class as a buffer, `String::String(int)` can be declared private:

```
class String {
        friend class Buf;
public:
        String( char* );
        String();
private:
        String( int );
        // ... rest of String class
};
```

Within the program, only the String member functions and the friend class Buf may declare String objects that take an argument of type `int`. There is no restriction on the declaration of String objects that take either no argument or an argument of type `char*`.

```
f()
{
    // ok: String::String( char* ) is public
    String search( "rosebud" );

    // error: String::String( int ) is private
    String inBuf( 1024 );
    ...
}

Buf::in()
{
    // ok: String::String( char* ) is public
    String search( "rosebud" );

    // ok: String::String( int ) is private
    // Buf is a friend to String
    String inBuf( 4096 );
    ...
}
```

A private class is one with no public constructors. Only the member functions and friends may declare objects of the class. The IntItem class defined in Section 4.2 (page 145) is an example of a private class. IntItem class objects can be defined only by the IntList class, which is declared a friend of IntItem.

Destructors

C++ supports a mechanism complementary to constructors for the automatic "deinitialization" of class objects. A special, user-defined member function, referred to as a *destructor*, is invoked whenever an object of its class goes out of scope or operator delete is applied to a class pointer. When a reference to a class object goes out of scope, however, no destructor is invoked. This is because a reference serves as an alias for an already defined object; it is not itself the class object. The destructor for String is declared as follows:

```
class String {
public:
    ~String(); // destructor
    ...
};
```

A member function is designated the class destructor by giving it the tag name of the class prefixed with a tilde ("~"). A destructor cannot take an argument (and therefore may not be overloaded). It must not specify a return type or return a value. The String class destructor is defined as follows:

```
String::~String() { delete str; }
```

A constructor, recall, does not actually allocate storage. Rather, a constructor serves to initialize the newly allocated storage associated with a class object. Similarly, a destructor does not actually deallocate storage. Rather, it "deinitializes" the class object prior to the normal deallocation of storage that occurs when an object goes out of scope. In this case, because str addresses memory allocated through operator new, the String destructor explicitly deletes it. The storage associated with the class member len, however, does not require any special handling.

There is no constraint on what can be done within the destructor. A common program debugging technique, for example, is to place print statements within both the constructors and destructor of a class:

```
String::~String() {
#ifdef DEBUG
    cout << "~String() "
         << len << " " << str << "\n";
#endif
    delete str;
}
```

Destructors, in short, can perform any operations that the programmer wishes to have executed just prior to a class object exiting scope.

A destructor is not invoked automatically for a pointer to a class object that exits scope. Rather, the programmer must explicitly apply the delete operator. The destructor for the class object addressed will then be invoked. For example,

```
#include "String.h"
String search( "rosebud" );

f() {
    // would not want destructor applied to p
    String *p = &search;

    // would want destructor applied to pp
    String *pp = new String( "sleigh" );

    // ... body of f()

    // String::~String() invoked for pp
    delete pp;
}
```

If the pointer to which delete is applied does not address a class object (that is, the pointer is set to 0), the destructor is not invoked. It is unnecessary to write

```
if ( pp != 0 )
    delete pp;
```

There is one case in which the programmer may need to invoke a destructor explicitly. This is the case where the programmer wishes to delete an object of the class but does not wish to delete the storage associated with the object. This occurs in cases where a class object is allocated at a specific address using operator new. For example,

```
#include <string.h>
#include <stream.h>
#include <new.h>
struct inBuf {
public:
    inBuf( char* );
    ~inBuf();
private:
    char *st;
    int sz;
};
```

```
inBuf::inBuf( char *s ) {
    st = new char [ sz = strlen(s)+1 ];
    strcpy( st, s );
}

inBuf::~inBuf() {
        cout<<"inBuf::~inBuf(): " <<st <<"\n";
        delete st;
}

char *pBuf = new char[ sizeof( inBuf ) ];

main() {
  inBuf *pb = new (pBuf) inBuf( "free store inBuf #1" );
  pb->inBuf::~inBuf();  // explicit destructor call

  pb = new (pBuf) inBuf( "free store inBuf #2" );
  pb->inBuf::~inBuf();  // explicit destructor call

  // ...
}
```

When compiled and executed, this program generates the following output:

```
inBuf::~inBuf(): free store inBuf #1
inBuf::~inBuf(): free store inBuf #2
```

An explicit call of a destructor requires the fully qualified name. For example,

```
pb->inBuf::~inBuf(); // correct
pb->~inBuf(); // error
```

Class Arrays

An array of class objects is defined in the same way as an array of a built-in data type. For example, tbl and tbl2 each define a String class array of sixteen class objects:

```
const int size = 16;
String tbl[ size ];
String *tbl2 = new String[size];
```

The individual elements are accessed using the subscript operator in the same way as for an array of a built-in data type. To access the class members of a particular array element, the class member selector operators are applied to the array element after the subscript operator is specified. Here is an example:

```
while ( cin >> tbl[ i ] )
        tbl[i].display();
```

The class objects of the array are initialized using the defined class constructors in the same way as are individual class objects. The arguments to the constructor are specified in a brace-enclosed array initialization list. In the case of multiple arguments, the full constructor syntax must be used; otherwise, either the full or shorthand constructor notation is acceptable.

```
String ar1[] = { "phoenix", "crane" };
String ar2[3] = {String(),String(1024),String("string")};
String ar3[2] = { 1024, String( 512 ); };

Screen as[] = { Screen(24,80,'#') };
```

A class that defines a default constructor (that is, a constructor with an empty argument list) will have that constructor applied in the case of a partial initialization list. If the class does not define a default constructor, the initialization list must supply a value for each element of the array. An array allocated from the free store cannot be explicitly initialized. The class must either not define any constructors, or define a constructor requiring no arguments.

Before tbl2 goes out of scope, an explicit delete is required to reclaim the free store. However, simply writing

```
delete tbl2;
```

is insufficient because it causes the String destructor to be applied to only the initial element of tbl2. delete does not know that tbl2 points not to one String object but to an array of String objects. The programmer must provide delete with the size of the array tbl2 addresses. This is done by writing

```
delete [ size ] tbl2;
```

Now, the String destructor is invoked for each of the size elements of tbl2.

Member Class Objects

Having introduced the String class, let's now redefine the Word class to replace its char* member with a member of type String, while remaining compatible with our previous public interface.

```
class Word {
public:
    Word();
    Word( char*, int = 0 );
    Word( String&, int = 0 );
private:
    int occurs;
    String name;
};
```

Two constructors must now be invoked for each Word object — its own and the constructor for its String class member. Two questions must be considered:

1. Is there a defined order of constructor invocation? If so, what is it?

2. How can the programmer pass arguments to the member class constructor?

There is a defined order of constructor invocation. The member class constructors are always executed before the constructor for the containing class. In the case where there are multiple member class objects, the order of constructor invocation follows the member class order of declaration. (The destructor order is the reverse.)

```
// first String::String( char * )
// then Word::Word( char * )
Word flower( "iris" );
```

Arguments are passed to member class constructors through the *member initialization list*, a comma-separated list of member name/argument pairs. For example,

```
Word::Word( char *s, int cnt ) : name( s )
{
    occurs = cnt;
}
```

The member initialization list follows the signature of the constructor and is set off by a colon. Each member may be named once in the list. The member initialization list can appear only in the definition of a constructor; it cannot be specified in the declaration of a constructor. In the preceding example name is passed the character pointer s, which in turn is passed as the argument to the String constructor. Data members of built-in types of the class may also be specified in the member initialization list. occurs, for example, is initialized to the value of cnt in the following example:

```
Word::Word( char *s, int cnt )
     : name( s ), occurs( cnt ) {}
```

The execution of a constructor consists of two phases — those of initialization and assignment. When the body of the constructor is null, there is no assignment phase. For example,

```
class Simple {
public:
    Simple( int, float );
private:
    int i;
    float f;
};


Simple::Simple( int ii, float ff )
        : i(ii), f(ff)  // initialization
        {}              // assignment
```

The assignment phase begins with execution of the body of the constructor. Implicit initialization occurs in the presence of a member class that defines a constructor that requires no argument. The member initialization list makes the initialization phase explicit. There is no initialization phase in the following redefined Simple class constructor:

```
Simple::Simple( int ii, float ff ) {
    i = ii; f = ff; // assignment phase
}
```

Under most circumstances, the distinction between the initialization and assignment phase of a constructor's execution is transparent to the programmer. The handling of const and reference class data members, however, is one instance in which the distinction is *not* transparent. The member initialization list is the only mechanism by which const and reference class data members can be initialized. The following constructor implementation, for example, is illegal:

```
class ConstRef {
public:
    ConstRef( int ii );
private:
    int i;
    const int ci;
    int &ri;
};
```

```
ConstRef::ConstRef( int ii )
{ // assignment
      i = ii;    // ok
      ci = ii;  // error: cannot assign to a const
      ri = i;    // error: ri is uninitialized
}
```

By the time the body of the constructor begins execution, the initialization of all `const` and reference class data members must already have taken place. This can be done only by specifying them in the member initialization list. For example,

```
ConstRef::ConstRef( int ii )
         : ci( ii ), ri( i ) // initialization
{ // assignment
         i = ii;
}
```

The initialization argument is not limited to a simple identifier or constant value. It may be any complex expression. For example,

```
class Random {
public:
    Random( int i ) : val( seed( i ) ) {}
    int seed( int );
private:
    int val;
}
```

The initialization argument to a class member object may be another object of its class.

```
Word::Word( String &str, int cnt )
        : name( str ), occurs( cnt )
        {}

String msg( "hello" );
Word greetings( msg );
```

A class member object must appear in a member initialization list if its constructor requires an argument list. Failure to provide a required argument list results in a compile-time error. The class SynAntonym, for example, contains three class member objects: `wd`, a Word class object, and `synonym` and `antonym`, both String class objects. All Word class objects require at least one argument of type `char*` or type `String&`. The member initialization list must provide an argument list for `wd`.

```
class SynAntonym {
public:
    SynAntonym(char* s) : wd(s) {}
    SynAntonym(char* s1, char* s2, char* s3)
            : wd(s1), synonym(s2), antonym(s3) {}
    ~SynAntonym();
private:
    String synonym;
    Word wd;
    String antonym;
};

SynAntonym sa1( "repine" );
SynAntonym sa2( "cause", "origin", "effect" );
```

The order of constructor invocation for sa1 and sa2 is the following:

1. In order of declaration within the class body, the constructor of each class member:

```
String();               // synonym String member
String( "repine" );     // String member of wd
Word( "repine" );       // wd Word member
String();               // antonym String member
// sa1( "repine" );

String( "origin" );     // synonym String member
String( "cause" );      // String member of wd
Word( "cause" );        // wd Word member
String( "effect" );     // antonym String member
// sa2( "cause", "origin", "effect" );
```

2. The constructor of the containing class is invoked.

A class member object itself containing a class member object will recursively apply these constructor-ordering rules. The order of destructor calls is the reverse of the constructor call order. That is, the destructor for the containing class is called before that of a member class object. If there are multiple class objects, the order of destructor calls is the reverse of the declaration order of the member class objects.

Exercise 6-2. Here is a skeleton definition of a Buffer class:

```
#include "String.h"
class Buf {
public: // ...
private: String buf;
};
```

Declarations can take any of the following forms:

```
String s1;

Buf();
Buf( 1024 );
Buf( s1 );
```

Implement the constructor and destructor set. □

An important abstract data type is the binary tree. A skeleton for one implementation of a binary tree class for integer values is presented below. The implementation of this class will evolve from the exercises at the end of this subsection and in the other sections of this chapter.

```
class BinTree;
class INode { // private class
    friend class BinTree;
    int val;
    BinTree *left;
    BinTree *right;
};

class BinTree {
public:
    // ... public interface
private:
    INode *node;
};
```

A binary tree can either be empty (node is set to 0) or point to an INode. An INode consists of three members: an integer value, a left child, and a right child. Each child is either empty or points to a binary tree.

Exercise 6-3. Discuss the benefits and/or drawbacks of defining the INode class as a private class.

□

Exercise 6-4. Define the constructor(s) and destructor for the INode class.

□

Exercise 6-5. Define the constructor(s) and destructor for the BinTree class.

□

Exercise 6-6. Discuss the design choices you made in exercises 6-4 and 6-5. □

6.2   Memberwise Initialization

There is one instance in which the constructors provided by the class designer are not invoked to initialize a newly defined class object — this is when a class object is initialized with another object of its class. For example,

```
String vowel( "a" );
String article = vowel;
```

The initialization of `article` is accomplished by copying in turn each member of `vowel` into the corresponding member of `article`. This is referred to as *memberwise initialization*.

The compiler accomplishes memberwise initialization by internally defining a special constructor of the following general form:

```
X::X( const X& );
```

In the case of the String class, the constructor is defined something like the following:

```
String::String( const String& s )
{
    len = s.len;
    str = s.str;
}
```

The initialization of a class object with another object of its class occurs in three program situations:

1. The explicit initialization of one class object with another. For example,

```
// String::String( char* );
String color( "blue" );

// memberwise initialization generated
String mood = color;
```

2. The passing of a class object as an argument to a function. For example,

```
extern int count( String s, char ch );

// local instance of s <== mood
int occurs = count( mood, 'e' );
```

3. The return of a class object as the return value of a function. For example,

```
extern String sub( String&, char, char );

main()
{
    String river( "mississippi" );
    cout << river << " "
         << sub( river, 'i', 'I' ) << "\n";
}
```

Neither the passing of a reference argument nor the return of a reference, however, results in object initialization. This is because pass-by-reference, unlike pass-by-value, does not result in the creation of a local copy of the class object. (Section 3.6 (page 118) discusses pass-by-reference.)

Memberwise initialization copies each built-in or derived data member from one class object to another. The member classes, however, are not copied; rather, memberwise initialization is recursively applied. For example, the Word class defines an integer member, occurs, and a String class member, name. Here are two Word object definitions:

```
Word noun( "book" );
Word verb = noun;
```

verb is initialized in the following two steps:

1. The occurs member is initialized with the value of noun.occurs.

2. The name member is memberwise initialized with the internally generated constructor for the String class.

Default memberwise initialization is sometimes insufficient. Fig. 6.1 illustrates the resulting storage allocation of noun and verb. There are two problems:

1. The occurrence count of noun must not be copied to the occurrence count of verb. In fact, the two values are disjoint. The default memberwise mechanism violates the semantics of the Word class.

2. The str members of both noun and verb address the same memory. This will cause a serious problem if the two class objects do not exit scope at the same time.

In general, default memberwise initialization is insufficient for classes that contain pointer members and also define a destructor. This is because the destructor is invoked for every class object, even those that are memberwise initialized rather than "constructed."

As Fig. 6.1 illustrates, this means that the storage addressed by two or more class objects is "destructed" two or more times. In one case, a

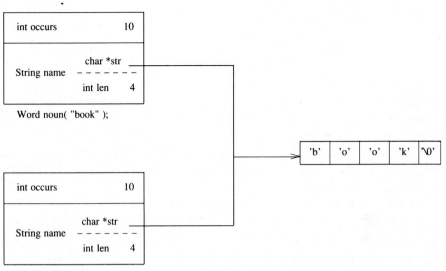

Figure 6.1 Memberwise Initialization

dangling reference may result. In another case, the result may be the destruction of storage subsequently reallocated for another purpose entirely. In either case, the program is likely to be in error. The solution is for the class designer to provide an explicit memberwise initialization constructor instance. This is the topic of the following subsections.

A Special Constructor: X(const X&)

As we have seen, under some circumstances, a class requires more control of initialization of one class object with another than is provided by default memberwise initialization. A class can assume this additional control by defining an explicit instance of the X(const X&) constructor. If explicitly defined within a class, it is invoked for each initialization of one class object with another. For example,

```
String::String( const String& s )
{
        len = s.len;
        str = new char[ len + 1 ];
        strcpy( str, s.str );
}
```

`String(const String&)` is now invoked whenever one String object is initialized with another. Each `str` member will address a distinct area of memory.

Exercise 6-7. Implement a `Screen(const Screen&)` constructor for the Screen class defined in Chapter 5. Illustrate three different situations in which the constructor is invoked.

□

Exercise 6-8. Implement an `IntList(const IntList&)` constructor for the IntList class defined in Chapter 4. Illustrate three different situations in which the constructor is invoked. □

X(const X&) and Class Member Objects

In this subsection, we examine two cases of `X(const X&)` for classes containing class member objects:

1. The containing class does not define an `X(const X&)` instance, but the member class does.

2. Both the containing and the member class define an `X(const X&)` instance.

In the first case, illustrated by the Word class definition, Word is without a `Word(const Word&)` instance. The member class, String, however, has been expanded to define `String(const String&)`.

```
class Word {
public:
    Word( char *s, int cnt = 0 )
        : name(s), occurs(cnt) {}
    Word( String& s, int cnt = 0 )
        : name(s), occurs(cnt) {}
private:
        int occurs;
        String name;
};
```

The initialization of one Word object with another defaults to memberwise initialization. The String class member, however, is initialized through an invocation of String(const String&). For example,

```
String mystery( "rosebud" );
Word resolve( mystery );


extern search( Word wd );
search( resolve );
```

String(const String&) is invoked to initialize the name member of resolve and the name member of the local copy of wd. In general, memberwise initialization is applied recursively to each class member object. For each member class that defines an X(const X&) instance, however, that instance — rather than memberwise initialization — is invoked.

The default memberwise initialization behavior is no longer applied with the introduction of an explicit Word(const Word&) instance. The String memberwise instance is no longer invoked automatically. The Word instance has assumed responsibility for the initialization of its members. Before we illustrate the correct implementation of the Word instance, let's look at the following incorrect implementation:

```
// this implementation is incorrect
Word::Word( const Word& w )
{
        occurs = 0;
        name = w.name;
}
```

This instance fails to correctly initialize the name String class member. Let's consider the following example step by step:

```
Word weather( "warm" );
Word feeling = weather;
```

The initialization steps occur as follows:

1. feeling is recognized as being initialized with a Word class object. Is there a Word(const Word&) instance defined? If yes, invoke it; otherwise, apply memberwise initialization. Word(const Word&) is found.

2. Is there a member initialization list? No.

3. Are there any class member objects? Yes. There is a String class object, name.

4. Does this String member class define a constructor that does not require arguments? If no, issue a compile-time error; otherwise, invoke it.

5. `String()` is invoked to initialize `feeling.name`.

6. `Word(const Word&)` is invoked. The assignment `name = w.name` is executed. By default, as with initialization, class object assignment is accomplished by memberwise assignment (See Section 6.3 (page 266) for a discussion). `String(const String&)` is never invoked.

This is the second instance in which the distinction between the initialization and assignment phases in the execution of a constructor becomes important. (Section 6.1 (page 243) describes the first — that of initializing `const` and reference class members.) In order for the String object constructor to be invoked, `name` must be initialized with `w.name`. This means that `name` must be placed in the member initialization list. The correct definition of the Word object initialization constructor is as follows:

```
Word::Word( const Word& w )
     : name( w.name ) // initialization
{ // assignment
     occurs = w.occurs;
}
```

In summary, if a containing class does not define an `X(const X&)` instance, each member class object is memberwise initialized. If the member class defines an `X(const X&)` instance, that instance will be invoked. If a containing class does define an `X(const X&)` instance, however, it becomes the responsibility of that class, through its member initialization list, to explicitly initialize its member class objects.

Exercise 6-9. Implement `Buf(const Buf&)` (Exercise `6.2`).

☐

Exercise 6-10. Implement an instance of both the `INode(const INode&)` and `BinTree(const BinTree&)` constructor. ☐

Summary of Constructors and Destructors

The special constructor and destructor mechanism allows for the automatic initialization and deallocation of class objects. Constructors can be overloaded to provide a set of initialization options; for efficiency, they can be defined as inline.

Member class objects have their constructors invoked before the constructor for the containing class. The order of member class object constructor invocation is the order of declaration of the member class objects. Destructor calls are invoked in the reverse order.

A constructor may specify a member initialization list which provides a mechanism for passing arguments to member object constructors. It may also be used to initialize data members that are not class objects, allowing const and reference class members to be initialized.

In one instance, a constructor is not invoked for a new class object: when the new class object is initialized with an existing class object. In this case, referred to as *memberwise initialization*, the value of each class member is copied in turn. If a class contains a member class object, memberwise initialization is recursively applied to that object.

Memberwise initialization may become a problem for classes with pointer members. The same area of memory may be "destructed" multiple times. A special object initialization constructor, X(const X&), can be explicitly defined to handle these cases. The initialization of one class object with another object of its class invokes this special constructor, if defined, rather than applying default memberwise copy.

6.3   Operator Overloading

In the previous section we defined the data members and member functions necessary to initialize and deallocate the String class. What additional functionality must a String class provide?

Users must perform tests on Strings: Is a String empty? Is one String equal to another? Is one String a substring of another? Users must also input and output a String object, assign one String to another, concatenate two Strings, determine the length of a String, index into a String, and iterate over a String. Code utilizing a String class might look as follows:

```
String inBuf;
while ( readString( cin, inBuf ))
{
    if ( inBuf.isEmpty()) return;
    if ( inBuf.isEqual( "done" )) return;

    switch ( inBuf.index(0) ) { /* ... */ }
    cout << "String is ";
    writeString( cout, inBuf );
}
```

Use of the String class is not quite as easy as is the use of the built-in data types. For example, the names chosen for the String operations, although both logical and mnemonic, are not easy to remember. In contrast, here is the same code fragment with overloaded operator instances replacing the named String operations.

```
String inBuf;

while ( cin >> inBuf )
{
    if ( !inBuf ) return;
    if ( inBuf == "done" ) return;

    switch ( inBuf[ 0 ] ) { /* ... */ }
    cout << "String is " << inBuf;
}
```

In the remainder of this section, we implement the set of operators necessary to support this style of String class programming.

Overview of Operator Overloading

A class designer can provide a set of operators to work with objects of the class. An operator function need not be a member function, but it must take at least one class argument. This prevents the programmer from overriding the behavior of operators for the built-in data types. An operator function is defined in the same way as an ordinary function except that its name consists of the keyword `operator` followed by one of the predefined C++ operators. For example,

```
String& String::operator=( const String& s )
{ // assign one String object to another
    len = s.len;
    delete str; // deallocate existing array
    str = new char[ len + 1 ];
    strcpy( str, s.str );
    return *this;
}
```

Each assignment of one String object with another String object will now invoke the String assignment operator.

```
#include "String.h"

String article( "the" );
String common;

main() {
    // String::operator=()
    common = article;
}
```

Operator functions for a class can be overloaded provided that their signatures are distinct. For example, users of our String class should be able to assign to a String object a value of type `char*`.

```
class String {
public:
    String &operator=( const String& );
    String &operator=( const char* );
    // ...
};
```

`strcmp()` is the standard library function to compare two character arrays for equality. Here is our String class equality operator for comparing two String class objects:

```
String::operator==( String& st )
{
    // strcmp returns 0 if both strings are equal
    // operator== returns 1 for equality
    return( strcmp( str, st.str ) == 0 );
}
```

Operator Function Definition

Only the predefined set of C++ operators can be overloaded. The designer of a class may not introduce a new operator ("`**`", for example, for exponentiation). Table 6.1 lists the operators that may be overloaded.

Overloadable Operators							
+	−	*	/	%	^	&	|
~	!	,	=	<	>	<=	>=
++	--	<<	>>	==	!=	&&	||
+=	-=	/=	%=	^=	&=	|=	<<=
>>=	[ ]	( )	->	->*	new	delete	

Table 6.1 Overloadable Operators

The predefined meaning of an operator for the built-in types may not be overridden. For example, the built-in integer addition operation cannot be replaced with an operation that checked for overflow. Nor may additional operators be defined for the built-in data types. Integer array addition, for example, cannot be added to the set of operations. The programmer may define operators only for class types. This is enforced by the requirement that an operator function take at least one class argument.

The predefined precedence of the operators (Section 2.9 (page 79)

discusses operator precedence) cannot be overridden. Regardless of the
class type and operator implementation,

```
x == y + z;
```

will always perform operator+ before operator==. As with the predefined operators, precedence can be overridden with the use of parentheses.

The predefined *arity* of the operator must be preserved. The unary logical NOT operator ("!"), for example, cannot be defined as the binary inequality operator for two String class objects. The following implementation is illegal:

```
// illegal: ! is a unary operator
operator!( String st1, String st2 )
{
    return( strcmp(st1.str, st2.str) != 0 );
}
```

Four predefined operators ("+", "−", "*", and "&") serve as both unary
and binary instances. Either or both arities of these operators can be
defined.

There can be only one instance of the unary increment ("++") and
decrement ("−−") operators. Overloading does not distinguish between
prefix and postfix instances of these operators.

In general, an operator function can be defined as either a member or
nonmember function. For example, to support the concatenation of two
String class objects,

```
String st1( "cobble" );
String st2( "stone" );
String st3 = st1 + st2;
```

the addition operator can be declared as either a nonmember friend of
String:

```
class String {
    friend String& operator+( String&, String& );
    // ...
};
```

or a String member function:

```
class String {
public:
    String& operator+( String& );
    // ...
};
```

The definition of both instances is likely to be ambiguous:

```
class String {
    friend String& operator+( String&, String& );
public:
    String& operator+( String& );
    // ...
};

String a( "hobby" ), b( "horse" );
String c = a + b; // error: ambiguous
```

A class member function always defines one fewer argument operands than does a friend function. This is because the first operand of a member function is the implicit class object that invokes it. For example,

```
st1 + st2
```

can be defined either as a member function, of the form

```
st1.operator+( st2 )
```

or as a nonmember function, of the form

```
operator+( st1, st2 )
```

The two definitions cannot both be present because the compiler has no way to choose between them.

There are four operator functions that *must* be defined as class member functions: the assignment operator ("="), the subscript (or index) operator ("[]"), the call operator ("()"), and the pointer member selector operator ("->"). These operators are discussed individually in subsequent subsections of this chapter.

A class member function requires an object of its class as its left operand. An operation that requires a left operand that is other than an object of its class *must* be defined as a nonmember. If the function requires access to the nonpublic class members, it must then also be declared a friend. For example,

```
class String {
    friend ostream&
    operator<<( ostream& os, String& s )
            { return ( os << s.str ); }
    // ...
};
```

Exercise 6-11. Declare the unary operator+() function prototype — first as a friend nonmember then as a member function of the String class.

☐

Exercise 6-12. The logical NOT operator returns 1 if the String object is empty; otherwise, it returns 0. Implement the logical NOT String operator.

□

Exercise 6-13. The binary `operator+()` function concatenates two Strings. Implement a nonmember instance of this operator.

□

Exercise 6-14. Implement the member instance of the binary `operator+()` function. □

Operator [ ]

Users of our String class need to have both read and write access of the individual characters of the `str` class member. We must support the following coding style using String class objects:

```
String sentence( "Ash on an old man's sleeve." );
String tempBuf( sentence.getLen() );

for ( int i = 0; i < sentence.getLen(); ++i )
    tempBuf[ i ] = sentence[ i ];
```

`String::getLen()` is a simple access function returning the length of a String object:

```
inline String::getLen()
{
    return len;
}
```

The subscript operator, slightly more tricky, must be able to appear on both the right- and the left-hand side of an expression. In order to appear on the left-hand side, its return value must be an lvalue. This is achieved by specifying the return value as a reference type:

```
inline char& String::operator[]( int elem )
{
    checkBounds( elem );
    return str[ elem ];
}
```

The return value of the subscript operator is the lvalue of the indexed element. This is why it can appear as the target of an assignment. For example, ple,

```
String st ( "mauve" );
st [0] = 'M';
```

assigns the character constant to the zeroth element of st.str.

checkBounds() verifies that the index passed to the subscript operator is within the bounds of the String array. If it is not, it reports an error and terminates the program. Its implementation looks as follows:

```
// pull in exit(int) prototype
#include <stdlib.h>

void String::checkBounds( int elem )
{ // check array bounds

    if ( elem < 0 || elem >= len )
    {
        cerr << "\nString Array Out of Bounds!! index: "
            << elem << " string length (0-"
            << len-1 << ")\n";
        exit( -1 );
    }
}
```

Operator ()

An iterator allows the user to iterate over the elements contained within a class type. Each invocation of the iterator returns a "next" element until each of the elements has been returned. The following program fragment illustrates how an iterator for a String class object might be used:

```
String inBuf;

// read in a String object
while ( cin >> inBuf )
{
    char ch;
    // iterate over the elements of inBuf
    while ( ch = inBuf() )
        // ... do something with ch
}
```

This subsection will consider how this program fragment can be implemented using two operator functions: the nonmember operator>>() and the String member operator()().

The input operator is overloaded to read a String object as follows:

```
istream& operator>>( istream& is, String& s )
{
    char inBuf[ STRING_SIZE ];

    is >> inBuf;
    s = inBuf; // String::operator=( char * )
    return is;
}
```

The String input function operator must assign a char* to a String object. This can be handled by a String::operator=(char*) instance.

```
String& String::operator=( const char *s )
{
    len = strlen( s );
    delete str;
    str = new char[ len + 1 ];
    strcpy( str, s );
    return *this;
}
```

The function call operator ("()") provides an easy way to define a class iterator, which returns the next class element with each call. After the entire array of elements is "iterated," the iterator returns a 0. This allows constructs such as

```
while ( ch = inBuf() ) // ... code
```

To implement a String iterator, an additional String data member, index, is required. index will address the next element to be returned. Each String constructor must initialize index to 0.

```
char String::operator()()
{
    // provide for an iterator operator
    if ( index < len )
        return str[ index++ ];

    // still here? completed iteration
    return ( index = 0 );
}
```

The following small program, which strips a String of punctuation, utilizes the iterator, subscript, and stream String operators.

```
#include "String.h"

const LINESIZE = 40;
enum {PERIOD='.',COMMA = ',',SEMI=';',COLON=':'};

main() {
    String inBuf( STRING_SIZE );
    int lineSize = 0;

    // operator>>( istream&, String& )
    while ( cin >> inBuf )
    {
        char ch;
        int i = 0;

        // String::operator()()
        while ( ch = inBuf() )
        {
            switch (ch) {
                case PERIOD:
                case COMMA:
                case SEMI:
                case COLON:
                    // String::operator[](int)
                    inBuf[ i ] = '\0';
                    break;
            }
            ++i; ++lineSize;
        }
        if ( lineSize >= LINESIZE )
        {
            cout << "\n";
            lineSize = 0;
        }
        cout << inBuf << " ";
    }
    cout << "\n";
}
```

The program's input is the following:

```
We were her pride of ten; she named us: benjamin,
phoenix, the prodigal, and perspicacious, pacific
Suzanne.  Benjamin, hush now.  Be still, child.
People are never just.
```

When compiled and executed, the program generates the following output:

```
We were her pride of ten she named us
benjamin phoenix the prodigal and perspicacious
pacific Suzanne Benjamin hush now Be still child
People are never just
```

Operators new and delete

By default, the free store allocation of a class object is provided by the predefined, global instance of operator new (discussed in Section 4.1 (page 135)). For example, the following program reads in a series of words from the terminal and sorts them by the length of the word. It makes use of a class called StringList.

```cpp
#include "String.h"
#include "StringList.h"

// maintain a pointer table indexed by length
const maxLen = 25;
StringList *stbl[ maxLen ];

main()
{ // read in and sort strings by length
    const inBuf = 512;
    char st[ inBuf ];
    StringList *p;

    while ( cin >> st ) {
        p = new StringList( st );
        int sz = p->getLen();
        if ( sz >= maxLen )
            // issue error message
            continue;
        p->next = stbl[ sz ];
        stbl[ sz ] = p;
    }

    for ( int i = maxLen - 1; i > 0; --i ) {
        StringList *tp;
        p = stbl[ i ];
        while ( p != 0 ) {
            cout << *p << "\n";
            tp = p;
            p = p->next;
            delete tp;
} } }
```

StringList defines two data members, a String class object named `entry` and a StringList pointer called `next`. The constructor takes one argument of type `char*`. This argument is passed to the String constructor for initialization of `entry`.

```
StringList::StringList( char *s )
            : entry( s ), next( 0 )
            { }
```

`getLen()` is an access function. It returns the length of `entry`.

```
StringList::getLen()
{
    return entry.getLen();
}
```

The String access function `getLen()` is called because the member functions of StringList have no access privilege to the nonpublic members of the String class. It is illegal for the StringList instance of `getLen()` to write the following:

```
StringList::getLen()
{
    // illegal: private member
    return entry.len;
}
```

The output operator is overloaded to accept a StringList reference:

```
ostream&
operator <<( ostream& os, StringList& s )
{
    return ( os << s.entry );
}
```

The input to the program is the theme of this subsection:

```
A class may provide new and delete
operator functions
```

When the program is compiled and executed, it generates the following output:

```
functions
operator
provide
delete
class
and
new
may
A
```

Once we are sure the program runs correctly, the next step is to try to speed up its performance. A probable area of improvement is in its memory management. Currently, new is called to allocate a new StringList object every time a word is read. If we could reduce that — say to every 24th word — we should see a considerable speed-up of our program.

A class can assume its own memory management by providing member class new and delete operators. If defined, they are invoked in place of the default instances. User programs need not change.

The memory strategy we'll use for StringList is to allocate a chunk of stringChunk objects at one time. These objects will be managed as a linked list of available class objects. Here are the declarations of freestore and stringChunk:

```
class StringList {
// ...
private:
    enum { stringChunk = 24; }
    static StringList *freeStore;
    // ...
};
```

stringChunk indicates the number of StringList objects to be allocated at one time. freeStore is a pointer to the linked list of available StringList objects. It is defined as a static class member of StringList.

A class member instance of operator new must specify a return type of void* and take a first argument of the system typedef size_t, defined in the stddef.h system header file. This argument is automatically initialized by the compiler with the size of the class type in bytes. Additional instances of operator new can also be defined, provided that each has a unique signature. Section 4.3 (page 164) presents a discussion of overloading operator new. When new is applied to a class name, the compiler looks to see if the class has provided its own instance. If it has, that instance is selected; otherwise, the predefined global instance is applied. Adding or backing out a class instance of new does not require a change to user code.

Here is an example of a StringList member instance of operator new. It checks to see if an object is available from freeStore. If one is available, the member instance returns it. If not, the global operator new is called to allocate a stringChunk of objects. Here is the implementation:

```
#include <stddef.h>

StringList *StringList::freeStore = 0;
void *StringList::operator new( size_t size )
{
        register StringList *p;

        // if the free store is exhausted
        // grab a new chunk of memory
        if ( !freeStore ) {
            long sz = StringChunk * size;
            freeStore = p =
                // the global new operator
                (StringList *)new char[ sz ];

            // initialize the StringList freeStore
            for ( ; p != &freeStore[ StringChunk-1 ];
                    p->next = p+1, p++ ) ;
            p->next = 0;
        }
        p = freeStore;
        freeStore = freeStore->next;
        return p;
}
```

The member operator delete restores the StringList object to the linked list of available objects. Here is its implementation:

```
void StringList::operator delete( void *p, size_t )
{   // restore p to freeStore
    ((StringList*)p)->next = freeStore;
    freeStore = (StringList *)p;
}
```

The delete operator must have a first argument of type void*. A second argument of the predefined system typedef size_t may be specified (remember to include stddef.h). If present, it is initialized implicitly with the size in bytes of the object addressed by the first argument. The delete operator must have a return type of void.

A class instance of operator new is invoked only for the allocation of individual class objects, not for the allocation of an array of class objects. For example,

```
StringList *p = new StringList;
```

invokes the StringList instance of new, while

```
StringList *pia = new StringList[10];
```

invokes the predefined instance that handles the allocation of an array of objects from the free store. Note, too, that the explicit definition of a class object, such as

```
StringList s;
```

does not invoke either instance of operator new.

The programmer can selectively invoke a nonclass instance of operator new through use of the scope operator. For example,

```
StringList *ps = ::new StringList;
```

invokes the default operator new. Similarly,

```
::delete ps;
```

invokes the default instance of operator delete.

The new and delete operator functions are static members of their class, and they obey the usual constraints for static member functions. In particular, recall that a static member function is without a this pointer and can therefore only directly access static data members of its class. (See Section 5.6 (page 208) for a discussion of static member functions.) These operators are made static member functions because they are invoked either before the class object is constructed (operator new) or after it has been destroyed (operator delete).

X::Operator=(const X&)

The assignment of one class object with another object of its class is performed as the memberwise assignment of the nonstatic data members; the mechanics are the same as those of memberwise initialization, described in Section 6.2 (page 247) of this chapter.

The compiler generates a class instance of the assignment operator, of the following form:

```
X& X::operator=( const X& );
```

to handle the default memberwise assignment of class objects. For example, given the following two String objects:

```
String article( "the" );
String common( "For example" );
```

the assignment

```
common = article;
```

is handled by the implicit memberwise assignment operator:

```
String& String::operator=( const String& s )
{
    len = s.len;
    str = s.str;
    index = s.index;
}
```

There are a number of problems with this assignment.

1. As with memberwise initialization, `article` and `common` both now
   address the same area of free store. The destructors for both String
   objects will be applied to that single area.

2. The free store allocated to contain *For example* is never reclaimed. It is
   lost in the memberwise assignment.

3. The semantics of the String class design prohibit a simple-minded copy
   of each data member. In Section 6.3 (page 260) we defined an `index`
   data member of the String class that allows a user to iterate through the
   String's character array. The value of `index` after a memberwise copy
   must be 0 for the target String class object — not the value of the
   source object's `index`. Default memberwise copy violates the String
   iterator semantics.

The designer of the class can resolve these problems by providing an
explicit instance of the memberwise assignment operator. The String class
instance might be defined as follows:

```
String& String::operator=( const String& s )
{
    index = 0;
    len = s.len;
    delete str;

    str = new char[ len + 1 ];
    strcpy( str, s.str );
    return *this;
}
```

StringList, defined in the previous section, contains a String class
member named `entry`. StringList does not define a memberwise

assignment operator. When a StringList object is assigned to another object of the StringList class, the string memberwise assignment operator is implicitly invoked to handle the memberwise copy of entry. For example,

```
#include "StringList.h"

main() {
StringList sl1( "horse" );
StringList sl2( "carriage" );

    // sl1.next = sl2.next
    // sl1.entry.String::operator=(sl2.entry)
    sl1 = sl2;
}
```

If StringList defines its own memberwise assignment operator, the String instance is invoked only if, within the body of the operator, an explicit String assignment takes place. For example,

```
StringList&
StringList::operator=( const StringList& s )
{
    // String::operator=(const String&)
    entry = s.entry;
    next = 0;
    return *this;
}
```

If the assignment

```
entry = s.entry;
```

is not specified, the String memberwise operator will not be invoked — entry will not be changed.

Initialization and assignment are often not adequately distinguished by programmers implementing class types. This can sometimes result in an unnecessarily inefficient class implementation. For example, given the following two class definitions:

```
class X {
public:
    X();
    X( int );
    X( const X& );
    X& operator=( const X& );
    // ...
```

```
class Y {
public:
    Y();
private:
    X x;
};
```

the following simple implementation of the Y class constructor:

```
Y::Y() { x = 0; }
```

causes the implicit invocation of two X class constructors plus the invocation of the assignment operator for X:

1. The default constructor

   ```
   X::X()
   ```

   is invoked before Y's constructor to initialize the member class object x.

   The assignment of x with 0 cannot be carried out directly since the class X does not define an assignment operator accepting an argument of type int. The assignment is carried out in two steps:

2. The constructor

   ```
   X::X( int )
   ```

   is invoked to convert the integer 0 into an object of type X. (The use of constructors in type conversion is discussed in Section 6.5 (page 286) later in this chapter.)

3. This newly created class X object is assigned to x by invoking

   ```
   X::operator=( const X& )
   ```

   The second and third invocations are unnecessary, and they are not invoked when the constructor for Y properly initializes its class member x, as follows:

   ```
   Y::Y() : x( 0 ) {}
   ```

Now, only

```
X::X( int )
```

is invoked with each invocation of the constructor for the Y class.

Operator ->

The member selection operator ("->") is handled as a unary operator of its left operand, which must be either a class object or a reference to a class object. The return value of the operator function must either be a pointer to a class object or a class object for which operator -> is defined. In the following example, an operator instance is declared that returns a `String*`.

```
#include "String.h"

class Xample {
public:
    String *operator->();
    // ...
private:
    String *ps;
    // ...
};
```

Here is a skeletal implementation of the operator. It returns the member ps after doing some processing of the object to which it points.

```
String* Xample::operator->() {
    if ( ps == 0 )
        // ... initialize ps
    // ... process ps
    return ps;
}
```

The member selection operator can be invoked for either a class object or a reference to an Xample class object. For example,

```
void ff( Xample x, Xample &xr, Xample *xp )
{
    int i;

    // invoke String::getLen()
    i = x->getLen();   // ok: x.ps->getLen()
    i = xr->getLen();  // ok: xr.ps->getLen()
    i = xp->getLen();  // error: no Xample::getLen()
}
```

The member selection operator cannot be invoked through an Xample pointer since there is no way for the compiler to distinguish between the predefined and overloaded instance.

Overloaded Operator Function Design

The only predefined operators for a class are the assignment ("=") and address of operators ("&"). For any other operator to have meaning when applied to a class object, the designer of the class must explicitly define it. The choice of which operators to provide is determined by the expected uses of the class.

Always begin by defining the public interface of the class. Which operations must the class provide for its users? These will be the minimum set of public member functions. Once this set is defined, it is possible to consider which operators the class type should provide.

Each operator has an associated meaning from its predefined use. Binary +, for example, is strongly identified with addition. Mapping + to an analogous operation within a class type can provide a convenient notational shorthand. For example, String concatenation, which adds one String to another, is an appropriate extension of +.

Once the public interface of the class is defined, look for a logical mapping between the operation and an operator. isEmpty() becomes the logical NOT operator, operator!(); isEqual() becomes the equality operator, operator==(); copy() becomes the assignment operator, operator=(); and so on.

Operator equivalency for overloaded operators must also be explicitly defined for a class. String operators, for example, support concatenation and memberwise copy:

```
String s1( "C" );
String s2( "++" );

s1 = s1 + s2; // s1 <== "C++"
```

These operators, however, do *not* support the equivalent compound assignment operator:

```
s1 += s2;
```

That operator must also be explicitly defined and provided with an equivalent semantics.

Exercise 6-15. Identify which member functions of the Screen class implemented in Chapter 5 are candidates for operator overloading.

☐

Exercise 6-16. Implement the Screen class overloaded operator functions identified in the previous exercise.

☐

Exercise 6-17. Section 4.2 (page 141) presents the integer list class, IntList. Identify and implement the overloaded operator functions for this class.

□

A binary tree class must provide the following general functionality: `isEmpty()`, `isEqual()`, `print()`, `addNode()`, `build()`. `copy()`, and `deleteNode()`,

Exercise 6-18. Which of these member functions are candidates for overloading? Which of these member functions are candidates for operator overloading? □

Exercise 6-19. Implement the binary tree member functions listed in the above paragraph. □

Exercise 6-20. INodes are generated quite frequently while managing a BinTree. Using operators `new` and `delete`, take over the memory management of INodes. □

6.4   A BitVector Class Example

In Section 2.8 (page 76) bit vectors were shown to be a useful method of encoding yes/no information. In the previous sections, the String class is used to introduce the concepts of operator overloading. In this section, we consider the implementation of a bit vector class, with particular emphasis on the design choices of overloaded operator functions. We shall name our class BitVector.

The internal representation of the BitVector class is defined as follows:

```
typedef unsigned int BitVecType;
typedef BitVecType *BitVec;

class BitVector {
private:
    BitVec bv;
    unsigned short size;
    short wordWidth;
};
```

`size` contains the number of bits the BitVector class object represents. `bv` points to the actual bit vector, stored as a contiguous sequence of one or more unsigned integers. `wordWidth` holds the number of unsigned integers pointed to by `bv`. For example, if an unsigned integer is 32 bits, a BitVector of 16 bits initializes its members with the following values:

```
// number of bits in bit vector
size = 16;

// number of unsigned ints to hold bit vector
wordWidth = 1;
```

A BitVector of 107 bits, however, cannot represent its bit vector with less than four unsigned integers. Its members are initialized with the following values:

```
size = 107;
wordWidth = 4;
```

In both cases, bv is initialized to an array of BitVecType of size wordWidth. For example,

```
bv = new BitVecType[ wordWidth ];
```

The bit and byte sizes of data types are guaranteed to vary among different machines, and so we want to localize the explicit references to these machine-dependent values in our code:

```
#ifdef vax
const BITSPERBYTE = 8;
const BYTESPERWORD = 4;
#endif

#ifdef sun
const BITSPERBYTE = 8;
const BYTESPERWORD = 2;
#endif

// The size of a machine integer
const WORDSIZE = BITSPERBYTE * BYTESPERWORD;
```

A user should have the option of selecting the bit vector's size but should not be required to indicate a size. The most logical default value for a bit vector is the size in bits of a single unsigned integer, the smallest unit that can be pointed to by bv. Here is the constructor for our BitVector class:

```
enum { OFF, ON };

// default values: sz => WORDSIZE, init => OFF
BitVector::BitVector( int sz, int init )
{
    size = sz;
    wordWidth = (size + WORDSIZE - 1)/WORDSIZE;
    bv = new BitVecType[ wordWidth ];

    // now initialize bv to either all 0's or 1's
    if ( init != OFF ) init = ~0;

    // assign 0 or -1 to each word of bv
    for ( int i = 0; i < wordWidth; i++ )
        *(bv + i) = init;
}
```

Users must be able to set() and unset() individual bits. These are binary operations, requiring a BitVector class object and an integer value representing the bit to be modified. A number of possible operators come to mind. For example, to set a single bit, the user might specify one of the following:

```
BitVector bvec;

// possible operators for set()
bvec | 12;
bvec |= 12;
bvec + 12;
bvec += 12;
```

Setting a bit to one is more similar to an addition operation than a bitwise OR operation. How do we choose, however, between the operators "+" and "+="? Or should we implement both? Let's consider what the operation actually does.

As a nonoperator set() function, the invocation looks as follows:

```
bvec.set(12);
```

bvec, that is, is modified by having its 12th bit set to 1. This means that the left operand of the expression stores the result of the expression. This is not the normal behavior of the "+" operator, but it does reflect the behavior of the "+=" operator. This is our choice of an operator. Here is our implementation:

```
void BitVector::operator+=( int pos )
{ // turn on bit at position pos

    checkBounds( pos );

    int index = getIndex( pos );
    int offset = getOffset( pos );

    // turn on bit offset at word index
    *(bv + index) |= (ON << offset);
}
```

getIndex() and getOffSet() are both private helping functions. getIndex() returns an index indicating which unsigned integer contains the bit. For example, bit 16 returns an index of 0; bit 33 returns an index of 1; and bit 107 returns an index of 3. Here is the implementation:

```
inline BitVector::getIndex( int pos )
{
    // return word bit is positioned in
    return( pos / WORDSIZE );
}
```

getOffSet() returns the position of the bit in the unsigned integer which contains it. For example, bit 16 returns an offset of 16; bit 33 returns an offset of 1; and bit 107 returns an offset of 11. Here is the implementation:

```
inline BitVector::getOffset( int pos )
{
    // return position of bit in word
    return( pos % WORDSIZE );
}
```

The implementation of BitVector::operator-=(int) is the same as that of the addition operator except for the bitwise operation to turn off the bit:

```
// turn off the bit
// in word index at position offset
*(bv + index) &= (~(ON<<offset));
```

The user should not be permitted to overstep the BitVector bounds. For example, the following assignment should be caught:

```
BitVector bvec( 16 );
bvec += 18; // error: out of bounds
```

Here is a possible implementation:

```
void BitVector::checkBounds( int index )
{
    // make sure index is within bounds of BitVector
    if ( index < 0 || index >= size )
    {
        cerr << "\nBitVector Index Out of Bounds: "
             << "<< " << index
             << ", size: " << size << " >>\n";
        exit( -1 ); // stdlib.h
    }
}
```

Users of a BitVector need to be able to test an individual bit. `isOn()` and `isOff()` are each binary operations with a left operand of a BitVector class object and an integer right operand representing an individual bit. We have chosen to represent these functions with the equality ("==") and inequality ("!=") operators.

For example, the user code to test whether bit 17 is set might look as follows:

```
BitVector bvec;

if (bvec == 17 )
    // ...
```

Here are the implementations:

```
BitVector::operator == ( int pos )
{
    // true if bit at position pos is 1
    checkBounds( pos );

    int index = getIndex( pos );
    int offset = getOffset( pos );

    return( *(bv + index) & (ON << offset) );
}

BitVector::operator != ( int pos )
{ // return the negation of operator==()
    return ( !(*this == pos) );
}
```

The user of a BitVector must be able to display class objects as well as to intermix the display of a BitVector object freely with the display of built-in data types. This is done by overloading the output operator ("<<") and making its return value of type `ostream&`. The BitVector user will then be able to write the following:

```
cout << "my BitVector: " << bv << "\n";
```

Were bits 7, 12, 19, 27, and 34 set, the output of bv would look as follows:

```
< 7 12 19 27 34 >
```

Were none of bv's bits set, it would look as follows:

```
< (none) >
```

The operator function can be defined like this:

```
ostream& operator<<(ostream& os, BitVector& bv)
{
    int lineSize = 12;
    os << "\n\t< ";

    for ( int cnt = 0, i = 0; i < bv.size; ++i ) {
        // BitVector::operator==(int)
        if ( bv == i ) {
            // worry about line format of output
            int lineCnt = cnt++ % lineSize;
            if ( lineCnt == 0 && cnt != 1 )
                os << "\n\t   ";
            os << i << " ";
        }
    }

    if ( cnt == 0 ) os << "(none) ";
    os << ">\n";
    return os;
}
```

An operation should sometimes not be translated into an operator function. Here is an example.

In order to reuse a BitVector object, the programmer must be able to reset() all its elements to 0. reset() could be implemented as a unary operation applied to a BitVector class object. It is represented by the logical NOT operator ("!"):

```
BitVector& BitVector::operator!()
{ // reinitialize all elements to 0
    for ( int i = 0; i < wordWidth; ++i )
        *( bv + i ) = 0;
    return *this;
}
```

This implementation of the logical NOT operator is counterintuitive and likely to be misused by the programmer. Here's why.

- In its predefined role, it returns a true value if its operand evaluates to 0. It does not modify its operand.

- In its BitVector implementation, it returns a reference to its operand. It resets all the bit elements of its operand to 0.

Here is a likely programmer error. In this example, testResults() returns a BitVector in which each bit represents the outcome of a test case. Each bit set to 1 represents the outcome of a test case. The programmer has confused the use of the BitVector logical NOT with its predefined use:

```
if ( !( bvec = testResults() ))
    cout << "All Tests passed!\n";
else
    reportFailures( bvec );
// ...
```

In our implementation, reset() is left as a named member function.

BitVectors are commonly used in compiler optimizers to aid in what is referred to as program data flow analysis. Two operations frequently performed are the bitwise ANDing and ORing of two bit vectors; both are essential to a BitVector class.

The operators & and | are used to represent these operations. For simplicity, the implementations presented assume that both BitVector objects are the same size.

```
#include "BitVector.h"

BitVector BitVector::operator | (BitVector& b)
{ // simplifying assumption: both have same size

    BitVector result( size, OFF );
    BitVec tmp = result.bv;

    for ( int i = 0; i < wordWidth; ++i )
        *(tmp + i) = *(bv + i) | *(b.bv + i);

    return result;
}
```

Notice that the operator & implementation is the same as that of the operator | except for the bit operation to perform the ANDing:

```
*(tmp + i ) = *( bv + i ) & *(b.bv + i );
```

Fig. 6.2 presents a small interactive program that uses a BitVector object to keep track of type attributes. For example, entering

```
unsigned const char * ;
```

will set four bits of the BitVector object `typeFlag`. To simplify the presentation of the program, strings rather than individual characters are read, requiring the user to enter each attribute and terminating semicolon separated by a space.

When compiled and executed, the program of Fig. 6.2 generates the following output:

```
Type in a declaration -- end with ';'
preceded by white space.  For example, try
      'unsigned const char * ;'
Hit ctrl-d to exit program

unsigned const char * ;

flags set for declaration are:
      unsigned
      const
      *
      char
```

Fig. 6.3 presents the `BitVector.h` header file for the BitVector class as implemented in this section.

Exercise 6-21. Modify the program listed in Fig. 6.2 to handle input of the following form:

```
const char * const ;
```

☐

Exercise 6-22. Add the `X(const X&)` and `operator=(const X&)` instances for the BitVector class.

☐

Exercise 6-23. Define an equality operator for two BitVector objects.

☐

Exercise 6-24. Modify the AND operator function to handle BitVectors of different sizes.

☐

Exercise 6-25. Modify the OR operator function to handle BitVectors of different sizes.

☐

```
#include <string.h>
#include "BitVector.h"

const int MAXBITS = 8;

enum { ERROR, CHAR, SHORT, INT, PTR,
       REFERENCE, CONST, UNSIGNED };

static char *typeTbl[] = {
    "OOPS, no type at slot 0",
    "char", "short", "int",
    "*", "&", "const", "unsigned" };

static char *msg =
"Type in a declaration -- end with ';' \
\npreceded by white space.  For example, \
try\n\t'unsigned const char * ;' \
\nHit ctrl-d to exit program\n";

main() {
    BitVector typeFlags( MAXBITS );
    char buf[ 1024 ];

    cout << msg;
    while ( cin >> buf ) {
        for ( int i = 0; i < MAXBITS; i++ )
            if (strcmp( typeTbl[i], buf ) == 0)
            { // a keyword?  BitVector::operator+=
                typeFlags += i; break;
            }

        if ( buf[0] == ';' ) { // end of entry
            cout << "\nflags set for declaration are:\n\t";

            for ( i = MAXBITS-1; i > 0; i -- )
                // BitVector::operator==
                if ( typeFlags == i )
                    cout << typeTbl[i] << "\n\t";
            cout << "\n";

            // reinitialize: BitVector::reset()
            typeFlags.reset();
        }
    }
}
```

Figure 6.2 Program Example Using BitVectors

```
#ifndef BITVECTOR_H
#define BITVECTOR_H

#ifdef vax
const BITSPERBYTE = 8;
const BYTESPERWORD = 4;
#endif

#ifdef sun
const BITSPERBYTE = 8;
const BYTESPERWORD = 2;
#endif

const WORDSIZE = BITSPERBYTE * BYTESPERWORD;
enum { OFF, ON };
typedef unsigned int BitVecType;
typedef BitVecType *BitVec;

#include <iostream.h>
class BitVector {
    friend ostream&
        operator<<(ostream&, BitVector&);
public:
    BitVector( int = WORDSIZE, int = OFF );
    ~BitVector() { delete [wordWidth] bv; }
    void operator+=( int pos ); // turn on pos
    void operator-=( int pos ); // turn off pos
    BitVector operator &( BitVector& );
    BitVector operator |( BitVector& );
    operator == ( int pos ); // pos is on
    operator != ( int pos ); // pos is off
    void reset(); // reinit to 0
private: // helping functions
    void checkBounds( int );
    inline getOffset( int );
    inline getIndex( int );
private: // internal representation
    short wordWidth;
    short size;
    BitVec bv;
};
#endif
```

Figure 6.3 BitVector.h

Exercise 6-26. Modify the BitVector output operator instance to condense multiple conscutive bits. For example, it currently prints out

```
< 0, 1, 2, 3, 4, 5, 6, 7 >
< 0, 2, 3, 4, 7, 8, 9, 12 >
```

Reimplement the output operator to group consecutive values as a hyphen-separated pair. For example,

```
< 0 - 7 >
< 0, 2 - 4, 7 - 9, 12 >
```

□

6.5   User-Defined Conversions

The predefined standard conversions for the built-in data types prevent a combinatorial explosion of operators and overloaded functions. For example, without arithmetic conversions, the following six addition operations each require a unique implementation:

```
char ch; short sh; int ival;

// without type conversion, each addition
// would require a unique operation
ch + ival;      ival + ch;
ch + sh;        sh + ch;
ival + sh;      sh + ival;
```

With arithmetic conversions, each operand is promoted to type int. Only one operation is necessary — the addition of two integer values. These conversions are handled implicitly by the compiler and are therefore transparent to the user.

In this section, we consider how the designer of a class can provide a set of user-defined conversions for that class. These conversions are implicitly invoked by the compiler when necessary. To illustrate our discussion, a SmallInt class is implemented.

A SmallInt class can hold the same range of values as an 8-bit unsigned char — that is, 0 – 255. Its additional functionality is that it catches under- and overflow errors. Other than that, we wish for it to behave in the same way as an unsigned char.

For example, we would like to add and subtract SmallInt objects both with other SmallInt objects and from the built-in arithmetic types. To support these operations, we must implement *six* SmallInt operator functions:

```
class SmallInt {
    friend operator+( SmallInt&, int );
    friend operator-( SmallInt&, int );
    friend operator-( int, SmallInt& );
    friend operator+( int, SmallInt& );
public:
    operator+( SmallInt& );
    operator-( SmallInt& );
    // ...
};
```

Only six operators are required because any built-in arithmetic type will be converted to match the operand of type int. For example, the expression

```
SmallInt si( 3 );
```

```
si + 3.14159
```

is resolved in two steps:

1. The double literal constant 3.14159 is converted to the integer value 3.

2. operator+(si,3) is invoked and returns a value of 6.

If we should wish to support the bitwise, logical, relational and compound assignment operators as well, the number of required operators becomes — well, daunting. What we would prefer instead is a way to convert a SmallInt class object into an int.

C++ provides a mechanism by which each class can define a set of conversions that can be applied to objects of its class. For SmallInt, we shall define a conversion of a SmallInt object to that of type int. Here is the implementation:

```
class SmallInt {
public:
    // conversion operator: SmallInt ==> int
    operator int() { return value; }
    // ...
private:
    int value;
};
```

User-defined conversions for a class type provide a set of conversion rules for a class. They define the allowable conversions that can be performed on individual class objects. In addition, they define for the compiler what the conversion means.

A SmallInt class object can now be used anywhere an int object can be used. For example, the expression

```
SmallInt si( 3 );

si + 3.14159;
```

is now resolved in the following two steps:

1. The SmallInt conversion operator is invoked, yielding the integer value 3.

2. The integer value 3 is promoted to 3.0 and added to the double literal constant 3.14159, yielding the double value 6.14159.

The following program illustrates the use of the SmallInt class:

```
#include <stream.h>
#include "SmallInt.h"
SmallInt si1, si2;

main() {
    cout << "enter a SmallInt, please:   ";
    while ( cin >> si1 )
    {
        cout << "\n\nThank you.\n";
        cout << "The value read is "
            << si1 << "\nIt is ";

        // SmallInt::operator int() invoked twice
        cout << (( si1 > 127 )
            ? "greater than "
            : (( si1 < 127 )
                ? "less than "
                : "equal to ")) << "127\n";

        cout << "\nenter a SmallInt, please \
(ctrl-d to exit):   ";
    }
    cout << "bye now\n";
}
```

When compiled and executed, the program generates the following results:

```
enter a SmallInt, please:   127

Thank you.
The value read is 127
It is equal to 127
```

```
enter a SmallInt, please (ctrl-d to exit):   126

Thank you.
The value read is 126
It is less than 127


enter a SmallInt, please (ctrl-d to exit):   128

Thank you.
The value read is 128
It is greater than 127


enter a SmallInt, please (ctrl-d to exit):   256
***SmallInt range error: 256 ***
```

The code implementing the SmallInt class looks as follows:

```
#include <stream.h>

class SmallInt {
    friend istream&
        operator>>(istream& is, SmallInt& s);
    friend ostream&
        operator<<(ostream& os, SmallInt& s)
        { return ( os << s.value ); }
public:
    SmallInt(int i=0) : value( rangeCheck(i) ){}
    int operator=(int i)
        { return( value = rangeCheck(i) ); }
    operator int() { return value; }
private:
    enum { ERRANGE = -1 };
    int rangeCheck( int );
    int error( int );
    int value;
};
```

The member functions defined outside the class body look as follows:

```
istream& operator>>( istream& is, SmallInt& si )
{
    int i;

    is >> i;
    si = i; // SmallInt::operator=(int)
    return is;
}
```

```
SmallInt::error( int i )
{
    cerr << "\n***SmallInt range error: "
        << i << " ***\n";
    return ERRANGE;
}

SmallInt::rangeCheck( int i )
{
// if any bits are set other than the first 8
// value is too large: report, then exit

    if ( i & ~0377 )
        exit( error( i ) ); // stdlib.h
    return i;
}
```

Exercise 6-27. Why is the overloaded input operator not implemented in the following manner?

```
istream& operator>>( istream& is, SmallInt& si )
{
    return ( is >> si.value );
}
```

□

A Constructor as a Conversion Operator

The collection of single-argument constructors for a class, such as SmallInt, defines the set of implicit conversions of non-SmallInt types into objects of type SmallInt. Standard conversions, if necessary, are applied to the types before the invocation of the constructor.

A constructor that takes a single argument, such as SmallInt(int), serves as a conversion operator between that argument type and the class. SmallInt(int), for example, converts integer values into SmallInt objects.

```
extern f( SmallInt );
int i;

// need to convert i into a SmallInt
// SmallInt(int) accomplishes this
f( i );
```

In the call f(i), i is convered into a SmallInt object by invoking

`SmallInt(int)`. A temporary SmallInt object is constructed by the compiler and passed to `f()`.

```
// a temporary SmallInt Object is created
{
    SmallInt temp = SmallInt(i);
    f(temp);
}
```

The braces in the example indicate the lifetime of the generated SmallInt temporary.

If necessary, a standard conversion is applied before the invocation of `SmallInt(int)`. For example,

```
double d;
f( d );
```

becomes

```
{
    // warning: narrowing conversion
    SmallInt temp = SmallInt( (int)d );
    f(temp);
}
```

The invocation of a conversion operator is applied only if no other conversion is possible. Were `f()` overloaded as follows, for example, `SmallInt(int)` would *not* be invoked.

```
f( SmallInt );
f( double );
int ival;

// matches f(double) by standard conversion
f( ival );
```

The argument may also be another user-defined class type. For example,

```
class Token {
public:
    // ... public members
private:
    SmallInt tok;
    // ... rest of Token members
};
```

```
// create a SmallInt object from a Token
SmallInt::SmallInt( Token& t ) { /* ... */ }

extern f( SmallInt& );
Token curTok;

main()
{ // invoke SmallInt( Token& )
    f( curTok );
}
```

Conversion Operators

A conversion operator, a special instance of a class member function, specifies an implicit conversion of a class object into some other type. SmallInt,
for example, might define the conversion of a SmallInt object into a value
of type unsigned int:

```
SmallInt::operator unsigned int()
{
    return( (unsigned)value );
}
```

A Token class, defined next, may choose to define multiple conversion
operators:

```
#include "SmallInt.h"

class Token {
public:
    Token( char *nm, int vl )
        : val( vl ), name( nm ) {}
    operator SmallInt() { return val; }
    operator char*() { return name; }
    operator int() { return val; }
    // ... rest of public members
private:
    SmallInt val;
    char *name;
};
```

Notice that the Token conversion operators for SmallInt and int are
the same. SmallInt::operator int() is implicitly applied to the
SmallInt object val in Token::operator int(). For example,

```
#include "Token.h"

void f( int i )
{
    cout << "\nf(int) : " << i;
}

Token t1( "integer constant", 127 );

main() {
Token t2( "friend", 255 );

    f( t1 ); // t1.operator int()
    f( t2 ); // t2.operator int()
}
```

When compiled and executed, this small program generates the following output:

```
f(int) : 127
f(int) : 255
```

A conversion operator takes the general form

```
operator <type> ();
```

where <type> is replaced by a specific built-in, derived, or class data type. (Conversion operators for either an array or a function are not allowed.) The conversion operator must be a member function. It must not specify a return type nor can an argument list be specified. Each of the following declarations, for example, are illegal:

```
operator int( SmallInt& ); // error: nonmember

class SmallInt {
public:
    int operator int();  // error: return type
    operator int( int ); // error: argument list
    ...
};
```

The programmer may explicitly invoke a conversion operator by using either form of cast notation. For example,

```
#include "Token.h"
Token tok( "function", 78 );

// function cast notation: operator SmallInt()
SmallInt tokVal = SmallInt( tok );

// type cast notation: operator char*()
char *tokString = (char *)tok;
```

If a class object is present and is not of the appropriate type, a conversion operator, if defined, will be applied implicitly by the compiler. For example,

```
#include "Token.h"
extern void f( char * );
Token tok( "enumeration", 8 );
enum { ENUM }; // token constant

main() {
    f( tok ); // tok.operator char*();

    // explicit functional cast notation
    switch ( int(tok) ) // tok.operator int()
    {
        case ENUM:
        {   // tok.operator SmallInt();
            SmallInt si = tok;
            // ...
        }
    }
}
```

Suppose that the required type does not match any of the conversion operator types exactly. Will a conversion operator still be invoked?

- Yes, if the required type can be reached through a standard conversion. For example,

```
extern void f( double );
Token tok( "constant", 44 );

// tok.operator int() invoked
// int ==> double by standard conversion
f( tok );
```

- No, if to reach the required type a second user-defined conversion operator must be applied to the result of the first user-defined conversion operator. (This is why Token defines both operator SmallInt() and operator int().)

For example, if Token did *not* provide an `operator int()` instance, the following call would be illegal:

```
extern void f(int);
Token tok( "pointer", 37 );

// without Token::operator int() defined,
// this call will generate a compile-time error
f( tok );
```

Without `Token::operator int()` defined, the conversion of `tok` to type `int` would require the invocation of two user-defined conversion operators.

```
Token::operator SmallInt();
```

would convert `tok` into a SmallInt object.

```
SmallInt::operator int();
```

would complete the conversion to type `int`.

The rule, however, is that only one level of user-defined conversions can be applied. If `Token::operator int()` is not defined, the call `f(tok)`, requiring an argument of type `int`, is flagged at compile time as a type violation.

Ambiguity

Ambiguity may arise in connection with the implicit invocation of conversion operators. For example,

```
extern void f( int );
extern void f( SmallInt );
Token tok( "string constant", 3 );

f( tok ); // error: ambiguous
```

Token defines a conversion operator for both SmallInt and `int`: both conversions are equally possible. The call `f(tok)` is ambiguous since there is no way for the compiler to choose between the two conversions, and the call is flagged at compile time as an error. The programmer can resolve the ambiguity by making the conversion explicit:

```
// explicit conversion resolves ambiguity
f( int(tok) );
```

Were `Token::operator int()` not defined, the call would not be ambiguous. It would resolve to `Token::operator SmallInt()`. The fact that SmallInt defines an int conversion operator is not considered. In determining the permissible conversions of an object, only the first level of user-defined conversion operators is examined.

If two conversion operators are possible, but one is an exact match while the other also requires a standard conversion, there is no ambiguity — the conversion operator that effects an exact match is chosen. For example,

```
class Token {
public:
    operator float();
    operator int();
    ...
};


Token tok;
float ff = tok; // ok: operator float()
```

However, if both conversion operators are equally applicable, the statement is flagged as ambiguous:

```
// errror: both operators float() and int()
long lval = tok;
```

Ambiguity can also occur when two classes define conversions between themselves. For example,

```
SmallInt::SmallInt( Token& );
Token::operator SmallInt();

extern void f( SmallInt );
Token tok( "pointer to class member", 197 );

// error: two possible user-defined conversions
f( tok );
```

In this case, there are two equally possible ways to convert tok into a SmallInt object. The call is ambiguous since there is no way for the compiler to choose between the two; the call is flagged at compile time as an error. The programmer can resolve the ambiguity by making the conversion explicit. For example,

```
// explicit conversion resolves ambiguity
// Token::operator SmallInt() invoked
f( (SmallInt)tok );
```

The programmer can also resolve the ambiguity by explicitly invoking the Token class conversion operator:

```
// explicit conversion resolves ambiguity
f( tok.operator SmallInt() );
```

Notice that the explicit cast in functional notation is still ambiguous.

```
// error: still ambiguous
f( SmallInt(tok) );
```

`SmallInt(Token&)` and `Token::operator SmallInt()` are equally possible interpretations of the call.

A second form of ambiguity relates to the human reader of a program making use of conversion operators. When a SmallInt object is converted to an `int` value, the meaning of that conversion is clear. When a String object is converted to a type `char*`, the meaning of that conversion is also clear. In both cases, there is a one-to-one mapping between a built-in data type and the internal representation of a class type. When there is no logical mapping between a conversion operator and the class type, however, the use of objects of that class may become ambiguous to the reader of the program. For example,

```
class Date {
public:
    // guess which member is returned!
    operator int();
private:
    int month, day, year;
};
```

What value should be returned by the `int` conversion operator of Date? Whatever choice is made for whatever good reason, the use of Date objects will be ambiguous to a reader of the program because there is no logical one-to-one mapping. In this case, it would be better *not* to define a conversion operator.

Exercise 6-28. What are the conversion operators necessary to support the following uses of a String class object?

```
extern int strlen( const char* );
const maxLen = 32;

String st = "a string";
int len = strlen( st );
if ( st >= maxLen ) ...
String st2 = maxLen;
```

□

Exercise 6-29. Discuss the benefits and drawbacks of supporting the conversion operation represented by

```
if ( st >= maxLen ) ...
```

□

Exercise 6-30. An interesting conversion operator for BinTree would return an IntArray class object of the Inode values (Section 1.8 (page 51) contains the definition of the IntArray class). Implement the following two conversion operations:

```
BinTree::BinTree( IntArray& );
BinTree::operator IntArray();
```

□

Note that the order of tree traversal must be the same in both operations. A preorder traversal of the following general form might be used:

```
BinTree::preOrder( /* ??? */ )
{
    if ( !node ) return;
    node->visit( /* ??? */ ); // do work
    if ( left ) left->preOrder( /* ??? */ );
    if ( right ) right->preOrder( /* ??? */ );
```

Exercise 6-31. The previous exercise provides for the handling of an expression involving objects of both the IntArray and BinTree classes. For example,

```
extern BinTree bt;
extern IntArray ia;

if ( ia == bt ) ...
```

The order of operations is as follows: The BinTree conversion operator is first invoked to convert bt into an IntArray class object. Then the IntArray equality operator is invoked to compare two IntArray class objects. What would happen, however, if the IntArray class defines the following two conversion operations?

```
IntArray::IntArray( BinTree& );
IntArray::operator BinTree();
```

□

Chapter 7: **Class Derivation**

Object-oriented programming extends abstract data types to allow for type/subtype relationships. This is achieved through a mechanism referred to as *inheritance*. Rather than reimplementing shared characteristics, a class can inherit selected data members and member functions of other classes. In C++, inheritance is implemented through the mechanism of *class derivation*, the topic of this and the next chapter.

In this section we answer the following questions: Why are type/subtype relationships important? What kinds of design problems led programmers to extend abstract data types? What is really meant by the terms inheritance and object-oriented programming? By way of illustration, let's return to the Screen class defined in Chapter 5.

Our Screen class represents an old technology. The newer generation of workstations and terminals supports the concept of windowing. A window serves as a screen, but with additional capabilities:

- A window can be made larger or smaller.

- A window can be moved from one position to another.

- Multiple windows can be defined on a single screen.

The author's terminal, for example, supports up to seven windows. In one, this chapter of the book can be written. In a second window, program examples can be implemented and edited. These programs can be compiled and executed in a third window. In a fourth window, electronic mail can be read. In short, each window can be used simultaneously in the same manner that a single screen was used on an older terminal.

A window must know not only its size, but also its position on the workstation screen. The window requires coordinates to locate itself, as well as member functions to resize and move itself. It will also need the same data members as defined for the Screen class. Some of the Screen member functions can be reused directly; others require reimplementation.

A window is a kind of specialized Screen. It is more an extended subtype of Screen than it is an independent abstract data type. On a conceptual level, Window and Screen represent two elements of a terminal display class. On an implementation level, they share data members and member functions.

Abstract data types cannot model this kind of type/subtype relationship. The closest representation would be to make Screen a member class of Window:

```
class Window {
public:
        // ... member functions go here
private:
        Screen base;
        // ... data members go here
};
```

One problem with this representation is that the Screen data members are private and therefore not directly accessible to Window. If the source for Screen is available, Window can be made a friend to Screen.

For programmers to use the Screen members directly, base must be a public member of Window:

```
Window w;
w.base.clear();
```

This violates information hiding. The programmer must know of the implementation of Window as well as which of the Screen member functions are active within the Window class and which have been redefined (since the calling syntax in the two cases is different). home(), for example, would be redefined in the Window class. The following two calls invoke different functions:

```
w.home();
w.base.home();
```

This design is too prone to programmer error.

To enforce information hiding and to maintain a uniform syntax, Window must define an interface function for each active Screen member function. For example, for the programmer to write

```
w.clear();
```

the class designer must define

```
inline void Window::clear() { base.clear(); }
```

This is tedious but feasible.

If a Window is extended further, however, the complexity of the implementation becomes a serious constraint on the design. For example, a Menu is a kind of Window. It will have its own data members and member functions. A menu will also share a subset of Window's members, and possibly a different subset of Screen's members than those used by Window. A better solution is needed — that of inheritance.

7.1 Object-Oriented Programming

Class inheritance allows the members of one class to be used as if they were members of a second class. Were Window to inherit the members from Screen, for example, all the operations a user could perform on a Screen class object could also be performed on a Window class object. No additional programming is required to implement Window except for those operations that either extend or replace the members inherited from the Screen class.

Inheritance is the primary characteristic of object-oriented programming. In C++, it is supported by the mechanism of *class derivation*. The derivation of Window from the Screen class allows Window to inherit the Screen class members. Window can access the nonprivate members of Screen as if they had been declared members of Window. For example,

```
Window w;
w.clear().home();
```

In order to derive a class, the following two extensions to the class syntax are necessary:

1. The class head is modified to allow a *derivation list* of classes from which to inherit members. The class head of the Window class looks as follows:

   ```
   class Window : public Screen { ... }
   ```

   The colon following Window indicates that Window is being derived from one or more previously defined classes. The keyword `public` indicates that Window is to be a publicly derived class. Derivations can be either public or private — the specification affects the visibility of the inherited members within the derived class. The class name Screen indicates the object of the derivation, referred to as a *base* class. We say that Screen is a public base class of Window.

2. An additional access level, that of `protected`, is provided. A `protected` class member behaves as a public class member to a derived class; to the rest of the program, the protected class member is private. The members of Screen must be changed from private to protected in order to allow the member functions and friends of Window to access them.

A derived class can itself be an object of derivation. Menu, for example, can be derived from Window:

```
class Menu : public Window { ... };
```

Menu, in turn, inherits members from both Window *and* Screen. The additional programming required is only for those operations that either extend or replace the inherited members. The syntax remains uniform:

```
Menu m;
m.display();
```

The special relationship between base and derived classes is recognized by a set of predefined standard conversions. A derived class can be assigned to any of its public base classes without requiring an explicit cast. For example,

```
Menu m;
Window &w = m;    // ok
Screen *ps = &w;  // ok
```

This special relationship between inherited class types promotes a "generic" style of programming in which the actual type of a class is unknown. The following declaration of dumpImage() is an example:

```
extern void dumpImage( Screen *s );
```

dumpImage() can be invoked with an argument of any class type for which Screen serves as a public base class, however far removed it occurs in the chain of class derivations. An attempt to pass it an argument of an unrelated class type, however, results in a compile-time error. For example,

```
Screen s;
Window w;
Menu m;
BitVector bv;

// ok: Window is a kind of Screen
dumpImage( &w );

// ok: Menu is a kind of Screen
dumpImage( &m );·

// ok: argument types match exactly
dumpImage( &s );

// error:  BitVector has no relationship with Screen
dumpImage( &bv );
```

Screen, Window, and Menu each provide an instance of the dumpImage() member function. The purpose of the nonmember dumpImage() function is to take an argument of any of these three class types and invoke the appropriate function. In a nonobject-oriented implementation, the main effort of this general `dumpImage()` function is to determine the actual data type of its argument. For example,

```
#include "Screen.h"
extern void error( const char*, ... );

enum { SCREEN, WINDOW, MENU };
// nonobject-oriented code
void dumpImage( Screen *s )
{
    // figure out the actual type of s
    switch( s->typeOf() )
    {
        case SCREEN:
            s->dumpImage();
            break;

        case WINDOW:
            ((Window*)s)->dumpImage();
            break;

        case MENU:
            ((Menu*)s)->dumpImage();
            break;

        default:
            error( "unknown type", s->typeOf() );
            break;
    }
}
```

The burden of type resolution, in this case, rests with the programmer. The second primary characteristic of object-oriented programming shifts the burden of type resolution from the programmer to the compiler. This characteristic is referred to as *dynamic binding*. Under dynamic binding, the implementation of `dumpImage()` is considerably simplified:

```
void dumpImage( Screen *s )
{
    s->dumpImage();
}
```

With each invocation of `dumpImage()`, the correct `dumpImage()` member function is invoked automatically. Not only does this reduce the complexity and size of the code; it also makes for *extensible* code: A subsequent derivation — Border, for example — can be added to a program without the need to change any existing code. A call of `dumpImage()`

with a Border class type is handled without problem once the code has been recompiled. In C++, dynamic binding is supported by the mechanism of *virtual member functions*. A member function is made virtual by preceding its declaration in the class body with the keyword `virtual`. For example,

```
class Screen {
public:
    virtual void dumpImage();
    // ...
};
```

A function is declared to be virtual under the following two conditions:

1. A class expects to be an object of derivation.

2. The implementation of the function is type-dependent.

Each member instance of `dumpImage()`, for example, is dependent on the representation of its class type — its implementation will differ for a Screen, Window, and Menu. The designer of the Screen class indicates this type implementation dependency by declaring `dumpImage()` to be a virtual member function.

The type/subtype relationship between a base and derived class is referred to as a *derivation* or *inheritance hierarchy*. A derivation from multiple base classes is referred to as a *derivation* or *inheritance graph*.

Object-oriented programming is built on the extended concept of an abstract data type that supports the definition of an inheritance hierarchy. `Simula` was the first programming language to recognize the need for and to provide the class mechanism for this extended abstract data type. The `Smalltalk` language originated the term "object-oriented," which is used to emphasize the encapsulated nature of the user-defined class type. In Smalltalk, object-oriented programming transforms information hiding from a design methodology into a model of the program world.

7.2   A Sorted Array Class

An array that is intended primarily for lookup is best stored in sorted order. The worst-case search time for a value in an unsorted array requires that the entire array be examined. On average, the search requires that half the elements be examined. When the number of elements in an array is large, this can be quite expensive. A better search time can be gained by using a binary search algorithm — if the array is guaranteed to be in sorted order. Both the average and worst-case time for a binary search is *log n*, where *n* represents the number of elements in the array. This is a significant gain provided that the array does not constantly have to be resorted.

Inheritance frees the programmer from entirely reimplementing a sorted array class. By deriving ISortArray from IntArray, we need only implement the differences between the two class types. The operations and data that are the same can be reused.

Dynamic binding also frees the programmer from having to distinguish between the two array classes in application code. By declaring as virtual the functions implemented differently by the two array classes, such as `min()`, `max()`, and `find()`, the programmer need not worry about the type of array being handled. This allows the programmer to introduce the sorted array class into an existing application without having to modify working code (which must, however, be recompiled).

To make a member function virtual, its declaration inside the base class must be prefixed with the keyword `virtual`. The data members and each of the member functions not declared as virtual will be reused by the derived sorted array class, with the exception that constructors and the memberwise assignment operator are not inherited. The modified IntArray class definition looks as follows:

```
const int ArraySize = 24; // default size

class IntArray {
public:
    IntArray( int sz = ArraySize );
    IntArray( const IntArray& );
    virtual ~IntArray() { delete ia; }

    IntArray& operator=( const IntArray& );
    int getSize() { return size; }
    void grow();

    virtual int& operator[]( int );
    virtual void sort( int, int );
    virtual int find( int );
    virtual int min();
    virtual int max();

protected:
    // visible to derived classes only
    int size;
    int *ia;
};
```

The `sort()` function is placed inside IntArray because it is a generally useful operation on an array. The difference between IntArray and the sorted array derivation is that ISortArray is guaranteed always to be in sorted order, a property essential to its look-up operations. These operations, not the `sort()` function, are the motivation behind the derivation.

The IntArray `sort()` member function instance is a translation of the `qsort()` nonmember function (see Section 3.9 (page 128) for its definition). It is not shown again since the changes required are minimal and make a good exercise for the reader.

The functions specified as virtual may be, but need not be, reimplemented by the derived class. A function is declared as virtual if its implementation is likely to differ in a subsequent derivation. A derived class that does not reimplement a particular virtual function, however, is not penalized. Such a class simply inherits any virtual functions it has not reimplemented. In the sorted array class, the IntArray virtual destructor is inherited (see Section 8.2 (page 348) for a discussion of virtual destructors) as is the virtual `sort()` function.

Here is the definition of the sorted array class:

```
class ISortArray : public IntArray {
public:
    ISortArray( int sz = ArraySize )
        : IntArray(sz) { dirtyBit = 0; }
    int& operator[]( int );
    int find( int );
    int min(){ checkBit(); return ia[0]; }
    int max(){ checkBit(); return ia[size-1]; }
private:
    void checkBit();
    char dirtyBit;    // if 1, need resort
};
```

The constructor for the base class is invoked before the derived class constructor. The member initialization list of the constructor is extended arguments to be passed to the base class. Since ISortArray does not contain a pointer data member and its semantics allow the copying of `dirtyBit`, default memberwise copy is sufficient. The initialization or assignment of one ISortArray object with another will cause the

```
IntArray( const IntArray& )
```

or

```
operator=( const IntArray& )
```

member function to be invoked to handle the base class.

The virtual instances to be defined in the derived class need not use the virtual keyword. The name, return type, and signature of each instance, however, must match exactly the virtual instance defined in the base class.

Here is the implementation of checkBit(). Its purpose is to check whether the array has been modified. If it has, the array must be resorted. checkBit() is called by each look-up function.

```
#include "ISort.h"
void ISortArray::checkBit()
{ // has array been possibly modified?
    if ( dirtyBit ) {
        sort( 0, size-1 );
        dirtyBit = 0;
    }
}
```

find() is a translation of the binSearch() function (see Section 3.10 (page 131) for its definition). This translation from a nonmember to a member function is also left as an exercise for the reader.

All that remains is to implement the index operator function. Each time it is invoked, the array has potentially been modified and will require resorting before lookup. One implementation might look as follows:

```
int& ISortArray::operator[]( int indx )
{
    dirtyBit = 1;
    return IntArray::operator[]( indx );
}
```

An operator function may be called explicitly, as is the IntArray index operator. An explicit call of a virtual function using the class scope operator is resolved statically and not at run time. (Invoking a virtual function through a class object is also resolved statically.)

Exercise 7-1. The current implementation of the ISortArray subscript operator unconditionally sets dirtyBit with each invocation. Why is this inefficient? What would be a better implementation?

□

Exercise 7-2. Modify ISortArray to keep track of how many times an object is touched before it is actually sorted.

□

Exercise 7-3. Modify ISortArray to keep track of how many times an object is sorted in its lifetime compared to how many times each look-up function is called.

□

Exercise 7-4. Modify the `sort()` routine to determine if the array actually required sorting. Keep track of the percentage of times it was called unnecessarily.

□

Exercise 7-5. Derive an IStatSort class from ISortArray to provide all the statistics of the three previous exercises. □

7.3   The Zoo Animal Representation

To help organize the discussion of class derivation in C++, an extended example will be presented that centers around the representation of animals maintained by a zoo.

Ling-ling, a giant panda from China, will be on loan to a local zoo for six months. The zoo anticipates a four-fold increase in visitor attendance during these months. Fearing a shortage of staff, the zoo proposes installing display terminals in its information center that will answer questions posed by visitors about the animals.

The zoo animals exist at different levels of abstraction. There are individual animals, such as Ling-ling. Each animal belongs to a species; Ling-ling, for example, is a giant panda. Species in turn are members of families. A giant panda is a member of the bear family. Each family in turn is a member of the animal kingdom — in this case, the more limited kingdom of a particular zoo.

The taxonomy of the zoo animals maps nicely into an inheritance hierarchy. Fig. 7.1 illustrates a subportion of the Bear family derivation. This inheritance hierarchy is referred to as *single inheritance*. In such a hierarchy, each derived class has only one immediate base class.

The taxonomy of the zoo animals does not provide a complete representation. For example, Panda is a species of Bear and is also an endangered species, although the Polar and Grizzly Bear species are not. The Leopard species of the Cat family is also endangered.

"Endangered" is an independent abstraction that randomly cuts across the taxonomy. A single inheritance hierarchy cannot represent the endangered nature of both a Leopard and a Panda, but multiple inheritance can. Fig. 7.2 illustrates a subportion of a multiply derived inheritance graph.

Multiple inheritance defines a relationship between independent class types. The derived class can be thought of as a composite of its multiple base classes. C++ supports both single and multiple inheritance.

Fig. 7.3 illustrates three levels of a zoo animal derivation.

The ZooAnimal class, referred to as an *abstract base class*, is designed

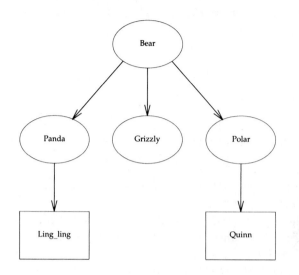

Figure 7.1 Single Inheritance

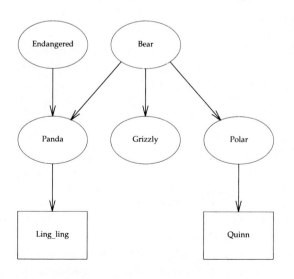

Figure 7.2 Multiple Inheritance

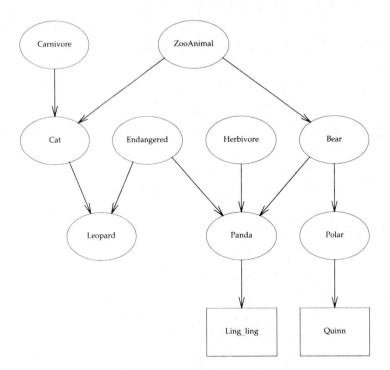

Figure 7.3 Zoo Animal Inheritance Graph

specifically as a class from which other classes can be derived. It can be thought of as an incomplete class that is more or less finished with each subsequent derivation.

ZooAnimal attempts to define the set of data and function members that are common to all zoo animals; derivations from ZooAnimal attempt to define what is unique to a particular class of animal. Subsequent derivations attempt to refine this even more. A Bear, for example, is a particular instance of ZooAnimal. A Panda is an even more particular instance.

In the course of building up the derivation hierarchy, the design of an abstract base class such as ZooAnimal will almost certainly be modified and extended many times. Although the design process originates with an abstraction and culminates with an implementation, the path connecting the two points is not a straight line, but rather a feedback loop.

A class that serves as the root class of a derivation hierarchy is referred to as an *abstract superclass*. ZooAnimal plays the role of an abstract superclass, serving as the root base class of all the animal class types.

The abstract superclass is central to the design of a derivation hierarchy. Regardless of how deeply nested and complex the hierarchy becomes, the relationship between classes is maintained by the common set of class members inherited from the abstract superclass.

"Endangered" is not currently a characteristic of all zoo animals, and thus it does not make sense either to derive ZooAnimal from Endangered or to declare an Endangered object as a data member of ZooAnimal. Endangered serves as an auxiliary abstract base class because Endangered is an independent class type rather than a subtype of ZooAnimal. ZooAnimal serves as the abstract superclass of the animal taxonomy. Multiple inheritance allows for the composition of particular class types, such as Panda, with auxiliary abstract base classes that fall outside the taxonomy.

The rest of this chapter and Chapter 8 consider how this representation might be implemented in C++ and the different design issues that need to be resolved.

Exercise 7-6. Geometric shapes are commonly used to illustrate class derivation. Such shapes minimally include a triangle, box, and circle. Draw an inheritance hierarchy for these shapes.

□

Exercise 7-7. How do a square and a rectangle fit into your shapes hierarchy? What about the different kinds of triangles such as the right triangle and the equilateral triangle? □

7.4   Derivation Specification

A skeletal implementation of a portion of the relationship pictured in Fig. 7.3 looks as follows.

```
// classes to serve as base classes
class ZooAnimal  { ... };
class Endangered { ... };
class Carnivore  { ... };
class Herbivore  { ... };

// Bear: single derivation
class Bear : public ZooAnimal { ... };

// Cat, Panda: multiple derivations
class Cat : public ZooAnimal, Carnivore { ... };
class Panda : private Endangered, public Bear,
              private Herbivore { ... };
```

Bear, Panda, and Cat are referred to as *derived* classes. Bear is an example of single inheritance. ZooAnimal is referred to as the *public base class* of Bear. Both Cat and Panda are examples of multiple inheritance. Panda is composed of one public base class (Bear) and two private base classes (Herbivore and Endangered). Cat is composed of one public base class (ZooAnimal) and one private base class (Carnivore). Without an explicit `public` or `private` attribute, a base class by default is handled as private. Thus,

```
class Cat : public ZooAnimal, Carnivore { ... };
```

declares Carnivore as a private base class of Cat.

`Ling_ling` is a Panda class object. A derived class object is declared in the same way as a nonderived class object:

```
Panda Ling_ling; // derived class object
```

A derived class may itself serve as a base class in a subsequent derivation. Bear, for example, derived from ZooAnimal, serves as a public base class of Panda.

The syntax for defining a base class is the same as that of an "ordinary" class with two exceptions:

1. Members intended to be inherited but not intended to be public are declared as protected members. These members would be declared as private in an abstract data type such as BitVector.

2. Member functions whose implementation depends on representational details of subsequent derivations that are unknown at the time of the base class design are declared as virtual functions.

Here is a simple, preliminary definition of ZooAnimal:

```
class ZooAnimal {
public:
    ZooAnimal( char*, char*, short );
    virtual ~ZooAnimal();
    virtual void draw();
    void locate();
    void inform();
protected:
    char *name;
    char *infoFile;
    short location;
    short count;
};
```

Exercise 7-8. The members of an abstract class represents the attributes common to the entire hierarchy. Outline what you think are the common data members and member functions of the Shape hierarchy. Identify which functions you believe should be declared as virtual. □

Exercise 7-9. Provide a definition of the Shape class outlined in the previous exercise. Note that the destructor of an abstract class should always be specified as virtual. □

Definition of a Derived Class

In this section let us examine the actual syntax of class derivation. Here is a simple, preliminary derivation of Bear from ZooAnimal:

```
#include "ZooAnimal.h"
class Bear : public ZooAnimal  {
public:
    Bear( char*, char*, short, char, char );
    ~Bear();
    void locate( int );
    int isOnDisplay();
protected:
    char beingFed;
    char isDanger;
    char onDisplay;
    char epoch;
};
```

The only necessary syntactic difference between a simple and a derived class definition lies in the class-head specification:

```
class Bear : public ZooAnimal
```

The colon following the class tag name indicates the presence of a *class derivation list*, a (possibly) comma-separated list of one or more base classes. There is no language-imposed limit on the number of base classes that may appear in the class derivation list; no class name, however, may appear more than once. Each listed base class must already have been defined.

A base class is either a private or a public base class. If the keyword private or public is unspecified, *the base class by default becomes private*. For example, the following two class heads both declare a private derivation of Bear:

```
// equivalent declarations of a private base class
class Bear : ZooAnimal
class Bear : private ZooAnimal
```

The preferred method of declaring a private base class is through explicit use of the keyword `private`. This coding style has proven less prone to misinterpretation, especially in the case of multiple base classes. (Most compilers issue a warning message if neither the `private` or `public` keyword is specified.)

In a multiple derivation, each base class must specify its own private or public attribute. A base class does not assume the attribute of the preceding base class. In the following class head, it is common to misinterpret Endangered as a public base class of Panda. In fact, Endangered is private by default.

```
// Endangered by default is private
class Panda : public Bear, Endangered
```

The public or private attribute of a base class is specific to the declaration list in which it appears. There is no constraint on declaring a class a public base class in one instance and a private base class in another. For example, although ZooAnimal is a public base class of Bear and Cat, there is no reason it cannot be declared a private base class of Rodent.

The meaning of public and private base classes and the reasons one might choose one or the other are discussed in Section 7.6 (page 317) later on in this chapter. The next subsection examines the syntax of accessing the inherited class members within the derived class.

Exercise 7-10. Provide a definition of a Circle class. □

Exercise 7-11. Provide a definition of a Box class. □

Exercise 7-12. Provide a definition of a Rectangle class derived from Box. □

Inherited Member Access

Bear inherits the following ZooAnimal class members: `name`, `location`, `count`, `infoFile`, `locate()`, and `inform()`. (Handling the virtual functions `draw()` and `~ZooAnimal()` is discussed in Chapter 8.) These inherited ZooAnimal members can be accessed as if they were members of Bear. For example,

```
void objectExample( Bear& ursus ) {
    if ( ursus.isOnDisplay() ) {
        ursus.locate(HIGH); // const HIGH
        if ( ursus.beingFed )
            cout << ursus.name << " is now being fed\n";
        ursus.inform();
    }
}
```

Although they may be accessed as if they were members of the derived class, the inherited members maintain their base class membership. Each can be accessed using the class scope operator. For example,

```
if ( ursus.beingFed )
        cout << ursus.ZooAnimal::name;
ursus.ZooAnimal::inform();
```

In most cases, use of the class scope operator is redundant. The compiler can find the intended member without the additional lexical aid. In two cases, however, this additional aid is necessary:

1. When an inherited member's name is reused in the derived class.

2. When two or more base classes define an inherited member with the same name.

Reuse of an inherited member's name within the derived class hides the inherited member. This is similar to a local identifier reusing the name of a variable defined at file scope. In both cases a reference to the name is resolved to mean the identifier defined in the most immediate scope. `Bear::locate(int)`, for example, hides the inherited ZooAnimal member. The statement

```
ursus.locate();
```

will always refer to `Bear::locate(int)` (and cause the error message *missing first argument* to be generated). To invoke the hidden inherited member function, the statement *must* read:

```
ursus.ZooAnimal::locate();
```

When a name is reused by the inherited members of two or more base classes, use of the unmodified name within the derived class is ambiguous and results in a compile-time error. The class scope operator must be used to disambiguate between the multiple instances of the inherited members. For example,

```
class Endangered { public: highlight(short); };
class Herbivore  { public: highlight(short); };

class Panda : public Bear, public Endangered,
              public Herbivore { public: locate(); };

// hides ZooAnimal::locate() and Bear::locate(int)
Panda::locate() {
    if ( isOnDisplay() ) {
        Bear::locate( LOW ); // const LOW
        highlight( location ); // error: ambiguous
        Endangered::highlight( location ); // ok
    }
}
```

This method of explicitly resolving the ambiguity has two significant drawbacks.

1. A virtual function called explicitly is invoked as a nonvirtual function. (Section 8.2 (page 352) considers this in detail.) In choosing this method of disambiguation, we have effectively disallowed highlight() to be specified as a virtual function.

2. The ambiguity is inherited by subsequent derivations. A rule of thumb about the design of a class hierarchy is that the derived class should not have to exhibit any implementation knowledge of classes in the hierarchy beyond that of its immediate base classes. This violates that rule.

When the inherited members that share the same name are all member functions, it is therefore a good design strategy to define a derived class member function of the same name. For example,

```
void Panda::highlight()
{
    // encapsulate the ambiguous inherited members
    Endangered::highlight( location );
    Herbivore::highlight( location );
}
```

The Panda instance of highlight() hides both inherited members at the same time that it provides the functionality of both. The ambiguity is resolved in a manner transparent to the user.

Exercise 7-13. A debug() member function is useful to the class designer. It displays the current values of the class data members. Implement a debug() member function for each class in the hierarchy of Shapes. □

Base Class Initialization

The member initialization list is used to pass arguments to a base class constructor. The tag name of a base class is specified, followed by its argument list enclosed in parentheses. (The member initialization list can appear only in the definition, not in the declaration, of the constructor.) For example, here is a member initialization list for Bear:

```
Bear::Bear( char *nm, char *fil, short loc,
            char danger, char age )
        : ZooAnimal( nm, fil, loc ),
          epoch( age ), isDanger( danger )
          {} // deliberately null
```

In the case of multiple base classes, each base class may be listed in turn. Here is a member initialization list for Panda:

```
// PANDA,MIOCENE,CHINA,BAMBOO: enumeration constants
Panda::Panda( char *nm, short loc, char sex )
         : Bear( "Ailuropoda melaoleuca",
                 "Panda", PANDA, MIOCENE ),
         Endangered( CHINA ), Herbivore( BAMBOO ),
         name( nm ), cell( loc ), gender( sex )
         {} // deliberately null
```

A base class that either does not define a constructor or that defines a constructor that does not require an explicit argument need not be specified on the member initialization list. A base class may be initialized with the argument list expected by a constructor. Alternatively, it may be initialized with another class object. This class object can be of the same base class type. For example,

```
Bear::Bear( ZooAnimal& z )
        : ZooAnimal( z ) { /* ... */ };
```

The class object can also be of a publicly derived class type. For example,

```
Bear::Bear( const Bear& b )
        : ZooAnimal( b ) { /* ... */ };
```

Here is an example of where the class object has no relationship to the base class, but defines a conversion operator which does:

```
class GiantSloth : public Extinct {
public:
    operator Bear() { return b; }
protected:
    Bear b;
};

// invokes GiantSloth::operator Bear()
Panda::Panda(GiantSloth& gs) : Bear(gs) {...}

// invokes GiantSloth::operator Bear()
Bear::Bear(GiantSloth& gs) : ZooAnimal(gs) {...};
```

The base class constructors are invoked prior to the constructor of the derived class. Because of this, the member initialization list of a derived class may not explicitly initialize an inherited base class member; the base class members at this point have already been initialized. The following, for example, is illegal:

```
// illegal:  explicit initialization of the
// inherited base class member ZooAnimal::name
Bear( char *nm ) : name( nm ) /* ... */
```

Exercise 7-14. Define the Shapes class constructor(s). □

Exercise 7-15. Define the Circle class constructor(s). □

Exercise 7-16. Define the Box and Rectangle class constructors. □

7.5   Information Hiding under Derivation

Inheritance introduces a second client group for a class — a design group intent on type extension. The public/private member division that serves the class user group is inadequate for derivation. Protected class members serve the needs of the design group while preserving the ability of the base class to declare private members.

A protected class member is public to the member functions and friends of a derived class; it is private to the rest of the program. A derived class has *no* access privilege to the private members of a base class. For example, here is a simplified ZooAnimal derivation:

```
class ZooAnimal {
    friend void setPrice( ZooAnimal& );
public:
    isOnDisplay();
protected:
    char *name;
    char onDisplay;
private:
    char forSale;
};


class Primate : public ZooAnimal {
    friend void canCommunicate( Primate* );
public:
    locate();
protected:
    short zooArea;
private:
    char languageSkills;
};
```

A derived class inherits all the members of a base class; however, the derived class has access privilege only to the nonprivate members of the base class. Primate, for example, cannot access the private ZooAnimal data member forSale. As a friend to ZooAnimal, setPrice() has access to all the members of ZooAnimal. What, however, is its relationship to Primate or any other ZooAnimal derivation? For example,

```
void setPrice( ZooAnimal &z ) {
    Primate *pr;
    if ( pr->forSale            // legal? yes.
         && pr->languageSkills ) // legal? no.
    // ...
}
```

Primate is a kind of ZooAnimal. setPrice() has the same access privilege to the ZooAnimal members inherited by a Primate class object that it has with a ZooAnimal class object. forSale can therefore legally be accessed within setPrice().

The member functions and friends of ZooAnimal have access privilege only to the members of Primate inherited from ZooAnimal. The access of languageSkills within setPrice() is therefore illegal.

Specifying ZooAnimal as a friend to Primate extends access privilege to the nonpublic members of Primate to all the member functions of ZooAnimal. It does not, however, extend access privilege to setPrice(). The only way setPrice() can access the nonpublic Primate members is to be explicitly made a friend to Primate. In this way, the member functions and friends of a class behave differently.

canCommunicate() is a friend of Primate and has full access to its members. Were Orangutan derived from Primate, canCommunicate() would have full access right to those Primate members inherited by an Orangutan class object. But what access privilege, if any, does canCommunicate() have with the members of ZooAnimal? For example,

```
void canCommunicate( Primate *pr ) {
    ZooAnimal za;
    if ( pr->onDisplay          // legal? yes.
         && za.onDisplay        // legal? no.
         && pr->forSale )       // legal? no.
    // ...
}
```

In general, a friend function has the same access privilege as the member functions of that class. The member functions of Primate can access the inherited nonprivate members of ZooAnimal but not the inherited private members. The access of onDisplay is therefore legal while the access of forSale is not.

The derived class has no special access privilege to *objects* of its base class. Rather, the derived class has access privilege to the nonprivate *inherited* members of a derived class object. For example,

```
Primate::locate() {
    ZooAnimal za;
    Primate pr;

    if ( onDisplay          // ok
         && pr.onDisplay // ok
         && za.onDisplay // error: no access
    // ...
}
```

Derivation is not friendship. Primate has no access privilege to the nonpublic members of a ZooAnimal class object. The same holds true for friends of Primate. The expression

```
za.onDisplay
```

within canCommunicate() is also illegal.

Derivation provides for type extension. Primate is a specialized instance of a ZooAnimal. It shares the characteristics of a ZooAnimal, but adds a set of attributes that apply only to itself. Friendship provides for data access of otherwise nonpublic members. It does not define a type relationship. Derivation is not a special form of friendship — one that provides access to the protected but not private members of individual base class objects. Only the friends and member functions of ZooAnimal, for example, can access the nonpublic members of a ZooAnimal class object.

Exercise 7-17. Should the debug() member function implemented in Section 7.4 (page 312) for the Shape hierarchy be made a private, protected, or public member of its class? Why? □

7.6 Public and Private Base Classes

The inherited members of a public base class maintain their access level within the derived class. name and isOnDisplay(), protected ZooAnimal members, are treated as protected members of Primate; a derivation of Baboon from Primate will inherit these members. In general, in a public derivation hierarchy, each subsequently derived class has access to the combined set of protected and public members of the previous base classes along the particular branch of the hierarchy. A public derivation from Panda, for example, can access the collection of Bear, ZooAnimal, Endangered and Herbivore public and protected members.

The inherited public and protected members of a private derivation become private members of the derived class. This has two effects:

1. The public members of the base class cannot be accessed through a derived class object.

2 The public and protected members of the base class are "sealed off" from subsequent derivations.

Private derivations serve to prohibit access to the public interface of the base class. In addition, there is no implicit conversion of a derived class object to an object of a private base class. Section 2.5 (page 71) illustrates one use of a private base class — IntStack reuses the IntArray implementation but not its set of public operations. Inheritance in this case is used to achieve code reuse, and not as a method of class subtyping.

Here is another example. The zoo administration wishes to keep track of its rodent population but does not wish that information to be generally available. The Rodent class is made a private derivation:

```
class Rodent : private ZooAnimal {
public:
    void reportSighting( short loc );
    // ...
};
```

The entire set of inherited ZooAnimal members are private members of Rodent. They can be accessed only by the member functions and friends of Rodent. For example, the following call of `locate()`, a public ZooAnimal member function, is illegal:

```
Rodent pest;
pest.locate(); // error: ZooAnimal::locate() is private
```

Because Rodent is a private derivation, it cannot be assigned to a ZooAnimal class object. Were the assignment permitted, the inherited members would no longer be private. For example, given the following declarations:

```
extern void locate( ZooAnimal& );
ZooAnimal za;
```

the following two uses of `pest` are illegal and result in errors at compile time:

```
locate( pest ); // error.
za = pest;      // error.
za.locate();    // ok.
```

All subsequent derivations from Rodent have no access privilege to any of the ZooAnimal members since access is restricted to the public and protected members of the base class. For example,

```
class Rat : public Rodent { ... };
Rat anyRat;

anyRat.reportSighting( CAFETERIA ); // ok
anyRat.locate(); // error: not visible to Rat
```

The class designer can exempt individual members of the base class from the effects of the private derivation. For example,

```
class Rodent : private ZooAnimal {
public:
    // maintain public access level
    // do not specify return type or signature
    ZooAnimal::inform;
};

pest.locate(); // error: locate() is private
pest.inform(); // ok: inform() is public
```

The specification of `ZooAnimal::inform` within a public section of Rodent causes `inform()` to be inherited at its original access level. Subsequent derivations also inherit `inform()` as a public member:

```
class Rat : public Rodent { ... };
Rat anyRat;

anyRat.locate(); // error: locate() is not visible
anyRat.inform(); // ok: inform() is a public member
```

The derived class can maintain the inherited member's access level only. The access level cannot be made either more or less restrictive than the level originally specified within the base class. It is illegal, for example, to declare the protected ZooAnimal class member `onDisplay` within a `public` section of Rodent or to declare `inform()` within a `protected` section.

7.7 Standard Conversions under Derivation

Four predefined standard conversions are applied between a derived class and its public base classes.

1. A derived class object will be implicitly converted into a public base class object.

2. A derived class reference will be implicitly converted into a public base class reference.

3. A derived class pointer will be implicitly converted into a public base class pointer.

4. A pointer to a class member of a base class will be implicitly converted into a pointer to a class member of a publicly derived class.

In addition, a pointer to any class object will be implicitly converted into a pointer to type `void*`. (A pointer to type `void*` requires an explicit cast in order to assign it to a pointer to any other type.)

For example, here is a simplified set of class definitions. In addition, a function `f()` is declared that takes as its argument a reference to an object of class ZooAnimal.

```
class Endangered { ... } endang;
class ZooAnimal { ... } zooanim;
class Bear : public ZooAnimal { ... } bear;
class Panda : public Bear { ... } panda;
class ForSale: private ZooAnimal { ... } forsale;

extern void f( ZooAnimal& );
```

`f()` may legally be called with a ZooAnimal, Bear, or Panda class object. In the latter two calls, an implicit standard conversion takes place:

```
f( zooanim ); // ok: exact match
f( bear );   // ok: Bear ==> ZooAnimal
f( panda ); // ok: Panda ==> ZooAnimal
```

The following two invocations of f() are both illegal. Each is flagged as a type mismatch at compile time.

```
f( forsale ); // error: ZooAnimal private
f( endang );  // error: ZooAnimal not a base class
```

Fig. 7.4 models the object layout of a derived class, using the following simplified ZooAnimal and Bear class definitions:

```
class ZooAnimal {
public:
    isA();
    // ...
protected:
    char *name;
    int typeOf;
    int someVal;
};

class Bear : public ZooAnimal {
public:
    locate();
    // ...
protected:
    short ZooArea;
    int someVal;
};

Bear b, *pb = &b;
ZooAnimal *pz = pb;
```

A derived class is pictured in Fig. 7.4 as consisting of one (or more) base class "parts" plus the members unique to the derived class. Both a derived and base class object contain a "base part" — only a derived class object is guaranteed to contain a "derived part."

The conversion of a derived class object into an object of a base class is considered safe because every derived class object contains a base class object. The reverse conversion, however, is not safe. This is why an explicit cast is required. For example,

```
// pb and pz both address the Bear object ``b''
// ok: Bear::locate()
pb->locate(); // ok: Bear::locate()
```

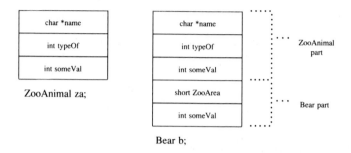

Figure 7.4 Class Object under Derivation

```
// error: locate() not a ZooAnimal member
pz->locate();

pb->someVal; // ok: Bear::someVal
pz->someVal; // ok: ZooAnimal::someVal
```

Except when virtual functions are being invoked, an explicit cast is necessary in order to access a derived class member through a base class object, reference, or pointer. For example,

```
// nonobject-oriented implementation
void locate( ZooAnimal* pZ ) {
    switch ( pZ->isA() ) {
        case Bear:
            ((Bear *)pZ)->locate();
            ...
        case Panda:
            ((Panda *)pZ)->locate();
            ...
    }
}
```

Note that the additional set of parentheses around the cast of pZ is necessary. The statement

```
// invoke the Zoo_Animal member locate(),
// cast its return value to Bear*
(Bear *)pZ->locate();
```

attempts to invoke the ZooAnimal instance of locate() and cast its return value to Bear*.

Initialization and assignment of a derived class to one of its base classes also require an explicit cast by the programmer. For example,

```
Bear *pb = new Panda; // ok: implicit conversion
Panda *pp = new Bear; // error: no implicit conversion
Panda *pp = (Panda *) new Bear; // ok.
```

A Panda object will always contain a Bear part. A Bear object may or may not actually be a Panda object depending on its last assignment. The cast of a base class object (or pointer) to that of its derived class is dangerous. For example, the following sequence assigns 24 to an undefined location in memory:

```
Bear b;
Bear *pb = new Panda; // ok: implicit conversion
pb = &b; // pb no longer addresses a Panda object
Panda *pp = (Panda *) pb; // oops: no Panda part
pp->cell = 24; // disaster! no Panda::cell ...
```

Pointers to class members behave in the reverse manner. It is always safe to assign a member of a public base class to a derived class pointer to class member. Assignment of a derived class member to a base class pointer to class member, however, is not safe. The reason is that the pointer to class member, when invoked, is bound to an object of its class.

For example, pm_Zoo is a ZooAnimal pointer to class member initialized to isA():

```
int (ZooAnimal::*pm_Zoo)() = ZooAnimal::isA;
```

It is invoked by binding it to a class object of its type:

```
ZooAnimal z;
(z.*pm_Zoo)();
```

isA() accesses members of ZooAnimal. Since a Bear class object is guaranteed to contain a ZooAnimal part, it is safe to assign the address of isA() to a Bear pointer to class member:

```
int (Bear::*pm_Bear)() = ZooAnimal::isA;
Bear b;
(b.*pm_Bear)(); // ok
```

Let's assign pm_Zoo the address of the Bear member function locate(). The assignment, because it is unsafe, requires an explicit cast:

```
pm_Zoo = (int (ZooAnimal::*)()) Bear::locate;
```

pm_Zoo must be invoked by binding it to a ZooAnimal class object. locate(), however, accesses members of Bear not contained in a ZooAnimal class object. Whether the invocation of pm_Zoo "crashes" the program depends on the actual type of the base class object. For example,

```
ZooAnimal *pz = &b;  // pz addresses a Bear
(pz->*pm_Zoo)();     // ok

pz = &z;             // pz address a ZooAnimal
(pz->*pm_Zoo)();     // disaster
```

Exercise 7-18. Given the following class hierarchy:

```
class Node { ... };
class Type : public Node { ... };
class Statement : public Type { ... };
class Expression : public Type { ... };
class Identifier : public Expression { ... };
class Function : public Expression { ... };
```

Which of the following initializations are illegal? Explain why.

```
(a) Node *pn = new Identifier( "i" );
(b) Identifier *pi = pn;
(c) Expression e = *pi;
(d) Statement s = e;
(e) Type *pt = &e;
(f) Identifier &ri = e;
(g) Function &rf = ri;
(h) Node n = rf;
```

□

Exercise 7-19. Define a nonmember function debug() which can accept any shape class derivation. It should invoke the correct debug() member function. (In Chapter 8, we will rewrite debug() as a virtual class member function.)

□

Exercise 7-20. Define a set of pointer to class members for Shape, Circle, Box, and Rectangle. Illustrate which assignments are permitted and which require an explicit conversion. □

7.8   Class Scope under Derivation

Inheritance provides for class scope nesting. As illustrated in Fig. 7.5, a derived class can be thought of as enclosed by the scope of its base classes.

Each class and external function is visible within file scope; their scopes are represented by boxes drawn with a dashed line. Each member function is visible within the scope of its class; its local scope is represented by boxes drawn with a dotted line. The arrows link each scope with its

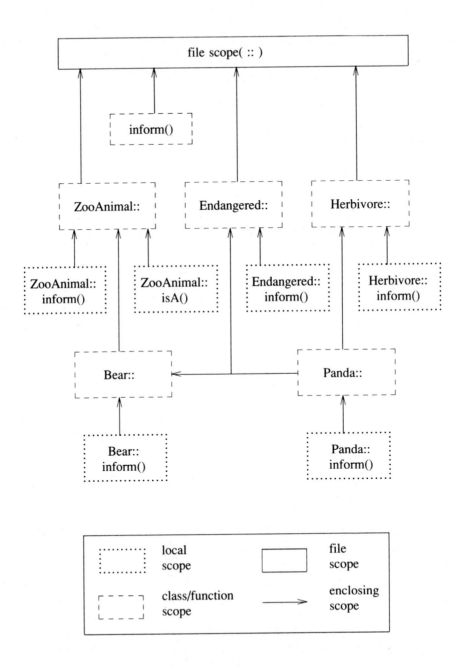

Figure 7.5 Class Scope under Derivation

enclosing scopes. In the case of multiple inheritance, there are multiple enclosing scopes. All of these multiple enclosing scopes must be searched within the same look-up step. Panda, for example, must search the Bear, Endangered, and Herbivore class scopes in the same look-up step. Fig. 7.5 is a representation of the following set of class definitions:

```
extern inform();

class ZooAnimal {
public:
    inform();
    isA();
};

class Endangered { public: inform( ZooAnimal* ); };
class Herbivore { public: inform( ZooAnimal* ); };

class Bear : public ZooAnimal
        { public: inform( short ); };

class Panda : public Bear, public Endangered,
                public Herbivore
        { public: inform( char * ); };
```

An occurrence of isA() within Panda::inform() initiates the following look-up search:

1. Is isA() declared within Panda::inform()? If yes, stop; otherwise, follow the scope arrow. It is not.

2. Is isA() declared as a class member of Panda? If yes, stop; otherwise, follow the scope arrows of the multiple base classes. It is not.

3. Is isA() an inherited member from one and only one of the Bear, Endangered or Herbivore base classes? If yes, stop. If it is inherited from two or more base classes, the reference is ambiguous. Issue an error message and stop. Otherwise, are any of these base classes also derived? If yes, follow the scope arrow to their base classes; otherwise, follow the scope arrow to file scope. Repeat until either the reference is resolved or file scope has been searched. If the reference is unresolved following the search of file scope, issue an error message and stop.

The reference to isA() within Panda::inform() is resolved to the inherited member ZooAnimal::isA().

Derivation Is Not Overloading

The inherited `ZooAnimal::locate()` member has a signature distinct from that of the renamed `Bear::locate(int)`. Users new to C++ often assume that the signature is sufficient to distinguish the two instances — that, in effect, inherited member functions with the same name are handled as an overloaded function set to be resolved at the point of call. For example,

```
// derivation is not overloading
Bear ursus;
ursus.locate( 1 ); // ok: Bear::locate(int)
ursus.locate(); // error: ZooAnimal::locate() is hidden
```

Derivation, however, is *not* a form of overloading. The ZooAnimal instance of `locate()` is hidden. The call `ursus.locate()` resolves to `Bear::locate(int)`. The call is flagged as an error. The instance of `locate()` that is found requires one argument.

Derivation preserves the scope of the base classes. Overloading requires that the entire function set be defined at the same scope. To overload `locate()`, a second Bear instance must be defined:

```
inline void Bear::locate() { ZooAnimal::locate(); }
```

7.9 Initialization and Assignment under Derivation

A class object initialized with another object of its class by default is memberwise initialized (see Section 6.2 (page 247) for a discussion). The same default behavior holds for derived class objects. In the same order as they are declared, memberwise initialization is applied first to each base class, then to each derived class member.

Memberwise initialization can be a source of problems in handling individual class objects which contain pointer members. Although the constructors are overridden in the initialization of the second object, the destructors are invoked twice, once as each object exits scope. This can result in dangling references and multiple attempts to delete the same free store.

To handle this problem, the class designer provides an explicit object initialization constructor, `X(const X&)`. In effect, the class provides its own memberwise initialization algorithm. The initialization of one class object with another is now handled with the invocation of the explicit `X(const X&)` constructor.

This section considers the handling of `X(const X&)` under class derivation. Three cases are discussed:

1. The derived class does not define an X(const X&) instance; one or more base classes do define an instance.

2. The derived class does define an instance; the base classes do not.

3. Both the derived and the base classes define an instance.

If the derived class does not define an X(const X&) instance, default memberwise initialization is applied whenever one object of the derived class is initialized with another. The base classes are memberwise initialized first; the order of initialization follows the declaration order of the base classes. X(const X&) is invoked for each base class for which it is defined. For example, given the following simplified set of class definitions,

```
class Carnivore { public: Carnivore(); };
class ZooAnimal {
public:
        ZooAnimal();
        ZooAnimal( const ZooAnimal& );
};
class Cat : public ZooAnimal,
        public Carnivore { public: Cat(); };

Cat Felix;
Cat Fritz = Felix;
```

The initialization of the Cat object Fritz with that of Felix will first invoke ZooAnimal(const ZooAnimal&). The Carnivore base class and members of Cat are then memberwise initialized.

If the derived class defines an X(const X&) instance, it is invoked for all initialization of a derived class object with another object of its class. The base class parts are not memberwise initialized. Handling of the base class parts becomes the responsibility of the derived X(const X&) instance. For example,

```
class Bear : public ZooAnimal {
public:
        Bear();
        Bear( const Bear& );
};

Bear Yogi;
Bear Smokey = Yogi;
```

Initialization of the Bear object Smokey with that of Yogi results in the following pair of constructor invocations:

```
ZooAnimal();
Bear (const Bear&);
```

A base class constructor is always invoked before execution of a constructor for the derived class. The handling of X(const X&) is no exception. If the base class constructor requires an argument, it must be provided in a member initialization list.

Since ZooAnimal defines its own instance of X(const X&), it is preferable that it be invoked. This can be done as follows:

```
Bear::Bear( const Bear& b )
        // ZooAnimal(const ZooAnimal&) invoked
        : ZooAnimal( b )
        { /* ... */ }
```

Initialization of Smokey with Yogi now results in the following pair of
constructor invocations:

```
ZooAnimal( const ZooAnimal& );
Bear( const Bear& );
```

If the base class does not define an X(const X&) instance, default
memberwise initialization is recursively applied to the base class.

In a similar manner, memberwise assignment (see Section 6.3 (page 266)
for a discussion) can be overridden by explicitly providing a memberwise
instance of operator=(const X&). Its handling parallels that of the
X(const X&) constructor.

If a derived class does not define operator=(const X&), then each of
its base class and member class objects that defines an object assignment
operator will have that operator invoked whenever one object of the
derived class is assigned to another. Each base class or member class object
without an operator=(const X&) defined is memberwise assigned.

If a derived class defines an instance of operator=(const X&), it will
be invoked to handle the initialization of a class object with another object
of its class. Base class and member class object assignment becomes the
responsibility of the derived class object assignment operator.

Given the following assignment of a derived class Bear object to a public base class object of ZooAnimal, which instance of the object assignment
operator is invoked? Both ZooAnimal and Bear define operator=(const
X&).

```
Bear ursus;
ZooAnimal onLoan;

onLoan = ursus;
```

The class type of the assignment's left operand determines the class type of the assignment. The ZooAnimal part of the Bear object ursus is assigned to onLoan. Therefore, it's as though two ZooAnimal objects are being assigned, and the ZooAnimal object assignment operator is invoked. The same holds true for object initialization. The declaration

```
Bear Fozzie;
ZooAnimal On_Loan = Fozzie;
```

also invokes the object initialization constructor of ZooAnimal, rather than that of Bear.

In general, if a class provides an explicit instance of either the initialization or assignment member, it should also provide the other. Explicit instances are usually necessary when either of the following conditions hold:

1. The semantics of the class representation invalidates value copying of one or more members. The String class index member, for example, must be reset to 0 with each copy.

2. The class contains pointer members and a destructor. Copying requires either the handling of a reference count or additional allocation and copying of memory.

Exercise 7-21. Define an X(const X&) and operator=(const X&) instance for the Shape class but not for the Circle class. What are the constructors invoked for the following two objects of type Circle?

```
Circle c1;
Circle c2 = c1;
```

☐

Exercise 7-22. Define an X(const X&) and operator=(const X&) instance for the Box class but not for the Rectangle class. What are the constructors invoked for the following class objects?

```
Rectangle r1;
Box b1 = r1;
Rectangle r2 = r1;
```

☐

7.10   Initialization Order under Derivation

Given the following simplified definition of Panda,

```
class Panda : public Bear,
    public Endangered, public Herbivore {
public:
    Panda();
    // ... rest of public members
protected:
    BitVector status;
    String name;
    // ... rest of Panda members
};
```

```
Panda yinYang;
```

The constructors for `yinYang` are invoked in the following order:

1. Each base class constructor in the order of base class declarations:

```
ZooAnimal(); // base class of Bear
Bear();
Endangered();
Herbivore();
```

2. Each member class object constructor in the order of member class declarations:

```
BitVector();
String();
```

3. The derived class constructor:

```
Panda();
```

The destructors for `yinYang` are invoked in the reverse order of the invocation of the constructors.

Although the fixed order of base and member class object constructor invocation is ordinarily of no concern to the user, the integrity of certain applications depends on this order. For example, a library that allows for arbitrarily complex user-defined class types to be written out and read from disk must be assured that objects will be constructed in the same order regardless of machines and regardless of compilers. The language guarantees uniformity across implementations by defining a fixed order of constructor (and destructor) invocation.

Chapter 8: **Object-Oriented P**

Object-oriented programming is characterized by inheritance and dynamic binding. C++ supports inheritance through class derivation — the subject of the previous chapter. Dynamic binding is provided by virtual class functions.

An inheritance hierarchy defines a type/subtype relationship between class types. A Panda is a type of Bear, for example, which in turn is a type of ZooAnimal. Similarly, both a sorted array and an array with range checking are types of IntArray. Virtual functions define *type dependent operations* within an inheritance hierarchy — the ZooAnimal `draw()` function, for example, or the subscript operator of the array classes. Virtual functions provide a method of encapsulating the implementation details of an inheritance hierarchy from programs that make use of it.

In this chapter, we look at virtual functions in detail. We also look at a special case of class inheritance, that of a virtual, or shared, base class. First, however, we reconsider the overloading of a function name in the presence of class arguments.

8.1   Overloaded Functions with Class Arguments

Often, a function is overloaded in order to introduce an instance of an existing function to handle objects of a class type. For example, having defined a Complex number class, the designer might next define an instance of the square root library function that handles a Complex class object:

```
extern Complex& sqrt( Complex& );
```

The original discussion of overloaded functions presented in Section 4.3 (page 155) did not consider argument-matching in the presence of class arguments. This is the subject of this section.

We will consider, in turn, the exact matching of a class argument, matching achieved by application of a standard conversion, and matching achieved by invoking a user-defined conversion operator.

Exact Match

A class object matches exactly only a formal argument of its own class type. For example,

```
ff( Bear& );
ff( Panda& );

Panda yinYang;

// exact match:.ff( Panda& )
ff( yinYang );
```

Similarly, a pointer to a class object matches exactly only a formal argument of a pointer to its own class type.

The argument-matching algorithm cannot distinguish between an object and a reference of a class type. Although the following two instances declare two distinct functions, the actual call is ambiguous and results in an error during compilation.

```
// warning: cannot be distinguished
// by the argument-matching algorithm
ff( Panda );
ff( Panda& );

// ok: ff( Panda& )
int (*pf)( Panda& ) = ff;

ff( yinYang ); // error: ambiguous
pf( yinYang ); // ok
```

Standard Conversions

If the class argument is not an exact match, a match is attempted through the application of a predefined standard conversion.

- A derived class object, reference or pointer is implicitly converted into a corresponding public base class type. For example,

  ```
  ff( ZooAnimal& );
  ff( Screen& );

  // ff( ZooAnimal& )
  ff( yinYang );
  ```

- A pointer of any class type is implicitly converted into a pointer of type void*.

```
ff( Screen* );
ff( void* );

// ff( void* )
ff( &yinYang );
```

A conversion of a base class object, reference, or pointer into its corresponding derived class type is *not* applied. The following call, for example, fails to achieve a match:

```
ff( Bear& );
ff( Panda& );

ZooAnimal za;

ff( za ); // error: no match
```

The presence of two or more immediate base classes results in the call being flagged as ambiguous. Panda, for example, is derived from both Bear and Endangered. Both conversions of a Panda class object require equal work. Since both conversions are possible, the call is an error.

```
ff( Bear& );
ff( Endangered& );

ff( yinYang ); // error: ambiguous
```

To resolve the call, the programmer must supply an explicit cast:

```
ff( Bear(yinYang));
```

A derived class is considered more nearly the type of its immediate base class than of a base class further removed. The following call is not ambiguous although a standard conversion is required in both instances. A Panda is treated as being more nearly a kind of Bear than a kind of ZooAnimal by the argument-matching algorithm.

```
ff( ZooAnimal& );
ff( Bear& );

// ff( Bear& );
ff( yinYang );
```

This rule extends to the handling of void*. For example, given the following pair of overloaded functions:

```
ff( void* );
ff( ZooAnimal* );
```

an argument of type Panda* matches ZooAnimal*.

User-Defined Conversions

A user-defined conversion can be either a constructor that takes one argument or an explicit conversion operator. User-defined conversions are applied only if no exact match or match by a standard conversion has been found. For this subsection, let's provide ZooAnimal with two user-defined conversions:

```
class ZooAnimal {
public:
    // conversion: long ==> ZooAnimal
    ZooAnimal( long );

    // conversion: ZooAnimal ==> char*
    operator char*();

    // ...
};
```

Given the following pair of overloaded functions:

```
ff( ZooAnimal& );
ff( Screen& );
```

a call with an actual argument of type `long` will be resolved to the ZooAnimal instance by invoking the user-defined conversion:

```
long lval;

// ff( ZooAnimal& )
ff( lval );
```

What if the call is made with an argument of type `int`? For example,

```
ff( 1024 ); // ???
```

There is still no match either by an exact match or through a standard conversion. There is one applicable user-defined conversion — almost. The problem is that the conversion constructor for ZooAnimal expects a value of type `long`, not of type `int`.

The argument-matching algorithm will apply a standard conversion to help it find an applicable user-defined conversion. In this case, `1024` is converted to type `long` and passed to the ZooAnimal constructor. The call is resolved to the ZooAnimal instance.

A user-defined conversion is applied only when no match is otherwise possible. Were an instance of `ff()` declared which accepted a predefined type, the ZooAnimal conversion operator would not be invoked. For example,

```
ff( ZooAnimal& );
ff( char );

long lval;

// ff( char );
ff( lval );
```

In this case, an explicit cast is necessary to resolve the call to the ZooAnimal instance:

```
// ff( ZooAnimal& )
ff( ZooAnimal( lval ));
```

In the following example, the ZooAnimal char* conversion operator is applied since there is no standard conversion from a base class object to a derived class object.

```
ff( char* );
ff( Bear& );

ZooAnimal za;

// za ==> char*
// ff( char* )
ff( za );
```

The argument-matching algorithm will apply a standard conversion to the result of a user-defined conversion, if doing so achieves a match. For example,

```
ff( Panda* );
ff( void* );

// za ==> char* ==> void*
// ff( void* )
ff( za );
```

Conversion operators (but not constructors) are inherited in the same way as other class members. Both Bear and Panda inherit the char* conversion operator of ZooAnimal. For example,

```
ff( char* );
ff( Bear* );

Bear yogi;
Bear *pBear = &yogi;
```

```
// ff( char* )
ff( yogi );

// ff( Bear* )
ff( pBear );
```

If two or more user-defined conversions can achieve a match, the call is ambiguous and results in a compile-time error. Conversion constructors and operator conversions share the same precedence. If one instance of each type can be applied, the call is ambiguous.

For example, let Endangered define a conversion operator of type int:

```
class Endangered {
public:
    // conversion: Endangered ==> int
    operator int();

    // ...
};
```

Then if Extinct defines a conversion constructor that accepts a reference to an Endangered class object, such as the following:

```
class Extinct {
public:
    // conversion: Endangered ==> Extinct
    Extinct( Endangered& );

    // ...
};
```

the following call is ambiguous. Both the conversion operator of Endangered and the conversion constructor of Extinct achieve a match.

```
ff( Extinct& );
ff( int );

Endangered e;

ff( e ); // error: ambiguous
```

Here is a second example of ambiguity involving user-defined conversions. In this case, the conversion constructors of SmallInt and BitVector are equally applicable — the call is flagged as an error.

```
class SmallInt {
public:
    // conversion: int ==> SmallInt
    SmallInt( int );

    // ...
};

class BitVector {
    // conversion: unsigned long ==> BitVector
    BitVector( unsigned long );

    // ...
};


ff( SmallInt& );
ff( BitVector& );

ff( 1 ); // error: ambiguous
```

8.2 Virtual Functions

A virtual function is a special member function invoked through a public
base class reference or pointer; it is bound dynamically at run time. The
instance invoked is determined by the class type of the actual object
addressed by the pointer or reference. Resolution of a virtual function is
transparent to the user.

draw(), for example, is a virtual function with an instance defined by
ZooAnimal, Bear, Panda, Cat, and Leopard. A function invoking draw()
might be defined as follows:

```
inline void draw( ZooAnimal& z )
{
        z.draw();
}
```

If an argument to this nonmember instance of draw() addresses a Panda
class object, the statement z.draw() will invoke Panda::draw(). A subsequent argument addressing a Cat class object will result in the call of
Cat::draw(). The compiler resolves which class member function to call
based on the class type of the actual object.

Before examining how virtual functions are declared and used, let's
look briefly at why we would want to use virtual functions.

Dynamic Binding is a Form of Encapsulation

The final screen of the zoo animal application paints a collage of the animals about which the visitor has requested information. This screen, a special favorite of children, has made the display terminal an attraction in its own right.

In order to produce the collage, a linked list of pointers to the animals about which the visitor has inquired is maintained. When the QUIT button is pressed, the head of the linked list of ZooAnimals is passed to finalCollage(), which displays the animals in an appropriate size and layout to fill the screen.

Maintaining the linked list is simple since a ZooAnimal pointer can address any publicly derived class. With dynamic binding, it is also simple to determine the derived class type addressed by the ZooAnimal pointer. finalCollage() might be implemented like this:

```
void finalCollage( ZooAnimal *pz ) {
        for ( ZooAnimal *p = pz; p; p = p->next )
                p->draw();
}
```

In a language without run-time type resolution, it becomes the programmer's responsibility to determine the derived class type addressed by the ZooAnimal pointer. Typically, this involves an identifying isA() class member and an if-else or switch statement that tests and branches on the value of isA(). Without dynamic binding, finalCollage might be implemented like this:

```
// nonobject-oriented implementation
void finalCollage( ZooAnimal *pz ) {
    for ( ZooAnimal *p = pz; p; p = p->next )
        switch ( p->isA() ) {
            case BEAR:
                ((Bear *)p)->draw();
                break;
            case PANDA:
                ((Panda *)p)->draw();
                break;
            // ... every other derived class
        }   // switch of isA
}
```

Programs written in this style are bound to the implementation details of the derivation hierarchy. If those details change, the program may cease to work, and it may become necessary to rewrite source code extensively.

After the pandas leave the zoo to return to China, the Panda class type must be removed. When the koalas arrive from Australia, the Koala class type must be added. For each modification of the hierarchy, every if-else and switch statement that tests on the class type must be identified and modified. The source code is subject to change with each change to the hierarchy.

Even moderately sized switch statements increase the size of program code dramatically. Conceptually simple actions become obscured under the conditional tests necessary to determine the class type of an object. Programs become more difficult to read (and to get *and keep* right).

Users of the hierarchy and its applications who wish either to extend the hierarchy or to customize the applications must have access to the source code. This makes distribution and support much more difficult and expensive for both the originator and the client of the system.

Run-time type resolution encapsulates the implementation details of the derivation hierarchy from the user. Conditional tests on the class type are no longer necessary. This simplifies user code and makes it less volatile. User code, no longer subject to change with each change to the hierarchy, is simpler to program and maintain.

In turn, this simplifies extension of the hierarchy. Adding a new ZooAnimal derivation does not require modification of existing code. The general draw() function need not know about future ZooAnimal derivations. Its code remains functional regardless of how the hierarchy is altered, which means that the application, except for header files, can be distributed in binary form.

Customization is also simplified. Since both the implementation of the class types *and* the implementation of the class hierarchy are encapsulated, either can be altered with minimum impact on client code, provided that both public interfaces remain unchanged.

Virtual Function Definition

A virtual function is specified by prefacing a function declaration with the keyword virtual. Only class member functions may be declared as virtual. The virtual keyword can occur only within the class body. For example,

```
class Foo {
public:
    virtual bar(); // virtual declaration
};

int Foo::bar() { ... }
```

The following simplified declaration of ZooAnimal declares four virtual functions: `debug()`, `locate()`, `draw()`, and `isOnDisplay()`.

```
#include <stream.h>
class ZooAnimal {
public:
    ZooAnimal( char *whatIs = "ZooAnimal" )
        : isa( whatIs ) {}
    void isA() { cout<< "\n\t" << isa << "\n"; }
    void setOpen(int status) { isOpen=status; }
    virtual isOnDisplay() { return isOpen; }
    virtual void debug();
    virtual void draw() = 0;
protected:
    virtual void locate() = 0;
    char *isa;
    char isOpen;
};

void ZooAnimal::debug() {
    isA();
    cout << "\tisOpen: "
        << ((isOnDisplay()) ? "yes" : "no") << "\n";
}
```

`debug()`, `locate()`, `draw()`, and `isOnDisplay()` are declared as member functions of ZooAnimal because they provide a set of routines common to the entire hierarchy of class types. They are declared as virtual functions because the actual implementation details are dependent on the class type and are not known at this time. The base class virtual function serves as a kind of placeholder for as-yet-undetermined derived class types.

Virtual functions defined in the base class of the hierarchy are often never intended to be invoked, as is the case with `locate()` and `draw()`. Neither function makes sense in an abstract class such as ZooAnimal. The class designer can indicate that a virtual function is undefined for an abstract class by initializing its declaration to 0.

```
virtual void draw() = 0;
virtual void locate() = 0;
```

`draw()` and `locate()` are spoken of as *pure virtual functions*. A class with one or more pure virtual functions can be used only as a base class for subsequent derivations. It is illegal to create objects of a class containing pure virtual functions. For example, the following two ZooAnimal definitions result in compile-time errors:

```
ZooAnimal *pz = new ZooAnimal; // error
ZooAnimal za; // error
```

Only an abstract class for which no class instances are intended can declare a pure virtual function.

The class that first declares a function as virtual must either declare it as a pure virtual function or provide a definition.

* If a definition is provided, it serves as a default instance for a subsequent class derivation should the derived class choose not to provide its own instance of the virtual function.

* If a pure virtual function is declared, the derived class *must* either define an instance of the function or again declare it to be a pure virtual function.†

For example, Bear must either provide definitions for `draw()` and `locate()` or else redeclare them as pure virtual functions.

What do we do, however, if we expect class objects of type Bear to be defined, but still wish to defer implementation of `draw()` until a particular species, such as Panda or Grizzly, is derived? We cannot declare `draw()` to be a pure virtual function and still define objects of the class. Here are three alternative solutions:

1. Define a null instance of the virtual function:

```
class Bear : public ZooAnimal {
public:
    void draw() {}
    // ...
};
```

2. Define an instance whose invocation results in an internal error:

```
void Bear::draw() {
        error( INTERNAL, isa, "draw()" );
}
```

3. Define an instance to log the unexpected behavior, while drawing a generic image of a Bear. That is, keep the system running, but also keep a record of run-time exceptions that need to be handled sometime in the future.

A derived class may provide its own instance of a virtual function or by default inherit the base class instance. In turn, it may introduce virtual

---

†This restriction has proved overly restrictive and has been lifted in Release 2.1. Release 2.1 allows for the default inheritance of pure virtual functions.

functions of its own. Bear, for example, redefines `debug()`, `locate()`, and `draw()`; it inherits the ZooAnimal instance of `isOnDisplay()`. In addition, Bear defines two new virtual functions, `hibernates()` and `feedingHours()`.

The Bear definition is simplified to highlight the declaration of virtual functions.

```
class Bear : public ZooAnimal {
public:
    Bear( char *whatIs = "Bear" )
        : ZooAnimal( whatIs ), feedTime( "2:30" )
        {} // intentionally null
    void draw(); // replaces ZooAnimal::draw
    void locate(); // replaces ZooAnimal::locate
    virtual char *feedingHours()
        { return feedTime; }
protected:
    void debug(); // replaces ZooAnimal::debug
    virtual hibernates() { return 1; }
    char *feedTime;
};
```

The redefinition of a virtual function in a derived class *must match exactly* the name, signature, and return type of the base class instance. The keyword `virtual` need not be specified (although it may be if the user wishes). The definition is that of an ordinary member function.

```
void Bear::debug()
{
    isA();
    cout << "\tfeedTime: "
        << feedingHours() << "\n";
}

void Bear::draw() {/*...code goes here */}
void Bear::locate() {/*...code goes here */}
```

The entire virtual mechanism is handled implicitly by the compiler. The class designer need only specify the keyword `virtual` for the first definition of each instance.

If the redeclaration in the derived class does not match exactly, the function is not handled as virtual for the derived class. If Bear, for example, declared `debug()` in either of the following ways:

```
// different return type
void *Bear::debug() {...}

// different signature
void Bear::debug( int ) {...}
```

debug() would not be a virtual function for the Bear class. For example,

```
Bear b;
ZooAnimal &za = b;
za.debug(); // invoke ZooAnimal::debug()
```

A class subsequently derived from Bear, however, can still provide a virtual instance of debug(), even if Bear does not. For example,

```
class Panda : public Bear {
public:
    void debug(); // virtual instance
    // ...
};
```

By exactly matching the virtual declaration of debug(), the Panda instance is also virtual:

```
Panda p;
ZooAnimal &za = p;
za.debug(); // Panda::debug()
```

Notice that the protection levels of two of the virtual functions differ between the base class and the derived class instance. The ZooAnimal instance of locate() is protected, while the Bear instance is public. Similarly, the ZooAnimal instance of debug() is public while the Bear instance is protected.

What, in general, are the protection levels of locate() and debug()? For example, our goal is to write general functions such as

```
void debug( ZooAnimal& z )
{
    // compiler resolves intended instance
    z.debug();
}
```

Since Bear::debug() is protected, does that make the following invocation illegal?

```
main()
{
    // outputs: Bear
    //             feedTime: 2.30
    Bear ursus;
    debug( ursus );
}
```

The answer is no: debug(ursus) is not illegal. The access level of a virtual function is determined by the class type of the pointer or reference through which the member function is invoked. Because debug() is a public member of ZooAnimal, each virtual invocation is treated as public. Note that both this example and the next presume ZooAnimal does not declare any pure virtual functions.

```
main ()
{
    ZooAnimal *pz = new Bear;
    pz->debug(); // invokes Bear::debug()

    pz = new ZooAnimal;
    pz->setOpen(1); // open the zoo
    pz->debug(); // invokes ZooAnimal::debug()
}
```

when compiled, outputs

```
Bear
feedTime: 2:30

ZooAnimal
isOpen: yes
```

Invocations of debug() virtual instances through a Bear class type, however, would all be treated as having protected access. The following invocation would be flagged as an illegal access of a protected class member:

```
main ()
{
    ZooAnimal *pz = new Bear;
    pz->debug(); // invokes Bear::debug()

    Bear *pb = (Bear *) new ZooAnimal; // dangerous

    // illegal: main has no access privilege
    // to the protected members of Bear!
    pb->debug();
}
```

Similarly, locate() is a protected member of ZooAnimal while a public member of Bear. Virtual invocations through a Bear pointer or reference would all be treated as having public access. Virtual invocations through a ZooAnimal pointer or reference, however, would all be treated as having protected access. The following invocation is flagged as an illegal access of a protected member unless the nonmember locate() is made a friend to ZooAnimal.

```
void locate( ZooAnimal *pz )
{
    // locate() has no access privilege;
    // unless made friend to ZooAnimal
    pz->locate(); // error
}
```

These two examples are chosen to illustrate that although virtual functions are resolved at run time, they still obey the access rules of information hiding. The only anomaly is that the access level of a virtual function is the level specified by the class type through which the call is being invoked.

Bear provides its own instances of three of the four virtual functions ZooAnimal defines; it also defines two additional virtual functions. A Panda class derivation inherits the six virtual functions visible within its base Bear class.

What of the three ZooAnimal virtual functions redefined within Bear? They remain inherited ZooAnimal members and can be invoked explicitly. For example, debug() can be reimplemented in the following way:

```
void Bear::debug()
{
    ZooAnimal::debug();
    cout << "Feed time: "
        << feedTime << "\n";
}
```

Panda is derived from three base classes, those of Bear, Endangered, and Herbivore. Endangered and Herbivore each define two virtual functions:

```
class Endangered {
public:
    virtual adjustPopulation( int );
    virtual highlight( short );
    // ...
};
```

```
class Herbivore {
public:
    virtual inform( ZooAnimal& );
    virtual highlight( short );
    // ...
};
```

Panda inherits the ten virtual functions defined within its three base classes. It can provide its own instances of any of its virtual functions. In addition, it can introduce virtual functions of its own.

Panda inherits two virtual functions named highlight() — one from its Endangered derivation and one from its Herbivore derivation. This is a problem only if highlight() is invoked from a Panda class type or if Panda is subsequently an object of derivation. In both cases, a reference to highlight() is ambiguous. For example,

```
RedPanda : public Panda { ... };
RedPanda pandy;
Panda &rp = pandy;

// ...
rp.highlight(); // error: ambiguous
```

To prevent the potential ambiguity, Panda defines its own instance of highlight() (see Section 7.4 (page 311) for a discussion of the problem). The following Panda class definition is simplified to highlight the declaration of virtual functions under multiple inheritance.

```
class Panda : public Bear, public Endangered,
        public Herbivore {
public:
    Panda( char *whatIs = "Panda" ) :
        Bear( whatIs ) {}
    virtual onLoan();
    inform( ZooAnimal& );
    void draw();
    int debug();
    void locate();
    hibernates() { return 0; }
protected:
    highlight( short );
    short cell;
    short onLoan;
};
```

A base class knows of the redefinitions of its virtual functions in subsequent class derivations. The virtual instance invoked is determined by the actual class type of the base class reference or pointer. A base class does not, however, know about virtual functions introduced in subsequent derivations. It is not possible, for example, to invoke `hibernate()`, introduced by Bear, through a ZooAnimal reference or pointer. The following, for example, is illegal:

```
int hibernate( ZooAnimal &za )
{
    // error: hibernate not a member of ZooAnimal
    return za.hibernate();
}
```

Bear is the "base clase" of the `hibernate()` virtual function. Only the classes on its branch of the inheritance hierarchy can access it. If `hibernate()` is an activity common to a wider set of classes in the inheritance hierarchy, then its definition does not belong in Bear. `hibernate()` must either be moved further up in the hierarchy (in this case becoming a member of ZooAnimal) or else the branches of the hierarchy must be redesigned. In either case, `hibernate()` needs to be accessible to all the classes within the hierarchy for which hibernation is a common activity.

Table 8.1 lists the active virtual functions within Panda. The second column lists the class in which the active function is defined; the third column, the class in which the virtual function is first defined.

Virtual Function	Active Definition	First Definition
isOnDisplay()	ZooAnimal	ZooAnimal
locate()	Panda	ZooAnimal
draw()	Panda	ZooAnimal
debug()	Panda	ZooAnimal
feedingHours()	Bear	Bear
hibernates()	Bear	Bear
adjustPopulation(int)	Endangered	Endangered
highlight(short)	Panda	Endangered/Herbivore
inform(ZooAnimal&)	Panda	Herbivore
onLoan()	Panda	Panda

Table 8.1 Panda Virtual Functions

The good design of an inheritance hierarchy is difficult. The designer can expect to go through many iterations. Hierarchy design is an area of active research (and some controversy) and as yet is without an agreed upon set of rules.

Exercise 8-1. There is a clearly misplaced virtual function introduced in the definition of Bear. Which virtual function is it? Where should it be placed? Why?

□

Exercise 8-2. Section 7.4 (page 308) presents first definitions of ZooAnimal, Bear, and Panda. These definitions are used to illustrate the derivation mechanism and do not necessarily represent the best design of a ZooAnimal hierarchy. Redefine these class definitions, including a set of virtual functions, and instances of X(const X&) and operator=(const X&).

□

Exercise 8-3. Redesign the debug() member function of the Shapes hierarchy described in Section 7.4 (page 312) to be a virtual member function.

□

Exercise 8-4. Reimplement the nonmember debug() function described in Section 7.7 (page 323) to handle the virtual implementation debug() member function of the Shapes hierarchy.

□

Exercise 8-5. Implement the draw() virtual function for the Shapes hierarchy.

□

Exercise 8-6. Implement a reSize() virtual function for the Shapes hierarchy. □

Virtual Destructors

The linked list of ZooAnimals passed to finalCollage() is no longer needed once that function is completed. Typically, a for-loop of the following sort is added to the end of finalCollage to free up storage:

```
for ( ZooAnimal *p = pz->next; p;
                 pz = p, p = p->next )
    delete pz;
```

Unfortunately, this strategy does not work. The explicit deletion of pz causes the ZooAnimal destructor to be applied to the object to which pz points. Each object, however, is not a ZooAnimal but some subsequently derived class type such as Bear; the destructor for the actual class type of

the ZooAnimal pointer must somehow be invoked. Any explicit invocation, however, reintroduces all the drawbacks that come with using the
representational details of the derivation hierarchy.

```
for ( ZooAnimal *p = pz->next; p;
                pz = p, p = p->next )
    switch ( pz->isA() )
    {
        case BEAR:
            // direct invocation of destructor
            ((Bear*)pz)->Bear::~Bear();
            break;


        case PANDA:
            // indirect invocation through delete
            delete (Panda *) pz;
            break;

        // ... more cases go here
    }
```

Although destructors do not share a common name, they can be
declared as virtual. The destructor of a class derived from a class that
declares its destructor virtual is also virtual. If ZooAnimal declares
ZooAnimal::~ZooAnimal() to be virtual, then every destructor in the
derivation hierarchy will be virtual. For example,

```
class ZooAnimal {
public:
    virtual ~ZooAnimal();
    // ... rest of ZooAnimal goes here
};


// ok: this will now correctly invoke the
// destructor for the class type pz addresses
for ( ZooAnimal *p = pz->next; p;
                pz = p, p = p->next )
    delete pz;
```

Specifying the destructors in a derivation hierarchy as virtual ensures
that the appropriate destructor is invoked whenever delete is applied to a
base class pointer. As a general rule of thumb, therefore, the destructor of
an abstract class should always be specified as virtual.

Exercise 8-7. Define the destructors for the Shapes hierarchy as virtual. □

Virtual Function Invocation

A virtual function is invoked through a pointer or reference of a particular class type. The set of potential virtual functions that may be invoked at each call consists of the following:

- The instance defined by the invoking class type.

- Those instances *redefined* by subsequent derivations.

The virtual function instance executed at any particular call is determined by the actual class type addressed by the pointer or reference.

The most inclusive class type through which to invoke a virtual function is the abstract base class of the derivation hierarchy — in our example, a pointer or reference of type ZooAnimal. ZooAnimal has access to the entire inheritance chain. That is the purpose of defining an abstract superclass.

For the purposes of illustrating the invocation of virtual functions, let us provide a simplified set of class definitions. ZooAnimal will define two virtual functions, print() and isA(), and a virtual destructor instance.

```
#include <stream.h>
enum ZooLocs { ZOOANIMAL, BEAR, PANDA };

class ZooAnimal {
public:
    ZooAnimal( char *s = "ZooAnimal" );
    virtual ~ZooAnimal() { delete name; }
    void link( ZooAnimal* );
    virtual void print( ostream& );
    virtual void isA( ostream& );
protected:
    char *name;
    ZooAnimal *next;
};

#include <string.h>
ZooAnimal::ZooAnimal( char *s ) : next( 0 )
{
    name = new char[ strlen(s) + 1 ];
    strcpy( name, s );
}
```

The idea is to build up a heterogeneous list of ZooAnimal derivations linked by the member next. The actual class types of the list need not be of concern to the programmer; the virtual function mechanism will determine the class type of each element.

The ZooAnimal `link()` function accepts an argument of type `ZooAnimal*` and assigns it to `next`. It is implemented as follows:

```
void ZooAnimal::link( ZooAnimal *za )
{
    za->next = next;
    next = za;
}
```

`isA()` and `print()` are each implemented as virtual functions. Each subsequent derivation will define its own instances of these two functions. `isA()` announces its class type; `print()` elaborates on the class type representation. Each takes an ostream reference as an argument. Here are the implementations:

```
void ZooAnimal::isA( ostream& os )
{
    os << "ZooAnimal name: "
        << name << "\n";
}

void ZooAnimal::print( ostream& os )
{
    isA( os ); // virtual invocation
}
```

One goal of our design is to support iostream output of any class type that is a member of the ZooAnimal inheritance hierarchy. To achieve that, we must overload the output operator to accept a ZooAnimal reference. This function is implemented as follows:

```
#include <stream.h>

ostream&
operator <<( ostream& os, ZooAnimal& za )
{
    za.print( os );
    return os;
}
```

The progammer can now direct any member of the ZooAnimal inheritance hierarchy to an output operator and have the correct virtual `print()` function invoked. We will see an example of this after we define the Bear and Panda class types. Note that the operator function has not been made a friend to ZooAnimal. It does not need to be a friend since its access is limited to the ZooAnimal public interface.

The Bear class definition looks as follows:

```
class Bear : public ZooAnimal {
public:
    Bear( char *s = "Bear", ZooLocs loc = BEAR,
          char *sci = "Ursidae" );
    ~Bear() { delete sciName; }
    void print( ostream& );
    void isA( ostream& );
protected:
    char *sciName; // scientific name
    ZooLocs zooArea;
};

#include <string.h>
Bear::Bear( char *s, ZooLocs loc, char *sci )
    : ZooAnimal( s ), zooArea( loc ) {
    sciName = new char[ strlen(sci) + 1 ];
    strcpy( sciName, sci );
}
```

Bear introduces two additional data members:

- `sciName`, the scientific name associated with the animal.

- `zooArea`, the general area in the zoo where the animal is housed.

The `isA()` and `print()` virtual instances that Bear provides reflect its representation. They are implemented as follows:

```
void Bear::isA( ostream& os ) {
    ZooAnimal::isA( os ); // static invocation
    os << "\tscientific name:\t";
    os << sciName << "\n";
}

static char *locTable[] = {
    "The entire animal display area",   // ZOOANIMAL
    "NorthWest: B1: area Brown",         // BEAR
    "NorthWest: B1.P: area BrownSpots"   // PANDA
    // ... and so on
};

void Bear::print( ostream& os ) {
    ZooAnimal::print( os ); // static invocation
    os << "\tZoo Area Location:\n\t";
    os << locTable[ zooArea ] << "\n";
}
```

There are three cases in which an invocation of a virtual function is resolved statically at compile time:

1. When a virtual function is invoked through an object of the class type.
    In the following code fragment, for example, the isA() function
    invoked through the ZooAnimal class object za is *always* resolved stati-
    cally. The isA() function invoked through the dereferenced pointer
    pz, however, is still resolved as a virtual call.

```
#include "ZooAnimal.h"

main() {
    ZooAnimal za;
    ZooAnimal *pz;

    // ...

    za.isA( cout );     // nonvirtual invocation
    (*pz).isA( cout ); // virtual invocation
}
```

2. When a virtual function is explicitly invoked through a pointer or refer-
    ence using the class scope operator. For example,

```
#include <stream.h>
#include "Bear.h"
#include "ZooAnimal.h"

main() {
    Bear yogi ( "cartoon Bear", BEAR,
                    "ursus cartoonus" );
    ZooAnimal circus( "circusZooAnimal" );
    ZooAnimal *pz;

    pz = &circus;
    cout << "virtual: ZooAnimal::print()\n";
    pz->print( cout );

    pz = &yogi;
    cout << "\nvirtual: Bear::print()\n";
    pz->print( cout );

    cout << "\nnonvirtual: ZooAnimal::print()\n";
    cout << "note: isA() is invoked virtually\n";
    pz->ZooAnimal::print( cout );
}
```

When compiled and executed, this program generates the following
output:

```
virtual: ZooAnimal::print()
ZooAnimal name: circusZooAnimal

virtual: Bear::print()
ZooAnimal name: cartoon Bear
        scientific name:        ursus cartoonus
        Zoo Area Location:
        NorthWest: B1: area Brown

nonvirtual: ZooAnimal::print()
note: isA() is invoked virtually
ZooAnimal name: cartoon Bear
        scientific name:        ursus cartoonus
```

3. When a virtual function is invoked within either the constructor or the destructor of a base class. In both cases, the base class instance of the virtual function is called since the derived class object is either not yet constructed or already destructed.

Panda introduces two additional data members: indName, the name of the individual animal, and cell, the cage location in which the animal is housed. Here is the Panda class definition:

```
#include <stream.h>

class Panda : public Bear {
public:
    Panda( char *nm, int room, char *s = "Panda",
           char *sci = "Ailuropoda Melaoleuca",
           ZooLocs loc = PANDA );
    ~Panda() { delete indName; }
    void print( ostream& );
    void isA( ostream& );
protected:
    char *indName; // name of individual animal
    int cell;
};

#include <string.h>
Panda::Panda ( char *nm, int room, char *s,
               char *sci, ZooLocs loc )
    : Bear( s, loc, sci ), cell( room ) {
    indName = new char[ strlen(nm) + 1 ];
    strcpy( indName, nm );
}
```

The isA() and print() virtual instances that Panda provides reflect its representation. They are implemented as follows:

```
void Panda::isA( ostream& os )
{
    Bear::isA( os );
    os << "\twe call our friend:\t";
    os << indName << "\n";
}


void Panda::print( ostream& os )
{
    Bear::print( os );
    os << "\tRoom Location:\t";
    os << cell << "\n";
}
```

Let's step through a number of examples to get a feel for how things work. Our first example illustrates the virtual invocation of print() through a ZooAnimal reference. Each class object is passed to the overloaded instance of the output operator ("<<"). Each call of

```
za.print( os );
```

within the output operator instance invokes the virtual instance defined by the actual class type of za.

```
#include <iostream.h>
#include "ZooAnimal.h"
#include "Bear.h"
#include "Panda.h"

ZooAnimal circus( "circusZooAnimal" );
Bear yogi("cartoon Bear",BEAR,"ursus cartoonus");
Panda yinYang("Yin Yang",1001,"Giant Panda");

main() {
    cout << "Invocation by a ZooAnimal object:\n"
         << circus << "\n";

    cout << "\nInvocation by a Bear object:\n"
         << yogi << "\n";

    cout << "\nInvocation by a Panda object:\n"
         << yinYang << "\n";
};
```

When compiled and executed, the program generates the following output:

```
Invocation by a ZooAnimal object:
ZooAnimal name: circusZooAnimal


Invocation by a Bear object:
ZooAnimal name: cartoon Bear
        scientific name:        ursus cartoonus
        Zoo Area Location:
        NorthWest: B1: area Brown


Invocation by a Panda object:
ZooAnimal name: Giant Panda
        scientific name:        Ailuropoda Melaoleuca
        we call our friend:     Yin Yang
        Zoo Area Location:
        NorthWest: B1.P: area BrownSpots
        Room Location:   1001
```

This next example illustrates the direct manipulation of pointers to class
objects. It invokes the isA() virtual function.

```
#include <stream.h>
#include "ZooAnimal.h"
#include "Bear.h"
#include "Panda.h"

ZooAnimal circus( "circusZooAnimal" );
Bear yogi("cartoon Bear",BEAR,"ursus cartoonus");
Panda yinYang("Yin Yang",1001,"Giant Panda");

main() {
    ZooAnimal *pz;

    pz = &circus;
    cout << "virtual: ZooAnimal::isA():\n";
    pz->isA( cout );

    pz = &yogi;
    cout << "\nvirtual: Bear::isA():\n";
    pz->isA( cout );

    pz = &yinYang;
    cout << "\nvirtual: Panda::isA():\n";
    pz->isA( cout );
}
```

When compiled and executed, the program generates the following output:

```
virtual: ZooAnimal::isA():
ZooAnimal name: circusZooAnimal

virtual: Bear::isA():
ZooAnimal name: cartoon Bear
        scientific name:        ursus cartoonus

virtual: Panda::isA():
ZooAnimal name: Giant Panda
        scientific name:        Ailuropoda Melaoleuca
        we call our friend:     Yin Yang
```

In this next example, the actual class type addressed by pz is known at compile time. Let's override the virtual mechanism and invoke each function statically:

```
#include <stream.h>
#include "ZooAnimal.h"
#include "Bear.h"
#include "Panda.h"

ZooAnimal circus( "circusZooAnimal" );
Bear yogi("cartoon Bear",BEAR,"ursus cartoonus");
Panda yinYang("Yin Yang",1001,"Giant Panda");

main() {
    ZooAnimal *pz = &yinYang;
    cout << "Nonvirtual invocation of Panda::isA():\n";
    ((Panda*)pz) ->Panda::isA( cout );

    pz = &yogi;
    cout << "\nNonvirtual invocation of Bear::isA():\n";
    ((Bear*)pz) ->Bear::isA( cout );
}
```

The nonvirtual invocation of Panda::isA() through a ZooAnimal pointer requires an explicit cast. ZooAnimal has no knowledge of its subsequent Panda class derivation; such knowledge is part of the virtual mechanism, not part of the base class itself. When compiled and executed, the program generates the following output:

```
Nonvirtual invocation of Panda::isA():
ZooAnimal name: Giant Panda
        scientific name:        Ailuropoda Melaoleuca
        we call our friend:     Yin Yang

Nonvirtual invocation of Bear::isA():
ZooAnimal name: cartoon Bear
        scientific name:        ursus cartoonus
```

This last example prints out a heterogeneous list of ZooAnimal pointers. It is implemented using the following nonmember `print()` function — because it must access the nonpublic ZooAnimal data member next, `print()` must be declared a friend to ZooAnimal.

```cpp
#include <iostream.h>
#include "ZooAnimal.h"

void print( ZooAnimal *pz, ostream &os = cout )
{
    while ( pz ) {
        pz->print( os );
        os << "\n";
        pz = pz->next;
    }
}
```

For our program example, we need a ZooAnimal pointer to head the linked list:

```cpp
ZooAnimal *headPtr = 0;
```

`main()` is defined as follows:

```cpp
#include <stream.h>
#include "ZooAnimal.h"

extern ZooAnimal *makeList( ZooAnimal* );
ZooAnimal *headPtr = 0;

main() {
  cout<< "A Program to Illustrate Virtual Functions\n";
  headPtr = makeList( headPtr );
  print( headPtr );
}
```

`makeList()`, in turn, is defined as follows:

```
#include <stream.h>
#include "ZooAnimal.h"
#include "Bear.h"
#include "Panda.h"

ZooAnimal circus( "circusZooAnimal" );
Bear yogi("cartoon Bear",BEAR,"ursus cartoonus");
Panda yinYang("Yin Yang",1001,"Giant Panda");
Panda rocky("Rocky",943,"Red Panda","Ailurus fulgens");

ZooAnimal *makeList( ZooAnimal *ptr )
{
    // for simplicity, hand code list
    ptr = &yinYang;
    ptr->link( &circus );
    ptr->link( &yogi );
    ptr->link( &rocky );
    return ptr;
}
```

When compiled and executed, the program generates the following output:

```
A Program to Illustrate Virtual Functions
ZooAnimal name: Giant Panda
        scientific name:        Ailuropoda Melaoleuca
        we call our friend:     Yin Yang
        Zoo Area Location:
        NorthWest: B1.P: area BrownSpots
        Room Location:   1001


ZooAnimal name: Red Panda
        scientific name:        Ailurus fulgens
        we call our friend:     Rocky
        Zoo Area Location:
        NorthWest: B1.P: area BrownSpots
        Room Location:   943


ZooAnimal name: cartoon Bear
        scientific name:        ursus cartoonus
        Zoo Area Location:
        NorthWest: B1: area Brown

ZooAnimal name: circusZooAnimal
```

Except for makeList(), the program is completely general, taking no account of the implementation details of the class objects, the member functions, or the inheritance hierarchy. Although simplistic, the example captures some of the spirit of object-oriented programming.

Exercise 8-8. Implement a nonmember draw() function which takes an argument of type Shape*. Have it draw a circle, a right triangle, and a rectangle.

□

Exercise 8-9. Implement a nonmember reSize() function which takes an argument of type Shape& (it will need a size argument as well). draw(), reSize(), then draw() a circle, an equilateral triangle, and a square.

□

Exercise 8-10. Add a virtual draw() instance which writes to a Screen class object.

□

Exercise 8-11. Implement the virtual functions save(), which writes an object of the Shapes hierarchy to an ostream, and restore(), which reads in the output of save(). □

8.3 Virtual Base Classes

Although a base class may legally appear only once in a derivation list, a base class can appear multiple times within a derivation hierarchy. This gives rise to a form of member ambiguity.

For example, there has been a debate, sometimes heated, within zoological circles for more than 100 years as to whether the Panda belongs to the Raccoon or the Bear family. From the computer science point of view, the best solution is to derive Panda from both families.

```
class Panda : public Bear, public Raccoon { ... }
```

Panda inherits a ZooAnimal base class from both Bear and Raccoon; that is, there are two base class parts to a Panda. Declaration of a Panda class object results in the invocation of two ZooAnimal constructors, in the following order:

```
ZooAnimal();   // base class of Bear
Bear();        // first Panda base class
ZooAnimal();   // base class of Raccoon
Raccoon();     // second Panda base class
Panda();       // derived class constructor is always last
```

For the purposes of this discussion, let's provide a simplified definition of ZooAnimal:

```
class ZooAnimal {  // simplified definition
public:
    void locate();
protected:
    short zooArea;
};

class Bear : public ZooAnimal    { /* ... */ };
class Raccoon : public ZooAnimal { /* ... */ };
```

Panda contains two sets of ZooAnimal data members: one `zooArea` data member inherited through Raccoon and one inherited through Bear. Fig. 8.1 illustrates the class object layout of this Panda class.

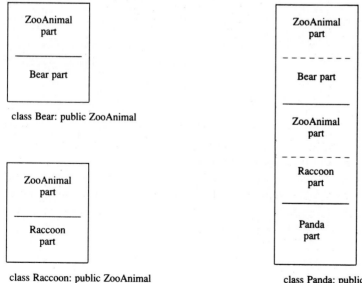

class Bear: public ZooAnimal

class Raccoon: public ZooAnimal

class Panda: public Bear, public Raccoon

Figure 8.1 Multiple Inclusion of a Base Class

zooArea cannot be directly accessed from within Panda. We must distinguish between the two instances of zooArea. The class scope operator can be used to disambiguate which instance is intended. Since the ambiguity rests in the multiple inclusion of the ZooAnimal base class part, however, writing ZooAnimal::zooArea is no less ambiguous than simply writing zooArea. To resolve the ambiguity, the qualification must indicate which of the two ZooAnimal instances is meant, either the one inherited through Bear or the one inherited through Raccoon; that is, either Bear::zooArea or Raccoon::zooArea. For example,

```
Panda::getArea()
{    // qualified reference to prevent ambiguity
     // BEAR is an enumeration constant
     return( (isA() == BEAR)
             ? Bear::zooArea : Raccoon::zooArea );

}
```

There is only one instance of ZooAnimal::locate(). Within Panda, both locate() and ZooAnimal::locate() access the intended inherited member function. Both, however, are flagged as ambiguous. Why?

Panda contains two ZooAnimal base class objects, one or the other of which must be bound to the function invocation (see Section 5.4 (page 194) for a discussion of the binding of a member function and the invoking class object through the this pointer). It is the programmer's responsibility to indicate which base class object, the one inherited through Bear or the one inherited through Raccoon. Once again, this is accomplished using the class scope operator. The programmer must indicate which class object: Bear::locate() or Raccoon::locate.

```
// qualified reference to prevent ambiguity
locate( Panda *p )
{
    // BEAR and RACCOON are enumeration constants
    switch( p->isA() ) {
        case BEAR:
            p->Bear::locate();
            break;

        case RACCOON:
            p->Raccoon::locate();
            break;
    }

}
```

Under certain applications, the occurrence of multiple base class instances is desirable. In this case, however, it is not:

These are unnecessary ambiguities. The user has to know the details of the multiple derivations so as to make the disambiguating calls. In addition, the space required for the additional base class instances is wasteful.

Panda requires only one base class instance of ZooAnimal. Conceptually, Panda can be thought of as a directed acyclic graph (DAG) with a shared ZooAnimal base class instance. The default inheritance mechanism, however, defines a tree derivation hierarchy in which each occurrence of a base class generates a base class instance (see Fig. 8.2).

It is necessary to find a way of overriding the default inheritance mechanism. It should be possible to specify a shared base class within a derivation hierarchy (that is, to define a DAG structure). Otherwise, a class of users (possibly quite small) will be penalized by its use of multiple inheritance.

Virtual base classes, a method of overriding the default inheritance mechanism, allow the class designer to specify a shared base class. Regardless of how often a virtual base class may occur in the derivation hierarchy, only one instance is generated. Panda, for example, would contain only one, shared ZooAnimal base class. Class member access would no longer be ambiguous.

Virtual Base Class Definition

A base class is specified as virtual by modifying its declaration with the keyword `virtual`. For example, the following declaration makes ZooAnimal a virtual base class of Bear and Raccoon.

```
// placement order of keywords public
// and virtual is not significant.
class Bear : public virtual ZooAnimal    { /* ... */ };
class Raccoon : virtual public ZooAnimal { /* ... */ };
```

A base class specified as virtual must, if it defines any constructors, define a constructor that does not require an argument list — either a constructor taking no arguments or one in which a default value is provided for each argument.† Apart from this, the definition of ZooAnimal need not be modified in order to specify it as a virtual base class. Here is the definition of ZooAnimal we will work with in our discussion of virtual base classes:

---

†This requirement has since been removed from the language, although the AT&T 2.0 Release enforces it. Under the current rules, if a default constructor is required and not present, a compile-time error results. The earlier constraint attempted to prevent just such a compile-time error.

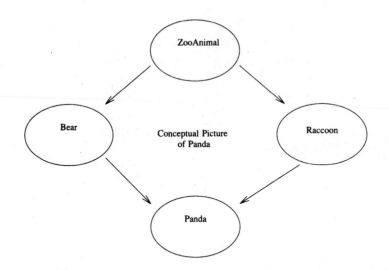

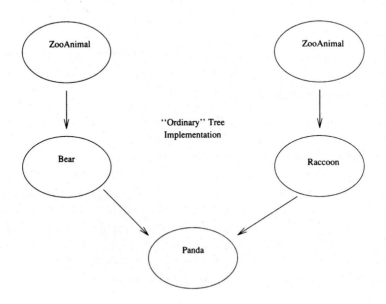

Figure 8.2 NonVirtual Multiple Inheritance

```
class ZooAnimal {   // simplified definition
public:
    ZooAnimal(){ zooArea = 0; name = 0; }
    ZooAnimal( char*, short );
    void locate();
protected:
    short zooArea;
    char *name;
};
```

The use of Bear and Raccoon class objects is unchanged. A virtual base class can be initialized in the same way as a nonvirtual base class:

```
Bear::Bear( char *nm)
    : ZooAnimal( nm, BEAR ) { ... }

Raccoon::Raccoon( char *nm)
    : ZooAnimal( nm, RACCOON ) { ... }
```

The declaration of Panda looks the same as its nonvirtual instance:

```
class Panda: public Bear, public Raccoon { ... };
```

Because both Bear and Raccoon have declared ZooAnimal as a virtual base class, however, each Panda class object contains only one ZooAnimal instance.

Ordinarily, a derived class can explicitly initialize only its immediate base classes. In a nonvirtual derivation of ZooAnimal, for example, Panda could not name ZooAnimal in the initialization list of its constructor. Virtual base classes, however, are an exception. The reason why is as follows.

Panda contains a single ZooAnimal instance shared between Raccoon and Bear. Raccoon and Bear, however, both explicitly initialize ZooAnimal. The Panda instance cannot be initialized twice.

A virtual base class is initialized by its *most derived* class. Panda, in this case, is more derived than either Raccoon or Bear. Panda can explicitly initialize ZooAnimal in the initialization list of its constructor. If its constructor does not explicitly initialize ZooAnimal, the default ZooAnimal constructor is invoked. The ZooAnimal initializations of Raccoon and Bear are never applied to the ZooAnimal portion of a Panda class object.

A Panda constructor might be defined as follows:

```
Panda::Panda( char *nm )
    : ZooAnimal( nm, PANDA ),
    Bear( nm ), Raccoon( nm ) { ... }
```

If the Panda constructor is defined as follows:

```
Panda::Panda( char *nm )
    : Bear( nm ), Raccoon( nm ) { ... }
```

the default ZooAnimal constructor is invoked.

Virtual Base Class Member Access

Each Raccoon and Bear class object maintains its own set of inherited
ZooAnimal members, which can be accessed exactly like the inherited
members of a nonvirtual derivation. An individual reading a program's
code could not distinguish between the use of an object of a virtual and a
nonvirtual base class derivation; the only difference lies in the method of
allocating the base class part.

In a nonvirtual derivation, each derived class object contains a contiguous base and a derived class part (see Fig. 7.4 in Section 7.7 (page 321)
illustrating the object layout of a derived class object). A Bear class object,
for example, has a ZooAnimal base and a Bear part. In a virtual derivation,
each derived class object contains a derived part and a pointer to the virtual base class part. The virtual base class is not contained within the
derived class object. The class model of a virtual derivation for the Bear,
Raccoon, and Panda class is illustrated in Fig. 8.3.

A virtual base class obeys the same public and private rules as a nonvirtual derivation:

- The inherited members of a public virtual derivation retain their same
  public and protected access levels in the derived class.

- The inherited members of a private virtual derivation become private
  members in the derived class.

What happens when a once-removed derivation, such as Panda,
includes both a public *and* a private instance of a virtual base class? For
example,

```
class ZooAnimal {
public:
    void locate();
protected:
    short zooArea;
};

class Bear : public virtual ZooAnimal { /* ... */ };
class Raccoon : private virtual ZooAnimal { /* ... */ };

class Panda : public Bear, public Raccoon { /* ... */ };
```

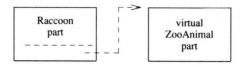

class Raccoon : public virtual ZooAnimal

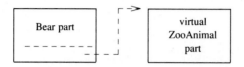

class Bear : public virtual ZooAnimal

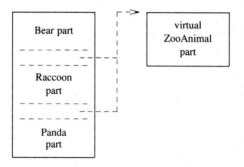

class Panda : public Bear, public Raccoon

Figure 8.3 Virtual Base Class Representation

Because ZooAnimal is a virtual base class, Panda inherits only one copy of `zooArea` and `locate()`. The question is whether Panda is allowed access to these members. Along the public path of the inheritance, Panda can access the two ZooAnimal members. These members, however, are not accessible to Panda along the private path of the inheritance. Which path predominates in a virtual derivation? Is the following call legal?

```
Panda p;
p.locate();
```

Yes, the call is legal. The public path always predominates. Panda can access both `zooArea` and `locate()`. In general, regardless of the number of virtual base class instances within the inheritance hierarchy, if there is a single public instance, the one shared instance of the derivation is considered public.

ZooAnimal defines a `locate()` member function that Raccoon inherits. The call

```
Raccoon r;
r.locate(); // inherited ZooAnimal instance
```

invokes the ZooAnimal instance. Imagine that Bear defines its own instance of `locate()`. The call

```
Bear b;
b.locate(); // Bear instance
```

invokes the Bear instance and not that of ZooAnimal. In a nonvirtual derivation, the call

```
Panda p;
p.locate(); // which locate()?
```

is ambiguous if Panda does not define its own instance of `locate()`. If ZooAnimal is a virtual base class of both Raccoon and Bear, however, the Bear instance of `locate()` is invoked. There is no longer an ambiguity. In a virtual derivation, the most derived instance of the member function *dominates*. The Bear instance of `locate()` dominates the ZooAnimal instance Raccoon inherits.

Constructor and Destructor Ordering

Virtual base classes are constructed before nonvirtual base classes regardless of where they appear in the derivation list. If a class has two base classes, and one of the base classes is virtual, the virtual base class constructor is *always* invoked first. Similarly, the destructor of the virtual base class is always invoked last. For example,

```
class TeddyBear : public Bear,
                  public virtual ToyAnimal { ... };


TeddyBear pooh;
```

The order of constructor invocations for pooh is the following

```
ToyAnimal();    // virtual base class
ZooAnimal();    // base class of Bear
Bear();         // nonvirtual base class
TeddyBear();
```

The destructor order for pooh is the reverse.

If a class has multiple virtual base classes, their constructors are invoked in the order the virtual base classes are declared. Following that, the normal ordering of constructor calls for a derived class object is observed

A more complicated case is when the virtual base class is nested within the inheritance hierarchy. Panda, for example, contains the shared virtual ZooAnimal base class of Bear and Raccoon. Detecting the presence of a virtual base class requires a search of the entire inheritance graph of the derived class. The actual definition of Panda, for example, does not suggest the presence of a virtual base class:

```
class Panda: public Endangered, public Herbivore,
             public Raccoon, public Bear { ... };

Panda yinYang;
```

The actual virtual derivation of ZooAnimal occurs at an earlier level of the inheritance graph, when Raccoon and Bear are defined. The order of constructor calls for yinYang is the following:

```
ZooAnimal();      // virtual base class
Herbivore();      // base class declaration order
Endangered();
Raccoon();
Bear();
Panda();
```

The inheritance hierarchy is searched for the presence of virtual base classes in the order of base class declarations. The Panda derivation presented here, for example, is searched in the following order:

- Endangered

- Herbivore

- Raccoon

- Bear

Were Endangered also to contain a virtual base class, the order of constructor invocation for multiple virtual base classes follows the search order of the hierarchy. For example, a virtual base class associated with Endangered is invoked before the ZooAnimal virtual base class associated with both Bear and Raccoon. The order of destructor calls is the inverse.

and Nonvirtual Instances

. contains both virtual and nonvirtual instances of a base
_ vase class object is created for each nonvirtual instance and
...other base class object is created for all virtual instances. For example, if
Endangered were modified to be a nonvirtual derivation of ZooAnimal,
Panda would contain two ZooAnimal instances, the virtual instance from
Bear and Raccoon and the nonvirtual Endangered instance.

There again exist two (or more) instances of the inherited base class
members. References must be qualified to indicate which instance is meant;
unqualified reference is again ambiguous.

Summary

The inheritance mechanism, by default, defines a tree derivation hierarchy
in which each occurrence of a base class generates a base class instance.
Virtual base classes provide a method of overriding this default mechanism. Regardless of how often a virtual base class may occur in a derivation hierarchy, only one instance of the virtual base class is generated. A
virtual base class serves as a single, shared instance. In our example,
ZooAnimal is a virtual base class of both Bear and Raccoon. Panda,
derived from both Bear and Raccoon, contains a single shared instance of
ZooAnimal.

Appendix A: **The C++ I/O Library**

Input/output facilities are not defined within the C++ language, but rather are implemented in C++ and provided as a component of a C++ standard library. The I/O library described here, referred to as the *iostream* library, is distributed with Release 2.0 of the AT&T C++ Language System. It replaces an earlier version of the I/O library referred to as the *stream* library, described in Stroustrup's *The C++ Programming Language*. Programs that use the earlier stream package are mostly upwardly compatible with the iostream package.

At its lowest level, a file is interpreted simply as a sequence, or *stream*, of bytes. One aspect of the I/O library manages the transfer of these bytes. At this level, the notion of a data type is absent.

At the user level, of course, a file consists of a sequence of possibly intermixed data types — characters, arithmetic values, class objects. A second aspect of the I/O library manages the interface between these two levels.

The iostream library predefines a set of operations for handling reading and writing of the built-in data types. In addition, the programmer can extend certain of these operations to handle class types. These two components of the iostream library form the subject of this appendix.

Input and output operations are supported by the *istream* (input stream) and *ostream* (output stream) classes. The *iostream* class is derived from both istream and ostream; it allows for bi-directional I/O. The ostream output operation, referred to as *insertion*, is performed by the left shift or insertion operator ("<<"). A value is said to be inserted into the output stream. The istream input operation, referred to as *extraction*, is performed by the right shift or extraction operator (">>"). A value is said to be extracted from the input stream.

A useful way of thinking about the two operators is that each "points" in the direction of its data movement. For example,

        >> x

moves the data *into* x, while

        << x

carries the data *out from* x.

Four stream objects are predefined for the user:

1. `cin`, an istream class object tied to standard input.

2. `cout`, an ostream class object tied to standard output.

3. `cerr`, an ostream class object tied to standard error and that provides for unbuffered output.

4. `clog`, an ostream class object also tied to standard error but that provides for buffered output.

Any program that uses the iostream library must include the header file `iostream.h`. Programs written under the earlier stream library, however, do not need to be changed. The `stream.h` include directive continues to be supported. It is treated as an alias for the `iostream.h` header file.

File manipulation using the input and output operations is also supported. A user can tie a particular file to the program by defining an instance of one of the following three class types:

1. *ifstream*, derived from istream, ties a file to the program for input.

2. *ofstream*, derived from ostream, ties a file to the program for output.

3. *fstream*, derived from iostream, ties a file to the program for both input and output.

The iostream library also supports "incore" formatting within character arrays. There are two associated class types:

1. *istrstream*, derived from istream, that fetches characters from an array.

2. *ostrstream*, derived from ostream, that stores characters into an array.

File manipulation and the use of incore operations are discussed later in this appendix following a general discussion of output and input.

A.1 Output

The general output method is to apply the insertion operator ("<<") to `cout`. For example,

```
#include <iostream.h>
main() {
    cout << "I am an output string\n";
}
```

will print as follows on the user's terminal:

```
I am an output string
```

A predefined set of insertion operators are provided that accept arguments of any of the built-in data types, including char*. Later in this appendix, we discuss how to extend this set of operators to accept class argument types.

Any complex expression can be specified that evaluates to a data type accepted by an insertion operator. For example,

```cpp
#include <iostream.h>
#include <string.h>

main() {
    cout << "The length of ''ulysses'' is:\t";
    cout << strlen( "ulysses" );
    cout << "\n";

    cout << "The size of ''ulysses'' is:\t";
    cout << sizeof( "ulysses" );
    cout << "\n";

    return 0;
}
```

will print as follows on the user's terminal:

```
The length of ''ulysses'' is:    7
The size of ''ulysses'' is:      8
```

The insertion operator can be concatenated into a single statement. For example, the preceding program can be rewritten as follows:

```cpp
#include <iostream.h>
#include <string.h>

main() {
    // insertion operations can be concatenated

    cout << "The length of ''ulysses'' is:\t"
         << strlen( "ulysses" ) << "\n"
         << "The size of ''ulysses'' is:\t"
         << sizeof( "ulysses" ) << "\n";
    return 0;
}
```

A predefined insertion operator for pointer types is also provided, allowing for the display of an object's address. By default, these values are displayed in hexadecimal notation. For example,

```
#include <iostream.h>

main() {
    int i = 1024;
    int *pi = &i;

    cout << "i:    " << i << "\t"
         << "&i:\t" << &i << "\n";

    cout << "*pi: " << *pi << "\t"
         << "pi:\t" << pi << "\n\t\t\t"
         << "&pi:\t" << &pi << "\n";
    return 0;
}
```

will print as follows on the user's terminal:

```
i:    1024        &i:     0x7ffff0b4
*pi: 1024         pi:     0x7ffff0b4
                  &pi:    0x7ffff0b0
```

To display an address value in decimal notation, an explicit cast of the value to type long is necessary. For example, the previous program could be modified as follows:

```
<< "&i:\t" << long( &i ) << "\n";
<< "pi:\t" << long( pi ) << "\n\t\t\t"
<< "&pi:\t" << (long) &pi << "\n";
```

This version of the program will print as follows on the user's terminal:

```
i:    1024        &i:     2147479732
*pi: 1024         pi:     2147479732
                  &pi:    2147479728
```

The following program presents something of a puzzle. Our intention is to print out the address value pstr contains:

```
#include <iostream.h>

char str[] = "vermeer";
main() {
    char *pstr = str;
    cout << "The address of pstr is: "
         << pstr << "\n";
    return 0;
}
```

When compiled and executed, however, the program unexpectedly generates the following output:

```
The address of pstr is: vermeer
```

The problem is that the type char* is interpreted not as an address value but as a string. To print out the address value pstr contains, we must override the default handling of char*. We do this with an explicit cast of pstr to type void*:

```
<< (void*) pstr << "\n";
```

When compiled and executed, the program now generates the expected output:

```
The address of pstr is: 0x116e8
```

Literal character constants are both easier to use and more readable when defined mnemonically. For example, here is the symbolic definition of a number of commonly used literal constants. They are placed in a header file named ioconst.h.

```
#ifndef IOCONST_H
#define IOCONST_H

const char *const sep =          ", ";
const char *const nltab =        "\n\t";
const char *const prefix1=       "[ ";
const char *const suffix1=       " ]";
const char *const prefix2=       "{ ";
const char *const suffix2=       " }";

const char bell =          '\007';
const char nl =            '\n';
const char tab =           '\t';
const char sp =            ' ';
const char comma =         ',';
const char lbrace =        '<';
const char rbrace =        '>';

#endif
```

The program can use these symbolic constants by including the header file. For example,

```
#include <iostream.h>
#include "ioconst.h"

main() {
    cout << bell
         << "I am an output string" << nl;
    return 0;
}
```

The put() member function provides an alternative method of inserting a character into the output stream. For example,

```
// put a newline to standard output
cout.put( nl );
```

will print a newline character on the user's terminal.

put() accepts one argument of either an unsigned or signed char and returns the ostream class object that invokes it. Occurrences of put() may be concatenated. For example,

```
cout.put( bell ).put( bell ).put( nl );
```

The write() member function provides an alternative method of inserting a string into the output stream. It has the following function signature:

```
write( const char *str, int length )
```

where length specifies the number of characters to display, beginning with the character addressed by str. write() returns the ostream class object that invokes it and may be concatenated. For example,

```
#include <iostream.h>
#include "ioconst.h"
#include <string.h>

inline void
putString( char *s ) {
    cout.put( tab ).write( s, strlen( s ) ).put( nl );
}

main() {
    putString( "Stately, plump Buck Mulligan" );
    putString( "Mr. Leopold Bloom" );
    return 0;
}
```

will print as follows on the user's terminal:

```
Stately, plump Buck Mulligan
Mr. Leopold Bloom
```

write() can also be used to output a noncharacter object in binary form;
the object's value is displayed as a sequence of bytes. The following program illustrates writing out the binary form of an integer as a sequence of
character values.

```
#include <iostream.h>
#include "ioconst.h"

const char byteSize = 8;
int ival = 'abcd';

main() {
    for ( int i = 0; i < sizeof(int); ++i ) {
        cout << "The integer value of ival: "
             << ival << nl
             << "The binary value of ival: ";

        // note cast of address to char*
        cout.write( (char*)&ival, sizeof(int) );

        // shift value one byte
        ival <<= byteSize;
        cout.put(nl).put(nl);
    }
    return 0;
}
```

When compiled and executed, the program generates the following output:

```
The integer value of ival: 1633837924
The binary value of ival: dcba

The integer value of ival: 1650680832
The binary value of ival: dcb

The integer value of ival: 1667497984
The binary value of ival: dc

The integer value of ival: 1677721600
The binary value of ival: d
```

cout is buffered: inserted values may accumulate before being written
to standard output (or some other ostream). Buffering follows from the
principle that, in general, it is more efficient to write one large collection of
values rather than to write a series of individual values. Buffering,

however, can become a problem in program situations, such as the following, in which the output is needed immediately:

1. Interactive programs in which input and output must alternate.

2. Program debugging in which print statements are used to trace execution.

The programmer can force the values inserted into an ostream to be written immediately by *flushing* the buffer. This is done by inserting a special value, `flush`. For example,

```
cout << "Hi.   What is your name?\n" << flush;
```

`flush` causes all previous values inserted into the ostream to be written.

`flush` is referred to as a *manipulator* because its insertion causes a particular action to be performed on the ostream. A particularly useful manipulator is `endl` (endline). `endl` causes a newline to be inserted into the ostream and its buffer to be flushed. Rather than writing

```
cout << j << "\n" << flush;
```

the user can write

```
cout << j << endl;
```

The following program presents something of a puzzle. Our intention is to display the larger of two values:

```
#include <iostream.h>
#include "ioconst.h"

char *str1 = "Of the values: ";
char *str2 = "The largest value is: ";

main() {
    int i = 10, j = 20;

    cout << str1 << i << ", " << j << nl;
    cout << str2
         << ( i > j ) ? i : j << nl;
    return 0;
}
```

When compiled and executed, however, the program generates the following incorrect results:

```
Of the values: 10, 20
The largest value is: 0
```

The problem is that the insertion operator has a higher precedence than the arithmetic `if` operator. The insertion operator shares the same precedence as the bitwise left shift operator. Section 2.9 (page 79) presents a discussion of operator precedence.) Parentheses are required to achieve the correct order of evaluation. The problem is that we did not parenthesize the full arithmetic `if` statement. The value output is the true/false value of the condition

```
( i > j )
```

which in this case evaluates to false, or 0. Here is the correct version of the operator subexpression:

```
<< ( i > j ? i : j ) << nl;
```

When the revised program is compiled and excuted, it generates the following correct output:

```
Of the values: 10, 20
The largest value is: 20
```

The safest method of inserting an expression is to place it within parentheses. This includes assignment expressions such as

```
cout << (i += j);
```

A.2   Overloading Operator <<

There are no predefined insertion operators for user-defined class types. The designer of a class, however, can overload the insertion operator to define output for that class. For example,

```cpp
#include <iostream.h>

class WordCount {
    friend ostream&
            operator<<(ostream&, WordCount&);
public:
    WordCount( char *, int = 1 );
    // ...
private:
    char *str;
    int occurs;
};
```

```
#include <iostream.h>
#include "ioconst.h"

ostream&
operator <<( ostream& os, WordCount& wd ) {
    os  << lbrace << wd.occurs
        << rbrace << sp << wd.str << endl;
    return os;
}
```

The WordCount instance of the insertion operator can now be intermixed freely with the predefined insertion operators. For example,

```
#include <iostream.h>
#include "ioconst.h"
#include "WordCount.h"

main() {
    WordCount wd( "sadness", 12 );
    cout << "wd: " << nl << wd << endl;
    return 0;
}
```

will print as follows on the user's terminal:

```
wd:
<12> sadness
```

Other examples of overloaded instances of the insertion operator can be found as follows:

- Section 5.5 (page 202) for the Screen class instance.

- Section 6.3 (page 257) for the String class instance.

- Section 6.4 (page 277) for the BitVector class instance.

The insertion operator is a binary operator that returns an ostream reference. The general skeleton of an overloaded definition looks as follows:

```
ostream&
operator << ( ostream& os, <ClassType>& )
{
    // ... any special logic for <ClassType>
    os <<  // ... output members
    return os; // ... return ostream object
}
```

Its first argument is an ostream reference; the second, a particular class type reference. The return value is the ostream argument.

Because the first argument is an ostream reference, the insertion operator must be defined as a nonmember function. (Section 5.5 (page 200)
discusses this in detail.) When the operator requires access to nonpublic
members, it must be declared as a friend to the class.

Loc is a class that holds the line and column number of each occurrence
of a word. Here is its definition (the header files are left off):

```
class Loc {
    friend ostream& operator<<( ostream&, Loc& );
public:
    Loc( int l, int c ) : line(l), column(c) {}
    Loc *next;
private:
    short line;
    short column;
};

ostream& operator <<( ostream& os, Loc& lc )
{ // output of a Loc object:  <10,37>
    os << lbrace << lc.line
        << comma << lc.column << rbrace;
    return os;
}
```

Let's redefine WordCount to contain both a Loc and a String class
object: It now contains two class members, each of which defines an
operator << instance.

```
class WordCount {
    friend ostream& operator<<(ostream&, WordCount&);
    friend istream& operator>>(istream&, WordCount&);
public:
    WordCount() : occurs(0), occurList(0) {}
    WordCount(char *s)
        : str(s), occurs(0), occurList(0) {}
    WordCount(char *s, int l, int c, int o=1)
        : str(s), occurs(o)
        { occurList = new Loc(l,c); }
    WordCount( String&, Loc&, int = 1 );
    void found( int, int );
private:
    String str;
    int occurs;
    Loc *occurList;
};
```

found() inserts a new Loc object into the list of locations at which the
word has been found. Here is its implementation:

```
void WordCount::found( int l, int c ) {
    Loc *tmp = new Loc( l, c );
    ++occurs;
    tmp->next = occurList;
    occurList = tmp;
}
```

WordCount now contains two class members, each of which defines an operator << instance. Here is the new definition of the WordCount insertion operator:

```
ostream& operator <<( ostream& os, WordCount& wd ) {
    Loc *tptr = wd.occurList;

    os  << lbrace << wd.occurs << rbrace << sp
        << wd.str << nl;          // os << String

    int tabCnt = 0, onLine = 5;
    while ( tptr ) {
        os << tab << *tptr;       // os << Loc
        if ( ++tabCnt >= onLine )
            { os << nl; tabCnt = 0;   }
        tptr = tptr->next;
    }
    return os;
}
```

Here is a program that utilizes the new definition of WordCount. For simplicity, the occurrences are hand coded.

```
#include <iostream.h>
#include "ioconst.h"
#include "WordCount.h"

main() {
    WordCount search( "rosebud" );

    // for simpilicity, hand code 6 occurrences
    search.found( 7, 12 ); search.found( 7, 18 );
    search.found( 14, 2 ); search.found( 34, 36 );
    search.found( 49, 17 ); search.found( 67, 51 );

    cout << "Occurrences: " << nl << search;
    return 0;
}
```

When this program is compiled and executed, it generates the following output:

```
Occurrences:
<6> rosebud
        <67,51> <49,17> <34,36> <14,2>   <7,18>
        <7,12>
```

The output of this program is stored in a file named `output`. In the section on overloading the input operator (">>") later in this appendix, we will read in this file.

The overloaded insertion operators are not class members, and so they are not inherited. Moreover, they cannot be made virtual functions directly. An example of how to provide virtual output functions while retaining the iostream insertion syntax is presented in Section 8.2 (page 351) using the ZooAnimal class hierarchy.

A.3   Input

iostream input is similar to output, except that the right shift operator (">>"), referred to as the *extraction* operator, is used. Predefined extraction operators for the built-in data types, including `char*`, are provided. The extraction operators can also be concatenated. For example,

```
#include <iostream.h>
#include "ioconst.h"
#include "Loc.h"

main()
{
    int line, col;
    cout << "Please enter two integers: " << flush;

    cin >> line >> col;

    Loc loc( line, col );
    cout << loc << endl;
    return 0;
}
```

will print as follows on the user's terminal:

```
Please enter two integers: 20 27
<20,27>
```

A more general method of reading from the input stream is to make the extraction operation the truth condition of a `while` loop. For example,

```
char ch;
while ( cin >> ch )
    // ...
```

reads a character at a time from standard input. When end-of-file is encountered, the truth condition evaluates as false and the loop terminates.

The character sequence

```
ab c
d        e
```

is treated by operator >> as a sequence of five characters ('a', 'b', 'c', 'd', 'e'). White space (blanks, newlines, and tabs) serve only to separate values on the input stream and are not themselves read as characters. The member functions get(), getline(), and read() can be used when the programmer wishes to also read white space characters. We will look at these later.

The extraction operator can also be used to read a sequence of strings from the input stream. For example,

```
char inBuf[ wordLength ];
while ( cin >> inBuf ) ...
```

A string is treated by the predefined char* instance of the extraction operator as being a sequence of characters delimited by white space. The presence of quotation marks does not cause embedded white space to be handled as part of an extended string. For example,

```
"A fine and private place"
```

requires five iterations of the preceding while loop to process. The sequence of strings read are the following:

```
"A
fine
and
private
place"
```

A null character is appended to a string during input. The size of a character array necessary to hold a string, therefore, is the length of the string plus one. For example,

```
char inBuf[ 4096 ];
while ( cin >> inBuf ) {
    char *pstr = new char[ strlen(inBuf) + 1 ];
    strcpy( pstr, inBuf );
    ...
}
```

The following program extracts a sequence of strings from standard input and determines which of the strings read is largest.

```
#include <iostream.h>
#include "ioconst.h"
#include "String.h"
#include <string.h>

char *msg[] = {
    "The number of words read is ",
    "The longest word has a length of ",
    "The longest word is " };

const bufSize = 24;
main() {
    char buf[ bufSize ];
    String largest;

    // hold statistics;
    int curLen, max = -1, cnt = 0;

    while ( cin >> buf ) {
        curLen = strlen( buf );
        ++cnt;

        // new longest word? save it.
        if ( curLen > max ) {
            max = curLen;
            largest = buf;
        }
    }

    cout << msg[0] << cnt << nl;
    cout << msg[1] << max << nl;
    cout << msg[2] << largest << nl;
    return 0;
}
```

The input to the program is the first few sentences of the novel *Moby Dick*:

```
Call me Ishmael.  Some years ago, never mind
how long precisely, having little or no money
in my purse, and nothing particular to interest
me on shore, I though I would sail about a little
and see the watery part of the world.  It is a
way I have of driving off the spleen, and
regulating the circulation.
```

When compiled and executed, the program generates the following output:

```
The number of words read is 58
The longest word has a length of 12
The longest word is circulation.
```

In the program, each string is stored in buf, declared to be an array of length 24. If a string were read which equaled or exceeded 24 characters, buf would overflow. The program would likely fail during execution.

The setw() manipulator can be used to prevent the overflow of an input character array. For example, the previous program might be modified as follows:

```
while ( cin >> setw( bufSize ) >> buf )
```

where bufSize is the dimension of the character array buf. setw() breaks a string equal to or larger than bufSize into two or more strings of a maximum length of

```
bufSize - 1
```

A null character is placed at the end of each new string. Use of setw() requires that the program include the iomanip.h header file.

If the visible declarations of buf do not specify a dimension,

```
char buf[] = "An unrealistic example";
```

the programmer can apply the sizeof operator — provided that the identifier is the name of an array:

```
while ( cin >> setw(sizeof( buf )) >> buf );
```

Use of the sizeof operator in the following example results in unexpected program behavior:

```
#include <iostream.h>
#include <iomanip.h>
#include "ioconst.h"

const bufSize = 24;
char buf[ bufSize ];

main() {
    char *pbuf = buf;

    // each string greater than sizeof(char*)
    // is broken into two or more strings
    while ( cin >> setw(sizeof(pbuf)) >> pbuf )
        cout << pbuf << nl;
    return 0;
}
```

When compiled and executed, the program generates the following incorrect results:

```
$ a.out
The winter of our discontent

The
win
ter
of
our
dis
con
ten
t
```

setw() is passed the size of the character pointer rather than the size of the character array to which it points. On this particular machine, a character pointer is four bytes, and so the input is broken into a sequence of strings three characters in length.

The following attempt to correct the mistake is an even more serious error:

```
while ( cin >> setw(sizeof(*pbuf)) >> pbuf )
```

The intention is to pass setw() the size of the array to which pbuf points. The notation

```
*pbuf
```

however, yields only a single char. setw(), in this case, is passed a value of 1. Each execution of the while loop will place a null character into the array to which `pbuf` points. Standard input is never read; the loop executes infinitely.

The member functions `get()` and `getline()` can be used when the programmer does not wish to skip over white space. There are two forms of the member function `get()`.

1. `get(char& ch)` extracts a single character from the input stream and stores it in `ch`. It returns the iostream object that invokes it. It serves as the inverse of the `put()` insertion function. For example,

```
#include <iostream.h>

main() {
    char ch;
    while (cin.get(ch)) // echo input
        cout.put(ch);
    return 0;
}
```

2. `get()` extracts and returns a single value from the input stream, including *EOF*, the end-of-file value defined in `iostream.h`. For example,

```
#include <iostream.h>

main() {
    int ch;
    while ( (ch = cin.get()) != EOF )
        cout.put(ch);
    return 0;
}
```

To distinguish EOF from the character set values, its associated value most often is −1. `ch` cannot safely be declared a `char` if it will hold both character values and EOF. The handling of signed `char` values is machine dependent. Were `ch` declared a `char`, the comparison of `ch` with EOF could not be guaranteed to work on all machines. For this reason, `ch` is declared an `int`.

Seven iterations of `get()` are required to read the following sequence of characters:

```
a b c
d
```

Seven characters are read ('a', blank, 'b', blank, 'c', newline, 'd'). The eighth iteration encounters EOF. Operator >>, because it skips over white space, reads the character sequence in four iterations.

The signature of getline() is the following:

```
getline( char *Buf, int Limit, char Delim = '\n' );
```

getline() extracts a block of characters and places them in the character array addressed by Buf. The invocation of getline will extract at most Limit - 1 characters. getline() appends a null character to Buf. If either the end-of-file is reached or the Delim character is encountered, getline() will extract less than Limit − 1 characters. By default, the delimiter for string termination is the newline. Delim is not placed within Buf.

The istream member function gcount() returns the number of characters actually extracted by the last call of getline(). Here is an example of using getline() and gcount():

```
#include <iostream.h>
#include "ioconst.h"

const lineSize = 1024;
main() {
    int lcnt = 0; // how many lines are read
    int max = -1; // size of longest line
    char inBuf[ lineSize ];

    // reads 1024 characters or up to newline
    while (cin.getline(inBuf, lineSize))
    {
        // how many characters actually read
        int readin = cin.gcount();

        // statistics: line count, longest line
        ++lcnt; if ( readin > max ) max = readin;

        cout << "Line #" << lcnt << tab
            << "Chars read: " << readin << nl;
        cout.write(inBuf, readin).put(nl).put(nl);
    }
    cout << "Total lines read: " << lcnt << nl;
    cout << "Longest line read: " << max << nl;
    return 0;
}
```

When run against the first few sentences of *Moby Dick*, the program generates the following output:

```
Line #1 Chars read: 45
Call me Ishmael.  Some years ago, never mind

Line #2 Chars read: 46
how long precisely, having little or no money

Line #3 Chars read: 48
in my purse, and nothing particular to interest

Line #4 Chars read: 50
me on shore, I though I would sail about a little

Line #5 Chars read: 47
and see the watery part of the world.  It is a

Line #6 Chars read: 43
way I have of driving off the spleen, and

Line #7 Chars read: 28
regulating the circulation.

Total lines read: 7
Longest line read: 50
```

The inverse of the ostream `write()` function is the istream `read()` function, whose signature is defined as follows:

```
read( char* addr, int size );
```

`read()` extracts `size` contiguous bytes from the input stream and places them beginning at `addr`. `gcount()` will also return the number of bytes extracted by the last call of `read()`. `read()` is most typically used to read values previously output by `write`.

The user should be aware of three other extraction operators:

```
// push character back into the iostream
putback( char c );

// returns next character (or EOF)
//      but does not extract it
peek();

// discards up to Limit characters
// stop if encounters Delim character
ignore( int Limit=1, int Delim=EOF );
```

The following code fragment illustrates how these operators might be used:

```
char ch, next, lookahead;

while ( cin.get(ch) ) {
    switch (ch) {
        case '/':
            // is it a line comment?  peek()
            // yes? ignore() rest of line
            next = cin.peek();
            if ( next == '/' )
                cin.ignore( lineSize, '\n' );
            break;

        case '>':
            // look for >>=
            next = cin.peek();
            if ( next == '>' ) {
                lookahead = cin.get();
                next = cin.peek();
                if ( next != '=' )
                    cin.putback(lookahead);
            }
```

A.4 Overloading Operator >>

Overloading of the extraction operator (">>") is similar to overloading the insertion operator. Fig. A.1 presents an implementation of the extraction operator for WordCount.

This example illustrates a number of issues with regard to possible iostream error states. These are as follows:

1. An istream that fails because of a bad format should mark the state of istream as *bad*. The expression

```
is.clear( ios::badbit|is.rdstate() )
```

does just that. Here is what it means.

The error state of an iostream is maintained as a bit vector. The member function rdstate() returns this vector. clear() resets the entire error state to 0. clear(ios::badbit) sets the badbit flag, which is what we want, but it resets the other error bit flags to 0. We want to retain the previous error state, whatever it is, while setting the badbit flag. We do this by *oring* ios::badbit with the previous error state — which is the reason we write

```
is.clear( ios::badbit|is.rdstate() )
```

```cpp
#include <iostream.h>
#include "ioconst.h"
#include "WordCount.h"

istream& operator >>(istream& is, WordCount& wd) {
/* format of WordCount object to be read:
 * <2> string
 *    <7,3> <12,36> */

    int ch;
    if ((ch = is.get()) != lbrace ) { // bad format
        is.clear( ios::badbit | is.rdstate() );
        return is;
    }

    is >> wd.occurs;
    while ( is && (ch = is.get()) != rbrace ) ;
    const bufSize = 512;
    char buf[ bufSize ];
    is >> buf;
    wd.str = buf;

    // read in the locations; build list
    // format of each location: <l,c>
    for ( int j = 0; j < wd.occurs; ++j )
    {
    Loc *tptr;
    int l, c;

        // extract values
        while (is && (ch = is.get())!= lbrace ) ;
        is >> l;

        while (is && (ch = is.get())!= comma ) ;
        is >> c;

        while (is && (ch = is.get())!= rbrace ) ;

        // build list
        tptr = new Loc( l, c );
        tptr->next = wd.occurList;
        wd.occurList = tptr;
    }
    return is;
}
```

Figure A.1 WordCount Extraction Operator

2. The insertion and extraction operations of an iostream in an error state are without affect. For example,

```
while ((ch = is.get()) != lbrace)
```

will loop forever if is is in an error state. This is why the condition of is is tested before each call of get():

```
// insure ``is'' is not bad
while ( is && (ch = is.get()) != lbrace)
```

is evaluates to 0 when its error state is set.

The following program reads in the WordCount class object previously written by the overloaded insertion operator defined earlier.

```
#include <iostream.h>
#include <stdlib.h>
#include "ioconst.h"
#include "WordCount.h"

main() {
    WordCount readIn;

    if ( (cin >> readIn) == 0 ) {
        cerr << "WordCount input error" << nl;
        exit( -1 );
    }
    cout << readIn << nl;
    return 0;
}
```

The expression

```
if ( (cin >> readIn) == 0 )
```

checks that the WordCount extraction operator was actually successful in reading from standard input.

When compiled and executed, the program generates the following output:

```
<6> rosebud
        <7,12>  <7,18>   <14,2>   <34,36> <49,17>
        <67,51>
```

A.5   File Input and Output

A user wishing to connect a file to the program for input and/or output must include the `fstream.h` header file in addition to `iostream.h`:

```
#include <iostream.h>
#include <fstream.h>
```

To open a file for output only, an *ofstream* (output file stream) class object must be defined. For example,

```
ofstream outFile( "copy.out", ios::out );
```

The arguments passed to `outfile` specify, in turn, the name of the file to be opened and the mode under which to open it. An ofstream file can be opened in either output (`ios::out`) or append (`ios::app`) mode.

If an existing file is opened in output mode, any data stored in that file is discarded. If the user wishes to add to rather than write over an existing file, the file should be opened in the append mode. Data written to the file will then be added at its end. In either mode, if the file does not exist, it will be created.

Before attempting to read or write to a file, it is always a good idea to verify that it has been opened successfully. Our test of `outFile` is coded as follows:

```
if ( !outFile ) { // opened failed
    cerr << "cannot open ''copy.out'' for output\n";
    exit( -1 );
}
```

ofstream is derived from ostream. All the ostream operations can be applied to an ofstream class object. For example,

```
outFile.put( '1' ).put( ')' ).put( sp );
outFile << "1 + 1 = " << (1 + 1) << nl;
```

inserts

```
1) 1 + 1 = 2
```

into the file `copy.out`.

The following program *gets* characters from the standard input and *puts* them into the file `copy.out`:

```
#include <iostream.h>
#include <fstream.h>
#include "ioconst.h"
#include <stdlib.h>

main() {
    // open a file copy.out for output
    ofstream outFile( "copy.out", ios::out );

    if ( !outFile ) { // open failed?
        cerr << "Cannot open ``copy.out'' for output"
            << nl;
        exit( -1 );
    }

    char ch;
    while ( cin.get( ch ) )
        outFile.put( ch );
    return 0;
}
```

User-defined instances of the insertion operator ("<<") can also be applied to an ofstream class object. The following program invokes the WordCount insertion operator defined in the previous section:

```
#include <iostream.h>
#include <fstream.h>
#include "ioconst.h"
#include "WordCount.h"

main() {
    // open a file word.out for output
    ofstream oFile( "word.out", ios::out );

    // test for successful open goes here ...

    // create and manually set
    WordCount artist( "Renoir" );
    artist.found( 7, 12 ); artist.found( 34, 18 );

    // invokes operator <<(ostream&, WordCount&);
    oFile << artist;
    return 0;
}
```

To open a file for input only, an *ifstream* class object must be defined. ifstream is derived from istream and inherits its nonprivate members. The following program reads copy.out and writes it to standard output:

```
#include <iostream.h>
#include <fstream.h>

main() {
    // open a file copy.out for input
    ifstream inFile( "copy.out", ios::in );

    // test for successful open goes here

    char ch;
    while ( inFile.get( ch ))
        cout.put( ch );
    return 0;
}
```

The enumeration constant ios::in specifies that copy.out is to be opened in input mode.

The following program copies an input file into an output file, placing each string on a separate line:

```
#include <iostream.h>
#include <fstream.h>
#include <iomanip.h>
#include "ioconst.h"

char *infile = "in.fil";
char *outfile = "out.fil";

main() {
    ifstream iFile( infile, ios::in );
    ofstream oFile( outfile, ios::out );

    // verify both files are open ...

    int cnt = 0;
    const bufSize = 1024;
    char buf[ bufSize ];

    while ( iFile >> setw( bufSize ) >> buf ) {
        oFile << buf << nl;
        ++cnt;
    }

    // display count of strings processed
    cout << "[ " << cnt << " ]" << nl;
    return 0;
}
```

Both an ifstream and an ofstream class object can be defined without specifying a file. A file can later be explicitly connected to a class object through the member function open(). For example,

```
ifstream curFile;
// ...
curFile.open( filename, ios::in  );
if ( !curFile ) // open failed?
// ...
```

where filename is of type char*.

A file can be disconnected from the program by invoking the member function close(). For example,

```
curFile.close();
```

In the following program, five files are in turn opened and closed using the same ifstream class object:

```
#include <iostream.h>
#include <fstream.h>

const fileCnt = 5;
char *fileTabl[ fileCnt ] = {
    "Melville","Joyce","Musil","Proust","Kafka"
};

main() {
    ifstream inFile; // not attached to any file

    for ( int i = 0; i < fileCnt; ++i ) {
        inFile.open( fileTabl[i], ios::in );
        // ... verify successful open
        // ... process file
        inFile.close();
    }
    return 0;
}
```

An *fstream* class object can open a file for either input *or* output. The fstream class is derived from the iostream class. In the following example, word.out is first read then written using the fstream class object file. The file word.out, created earlier in this section, contains a WordCount object.

```
#include <iostream.h>
#include <fstream.h>
#include "ioconst.h"
#include "WordCount.h"

main() {
    WordCount wd;
    fstream file;

    file.open( "word.out", ios::in );
    file >> wd;
    file.close();

    cout << "Read in: " << wd << nl;

    file.open( "word.out", ios::app );
    file << nl << wd;
    file.close();
    return 0;
}
```

An fstream class object can also open a file for *both* input and output. For example, the following definition opens word.out in both input and append mode:

```
fstream io( "word.out", ios::in|ios::app );
```

The bitwise OR operator is used to specify more than one mode.

All the iostream class types can be repositioned using either the seekg() or seekp() member function, which can move to an "absolute" address within the file or move a byte offset from a particular position. Both seekg() and seekp() take the following two arguments:

```
typedef long streampos;

seekg( streampos p, seek_dir d=ios::beg );
```

where seek_dir is an enumeration that defines three elements:

1. ios::beg, the beginning of the file.

2. ios::cur, the current position of the file.

3. ios::end, the end of the file.

A call with two arguments moves some offset. The following example positions the file at the *i*th Record entry for each iteration:

```
for ( int i = 0; i < recordCnt; ++i )
    readFile.seekg( i * sizeof(Record), io::beg );
```

A negative value can also be specified for the first argument. For example, the following moves backwards 10 bytes from end-of-file:

```
readFile.seekg( -10, ios::end );
```

If supplied with only one argument, the file is positioned n bytes from the beginning of the file. Thus, whenever the second argument is ios::beg, it can be omitted.

The current position in a file is returned by the member function tellg(). For example,

```
// mark current position
streampos mark = writeFile.tellg();

// ...
if ( cancelEntry )
    // return to marked position
    writeFile.seekg( mark );
```

A programmer wishing to advance one Record from the current file position might write either of the following:

```
// equivalent repositioning seek invocations
readFile.seekg( readFile.tellg() + sizeof(Record) );

// this is considered the more efficient
readFile.seekg( sizeof(Record), ios::cur );
```

Let's go through an actual programming example in some detail. Here is the problem. We are given a text file to read. We are to compute the byte size of the file and store it at the end of the file. In addition, each time we encounter a newline character, we are to store the current byte size, including the newline, at the end of the file. For example, given the following text file,

```
abcd
efg
hi
j
```

the program should produce the following modified text file:

```
abcd
efg
hi
j
5 9 12 14 24
```

Here is our initial implementation:

```cpp
#include <iostream.h>
#include "ioconst.h"
#include <fstream.h>

main() {
    // open in both input and append mode
    fstream inOut( "copy.out", ios::in|ios::app );

    int cnt=0; // byte count
    char ch;

    while ( inOut.get( ch ) ) {
        cout.put( ch ); // echo on terminal
        ++cnt;
        if ( ch == nl ) {
            inOut << cnt ;
            inOut.put( sp );
        }
    }

    // write out final byte count
    inOut << cnt; inOut.put( nl );
    cout << "[ " << cnt << " ]\n";
    return 0;
}
```

inOut is an fstream class object attached to the file copy.out, which is opened in both input and append mode. A file opened in append mode will write all data to the end of the file.

Each time we read a character, including white space but not end-of-file, we increment cnt and echo the character on the user's terminal. The purpose of echoing the input is so that we have something to look at and measure in the off chance that our program does not work as expected.

Each time we encounter a newline, we write the current value of cnt to inOut. Reading end-of-file terminates the loop. We write the final value of cnt to inOut and also to the screen.

The program compiles. It seems correct. The file contains the first few sentences of *Moby Dick* that we have used previously in this appendix. When we execute the program, the output generated is the following:

```
[ 0 ]
```

No characters are displayed and the program believes the text file is empty.

The problem is that the file, being opened in append mode, is positioned at its end. When

```
inOut.get( ch );
```

is executed, end-of-file is encountered and the `while` loop terminates, leaving `cnt` with a value of 0.

We can solve this problem by repositioning the file back to the beginning before we begin to read. The statement

```
inOut.seekg( 0, ios::beg );
```

accomplishes just that. The program is recompiled and rerun. This time, the following output is generated:

```
Call me Ishmael.  Some years ago, never mind
[ 45 ]
```

The display and byte count are generated for only the first line of the text file. The remaining six lines are ignored. Can you see what the problem is?

The problem is that the file is opened in append mode. The first time `cnt` is written, the file becomes repositioned at its end. The subsequent `get()` encounters end-of-file and once more prematurely terminates the `while` loop.

The solution this time is to reposition the file to where it was prior to the writing of `cnt`. This can be accomplished with the following two additional statements:

```
// mark current position
streampos mark = inOut.tellg();
inOut << cnt << sp;
inOut.seekg( mark ); // restore position
```

When the program is recompiled and executed, the output to the terminal is correct. Examining the output file, however, we discover another problem. The final byte count, although being written to the terminal, is *not* being written to the file. The insertion operator following the `while` loop is not being executed.

The problem this time is that `inOut` is in the "state" of having encountered end-of-file. As long as `inOut` remains in this state, input and output operations are *not* performed. The solution is to `clear()` the state of the file. This is accomplished with the following statement:

```
    inOut.clear(); // zero out state flags
```

The complete program looks as follows:

```
    #include <iostream.h>
    #include <fstream.h>

    main() {
        fstream inOut( "copy.out", ios::in|ios::app );
        int cnt=0;
        char ch;

        inOut.seekg(0, ios::beg );
        while ( inOut.get( ch ) ) {
            cout.put( ch );
            cnt++;
            if ( ch == '\n' ) {
                // mark current position
                streampos mark = inOut.tellg();
                inOut << cnt << ' ';
                inOut.seekg( mark ); // restore position
            }
        }

        inOut.clear();
        inOut << cnt << '\n' ;

        cout << "[ " << cnt << " ]\n";
    }
```

When the program is recompiled and executed, at last it generates the expected output.

A.6   Condition States

An iostream library object maintains a set of condition flags through which the ongoing state of the stream can be monitored. The following four predicate member functions can be invoked:

1. eof(): returns true if the stream has encountered end-of-file. For example,

```
        if ( inOut.eof() )
            inOut.clear();
```

2. bad(): returns true if an invalid operation, such as "seeking" past end-of-file, has been attempted.

3. `fail()`: returns true either if an operation has been unsuccessful or if `bad()` is true. For example,

```
ifstream iFile( filename, ios::in );

if ( iFile.fail() ) // unable to open
    error( ... );
```

4. `good()`: returns true if none of the other conditions is true. For example,

```
if ( inOut.good() )
```

The stream classes define an overloaded instance of the logical NOT operator ("`!`"):

```
if ( !inOut )
```

that provides a shorthand notation for the following equivalent compound expression:

```
if ( inOut.fail() )
```

The reason the truth condition of a `while` loop of the following form

```
while ( cin >> buf )
```

evaluates to 0 on encountering end-of-file is because of a stream member conversion operator which is generally equivalent to the following compound expression:

```
// predefined logical NOT operator
if ( !( cin.bad() || cin.fail() ))
```

It is also possible to test a file stream object explicitly to learn if it has yet been opened. For example,

```
ifstream ifile;
```

defines an unattached ifstream class object. Before writing

```
ifile << "hello, world\n";
```

it is a good idea to verify that `ifile` has been attached to some file. Since no operations have been attempted, the test

```
if ( ifile.good() )
    // ...
```

evaluates to true even though the file may as yet be unopened. The following predicate tests whether ifile is open:

```
if ( ifile.rdbuf()->is_open == 0 ) {
    // no file attached
    ifile.open( filename, ios::in );
    // ...
```

rdbuf() is a member function which accesses the internal buffer associated with the file stream.

A.7   Format State

Each iostream library class object maintains a *format state* that controls the details of formatting operations, such as the conversion base for integral numeric notation or the precision of a floating point value. The programmer can set and unset format state flags using the setf() and unsetf() member functions. Additionally, a set of manipulators is available to the programmer for modifying the format state of an object.

By default integers are written and read in decimal notation. The programmer may change the notational base to octal, hexadecimal or back to decimal. To change the conversion base for a value, the manipulators hex, dec, and oct can be inserted between the stream object and the value to be handled. For example,

```
#include <iostream.h>

main() {
    int i = 512;
    cout << "Default: " << i << "\n";

    // applying oct changes base to octal
    cout << "Octal:   " << oct << i;
    cout << "\t" << i << "\n";

    // applying hex changes base to hexadecimal
    cout << "Hex:     " << hex << i;
    cout << "\t" << i << "\n";

    cout << "Decimal: " << dec << i;
    cout << "\t" << i << "\n";
    return 0;
}
```

When compiled and executed, the program generates the following output:

```
Default: 512
Octal:    1000    1000
Hex:      200     200
Decimal: 512      512
```

The application of one of hex, oct, or dec changes the default interpretation to the specified notational base for subsequent integer values. The program illustrates this by printing the value a second time without use of a filter.

To read in those values, the programmer inserts the appropriate conversion filter. For example,

```cpp
#include <iostream.h>

main() {
    int i1, i2, i3, i4, i5, i6, i7;
    cin >> i1
        >> oct >> i2 >> i3
        >> hex >> i4 >> i5
        >> dec >> i6 >> i7;
}
```

By default, a floating point value is output with six digits of precision. This can be modified by setting the precision(int) member function. precision() returns the current precision value. For example,

```cpp
#include <iostream.h>
#include "ioconst.h"
#include <math.h>

main() {
    cout << "Precision: "
         << cout.precision() << nl
         << sqrt(2.0) << nl;

    cout.precision(12);
    cout << "\nPrecision: "
         << cout.precision() << nl
         << sqrt(2.0) << nl;
    return 0;
}
```

When compiled and executed, the program generates the following output:

```
Precision: 6
1.41421

Precision: 12
1.41421356237
```

The `setprecision()` stream manipulator can also be used provided that the `iomanip.h` header file is included. For example,

```
#include <iostream.h>
#include <iomanip.h>
#include "ioconst.h"
#include <math.h>

main() {
    cout << "Precision: " << cout.precision()
         << nl << sqrt(2.0) << nl
         << setprecision( 12 )
         << "\nPrecision: " << cout.precision()
         << nl << sqrt(2.0) << nl;
    return 0;
}
```

The `setf()` member function sets a specified format state flag. There are two overloaded instances:

```
setf( long );
setf( long, long );
```

The first argument can be either a format bit flag or a format bit field. Table A.1 lists the format bit flags that we will look at in this section.

Flag	Meaning
ios::showbase	display numeric base
ios::showpoint	display decimal point
ios::dec	decimal numeric base
ios::hex	hexadecimal numeric base
ios::oct	octal numeric base
ios::fixed	decimal notation
ios::scientific	scientific notation

Table A.1 Format Flags

The second argument is a format bit field associated with a particular set of format flags. Table A.2 lists the two format bit fields that we will consider in this section.

Bit Field	Meaning	Flags
ios::basefield	integral base	ios::hex ios::oct ios::dec
ios::floatfield	floating point notation	ios::fixed ios::scientific

Table A.2 Format Bit Fields

For example, to have `cout` show the numeric base of integral values, one would write the following:

```
cout.setf( ios::showbase );
```

Similarly, to set the numeric base for integral values to octal, one would write the following:

```
cout.setf( ios::oct, ios::basefield );
```

`setf(long,long)` first resets the format field to 0, then sets the format bit of its first argument. It returns the previous state as a `long` integer value. This allows that state to be saved. We can restore it later by passing it as the first argument to `setf(long,long)`. For example,

```
#include <iostream.h>
#include "ioconst.h"

main() {
    int ival = 1024;
    long oldbase;

    cout.setf( ios::showbase );
    cout.setf( ios::oct, ios::basefield );
    cout << "ival: " << ival << nl;

    // save previous notational base
    oldbase = cout.setf( ios::hex, ios::basefield );
    cout << "ival: " << ival << nl;

    // restore previous notational base
    cout.setf( oldbase, ios::basefield );
    cout << "ival: " << ival << nl;

    return 0;
}
```

When compiled and executed, this program generates the following output:

```
ival: 02000
ival: 0x400
ival: 02000
```

The reason we don't simply write

```
cout.setf( ios::hex );
```

is that this instance of setf() does not clear the previous state. Were ios::basefield previously set to decimal, it would now be set to *both* hexadecimal and decimal. If ios::basefield is set to more than one base, or if no base at all is set, output defaults to decimal notation.

By default, the trailing zeros of a floating point value are discarded when the value is displayed. For example,

```
cout << 10.70 << nl
```

will print on the user's terminal as

```
10.7
```

while

```
cout << 10.0 << nl
```

will print as 10 without either the trailing zero or the trailing decimal point.

In order to display trailing zeros and the trailing decimal point, the programmer must set the ios::showpoint flag. For example,

```
cout.setf( ios::showpoint );
```

The ios::floatfield format state controls the display of floating-point values. The programmer can explicitly set or unset it by using one of the following enumeration constants:

1. ios::fixed: display value in decimal notation.

2. ios::scientific: display value in scientific notation.

For example,

```
#include <iostream.h>
#include <iomanip.h>
#include "ioconst.h"
#include <math.h>

main() {
    cout << setprecision( 8 ) << "Precision:   "
         << cout.precision() << nl
         << "Default:    10.0: " << 10.0 << nl
         << "Default:    pow(18,10): "
         << pow( 18, 10 ) << nl;

    cout.setf( ios::fixed, ios::floatfield );
    cout << "\nPrecision:   " << cout.precision()
         << nl << "Fixed:      10.0: " << 10.0
         << nl << "Fixed:      pow(18,10): "
         << pow( 18, 10 ) << nl;

    cout.setf( ios::scientific, ios::floatfield );
    cout << "\nPrecision:   " << cout.precision()
         << nl << "Scientific: 10.0: " << 10.0
         << nl << "Scientific: pow(18,10): "
         << pow( 18, 10 ) << nl;
    return 0;
}
```

When compiled and executed, the program generates the following output:

```
Precision:   8
Default:    10.0: 10
Default:    pow(18,10): 3.5704672e+12

Precision:   8
Fixed:      10.0: 10.00000000
Fixed:      pow(18,10): 3570467226624.00012000

Precision:   8
Scientific: 10.0: 1.00000000e+01
Scientific: pow(18,10): 3.57046723e+12
```

A.8 Incore Formatting

The iostream library supports incore operations on arrays of characters. The ostrstream class inserts characters into an array while the istrstream class extracts characters from an array. To define objects of either class, the

strstream.h header file must be included. For example, the following
program fragment reads the entire file words into a character array
dynamically allocated by the buf ostrstream class object:

```
#include <iostream.h>
#include <fstream.h>
#include <strstream.h>

ifstream ifile("words", ios::in);
ostrstream buf;

processFile() {
    char ch;
    while (buf && ifile.get(ch))
        buf.put(ch) ;
    // ...
}
```

The str() member function returns a pointer to the character array
associated with the ostrstream class object. For example,

```
char *bp = buf.str();
```

initializes bp with the address of the array associated with buf. The array
can now be manipulated through bp in the same way as any "ordinary"
character array.

Invoking str(), in effect, hands off the character array from the
ostrstream to the programmer. Calling str() has the effect of "freezing"
the array — subsequent insertions using the ostrstream operators are not
permitted. str(), therefore, should be invoked only after character insertion is complete.

If the ostrstream goes out of scope and str() has not been invoked,
the array is automatically deleted by the ostrstream destructor. Once
str() is invoked, however, deletion of the array becomes the responsibility of the programmer. Before bp goes out of scope, therefore, the array it
addresses must be explicitly deleted:

```
delete bp;
```

Let's look at an example. In the following program, the ostrstream
inStore is used to store the file words. (words, recall, contains the
opening sentences of *Moby Dick*.) Unlike the previous example, however,
the file is stored as a sequence of null-terminated strings. ends is a predefined manipulator that inserts a null character.

```
#include <iostream.h>
#include <fstream.h>
#include <strstream.h>
#include <iomanip.h>
#include <string.h>

ifstream ifile("words", ios::in);
ostrstream inStore;
const len = 512;
main() {
    char inBuf[len];
    int wordCnt = 0;

    while ( inStore &&
            ifile >> setw(len) >> inBuf )
    {
        ++wordCnt;
        inStore << inBuf << ends;
    }
    char *ptr = inStore.str(); // grab hold of array
    char *tptr = ptr; // keep track of beginning

    // words is an array of character pointers
    // its size is the number of strings read from ifile
    char **words = new char*[wordCnt];
    wordCnt = 0;

    // initialize each element of words
    //    to address a string within inStore
    while ( *ptr ) {
        words[ wordCnt++ ] = ptr;
        ptr += strlen(ptr) + 1;
    }

    // print out the strings in reverse order
    // in lines of length lineLength
    const lineLength = 8;
    for ( int i=wordCnt-1, cnt=0; i >= 0; --i ) {
        if ( cnt++ % lineLength == 0 ) {
                cout << endl;
                cnt = 1;
        }
        cout << words[i] << " ";
    }
    cout << endl;
    delete tptr;
}
```

When compiled and executed, the program generates the following output:

```
circulation. the regulating and spleen, the off driving
of have I way a is It world.
the of part watery the see and little
a about sail would I though I shore,
on me interest to particular nothing and purse,
my in money no or little having precisely,
long how mind never ago, years Some Ishmael.
me Call
```

A second use of ostrstream is to provide the class object with the address of a preallocated character array. This instance of an ostrstream class object requires three arguments:

1. A character pointer, char *cp, to a preallocated array.

2. A long containing the size in bytes of the array.

3. An open mode, either ios::app or ios::out. If ios::app is passed, cp is assumed to be a null termined string; insertion begins at the null character. Otherwise, insertion begins at cp.

For example, the following program converts a value into a string, first in hexadecimal, then in octal notation. Note the use of seekp() to reposition the ostrstream to be beginning of the array before the second insertion:

```
#include <iostream.h>
#include <strstream.h>

const bufLen = 25;
main() {
    char buf[bufLen];
    long lval = 1024;
    ostrstream oss(buf,sizeof(buf),ios::out);
    oss.setf( ios::showbase );

    oss << hex << lval << ends;
    cout << "buf: " << buf << endl;

    oss.seekp( ios::beg );
    oss << oct << lval << ends;
    cout << "buf: " << buf << endl;
}
```

When compiled and executed, the program generates the following results:

```
buf: 0x400
buf: 02000
```

Here is a second example in which a numeric value is converted into a string. Its first and second characters are examined to determine its notational base.

```cpp
#include <iostream.h>
#include <strstream.h>
#include <string.h>

const bufLen = 25;
main() {
    char buf[bufLen];
    long lval = 1024;
    ostrstream oss(buf,sizeof(buf),ios::out);

    oss.setf( ios::showbase );
    oss << hex << lval << ends;

    cout << "lval: " << lval << endl;
    if ( strlen(buf) > 1 ) {
        switch( buf[0] ) {
            case '0':
                if ( buf[1] == 'x' || buf[1] == 'X' )
                    cout << "hexadecimal notation: ";
                else cout << "octal notation: ";
                break;
            default:
                cout << "decimal notation: ";
        }
    }
    cout << "buf: " << buf << endl;
}
```

The istrstream class extracts characters from a character array. An istrstream class object takes two arguments:

1. A character pointer to a preallocated array.

2. The size, in bytes, of the array.

The istrstream object can be either anonymous or named. For example, in the following program, an anonymous istrstream object is used to transform a character string into an integer value:

```
#include <iostream.h>
#include <strstream.h>

char s[] = "400";
main() {
    int hexVal;
    istrstream (s,sizeof(s)) >> hex >> hexVal;
    cout << "hexVal: " << hexVal << endl;
}
```

This final example uses a named istrstream class object to set in turn a hexadecimal, octal, and decimal value. The second and third extractions require the programmer to reposition iss to the beginning of its array.

```
#include <iostream.h>
#include <strstream.h>

char s[] = "400";
main() {
    int hexVal;
    int octVal;
    int decVal;

    istrstream iss (s,sizeof(s));
    iss >> hex >> hexVal;
    iss.seekg(ios::beg); iss >> oct >> octVal;
    iss.seekg(ios::beg); iss >> dec >> decVal;

    cout << "hexVal: " << hexVal << endl;
    cout << "octVal: " << octVal << endl;
    cout << "decVal: " << decVal << endl;
}
```

When compiled and executed, the program generates the following results:

```
hexVal: 1024
octVal: 256
decVal: 400
```

A Strongly Typed Library

The iostream library is strongly typed. The attempt, for example, to read from an ostream, or to assign an ofstream to an istream are both caught at compile time and flagged as type violations. For example, given the following set of declarations:

```
#include <iostream.h>
#include <fstream.h>
class Screen;

extern istream& operator>>( istream&, Screen& );
extern void print( ostream& );
ifstream inFile;
```

the following two statements result in compile-time type violations:

```
main() {
    Screen myScreen;

    // error: expects an ostream&
    print( cin >> myScreen );

    // error: expects >> operator
    inFile << "error: output operator";
}
```

A.9   Summary

Input/output facilities are provided as a component of the C++ standard library. Beginning with Release 2.0, they are supported by the library component referred to as the *iostream* library, the subject of this appendix.

The appendix does not describe the entire iostream library — in particular, the creation of user-derived buffer classes are beyond the scope of a primer. The author has chosen instead to focus on the portion of the iostream library fundamental to providing program I/O.

The iostream library implementation is built on multiple inheritance, and makes use of the virtual base class mechanism. The iostream library source provides an excellent case study of the design and implementation of an inheritance hierarchy in C++. Those of you with access to the source are encouraged to read through it.

Appendix B: **Future Directions for C++**

C++ is a relatively new language, first released commercially in late 1985. As users have increased in number and broadened in type, the language has evolved. Protected class members and pointers to class members were introduced in 1986. Multiple inheritance and the ability to overload operators new and delete as class members were introduced experimentally in early 1988. These language extensions addressed the needs of large systems development and served to round out the language.

As the use of C++ continues to grow, two additional areas of probable language support have become clear:

1. Parameterized types.

2. Exception handling.

Type parameterization provides a general facility for defining "container classes" such as lists and arrays as well as generic functions such as `sort()` and `max()`. The development of extensive class and algorithmic libraries is facilitated by the presence of parameterized types.

Exception handling provides a standard method for managing exceptions, which are program anomalies such as division by zero, arithmetic or array overflow, and the exhaustion of free store. The presence of an exception-handling mechanism can significantly reduce the size and complexity of program code, eliminating the requirement of testing anomalous states explicitly. By analogy, think of the amount of code reduction that results from the use of virtual functions and the elimination of explicit `switch` statements for determining the actual type of a class object.

In theory, each class definition provides its own error checking. Without a standard mechanism through which to raise an exception, however, it is more difficult to build and use large collections of class libraries. What does our BitVector class do when it addresses a nonexistent bit? Is it the same behavior as that defined for our IntArray class? Can these individual methods of error handling be tuned or turned off by the user?

Parameterized types and exception handling are important to the development of large C++ libraries. Bjarne Stroustrup is currently investigating possible definitions and implementations of both features.

The difficulty with exception handling is the need to unwind the run-time stack. It must be done in such a way as to guarantee the invocation of class destructors for class objects occurring on the unwound portion of the stack. The syntax of exception handling has not yet been publicly defined, and so we cannot consider it in any detail at this time.

An experimental design of parameterized types, however, has been publicly defined. We consider this design in the sections that follow. Stroustrup refers to the parameterized types mechanism as *templates*. Bear in mind that the design described is experimental and may change. Moreover, there is no guarantee that either parameterized types or exception handling will become part of the C++ language.

The description of parameterized types is based on discussions between the author and Stroustrup, as well as the paper written by Stroustrup:

Parameterized Types for C++, Bjarne Stroustrup, Proceedings of the Usenix C++ Conference, Denver, 1988.

B.1 Parameterized Types

A programmer wishing to provide a function that returns the maximum of two values must provide an overloaded instance for each distinct type. What soon becomes clear is that the basic algorithm of the function remains constant for each type. What changes is the type itself, and possibly the meaning of the greater-than ("$>$") operator. For example,

```
int max( int i, int j ) {
    return( (i > j) ? i : j ); }

double max( double i, double j )
    return( (i > j) ? i : j ); }

Complex max( Complex i, Complex j ) {
    return( (i > j) ? i : j ); }

String max( String i, String j ) {
    return( (i > j) ? i : j ); }
```

If it were possible to *parameterize* the argument and return type of the function, the programmer would need only provide one definition of max(); particular instantiations would be provided by the compiler as required. For example,

```
// a parameterized definition of max
// where Type serves as a type place-holder

template <class Type> Type
max( Type i, Type j ) {
    return( (i > j) ? i : j );
}


// require an instance of max<Complex>
Complex a, b;
Complex c = max( a, b );

// require an instance of max<int>
int i;
int j = max( 10, i );
```

A probable extension to C++ would provide just such a mechanism, referred to as both *parameterized types* and *templates*. Its usefulness extends to the parameterization of class types.

The class designer attempting to implement an array class is confronted with the same problem as that faced by the programmer attempting to provide the set of max() functions. The class designer is constrained to provide a unique array class for each distinct type: ArrayInt, ArrayComplex, ArrayDouble, and so on. Parameterized types also provide a solution for the class designer:

```
// a parameterized definition of Array
// where Type serves as a type placeholder

template <class Type>
class Array {
public:
    Array( int );
    Type& operator[]( int );
private:
    Type *ap;
    int size;
}
```

Instances of the Array class are instantiated by declaring the Array tag name followed by an actual type specifier:

```
// instantiate an Array of integers
Array<int> ia( 24 );

// instantiate an Array of BitVectors
Array<BitVectors> ba( SZ );
```

The Array objects ia and ba can be used in the same way as though their particular Array classes had been implemented by hand. The next section considers the proposed syntax in more detail.

B.2   Parameterized Classes

Parameterized types introduce a new keyword, template. The general form of a parameterized type is

```
template <class Parameter_tag_name>
```

where Parameter_tag_name may be any legal identifier. A parameterized class definition looks the same as an ordinary class definition except for this parameter template. The parameter tag name is used within the class definition as an ordinary type specifier. For example, here is a definition of a parameterized list class:

```
template <class PT>
class List {
public:
    List( PT *pt = 0, List<PT> *lpt = 0 )
            : val( pt ), next( lpt ) {}
    PT *append( List<PT>* );
private:
    PT *val;
    List<PT> *next;
};
```

PT is the tag name of the parameter type. The parameter tag name serves as a placeholder for particular type instances provided by the user. For example, the user may declare a List of integers and a List of Strings. Each particular type of List is referred to as an instantiation.

val is declared to be a pointer to type PT. Were the List class instantiated to be a list of integers, val would be of type int*. A List of Strings would have val point to a String class object. Similarly, the return type of append() varies with the List class instantiation.

The tag name of the parameterized List class is composed of the two tag names List and PT. The parameter tag name is enclosed in a bracket pair. List<PT> is the tag name of the parameterized List class. lpt points to another parameterized List class object. If the List class is instantiated as a list of integers, the name appears as List<int>. Similarly, a List class instantiated as a list of Strings has the tag name List<String>.

It may be preferable in some cases to provide a hand-coded instance of a parameterized class member function for a particular data type. This hand-coded instance could take advantage of type-specific knowledge that might speed up or otherwise optimize the implementation that the general template instance cannot know. Here is the syntax for an append member function explicitly defined for an integer instantiation of List, List<int>.

```
// type-specific instance defined by user
int *List<int>::append( List<int> *pt )
    { /* ... */ }
```

The definition of List<PT> does not result in a class type from which objects may be declared; the parameterized class template is only a prescription for creating a particular type of List class. Only the type instantiations of the List class may serve as type specifiers. The following, for example, is illegal:

```
List<PT> myList; // error
```

The programmer instantiates a List class type by specifying a type argument, which may be either a built-in or a class type. For example, here is the instantiation of a Screen List class and a List class of type int.

```
List<Screen> slist, *Pslist;
List<int> ilist, *Pilist;
```

A type argument is specified by replacing the parameter tag name with a type specifier. It is enclosed in a bracket pair and concatentated with the name of the parameterized class. Here are some additional instantiations of List classes:

```
List<BitVector> blist;
List<double> dlist;
List<String> stList;
```

If the type specifier denotes a class name, the class definition must have been seen. Objects of a particular instantiation may be used in the same way as ordinary class objects. For example,

```
Pilist->append( &ilist );
```

The use of a typedef can make the declaration of a parameterized instance seem more "natural." For example,

```
typedef List<Screen> ScreenList;
typedef List<int> iList;

ScreenList *ps;
iList hdr;
```

Parameterized Class Derivation

A parameterized class may serve as either a derived or a base class. The normal rules of inheritance apply. For example,

```
template <class Type>
class SortedArray : public Array<Type>
{ /* ... */ };
```

Instances of the derived class are declared with the same syntax as instances of nonderived parameterized classes.

```
// SortedArray<String> : public Array<String>
SortedArray<String> sa( 100 );

// SortedArray<int> : public Array<int>
SortedArray<int> ia( ARRAY_SIZ );
```

B.3   Parameterized Functions

The definition of a parameterized function, referred to as a *function template*, also begins with the keyword template followed by the type parameter enclosed in a bracket pair. For example,

```
template <class Type> Type&
min( Array<Type>& a ) {
    // return the smallest element of an Array
    Type smallest = a[ 0 ];
    for (int i = 1; i < a.size; ++i)
        if ( a[i] < t )
            smallest = a[i];
    return smallest;
}
```

min() is a function template parameterized on the type Type. It returns the smallest element in an Array of Type. Its argument is an instantiation of the parameterized Array class type.

The function template defined for min() in effect declares a set of overloaded functions, each of a distinct Type. In the case of min(), however, there is one constraint on Type: Each instantiation of min() must provide a Type that defines the less-than operator ("<"). int, double, and String, for example, may each become instances of min(). BitVector and Screen, however, as we have defined them, cannot; neither defines an instance of the less-than operator.

min() is invoked in the same way as an ordinary function. The proper instance is resolved through an analysis of the argument type. For example, given the following three instantiations of the parameterized Array class,

```
Array<int> ia( 24 );
Array<String> sa( 1024 );
Array<double> ia( ARRAY_SIZ );
```

min() may be invoked as follows:

```
int i = min( ia ); // int& min(Array<int>);
String s(min(sa)); // String& min(Array<String>);
double d = sqrt(min(da)); // double& min(Array<double>);
```

Pointers to a parameterized function can be declared for a particular instantiation. For example,

```
int& (*pf)(Array<int>) = &min;
```

Given the following declaration of a parameterized print() function,

```
template <class Type> void
print( Array<Type>&, Type& (*)( Array<Type> ) );
```

the function pointer pf may be passed to an invocation of print() as follows:

```
print( ia, pf );
```

Appendix C: **Compatibility of C++ with C**

An important factor in the rapid spread of C++ has been the ease of using C++ with the C language. There is language compatibility: the ability to use C++ with existing C-based systems; and there is a programmer compatibility: the ease with which C programmers can learn and make effective use of C++.

A C programmer first learning C++ can use it as C with strong type checking. (The function prototype introduced in C++ has been adopted by ANSI C.) Within a day, a C programmer can begin writing C-like C++ programs.

- The C standard I/O library can be used rather than the C++ iostream library. The programmer simply includes `stdio.h`.

- The C struct can be used in place of the C++ class. Associated functions may or may not be declared as member functions of the struct. The following two declarations are equivalent in C++:

```
class foo_1 {
public:
    /* ... */
};

struct foo_2 {
    /* ... */
};
```

- Under the UNIX operating system, all the C library and system calls can be invoked from a C++ program provided that the proper header file is included. The CC command by default includes `libc.a`, the standard C library. Additional C libraries are included by providing a `-l` option on the command line, the same as for the `cc` command.

The C++ programmer relies less on the C preprocessor (`cpp`) than does the C programmer, using it primarily for conditional compilation and the inclusion of header files. The introduction of the inline function facility has made the use of `cpp` macros largely unnecessary. Also, the introduction of the `const` read-only data type has made the use of `#define`s to declare constant values largely unnecessary. A "gotcha" in the use of `cpp` with C++ is that most instances of the preprocessor do not recognize the

C++ double slash as a comment and therefore interpret the C++ comment as part of the value to be substituted. The following #define, for example,

```
#define BUFSIZ  1024 // default buffer size
```

expands as

```
1024 // default buffer size
```

If by habit you find yourself using #defines, it is a good rule of thumb to stick with the C comment style of "/*,*/" pairs.

```
#define BUFSIZ  1024 /* default buffer size */
```

The primary difference between C++ and C is the support C++ provides for the following:

- Function name overloading.
- Argument pass-by-reference (in addition to the C language default pass-by-value).
- The new and delete free store operators (in place of direct calls of malloc() and free()).
- Support of abstract data types through the class mechanism. This includes the following:

    1. Information hiding.
    2. Automatic initialization.
    3. Operator overloading.
    4. User-defined conversions.

- Support of object-oriented programming through the mechanisms of inheritance and dynamic binding.

C.1   The C++ Function Prototype

C++ is based on the C programming language as described by Kernighan and Ritchie's *The C Programming Language*. Most of the changes to C specified by the ANSI C report will be adopted by C++. A program written in a subset of the language common to both C++ and C has the same meaning when compiled in either language. Most ANSI C programs are also legal C++ programs. The most visible difference between the original C language and C++ is in the declaration of external functions. For example, here are their respective declarations of the same function, min():

```
extern min();                // C
extern min( int*, int ); // C++
```

In C++, the type and number of each argument must be specified in the declaration of the function, referred to as the *function prototype*. Because of the function prototype, C++ can flag both of the following incorrect calls of min() at compile-time as errors. In C, both calls are accepted. The burden of finding the mistakes is left to the programmer.

```
int i, j, ia[10];
main() {
    min( i, j ); // illegal first argument
    min( ia );   // missing second argument
}
```

The main work in having a C program run under C++ is in converting the extern declarations of functions. (ANSI C, however, has adopted the C++ function prototype. The main difference between the C and C++ languages, therefore, will disappear as ANSI C compilers become available.)

Distributions of C++ provide a C++-style set of system header files with explicit function prototypes. In the C++ supplied stdio.h, for example, printf() is declared

```
int printf(const char* ...)
```

A C program which does not make use of standard header files for providing function declarations is likely not to compile under C++. For example,

```
struct node {
    int val;
    struct node *left, *right;
};

struct node *get_node( val )
int val;
{
    /* in C++, this means malloc takes no arguments */
    char *malloc();
    struct node *ptr;

    /* deliberately left out check for 0 return */
    ptr = ( struct node * )malloc( sizeof( *ptr ) );
    ptr->val = val;
    ptr->left = ptr->right = 0;
    return ptr;
}
```

```
main() {
struct node *p = get_node( 1024 );
    /* ... rest of program ... */
}
```

This program will not compile under C++ because of the explicit declaration of malloc() within get_node(). Why? Because malloc() is declared with an empty argument list. In C++, that means that it takes no arguments. The call of malloc() with the sizeof() argument value will be flagged at compile time as a type violation. The preferred solution is to remove the local declaration of malloc() and instead include the standard header file malloc.h. That done, the program will now compile under both C and C++.

The equivalent C++ program, both shorter and easier to read, replaces the use of malloc() with new and replaces get_node() with a Node constructor.

```
/* equivalent C++ version of program
 * new replaces explicit call of malloc()
 * Node constructor replaces get_node() */
class Node {
public:
    Node( int i = 0) {
        left = right = 0;
        val = i;
    }
    int val;
    Node *left, *right;
};


main() {
Node *p = new Node( 1024 );
    /* ... rest of program ... */
}
```

C++ and ANSI C interpret the empty argument list differently. In ANSI C, the empty argument list suspends type checking. The declaration

```
char *malloc();
```

is interpreted to mean that malloc() takes zero or more arguments of any data type. This means K&R C programs will continue to compile without change. This also means that there is a *huge* hole in the type checking of ANSI C programs. For example, neither of the following invalid calls of malloc() are caught by an ANSI C compiler that has accepted the empty argument declaration:

```
char ac[] = "any old string";

/* both these calls are invalid */
malloc( ac );
malloc();
```

In C++, the empty argument list means that the function takes no arguments. In ANSI C, this is indicated by the keyword `void`.

```
// ff takes no arguments
extern ff( void );
```

The argument list with an explicit `void` is also accepted by C++. Programs expected to run under both compilers should always use an explicit `void` in the argument list of a function taking no arguments.

C programmers can "escape" the C++ type system for individual function declarations by placing ellipses within the empty argument list. For example, the following C program does not compile under C++ because the declaration and call of `maxVal()` do not match:

```
extern maxVal();

main() {
    int ia[ 10 ];
    int max;

    /* ... */

    max = maxVal( ia, 10 );
}
```

By changing the declaration of `maxVal()` as follows:

```
extern maxVal( ... );
```

the program will now compile under C++, but it will do so at the cost of suspending all type checking.

In general, it is best to take the time up front to provide a correctly typed argument list:

```
extern int maxVal( int*, int size );
```

Use of a common header file greatly simplifies the task of converting and maintaining function declarations.

C.2   Where C++ and C Differ

In a very small number of areas, C++ and ANSI C diverge in their handling of a language feature. One example, as we just saw, is in the interpretation of the empty argument list of a function. Stronger compile-time type checking and the greater functionality of C++ motivate the small number of differences between the two languages. These differences are the subject of this section.

Greater Functionality

The following are a list of differences between C++ and ANSI C that result from the greater functionality of C++ exhibited in its support of function name overloading, abstract data types and object-oriented programming.

- C++ reserves additional keywords:

catch	new	public
class	operator	template
delete	overload	this
friend	private	try
inline	protected	virtual

- In C++, the type of a literal character constant is char; in C, it is int. For example, on a machine with a four-byte word,

    ```
    sizeof( 'a' );
    ```

    evaluates to 1 in C++ and to 4 in C. This distinction is necessary in C++ in order to allow functions to be overloaded by an argument of type char.

- A local structure name hides the name of an object, function, enumerator, or type in an outer scope. For example,

    ```
    int ia[ iaSize ];
    void fooBar() {
        struct ia { int i; char a; };

        // C++: size of the local struct
        // ANSI C: size of ::ia
        int sz = sizeof( ia );
        int ln = sizeof( ::ia ); // equivalent C++
    }
    ```

This is because structure names and identifiers occur in a single name space within C++. The single name space allows for the class constructor notation:

```
class Complex {
public:
    Complex( double, double );
    // ...
};

Complex a = Complex( 1.0, 1.0 );
```

- In C++, the elements of an enumeration are local to the scope of the struct in which they are defined. In ANSI C, structs do not maintain an associated scope. For example,

```
struct iostream {
    enum { bad, fail, good };
    /* ... */
};

// C++: ok: no name conflict
// ANSI C: reuse of an identifier
double fail;
```

- In C++, a goto statement cannot jump over a declaration with an explicit or implicit (that is, a class constructor) initializer unless the declaration is contained in a block and the entire block is jumped over. This constraint is not present in ANSI C

- In C++, a variable declaration without an explicit extern is considered a definition of that variable. In ANSI C it is considered a "tentative" definition. The occurrence of multiple tentative definitions within one file is resolved to a single definition. For example,

```
struct stat { /* ... */ };

// ANSI C: ok.
// C++: error: two definitions of stat
struct stat stat;
struct stat stat;
```

- In C++, the default linkage of a constant is static. In ANSI C, the default linkage of a constant is extern. An explicit extern or static in the declaration will provide the desired semantics:

```
class Boolean { /* ... */ };

extern const Boolean TRUE(1);    // ANSI C default
static const Boolean FALSE(0);   // C++ default
```

Stronger Type Checking

The following are a list of differences between C++ and ANSI C that are due to stronger type checking within C++.

- In C++, the use of an undeclared function is an error. In C, undeclared functions are permitted; type checking is suspended. For example,

```
main() {
    // C++: error, printf is undeclared
    // C: ok, taken to mean: int printf()
    printf( 3.14159 ); // interface error
}
```

- In C++, the assignment of a pointer of type void* to a pointer of any other type requires an explicit cast since it is potentially very dangerous. In ANSI C, the conversion is implicit. For example,

```
main() {
    int i = 1024;
    void *pv = &i;

    // C++: error, explicit cast required.
    // ANSI C: ok.
    char *pc = pv;
    int len = strlen( pc ); // bad pointer
}
```

- C++ and ANSI C interpret differently the type of a string constant used to initialize a character array. In C++, the following initialization is illegal because it does not provide space for the null character that terminates a literal string constant:

```
// C++: error
// ANSI C: no error
char ch[2] = "hi";
```

In ANSI C, the string initializer is interpreted as a shorthand notation for the character elements 'h' and 'i'. A terminating null is supplied if the array has sufficient size to accommodate it.
The following general form of array initialization:

```
char ch[] = "hi";
```

creates an array of three elements in both C++ and ANSI C Programmers are encouraged to use this form if they intend to move code between the two languages.

C.3   Linkage Between C++ and C

C programmers can "escape" the C++ type system for argument declarations by adding ellipses. This will "C++-ify" their C programs.

```
struct node *get_node( val )
int val;
{
    /* turns off C++ type checking */
    char *malloc( ... );
}
```

Although this program will now compile under C++, it will *not* link. This is because all function names in C++ are internally encoded. The programmer must explicitly inform the compiler not to encode the function name. This is done by a linkage directive. (Section 4.5 (page 171) considers the linkage directive in detail.) For example,

```
extern "C" char *malloc( unsigned );
```

The linkage directive informs the compiler not to encode the function name. malloc() will now link with the libc.a instance. The recommended solution is to include malloc.h.

If the programmer wishes to define the program so that it runs under *both* C++ and C, the predefined __cplusplus (double underscore) can be used.†

```
#include <stdio.h>

#ifdef __cplusplus
extern "C" char *malloc(long);
#endif

struct node *get_node( val )
int val;
{
    struct node *ptr;
#ifndef __cplusplus
    char *malloc();
#endif

    /* ... */
}
```

---

†Prior to Release 2.0, c_plusplus was the name of the predefined macro. It was changed to __cplusplus for ANSI C compatibility. Both macro definitions are supported under Release 2.0.

`__cplusplus` allows for the intermixing of C-style and C++-style function declarations through the use of the `#ifdef` and `#ifndef` conditional preprocessor directives.

C.4   Moving from C to C++

An important factor in the rapid acceptance of C++ has been the ease of using C++ with C. There are two aspects to this compatibility: the ability to use C++ with existing C based systems and the ease with which C programmers can learn and make effective use of C++. Typically, new users of C++ have been programming in C and often the initial use of C++ is to provide some new functionality to an existing program. Some of the lessons learned from the experience of melding C and C++ include the following:

- Keep the interface between the C and C++ parts clear and clean.

- "If it ain't broke, don't fix it" — that is, there is likely to be insufficient payoff to justify converting an existing system unless some substantial new development is undertaken at the same time.

- Use the new features of C++ gradually rather than all at once. You can get "spaghetti" classes just as you can have "spaghetti" code.

- Effective use of C++ comes with better design. You will get big payoffs from having some of the more experienced people spend the time to design a few classes that are fundamental to your application.

- Most users can start with a minimal knowledge of C++ and yet make effective use of general-purpose or application-specific class libraries.

Appendix D: **Compatibility with Release 1.2**

In this section, the differences between Release 2.0 and Release 1.2 of C++ are detailed. This appendix should be of primary interest to two categories of readers. For those without access as yet to a Release 2.0 implementation, the appendix notes those elements of the language described in the body of this book that do not apply to implementations based on Release 1.2. For those who have written code based on an implementation of Release 1.2 and wish to migrate the code to Release 2.0, this appendix can be used as a guidepost for making the transition.

The differences between Release 2.0 and Release 1.2 fall into two major categories:

1. Language extensions introduced in Release 2.0, including multiple inheritance, virtual base classes, type-safe linkage, const and static member functions, and the ability to overload operators new and delete for individual classes.

2. Modifications to the language semantics of Release 1.2 introduced in Release 2.0. For example, the overload function matching algorithm is modified to be order-independent; class object initialization and assignment are changed from bitwise- to memberwise-copy.

What are the motivations behind the changes in Release 2.0? The primary aim is to improve C++'s support for large-scale library building. Parameterized types and exception handling, discussed in Appendix B, will further enhance C++ in this regard. A second aim is to correct an existing or potential problem in the language as defined in Release 1.2. Memberwise-copy is an example of this kind of change.

D.1 Features Not Supported in Release 1.2

The following list summarizes the features added to C++ in Release 2.0. These features are *not* supported in Release 1.2.

- Multiple inheritance.

- Virtual base classes.

- Pure virtual functions.

- Type-safe linkage.

- Static member functions.

- Const member functions.

- Explicit initialization of static members.

- Overloading of operators `new` and `delete` both at file-scope and within an individual class.

- Explicit placement of objects using operator `new`.

- Overloading of the `->` and `,` (comma) operators.

- Class objects may be explicitly deleted by a direct call of the class destructor.

In the following subsections, we look at how the absence of these features affects users of Release 1.2.

Multiple Inheritance

The material on class derivation and inheritance can be found in Chapters 7 and 8. Readers unfamiliar with either of these terms and how they apply to the C++ language might benefit by first reading Chapter 7.

In Release 1.2, a class can be derived only from a single base class. In a number of cases, the rules regarding the declaration and initialization of the base class are more restrictive than those in Release 2.0:

1. The user may not explicitly declare a base class derivation as `private`. In Release 1.2, the declaration of a private ZooAnimal derivation can only be specified implicitly as follows:

   ```
   class Bear : ZooAnimal {} // legal in 1.2, 2.0
   ```

   With Release 2.0, the keyword `private` may be used explicitly:

   ```
   class Bear : private ZooAnimal{} // legal in 2.0
   ```

   The explicit use of the `private` keyword removes the possibility of the human reader of the program misinterpreting the derivation.

2. The user may not explicitly name the base class in the member initialization list of the derived class constructor. In Release 1.2, the initialization of a base class must be specified as follows:

```
class Bear : public ZooAnimal { /* ... */ };

// name is a data member of Bear
Bear::Bear( char *s, short ZooArea )
     : (ZooArea), name(s) {} // legal in 1.2, 2.0
```

The unnamed argument-list is understood to refer to the base class. In Release 2.0, the base class can be explicitly named by its tag:

```
Bear::Bear(char *s, short ZooArea)
     : ZooAnimal(ZooArea), name(s) {} // legal in 2.0
```

3. In Release 1.2, a base class can be initialized with another base class object only if the base class has defined an X(const X&) constructor. In Release 2.0, this restriction is lifted. For example,

```
class ZooAnimal {
public:
    ZooAnimal( short );
    // ...
};

class Bear : public ZooAnimal { /* ... */ };

Bear::Bear( short ZooArea )
     : ( ZooArea ) {} // legal in 1.2, 2.0

Bear::Bear( ZooAnimal& z )
     : ZooAnimal( z ) {} // legal only in 2.0

Bear::Bear( const Bear& b )
     : ZooAnimal( b ) {} // legal only in 2.0
```

4. Virtual base classes are not supported in Release 1.2. The presence of the virtual keyword in the derivation list is illegal:

```
class Base { ... };

// 2.0: ok
// 1.2: illegal.
class Derived : virtual public Base { ... };
```

5. Pure virtual functions are not supported in Release 1.2. An abstract class such as ZooAnimal must provide a definition for each of its virtual functions. For example,

```
class ZooAnimal {
public:
    // 2.0: pure virtual function
    virtual void draw() = 0;

    // 1.2: requires definition
    virtual void draw() {}
}
```

Apart from these changes and the handling of multiple base classes in general, the discussions of class derivation and inheritance in Chapters 7 and 8 hold for Release 1.2.

Linkage to Other Languages

This section discusses the handling of linkage to other languages in Release 1.2, as well as some of the reasons for the introduction of type-safe linkage with Release 2.0. Linkage to other languages is tied to the support C++ provides for the overloading of function names. Those readers unfamiliar with function name overloading should read Section 4.3 (page 151) before continuing with this section. Section 4.5 (page 171) contains a discussion of type-safe linkage.

Function name overloading gives the appearance of permitting multiple occurrences of the same nonstatic function identifier. This is a lexical convenience that holds at the program source level. Typical commercial link-editor technology cannot support multiple external symbols. If the link editor sees two or more instances of the identifier print, for example, it will flag print as multiply defined and quit. To handle this problem, all but one overloaded function identifier in Release 1.2 is encoded with a unique internal name.

If an instance of the overloaded function identifier is a library instance written in some other language, notably C, then a linkage problem will occur. The non-C++ function name was not encoded. If, for example, the complex class library overloads the C math library routine abs(), then how is the C instance to be accessed? Before Release 2.0, the solution was two-fold:

1. In order to overload a function name, the overload keyword has to be specified, in the form

   ```
   overload abs;
   ```

2. The first instance of the set of overloaded functions for a particular name is not encoded. That is, in order to overload a function name with

a C language instance, the programmer must make sure to list its name first. For example,

```
overload abs;
#include <math.h>
#include <complex.h>
BigNum& abs( BigNum& );
```

In Release 2.0, neither of these two constraints hold. For compatibility with earlier releases, however, the presence of the overload keyword, although without effect, is still accepted.

In Release 1.2, a function name can be overloaded only after the overload keyword declares it to be an overloaded function. The function may not be declared to be an overloaded function after a declaration of the function has been seen. It is an error to write, for example,

```
#include <math.h>
overload abs;
#include <complex.h>
```

A list of overloaded functions may be declared in a single list, provided that they share the same return type. For example,

```
overload double sqrt( double ), sqrt( complex );
overload f( int ), f( double ), f( Screen );
```

There are two problems with this strategy. First, an order dependency exists in the handling of the overloaded function set. If the C language instance does not occur first, it will not be linked to the program.

The second problem has to do with combining libraries. Providing large sets of class libraries is an important goal of a C++ programming environment. In general, we want to combine libraries from multiple, unrelated sources.

What is the problem with combining libraries under Release 1.2? The requirement that the overload keyword be seen before an instance of the function name. For example, complex.h overloads sqrt():

```
// complex.h
overload sqrt;
#include <math.h>
complex sqrt( complex );
```

A three-dimensional math library overloads atan().

```
// 3d.h
overload atan;
#include <math.h>
```

If a programmer writes

```
#include <complex.h>
#include <3d.h>
```

the statement

```
overload atan;
```

in 3d.h is flagged as an error because complex.h, which occurs first, includes math.h which contains a declaration of atan(). The overload keyword must be specified before a declaration of the function is seen. A similar problem with regard to sqrt() occurs if the include order is reversed. This means that the programmer potentially must examine every included header file to determine which functions are being overloaded and what the order dependencies are among the headers. Eventually, the programmer works out a correct header:

```
// mylib.h
overload sqrt;
overload atan;
#include <3d.h>
#include <complex.h>
```

A programmer wishing to add mylib.h to an application will need to go through the same process. The solution Release 2.0 provided is three-fold:

1. Encode all function names, removing any order dependency.

2. Make overloading implicit; that is, the overload keyword is no longer necessary. A function declared twice with different argument types is treated as an overloaded function.

3. Provide a general escape mechanism for linkage to other language functions (or to allow other languages to call C++ functions):

```
extern "C" void exit(int);
extern "C" {
  strlen( const char* );
  char *strcpy( char*, const char* );
}
```

Static Class Members

Release 1.2 does not support static member functions. Additionally, there is no way to explicitly initialize a static class member. The following Release 2.0 program fragment, for example, is unsupported under Release 1.2:

```
class X { public: X(int); };
class Y {
public:
    // 2.0 : ok: static member function
    // 1.2 : unsupported
    static getVal() { return val; }
private:
    static X xx;
    static int val;
};

// 2.0: ok: explicit initialization
// 1.2: unsupported
X Y::xx( 1024 );
int Y::val = 1;
```

D.2   Features Modified in Release 2.0

The behavior of a number of features differs somewhat between Releases 2.0 and 1.2. These include the following changes:

- Default bitwise-copy of class objects has been changed to memberwise-copy.

- The overload keyword need no longer be specified before overloading a function.

- The argument-matching algorithm for resolving the call of an overloaded function has been made order-independent.

- The argument-matching algorithm now distinguishes between const and nonconst pointer and reference arguments. It now also distinguishes between the small integral types and int and between the types float and double.

- Literal character constants, such as 'a' are evaluated as type char, not as type int.

- The initialization of a variable defined at file scope is no longer restricted to a constant expression.

- A function can no longer be used before it has been declared.

- Default argument initializers may be specified only once in a file.

- The elements of an enumeration defined at class scope are local to the scope of that class.

- Anonymous unions defined at file scope must be declared as static.

For each modification, the differences are considered, and a rationale for the change is provided.

Default Bitwise Copy

The reader should be familiar with Chapters 5 and 6 before continuing with this subsection, and especially with the discussion presented in Section 6.2 (page 247) and Section 6.3 (page 266) of Chapter 6.

In one instance, the constructor for a class is not called to initialize a newly declared class object — when an object is initialized with another object of its class. Before Release 2.0, initialization is accomplished by bitwise copy. In 2.0, it is accomplished by memberwise copy. The difference between these two copy methods is significant when the class object is a derived class or contains a class member object.

The class designer may override the default application of either copy method by defining two special member functions. For initialization, a constructor of the form

```
X::X( const X& );
```

will be invoked whenever one object of class X is initialized with another. For assignment, an assignment operator of the form

```
X& X::operator=( const X& );
```

will be invoked whenever one object of class X is assigned to another. Overriding either default copy method is necessary when the class contains a pointer member.

A bitwise copy does not examine the members of the class object to which it is being applied; rather, it copies the object bit by bit. Under bitwise copy, only two conditions hold:

1. Either the class defines a special object constructor, in which case it is called, or

2. the class object is initialized by bitwise copy.

Let's look at an example. Here is the definition of a Word class, containing a String class data member. String has defined a special object constructor to handle copying of its char* data member.

```
class Word {
public:
   Word(char* s): name(s), occurs(0) {}
   Word(String& s): name(s), occurs(0) {}
   // ...
private:
   String name;
   int occurs;
};

Word color( "blue" );
Word mood = color;
```

Under bitwise copy, `color` is copied in its entirety. The String data member of `mood`, therefore, points to the same character array as that of the String data member of `color`. This is the very condition that the String object constructor was defined to prevent. Under bitwise copy, however, it is not invoked.

Although the Word class does not itself require a special object constructor, it must define one to ensure that its class member instance is invoked:

```
Word::Word( const Word& w ):
       name( w.name ) { /* ... */ }
```

The same would hold true were Word derived from String. Under memberwise copy, this is no longer necessary. If the base or member class defines the special object handlers, it will be invoked in place of memberwise copy.

Overloaded Functions

In Release 1.2, a function intended to be overloaded must be announced as such to the program before any declaration of the function is seen. For example, to overload `sqrt()`, we would write the following:

```
overload sqrt;
#include <math.h>
Complex& sqrt( Complex& );
```

where `math.h` contains the following library declaration:

```
double sqrt( double );
```

It would be an error to write

```
#include <math.h>
overload sqrt;
```

since the predefined instance is declared in `math.h`. A shorthand form of the `overload` specification is the following:

```
overload void print( int ),
             print( char& ),
             print( double );
```

Under Release 2.0, the use of the `overload` keyword is no longer necessary. Any two functions with the same name and distinct signatures are considered overloaded instances.

Release 2.0 introduced a modified argument-matching algorithm for the resolution of overloaded function calls (Section 4.3 (page 155) provides a detailed discussion). There are a number of differences between the two argument matching algorithms. Let us consider each difference in turn.

In the Release 1.2 argument-matching algorithm, a standard conversion will not be applied if it involves a truncation. This causes overloaded and nonoverloaded functions to behave differently in terms of argument passing and introduces an incompatibility with the C language. In the modified matching algorithm, truncation is permitted (a warning message is issued). For example,

```
class X;

overload f; // required for Release 1.2
f( X& );
f( int );

// in Release 1.2: error: no match
// in Release 2.0: match on f(int) with warning
f( 3.14159 );
```

In the Release 1.2 argument-matching algorithm, the `const` modifier by itself does not make two pointer or reference arguments distinct. For example, the following call under Release 1.2 is ambiguous. Under Release 2.0, the `const` instance is invoked.

```
const String str;
overload ff;
ff( const String& );
ff( String& );

// 1.2: error: ambiguous
// 2.0: ff( const String& )
ff( str );
```

In the Release 1.2 argument-matching algorithm, if two or more matches are possible through a standard conversion, the first occurring instance is chosen. This behavior is clearly order-dependent and may result in nonintuitive matches. In the modified matching algorithm, this order-dependence is removed. If more than one standard conversion is possible, the call is flagged as ambiguous. The existence of a potential ambiguity is best made known to the programmer at compile time. For example,

```
overload ff; // required by Release 1.2
// from "a.h"
ff( double );

// from "b.h"
ff( char* );

// Under Release 1.2,
// if "a.h" included first: ff(double) matches
// if "b.h" included first: ff(char*) matches
// Under Release 2.0, the call is ambiguous
ff( 0 );
```

If a programmer is converting to Release 2.0 and is faced with a suddenly ambiguous function call, the call can be resolved through an explicit cast:

```
ff( double(0) );
```

In the Release 1.2 argument-matching algorithm, the small integrals (char, unsigned char, short, and unsigned short) are treated as forming an equivalence set of type int (reflecting the promotion rules for C). In effect,

```
overload ff; // required in Release 1.2

ff( char );
ff( int );
```

defines two instances of ff() that exactly match an argument of any of the five small integral types. (A warning message is issued at the declaration of the second instance.) In the case where two or more function instances may match exactly, the instance listed first is chosen. float and double form a second equivalence set.

In the modified matching algorithm, the C rules for promotion are applied if and only if there is no formal argument of the small integral type. This finer granularity of argument matching may cause some previously acceptable programs to break, such as the following program:

```
overload f; // required for 1.2
void f(int);
void f(float);

void
foo ()
{
        int a = 0;
        float b = 0.0;

        f(a);             // match: f(int)
        f(b);             // match: f(float)
        f(0);             // match: f(int)

        // two calls with arguments of type double
        f(0.0);           // 1.2: ok; 2.0: error
        f(1.2);           // 1.2: ok; 2.0: error

}
```

Why are the last two calls no longer unambiguous? In Release 1.2, only one instance of a function taking an argument of either float or double can be defined. The second instance is not recognized since float and double form an equivalence set. All calls of either type exactly match the first listed instance. This is why the last two calls, with literal arguments of type double, exactly match f(float) under Release 1.2.

Under Release 2.0, the function-matching algorithm distinguishes between the two argument types. Arguments of type double no longer exactly match a formal argument of type float. In this case, this means that

```
    f(0.0);
```

can match f(float) only through application of a standard conversion. Through application of a standard conversion, however, the call can also be made to match f(int) — the call is now ambiguous.

How can the programmer resolve code that, as in the preceding case, no longer compiles?

- The programmer could provide an instance that accepts an argument of type double. The f(float) declaration under Release 1.2, in fact, really provides for both cases. In Release 2.0, providing a float instance requires a separate double instance.

- The programmer could provide the explicit float notation for constant literals or an explicit cast:

```
f( 0.0f ); // 2.0: ok
f( float(1.2)); // 2.0: ok
```

- If the programmer did not originally mean `float`, but simply all floating-point values, then the instance could be changed to take an argument of type `double`. Now all arguments of type `float` and `double` will match that instance exactly under Release 2.0.

Literal Character Constants

A literal character constant is evaluated as a `char` under Release 2.0. Under Release 1.2, following the C language promotion rules, a literal character constant is evaluated as an `int`. This impacts programs in the following two ways:

1. The size of a literal character constant under Release 2.0 is 1 byte; under Release 1.2, it is the size in bytes of an `int`.

2. The output operator ("`<<`") under Release 2.0 can write a literal character constant; under Release 1.2, it writes the integer representation of the character. For example,

```
#include <stream.h>
main() {
    cout << 'a' << '\n';
}
```

generates the following output under Release 1.2:

```
$ a.out
9710$
```

Under Release 2.0, the program generates the following output:

```
$ a.out
a
$
```

where $ represents the system prompt.

A programmer wishing to print out a literal character constant under Release 1.2 can either use the `put()` function:

```
main() {
    cout.put('a').put('\n');
}
```

or enclose the character constant in double quotations in order to have it printed as a string:

```
main() {
    cout << "a" << "\n";
}
```

Static Initialization

Under Release 1.2, identifiers declared at file scope may be initialized
only by a constant expression (that is, one that may be evaluated at compile time). With Release 2.0, identifiers declared at file scope may be initialized with any general expression. For example,

```
#include <math.h>
extern f( double );

// ok: 2.0; illegal: 1.2
double e = exp( 1 );
int i = f( e );
int j = i;
```

Function Declaration Constraint

In Release 1.2, a function, unlike a variable, can be used before its declaration has been seen. The function is treated as having the following default
prototype:

```
int foo( ... );
```

A message is issued that warns about the use of the undeclared function,
but a program like the following will compile:

```
void f1() { double d = ff(); }
void f2() { unsigned char ch = ff(1); }
```

In effect, the argument list of an undeclared function is outside the C++
type system. The two calls may or may not both be legal; the compiler has
no way to decide. Under Release 2.0 this program will *not* compile
because a function can be used only after it has been declared. Otherwise,
it is a compile-time error.

Default Argument Initializers

The rules on specifying default argument initializers were not rigorously
defined in the original language reference manual. They have been clarified under Release 2.0. It is not permissible to specify a default value for

an argument more than once in a file. This rule clarifies an aspect of the language previously defined only by implementation. Under Release 1.2, an argument is allowed to have its default initializer specified multiple times in a file if and only if that initializer is a constant expression. Under Release 2.0, this is no longer supported. In cases where the initializer requires run-time evaluation, multiple instances are never legal. For example,

```
int val;

extern foo( int i = 0 );
extern bar( int i = val );

// ok: 1.2, error: 2.0
foo( int i = 0 ) { return i*2; }

// error: 1.2 and 2.0
bar( int i = val ) { return i+2; }
```

The convention is to place the default argument in the class definition or function declaration stored in a header file. This is generally the public instance seen by the user.

Enumerations at Class Scope

The behavior of enumerations defined as local to the class has been formally defined with Release 2.0. The elements of the enumeration are at class scope. They assume the level of protection of the class section in which the enumeration is defined; therefore, the elements of the enumeration may be `public`, `private`, or `protected` members of the class. Outside the class, the class scope operator is required to access them.

Before Release 2.0, the behavior of locally defined enumerations was defined by the implementation. One difference that may affect existing programs is that under Release 1.2, access rules for elements of the enumeration are not enforced.

Anonymous Unions at File Scope

Under Release 2.0, anonymous unions at file scope must be specified as static, which means that the elements of the union have internal linkage. Internally generated names are associated with anonymous unions. Declaring these names static will prevent collisions across compilation units.

```
// 1.2: ok
// 2.0: error, implicit extern
union { int i; double d; };

// 1.2, 2.0: ok
static union { int i; double d; };
```

Bug Fixes in Release 2.0

The rest of this section lists some differences between the behavior of
Release 2.0 and earlier releases that result from a more rigorous implementation of the C++ language definition. They can be thought of as bug
fixes and not modifications of the language. They do, however, change
how some existing programs may work, and so are listed here.

Operator Member Function Protection

Under Release 1.2, the protection level of operator member functions is
not enforced. This permits illegal programs such as the following to compile.

```
class SmallInt {
public:
    SmallInt( int );
    // ...
private:
    operator+( int );
    int val;
};

SmallInt myInt( 127 );
main() {

    // 1.2: not caught
    // 2.0: error: operator+ private
    int i = myInt + 1;
    // ...
}
```

If the programmer intends to allow public access to the addition operator
of class SmallInt, it is necessary to place the operator in a public section of
the class definition.

Const Linkage

Default linkage for all `const` objects has always been defined to be static. To define a `const` object at global scope requires an explicit `extern` specifier in its definition. For example,

```
extern const TRUE = 1;
```

Under Release 1.2, however, both a `const` class object and a `const` pointer are treated by default as `extern`. Under Release 2.0, this has been corrected. For example,

```
// 1.2: external linkage
// 2.0: static linkage
const X xObject( 2 );
char *const cp = "abc";

// 1.2: external linkage
// 2.0: external linkage
extern const X xObject( 2 );
extern char *const cp = "abc";
```

Note that the following declaration statement

```
const char *pc = "abc";
```

does *not* define pc to be a constant but, rather, a pointer to a constant array of characters. The linkage of pc is extern.

const Reference Arguments

Under Release 1.2, the checking of `const` is incomplete. The following call of bar(), for example, should not be permitted since the reference argument of bar() is not specified as `const`.

```
extern bar( int& );

int foo( const int &r )
{
    // 1.2: ok.
    // 2.0: error: r is a constant object
    return bar( r );
}
```

INDEX

CODE DISK

A disk (in 5 1/4 inch format) containing the C++ code appearing in this book is available from Addison-Wesley. To order the disk, simply clip or photocopy this entire page and complete the form below. Enclose a check for $12.75 (includes shipping and handling) made out to Addison-Wesley Publishing Company, and mail to:

> Addison-Wesley Publishing Company
> Attn: Order Department
> Reading, MA 01867-9984

Please send me the code disk (# 54783) that accompanies *A C++ Primer* by Stanley B. Lippman. I enclose a check for $12.75 made out to Addison-Wesley Publishing Company.

Name _____

Address _____

City _____ State _____ Zip _____